D0045283

❧ All That Glittered

❧ Other Works on the Theatre by Ethan Mordden

All That Glittered

❧ *The Golden Age of*
Drama on Broadway,
1919–1959

Ethan Mordden

ST. MARTIN'S PRESS
NEW YORK

www.stmartins.com

Photographs reprinted by permission of private collections; the Billy Rose Theatre Collection, the New York Public Library for the Performing Arts; and the Astor, Lennox, and Tilden Foundations.

Title page photograph: The cast of Alfred Lunt's *The Taming of the Shrew* in 1935 takes its final call. Center group, from left: Sydney Greenstreet, Lynn Fontanne, Lunt, Dorothy Matthews, Alan Hewitt. Photograph courtesy of the New York Public Library for the Performing Arts.

Book design by Jennifer Ann Daddio

Library of Congress Cataloging-in-Publication Data
Mordden, Ethan.
    All that glittered : the golden age of drama on Broadway, 1919–1959/Ethan Mordden.
    —1st ed.
        p. cm.
    ISBN-13: 978-0-312-33898-5
    ISBN-10: 0-312-33898-8
    1. Theater—New York (State)—New York—History—20th century.   2. American drama—20th century—History and criticism.   I. Title.

PN2277.N5M54 2007
792.09747'10904—dc22   2006051178

First Edition: April 2007

10 9 8 7 6 5 4 3 2 1

✻ To Erick Neher

✖ Contents

❧ Acknowledgments

To the staff upstairs at the New York Public Library at Lincoln Center; to my excellent copyeditor, Adam Goldberger; to my wonder-working agent, Joe Spieler; and to my marvelous editor, Michael Flamini.

❦ Introduction

One cannot do justice to all the famous, important, or even ephemerally interesting plays and people of Broadway during the four decades of its most expansive activity—not in a single volume. Therefore, this is a theme-driven text rather than one meticulously collecting titles and names. All the influential developments in the non-musical American theatre between World War I and the Vietnam Era are here. What is missing— or treated in passing—is a portion of the works and personnel that some readers might expect to encounter.

In fact, this is less a theatre history than an

examination of our theatregoing culture in its Golden Age: a time when Broadway and Hollywood enjoyed an extremely stimulating relationship, when the nature of celebrity underwent a provocative evolution, when the national sense of humor changed from folk-rural to urban-minority, and when our playwrights were the archons of social examination, the ones who asked the pertinent questions about how we live.

The symbiosis of theatre and film is especially arresting because it no longer exists in even vestigial form (except for movie stars' new interest in making pilgrimages to the places of Actors Equity). The most obvious benefit, to Broadway, was Hollywood money, for even a flop might pay off on its sale to story-hungry studios. And Hollywood of course benefited from Broadway's discovery of new acting and writing talent. However, the two different sources of entertainment were intimate in less apparent ways. For instance, one of American art's happiest inventions is the screwball comedy. It is entirely a creation of the movie industry: yet the materials were furnished by the stage. As we'll see, it is as if neither theatre nor film could have managed without the other in this and many other projects.

There is as well a striking change in the meaning of the word "Broadway" in this time. In the years just after World War I, especially during Prohibition but also after, Walter Winchell and Damon Runyon were town criers and "Broadway" meant not only the real estate of theatres from the Garrick on Thirty-fifth Street to Jolson's Fifty-ninth Street Theatre, nor yet the nation's highest level of thespian craft—"Broadway" as a guarantee of quality—but rather a culture in West Central Manhattan that fascinated the entire nation. This was a world in which gangsters, prizefighters, and the press mixed with artists, socialites, and the famous. Restaurants and nightclubs were Broadway; the Astor Hotel and certain bars and barber shops were Broadway. The term denoted a belief system of almost lawless independence; and a language we might call Fluent Wisecrack; and a prominence in the very meaning of America that made periodic visits essential to anyone—save politicians—who thought of himself as notable. Much of our narrative art—fiction, drama, and cinema—was set in and around this milieu, because that was where our society was developed and revealed.

Today, that setting is Southern California, just as the young genius of the 1920s who grew up wanting to be a playwright finds in his modern counterpart the would-be moviemaker. Ironically, even after the technology to record and reproduce sound liberated the movies to compete with theatre on an intellectual instead of merely sensual level, it was not till Hollywood made faithful renderings of important plays in the early 1930s that the stage began to lose its prestige superiority and devolve over the following decades into a kind of powerless older brother to the true inheritor. MGM made *Grand Hotel* and *Dinner at Eight* with people like Greta Garbo, Joan Crawford, Jean Harlow, Marie Dressler, and two Barrymores. Can anyone today name who played the original shows on Broadway?

One

Lightnin' Has Struck!

When Frank Bacon left school at the age of fourteen, his native California counted more jobs to fill than skilled labor qualified to fill them. If not exactly the anarchic frontier of legend, California in the 1880s nevertheless offered opportunity to anyone with—as they put it then—gumption. Young Bacon tried sheepherding, advertising soliciting, and newspaper editing, and even ran an unsuccessful campaign for the state assembly. Then he fell into acting.

It was easy to do at the time, for people went to theatre then almost as casually as they turn on the television today, and playhouses were literally everywhere. Some were operated by resident repertory troupes, the "stock" companies that sustained public interest with a constantly changing bill. Certain theatres in a given region were linked to form "wheels" of companies not resident but traveling as wholes from one house to another every six weeks or so; unlike the stock companies, who played everything, the wheels played host to certain genres, for instance in thrill melodrama or society comedy.

The expansion of the railroad doomed stock and eventually closed down the wheels, for now the "combination" troupe dominated the national stage: one unit of actors giving a single work and touring with all the necessary sets and costumes. A success in this line meant moving from one theatre to the next (with perhaps a hiatus in summer) for months or even years. Along with bookings in small towns and provincial capitals lay the possibility of an extended run in Chicago or New York.

Bacon ended up in one of the last stock companies, in San Jose, for seventeen years, during which he is alleged to have assumed over six hundred roles. One sort of character in particular seems to have caught his interest—the uneducated rustic, innocent of fancy fashion, who somehow gets the better of popinjays and rogues. It was a national stereotype, just then reaching its apex in the career of the third Joseph Jefferson (acting was a family trade), especially in *Rip Van Winkle* (1866). During his galley years in San Jose, Bacon envisioned a vehicle for his own version of the trope, a small-time hotelier named Bill Jones and ironically nicknamed "Lightnin'" for his life tempo, as slow as paste and a kind of objective correlative for his low-key yet fierce sense of independence. No one crowds Bill Jones. "Lightnin'" has wife troubles, money troubles, and to every question a set of deadpan retorts that exasperate all those in the vicinity yet—Bacon hoped—amuse the public. "Lightnin'"'s hotel straddles the California-Nevada border, the state line running through the middle of the lobby: so women can shield their reputations by claiming to be on holiday in California while more truly seeking one of those quickie Nevada divorces.

Bacon called his play *The Divided House,** and found no takers. Were managers—the contemporary term for "producers"—leery of a character that had held the stage for over a century, or did Bacon fail to set him off properly?

---

* Not *A House Divided,* as is sometimes reported.

By 1912, Bacon had made it to New York, then as now the goal of virtually any working actor; but Bacon's New York was vaudeville or plays of no professional importance. Now forty-eight, he had been acting for twenty-two years and had every reason to assume that he would never be anything more than one of the many who got a modest living out of it but made no mark.

And then Bacon happened to tell the extremely successful playwright Winchell Smith about *The Divided House,* and how nobody wanted it, and how Bacon had sold it to the movies.

"Buy it back," said Smith. He then rewrote Bacon's script, and with manager John Golden opened it at the Gaiety Theatre (at the southwest corner of Broadway and Forty-sixth Street, now demolished) on August 26, 1918. The renamed *Lightnin'* was a smash. In fact, Bacon was the star and co-author of the biggest hit that Broadway had had to that time. More important, it was general belief that Frank Bacon *was* Lightnin'. Critics likened his warmth and "business" to that of Joseph Jefferson—who also had had to apply to an extremely successful playwright, Dion Boucicault, for assistance before his *Rip Van Winkle* went over.

Up to *Lightnin',* the record for a New York run belonged to J. Hartley Manners, whose *Peg O' My Heart* (1912) held New York for about twenty months. Three other titles (*A Trip To Chinatown* [1891], *Adonis* [1884], and *The Music Master* [1904]) trailed *Peg* by a month or so. *Lightnin'* played New York for *three years,* and, had Bacon got his way, he would have led every single performance. Eventually persuaded to take a vacation, Bacon spent it in the Gaiety Theatre watching his replacement, Milton Nobles, who was getting in shape to head the first national company.

It was as though Bacon feared even momentary separation from the individualizing event of his life. He was a husband and father, yes: who wasn't, in those days? But in *Lightnin',* Bacon had created something typical yet unique, a play made of hokum that seemed the most honest good time the public ever had. And as Bill Jones, Bacon topped even Joseph Jefferson perhaps, and he could look forward to playing the show he so loved up and down the country for the rest of his working life. Indeed, they had had no little trouble auditioning Bacon's successor; Nobles was something like seventy, coaxed out of retirement to save the day.

We must get the measure of *Lightnin'* if we are to organize our perspective on how Broadway's Golden Age began: what it invented but also what it eliminated, because Bill Jones was one of the casualties. In a prologue and three acts, the play moves from the hotel to a courtroom and back, and the plot involves the usual bad guys' attempt to execute a swindle, the objective being Jones' hotel. The good guy is the young lawyer (Ralph Morgan, brother of Frank Morgan, the Wizard of Oz in the 1939 movie) determined to unmask the bad guys; he is also The Boy, and The Girl is the Joneses' foster daughter (Beatrice Nichols). She is loyal to Mrs. Jones (Jessie Pringle), who seeks to divorce Bill, complicating the young romance.

All ends well, though the show gets by on no more plot than that. *Lightnin'* seeks entertainment entirely in Bill Jones' personality, so it's odd to note that it's one of the shortest lead roles ever. Like Andrew Lloyd Webber's *Phantom*, Bill makes a great deal out of relatively brief stage time—not in the Big Effect but in the now lost art of underplaying. The aim is to give a detached and casual reading, to take all emotion way down to a point of intimacy between the performer and a public that, denied today's microphoned overstatement, must concentrate.

The object of all this attention is a ne'er-do-well drunk who drives everybody crazy by letting nothing perturb him. He's uncooperative, as here when one of the bad guys, Mr. Thomas, comes in:

> THOMAS: (beckoning Bill to him) Oh, Bill, I want to see you for a minute.
> BILL: Can't you see me from there?

He's a smart alec:

> BILL: Came out [to the West] during the gold excitement.
> HARPER: The gold excitement was back in '49.
> BILL: Well, they was still excited when I got here.

He's not paying attention even when things of value are at stake, as when he takes over questioning the other bad guy, Mr. Hammond, during the trial scene:

> BILL: Who controls the Golden Gate Land Company?
> HAMMOND: (lying) I don't know.
> BILL: Don't you know it's controlled by you and Mr. Thomas?

THOMAS: Your Honor, I object!

BILL: And that all your stock's in the name of rummies?

THE YOUNG LAWYER: (correcting him in a stage whisper) Dummies! Dummies!

BILL: Dummies! Dummies!

Worst of all, you name it and he's done it, which makes all of life's striving a fantasy, a jest. Buffalo Bill? "I learned him all he knew about killing Indians." Detectives? "I used to be a detective." Even bees can be claimed for Bill's curriculum vitae:

BILL: I used to be in the bee business. Why, I drove a swarm of bees across the plains in the dead of winter. (Audience titters.) And never lost a bee. (Audience laughs full out. Bacon lets the laughter die to twenty percent while staring at the other player. Then:) Got stung twice. (Audience roars.)

It's like a humorous version of Bacon's own odd-jobbing past.

But isn't that the point? The white-haired Bacon, in his rumpled jacket and tie and battered hat, made no stab at notching Bill up for charm. Bill was what he was, a loser having a good time. So Bacon *wasn't* Lightnin'. Bacon was a "barely made it" who never stopped struggling to get there. A striver. In an age of matinee idols, professional Brits, Heavy Fathers,* light comics, and Shakespeareans, Frank Bacon was almost not an actor. Not a type: because his type was all but retired by 1900 or so. One can only imagine how proud and relieved Bacon must have been to play *his* character in *his* style and make such a hit out of it.

He might easily have failed, with such superannuated material. It's flattering to be compared to one of the great names of the past; is it good for business? Jefferson enjoyed a very long career, but he was born the year

---

* A mainstay of the old stock company, the Heavy Father was played by an older male who combined the functions of Leading Man and Character Actor. He was not an older version of the Romantic Lead, but rather a strong personality entirely lacking in glamor but claiming a proud sense of authority. Most typically, he would be seen at the open doorway looking out on a blizzard, ordering out of his house an unfortunate young woman—often his own daughter—who is carrying her bastard infant. "Go!" he thunders. "And never darken my towels again!"

that President Andrew Jackson took office. That's an awfully old tradition to be a part of. Then, too, Bacon didn't just look rumpled and battered: he *was*, having lived at the bottom of a profession made of two distinct social groups—one, big stars; and, two, everyone else. By chance, Bacon's arrival in New York in 1912 coincided with the formation of Actors Equity, a group determined to reform managerial abuses.

These were, frankly, astonishing. In a time when a hit show played most of its run in weekly bookings around the country for one or two years, it was perhaps no more than unhappy that a production might close with the cast stranded many miles from home. It could be called regrettable that managers did not pay actors for the extra performances added on during holidays.* But it is simply unbelievable that rehearsals—which lasted as long as the manager wanted them to—went entirely unpaid. How on earth did the penniless see themselves through a rehearsal period? As it was, Equity sought no more than half salary for rehearsals, along with certain other modest concessions.

The Producing Managers Association had every reason to resist, because the actors were powerless. True, the stars weren't—but why would stars make common cause with grunts? The two groups dwelled on separate planets. The thespian solidarity that exists among actors today is relatively new, in part based on the development of the integrated acting ensemble, in which leads and support alike see themselves as working within a single entity. Ensemble acting did not exist in 1919: production tilted the room, as Hollywood now phrases it, toward the star. Everybody else was infinitely replaceable.

But something happened in around 1915. For some reason—probably the lower-middle-class acculturation of cinema and a concomitant falloff in playgoers' ticketbuying—the road began to close down. True, not till the late 1920s could one say that the road Just Wasn't What It Was; not till the 1950s was it genuinely vanishing; not till the 1960s was it gone but for the odd tour of some recent Broadway hit or a classic wrapped in a star package. Still, by 1915 the average actor's life had changed from difficult to impossible.

And something else happened. While many of the stars believed that theatre was a privileged profession, art rather than commerce, and were thus hostile to joining a labor union, other stars declared themselves absolutely in

---

* Ironically, many actors did not mind working for free, for these holiday shows were the best attended performances of the year, thus guaranteeing that the manager would have enough to pay his cast and not have to cheat them that week.

sympathy with Equity and its agenda. Some of them had come up the hard way, like Frank Bacon, and viewed with compassion those who were still struggling. Some held that theatre was made not by managers but by actors, and saw in that notion a dislocation of the makers' right to profit. And some of them simply knew fair from unfair. The managers were unfair, and I mean *to a man*.

So the acting profession was divided, and that made the managers feel secure. Unions serve the drudge, the work horse. Actors were dolls, and Equity was nonsense. The very business of American theatre was founded on a lack of equity: on the manager's more or less coddling his stars and exploiting the grunts. At that, few actors belonged to Equity in the first place. What was Equity going to do, strike? Pull out a couple of First Gravediggers? Besides, the tyrant of vaudeville, Edward F. Albee (grandfather of the playwright), faced his own strike in 1916, and not only did he crush the strike: he blacklisted its leaders.

Nevertheless, by the summer of 1919, having continually failed even to get recognition from the Producing Managers Association, Equity was seriously contemplating a strike. The timing could not have been worse, for 1919 was a year of social unrest and extremely unpopular labor actions. Beginning on January 21, a general strike in Seattle, believed to be the result of agitation by the radical Industrial Workers of the World, was defeated only by ferocious resistance from Mayor Ole Hanson, backed by the police and the army. On the other hand, a five-day strike of telephone operators in Boston starting on April 15 that froze communication throughout most of New England found almost all the public in sympathy with the strikers. These women put in long days deftly maneuvering in complex operations for very low pay. Wasn't their situation comparable to that of the actors?

However, the rest of that spring saw not just labor actions but the mailing of bombs disguised as packages from Gimbel's department store and the planting of bombs on the doorsteps of officials' houses. Through blind luck and the vigilance of one postal clerk, the mailings claimed but one casualty, blowing off the hands of Senator Thomas R. Hardwick's black maid; and the second terrorist wave took out only the front of Attorney General A. Mitchell Palmer's house and the terrorist himself.*

---

* Such other events of the unstable period of 1919–20 as the Boston Police Strike, the deportation of radicals on the *Buford,* the Wall Street bombing that killed thirty-eight, and

Another problem was that no one, in or out of Equity, knew even vaguely how an actors' strike would fare when something like one-third of the stars were pro-union, one-third anti-union, and one-third waiting to see what happened. If a star went on but the support struck his show, would understudies scab for an opportunity? How would the public react to being shut out of its most basic form of entertainment? Would the managers black-list ringleaders, in the Albee manner? In fact, the managers thought the actors too uncertain and infantile to do more than talk strike. "I honestly didn't think," said George M. Cohan's producing partner, Sam H. Harris, "the boys would go so far."

Because they did strike. It started on the evening of August 6, in utter confusion. Some actors struck and some didn't. Some managers did send un-derstudies on, but some *understudies* struck. Some stars prepared to walk, then changed their minds. Some stars refused to walk, learned that the the-atre across the street was going dark that night, and promptly led their companies out into the night. Broadway became its own theatre, as crowds watched the doings and passed along the latest reports and rumors. Some twelve shows ended up forking out refunds, including one, a bedroom farce called *Nightie Night,* that was to have had its premiere that day.

On August 7, star Holbrook Blinn, who had walked out of *The Challenge* the night before, reopened the piece and resigned from Equity. The wrathful George M., who took the strike as an act of treachery aimed personally at himself, forced *The Royal Vagabond* onstage with himself and understudies. The crafty Shuberts kept *Shubert Gaieties of 1919* running through the ex-pedient of turning it into a variety show of pickup talent. Other stars de-serted Equity—Zelda Sears, Laura Hope Crews, Janet Beecher. Ziegfeld got an injunction to keep the *Follies* running. The Shuberts got injunctions, too, though they preferred suing individual members of Equity, including those then working in Hollywood and even dead people. The actors put on monstrous all-star benefits at the Lexington Avenue Opera House—Eddie Cantor, Lillian Russell, John Charles Thomas, Eddie Foy and the seven little Foys, Charles Winninger, Ed Wynn (who was blocked by Shubert injunction from appearing onstage and so did his act in the audi-ence, like the cast of *The Cradle Will Rock,* eighteen years later), Lionel

---

the trial of Sacco and Vanzetti all occurred *after* the actors threatened to walk out if the managers refused to negotiate.

and Ethel Barrymore in a scene from *Camille* (as we call *La Dame aux Caméllias*), W. C. Fields as emcee, and Marie Dressler teaching two hundred fifty choristers a dance number in ten minutes, where a manager's idea of a musical's learning curve—without pay, remember—was six weeks at the minimum.

George M. tried to crush Equity by making every requested concession . . . to his own creation, the Actors' Fidelity League. Famous managers threatened to retire if Equity prevailed, as the strike spread beyond theatre capitals to Providence, Atlantic City (an important tryout stop), St. Louis, Washington, D. C. In New York, every single theatre eventually went dark except for the Garrick, the Nora Bayes, and the Hippodrome: the first because *John Ferguson* was produced by the Theatre Guild, run by a kind of socialist committee that was not a P.M.A. member and in any case was happy to recognize Equity, the first management to do so; the second because *The Greenwich Village Follies* was more roof-garden cabaret than theatre and fell under a distinct labor jurisdiction; and the last because it was technically a vaudeville house. Then, three weeks along, the walkout was swelled by the musicians and stagehands—four hundred of the latter at the Hippodrome alone.

It now went dark as well. When the Hippodrome's management made a separate peace with Equity, it was obvious to all that the managers had lost. The PMA signed its contract with Equity exactly a month after the strike had begun, at something like 2 A.M. on September 6. George M. sailed to London in a hopeless attempt to transfer his activities to the West End. And the strike was over.

It had been colorful and crazy fun, but it might well have ended in disaster. One act in particular is credited with having got the strike off to a crucial start: Frank Bacon closed *Lightnin'*.

True, the show had been running for a year by then. But we have seen how much it meant to Bacon; closing his show was like closing himself. Yet the single line *"Lightnin' has struck!,"* passed from Forty-sixth Street up and down the theatre district, seemed to put a kind of patriarchal imprimatur upon the strike while infusing it with energy. It's amazing to think that someone who, two years before, was one of the great unknown had become an archon of his profession, all the more so in that the profession immediately began to discard its Frank Bacons after 1919. It's a historians' favorite year, with the Versailles Peace Conference as its symbol and a shift in power from morning-coat feudalism to middle-class voting blocs as its content. But 1919 is a significant year also in the history of American theatre, which underwent an evolution from its early modern history of Mrs. Fiske and Henry Miller, of *Alias Jimmy Valentine* and *The Bird of Paradise,* into the days of Eugene O'Neill and the Group Theatre, of *Our Town* and *You Can't Take It With You.*

Why 1919 in particular? There are illustrative resonances, as in the founding of the Theatre Guild, whose output defined a strictly artistic viewpoint within a business regarded as lacking art. Some might prefer 1916, for the founding of *Theatre Arts* magazine, defining an intellectual viewpoint, with its unadorned yellow masthead cover and articles of academic and technical interest (till it went glossy and popular, in 1948). However, it would seem that, directly after World War I, everyone in the theatre embarked on an overnight revolution.

It was not, of course, an absolute one. Both Mrs. Fiske and Henry Miller were active after 1919. Then, too, Broadway's community of theatregoers seems to have become more united in this era precisely because film and then television kept drawing away the riffraff, "purifying" the atmosphere in which writers addressed a public.

Still, American culture unmistakably lurched from one place to another place. D. W. Griffith must give way to Warner Bros., Richard Barthelmess to James Cagney. In place of Lightnin' Bill Jones, we find the urbanized wise guy and fast talker, *real* lightning—the Lee Tracy of *Broadway* and *The Front Page,* for instance.

Still, for now, *Lightnin'* was so imposing—or, rather, its unexpected success was—that, on its last night in New York, President Harding's secretary of labor, James J. Davis, took the stage after the middle act to read a letter of congratulation from the Commander in Chief: because *Lightnin'* had struck. The rest of the intermission was deliberately drawn out to allow players from other shows time to reach the Gaiety Theatre (some still in costume and makeup) and rush the stage in jubilation after the third curtain. *Lightnin'* went on to a modest success in London, with the well-established Horace Hodges, at the Shaftesbury Theatre, in 1925. Back home, that same year, John Ford directed the first film version, with the unknown Jay Hunt; Will Rogers led the talkie remake, in 1930. That wasn't quite the end, for Fred Stone starred in a *Lightnin'* tour through the Northeast in 1938.

Nevertheless, America was losing *Lightnin'*, both the kind of entertainment it represented and the audience it played to. Ironically, Frank Bacon carried the seed of that destruction in his blood, for his son Lloyd drifted into movie acting and then directing. It was Lloyd Bacon who directed the first part-talking film that really had impact, Al Jolson's *second* movie, *The Singing Fool* (1928). Jolson's first, *The Jazz Singer* (1927), had played few theatres, for the equipment needed to project these films-with-soundtrack was not readily available. It was *The Singing Fool* that told Hollywood that Sound Had Arrived, empowering the movies to compete with theatre on theatre's terms while doing things beyond the limited resources of the stage.

Lloyd Bacon also directed *Moby Dick* (1930), one of talking Hollywood's first successful attempts to challenge the theatre's cultural hegemony by setting the reigning Hamlet into an American literary classic. True, it's an empty paradigm: John Barrymore had filmed the novel but five years earlier as *The Sea Beast,* and silent and talkie alike stray far from Melville, as Barrymore played a kind of Ishmael-Ahab, with a girl friend. However, we are talking not of authentic artistic value, but of perception, of how Hollywood appeared to most eyes to be able to rival the stage.

And it was Lloyd Bacon again who directed *42nd Street* (1933), which revived the moribund movie musical with a tense and grabby naturalism that the stage musical itself could not match. Broadway invented the musical, but here was Hollywood—here was Frank Bacon's son—reinventing it.

Frank did not live to see it. After closing *Lightnin'* in New York, he took his company to Chicago to begin what he believed might be an even bigger triumph, for *Lightnin'* was old-fashioned and Chicago liked its theatre well broken in. But after that lifetime of striving, a heart condition caught up with Bacon early in the run, and he gasped, "I am tired out" as he died in his wife's arms.

Two

I'll Be All Right When I'm Acclimatized:

OLD BROADWAY

The most noticeable difference between theatregoing today and theatregoing in the first
few seasons after the actors' strike is the
number of productions. Twenty-six new theatres
went up along The Street during the 1920s, and to
amortize the capitalization more plays had to be
staged.

There was a lot of variety in the kinds of plays on
offer, but there was almost nothing *but* kinds. Genre
was the playwright's muse—the "old dark house"
thriller, say, or the costume romance translated from
French or Italian, or society comedy, farce comedy,
sex comedy, domestic (i.e., middle-class family)

comedy. There were few out-of-genre one-offs, because critics and audiences alike entertained expectations, and failing to fulfill them risked baffling or even irritating one's clientele.

The oldest of the forms was melodrama. The term has a confused lineage; at one time it referred to a passage or even a full-length work of underscored declamation. By 1919, melodrama denoted theatre in which sensational effects and implausible surprises overruled character content in driving the narrative. The noble hero, chaste heroine, "errant foster sister," and hissable villain we see carrying on in *The Parson's Bride* during the first act of *Show Boat* (1927) preserve the conventions in their primitive state; the kind of melodrama practiced by 1919 was a little more textured. Still, it was sentimental and intense to the point of violence, and it gave the more outgoing performers plenty of opportunities. When a stagehand told Sir Henry Irving, "I 'ave 'eard many play 'Amlet, sir, but you have raised it to the level of a mellerdramer," he was paying a compliment.

Melodrama was also useful for the personality star, less a thespian than a celebrity making a personal appearance. When Theda Bara found that Hollywood's vamp cycle had ended, she turned to the stage to exploit her notoriety in *The Blue Flame* (1920). Not fewer than three writers contributed to this ludicrous fantasy in which Bara played a saintly young woman, struck dead by lightning, who is "raised" by her God-scorning scientist of a boy friend. He believes his atheism to be more powerful than Creation, but ho! The heroine's physical entity can be revived, but not her soul: and Bara awakes as the character familiar to her movie fans, the bad girl who lives to destroy and destroys to live. "Gimme a kiss" are her first words when brought back among the quick, and audiences that took the line in their stride might have gasped later, when she greeted one of her victims with "Have you brought the cocaine?" Later, Bara threatened yet another of her fools with "I'll shake you like I shake my shimmy!" In the end, it was all a dream—and, incidentally, a kind of digest of Bara herself, a nice middle-class girl from Cincinnati who impersonated the sinner in thirty-nine silent films for five years, made a brief return in the mid-1920s, and spent the remaining thirty-five years of her life At Liberty. It was all a dream.

In 1920, at least, Bara was a draw, and the curious came to call, if only to hear what a vamp *sounded* like. Alan Dale of the *New York American* noted a "pass-me-the-salt-please" vocal delivery, though Bara had started on the stage. She had even played Broadway, in one of the two productions of Ferenc Molnár's *The Devil* that ran simultaneously in 1908, appearing as Theodosia de Coppet. *The Blue Flame* lasted only 48 performances in New York, but it toured very well considering that Bara was a novelty whose trend was over.

The more typical melodrama was made of blood and guts, rather than *The Blue Flame*'s fantasy science. Laurence Eyre's *Martinique* (1920) brought its public to 1842 and the world of Creoles and mulattoes, in a script rich with racist attitudes. Hero Stephane loves heroine Zabette, but is forced to marry Zabette's snobby half sister. The usual insidious half-breed, hot for Zabette, attacks Stephane, but at least he and Zabette have produced an heir, even if Stephane dies of his wounds and Zabette enters a convent for no reason in particular. When the half-breed first made his advances to the heroine, one heard the passionate retort of "Leave this house . . . *negro!*" from Zabette. "It is at such great moments," observed Alexander Woollcott in the *New York Times*, "that one misses the gallery."*

Martinique lasted about as long as *The Blue Flame* and, like it, vanished forever. But when Austin Strong's *Seventh Heaven* (1922) finished its 704 performances, it was on its way to a 1927 film version with Janet Gaynor and Charles Farrell that won Gaynor the first Best Actress Oscar (the movie itself got a nomination), not to mention a 1937 remake with Simone Simon and James Stewart. On Broadway, Helen Menken and George Gaul played Diane and Chico, the sewer man who takes Diane to the heights— a seventh-floor walkup. Violence or its threat was endemic to melodrama, though this title limits it to Diane's abuse by her whip-wielding sister. But for the whipping scenes, *Seventh Heaven* might be a simple romance of life and love in Paris, for the bulk of the tale follows the arc of Diane's love for Chico, interrupted when he goes off to fight in the Great War. Now a complication: a wealthy interloper (Frank Morgan) convinces Diane that Chico is dead, and the destroyed Diane numbly submits to him. But wait! Chico *isn't* dead! He bursts into the room as Diane and the moneybags are embracing. Oh, no! Except Chico has seen nothing: he is blind! And true love reunited can rise above every misfortune.

---

* Those seated in the gallery—encompassing the cheapest seats, at the top of the house—were in olden days notoriously eager to comment on the quality of the evening's playwrighting.

Broadway got a taste of the violence that stormed through old-time melodrama when George Dibdin Pitt's nineteenth-century blood banquet *Sweeney Todd* was put on, in 1924, in a double bill with a short afterpiece of an opera spoof called *Bombastes Furioso*. Robert Vivian played Sweeney and Raffaella Ottiano was Mrs. Lovett; he was uncelebrated, but some of my readers may remark Ottiano, who played the ballerina's maid in *Grand Hotel* the play (1930) and movie (1932) and who lent her name (in an alteration as Ottanio) to the character in the musical (1989). For all that, note that both *Seventh Heaven* and *Sweeney Todd* also eventually became musicals. As we'll see, a Golden Age has plenty of chances to exploit its materials, keeping the art vital by trying it in different forms.

Sweeney Todd was apparently played straight rather than for laughs. But then, melodrama was still a vital form in the 1920s. It was never guyed—not even John Colton's *The Shanghai Gesture* (1926). This was the most extreme example of the genre to make hit status, with its "babies switched at birth" ruse and one of those revenge plots in which the plotter patiently waits twenty years to execute the humiliation of the English lord who wronged her.

Wronged her? He sold her into slavery! But all the torture and degradation that colonial China might visit upon an innocent girl did not impede her progress from whore to brothelkeeper—aye, to Mother Goddamn, the impassive custodian of all the government spy secrets and sex manias in China. *The Shanghai Gesture* is set entirely on the afternoon and evening of a single New Year's Day in four different parts of Mother Goddamn's establishment—the Gallery of Laughing Dolls, the Grand Red Hall of Lily and Lotus Roots, the Little Room of the Great Cat, and the Green Stairway of the Angry Dragon—and the slim plot slowly reaches what Mother Goddamn has waited so long to give to her betrayer of long ago. This is the sight of his own daughter (by a respectable English bride) being sold into slavery. Appealing to the tastes of one of the bidders, a certain Mr. Shu Ki, Mother Goddamn eggs him on with "Think of your hairy chest against her lovely young breasts." So it was with the young Mother Goddamn; so now with this poor innocent. Revenge is not only sweet but symmetrical.

To add to the fun, director Guthrie McClintic and star Florence Reed worked out a characterization for Mother Goddamn in a monotone pitched between an ironic servility and a coiled-spring hatred for men. The critics found it . . . well, monotonous. That is, until Reed got to the role's big set piece, the stupendous "Yet I survived!" speech. This swirling crescendo of a mad scene catalogued all the terrors of the life that Sir Guy Charteris (McKay Morris) exiled Reed to, each culminating in the frenzied spit of the three-word refrain. "Yet I survived! Yet I *survived!*" It was the talk of the town; and after Mother Goddamn's daughter (Mary Duncan), raised by Sir Guy, came reeling out of a passion suite having debauched herself, what could Mother Goddamn do but murder her? It's more symmetry.

One reason why this hoary genre still held the stage was the opportunity it gave the actor. When the young Brian Aherne was offered the juvenile lead in the West End staging of *White Cargo,* Aherne jumped at it, because this tale of life on a West African rubber plantation was built around the breakdown of an idealistic and energetic young chap—Aherne's role—amid the heat and boredom, and, as well, the sensual temptation of Tondelayo, native girl. (Technically, she's half French and half African, full-scale miscegenation being too controversial for love plots in conventional drama at this time.) The boy makes a strong entrance, all hope and vigor as he announces to the others, "I'll be all right when I'm acclimatized."

No, he won't. By the play's end, he is so depleted both physically and emotionally that he is loaded upon a boat bound for England in a comatose state, just so much "white cargo." It's a colorful exit, certain to pay off in the curtain calls a few minutes later.

Of course, Aherne got his shot at *White Cargo* only after Richard Stevenson originated the role, that of Allan Langford, on Broadway. True, all the white characters are English, and they speak in that stage patois of Trench War Teatime that was invented by English dramatists. (You'll hear it the next time someone revives R. C. Sherriff's war play *Journey's End* [1928].) *White Cargo*'s author, Leon Gordon, both acted and wrote; this was his one great moment. He had had trouble interesting a manager in the work because of its sensual devilry, but Earl Carroll, who had recently launched his *Vanities* revues on a foundation of sensual devilry, took an option. For some reason, Carroll opened *White Cargo,* in 1923, at the Greenwich Village Theatre, at Seventh Avenue and West Fourth Street. Was it to be publicized as too hot for Broadway? It was cheaper than Broadway, at least: a popular rumor told that Carroll had spent less than one hundred dollars on the production.

Surely not; though with one cheesy little set and only nine players, *White Cargo* would have run Carroll two thousand dollars at most had he launched it on Broadway. As it was, its flash success took it uptown, at first to the thousand-seat Daly's Sixty-third Street Theatre, where Carroll re-billed it as "a vivid play of the primitive." *The Shanghai Gesture* lasted some ten months—a very strong showing then—but *White Cargo* ran over twice as long, because Aherne was partly right. Langford is a no-fail part, but, mainly, *White Cargo* is a no-fail play, not least because everyone likes to watch a nice boy fall for a bad girl. Carroll liked to watch bad girls, period, especially because they wore so little, at least in his plays. And Tondelayo (Annette Margules, succeeded in the move uptown by Betty Pierce) is not only bad but homicidal. After all, if this is melodrama, someone has to be.

Then, too, Gordon troubled to frame his piece with an interesting, if familiar, irony: when men of the civilization of Dante and Goethe are cut off from cultural nourishment, they degenerate. Of course, there would be a seen-it-all Doctor (Conway Wingfield; in London it would be Horace Hodges, whom we saw playing Bill Jones in the West End *Lightnin'*). He provides ironic commentary, like the doctor in *Grand Hotel*. Traditionally, there must be a subsidiary anti-hero, here a man named Witzel (A. E. Anson), who survives in this atmosphere because he has no ideals to maintain.* The doctor is usually a drinker (in *Grand Hotel* a drug addict), and Langford is not only clean-cut and upright but firm in his morals: so we can marvel at his decline when, in the second act, he appears messy and unshaven and vacillating. Acclimatized. Not only is Langford Tondelayo's lover, but he marries her, which leads to further degradation. Finally, Tondelayo tires of respectability and tries to poison Langford, weakened by fever. But Witzel catches her and forces the venom—culled from the junna leaf—down her own throat.

It's a fine, tense scene. But more: thus the "beachcomber" atones for his life of aimless exile, for only the unbeliever has the freedom to play God and kill evil to save the good. The Doctor, so busy dispensing pills and wisdoms, would be ineffectual here.

Thus neutralized, Tondelayo runs off in terror to die in the bush as Witzel packs Langford onto the boat home. To round off the play, this same boat

---

* This was a common theatrical figure then; one thinks of the role of the beachcomber offered to the faded matinée idol in Kaufman and Ferber's *Dinner at Eight* (1932). We learn virtually nothing about the character, but we know him all the same: a wastrel with a point of view, cynical but capable of pretty sarcasms.

has brought the next Langford, this one called—of course—Worthy (Harris Gilmore). He tells one and all, "I'll be all right when I'm acclimatized."

"God almighty!" thunders the Doctor, as the curtain falls.

Interestingly, both *The Shanghai Gesture* and *White Cargo* were filmed as late as the early 1940s; they can't have been *that* outdated. Also, *White Cargo* tends to attract PR-building controversy wherever it goes, and controversy knows no age. During the original New York run, Ida Vera Simonton brought successful legal action against the production, claiming plagiarism of her novel *Hell's Playground*. (MGM's 1942 *White Cargo* film had to bill Simonton and her book right below Gordon and his play as the script's sources.) A 1961 revival took the piece back to its off-Broadway origin, meanwhile resetting it in Brazil. What can a modern-day Tondelayo (Marcia Howard) do but play at least a moment in the nude, albeit facing upstage? One night, a man reportedly leaped onto the stage in protest and had to be removed from the theatre. In fact, he had simply risen to object from his second-row seat. The man, Frank Lynn, explained that he and his wife had taken an oath to the Roman Catholic Legion of Decency to denounce all entertainment that they saw as objectionable.

Nudity in 1961! One would have expected a typhoon of ticketbuyers, but *White Cargo* simply closed. It had taken two generations to accomplish, but twenties melodrama had finally cooled off.

Another form popular in the early 1920s was a sort of faux theatre, works whose setting and actions stood beyond the physical potential of the stage. They needed to be movies. Describing *Aloma of the South Seas* (1925), the *Times'* Stark Young outlined a place of "swimming, strange fruits, sea weeds and sea shells." Moreover, "the islands themselves are plainly magical in their naive sexual allusions and loving vehemences. . . . They invent the most singularly disconcerting images from the love life of the animals." What, right there on stage?

In fact, authors John B. Hymer and LeRoy Clemens shoehorned *Aloma* into playhouse proportions by leaving all the interesting parts offstage. What remained in view was a feverish melodrama with the usual East of Suez romance between native girl Aloma and a Westerner. Actually, he loves another, a white woman—married, at that. So far, so good: but trailing Aloma is a fierce suitor who keeps the courtship tidy by taking his rivals for a ride—in a canoe, to the sharks' feeding ground. As with *White Cargo,* interracial romance must fail. So the suitor kills the supererogatory husband (he was a drunk, so he had it coming), leaving the white pair to marry and head for home.

Most typically, the "oversized" form of theatre capitalized on a popular literary work, staging it if only because the pubic wanted to *see* the account, and cinema had not yet become *embourgeoisé.* Three such examples turned up in September of 1921. Edgar Rice Burroughs' *Tarzan* had actually enjoyed some half dozen movie features and serials; nevertheless, English actor Ronald Adair, who claimed a boxing background, was imported for *Tarzan of the Apes,* which also included jungle beasts and two men in ape costumes. It lasted two weeks. *The Blue Lagoon,* previously a hit in London, lasted three. "The audience," Alexander Woollcott reported, greeted it "with yawns, titters, and occasional murmurs of mutiny." There was a great deal of mime and incidental music* to help the tale along, but how is one to re-create the book's innocent sexuality without the geography of ocean and isle?

Neither Edgar Rice Burroughs nor H. De Vere Stacpoole is regarded as a literary eminence, but Vicente Blasco Ibañez's novels were read around the world. *The Four Horsemen of the Apocalypse* was enjoying its first seasons of fame when the other famous Ibañez title, *Blood and Sand,* came to Broadway as the third of this set. The tale depends very strongly on the drama of the bull ring; how is one to "play" that on stage? Worse, the production starred the sixty-three-year-old Otis Skinner, though there are no

---

* Through the 1920s, all Broadway theatres included orchestral music with the performance. Classic works from Shakespeare to *Peer Gynt* made use of incidental scores, and a few modern works called for the like, but most plays offered if nothing else a bit of concertizing before the show, during intermissions, and after the curtain. It was an amenity that seemed logical in a culture that for the most part had to leave the home to hear more than the parlor piano. The record player and its software were not truly acculturated till the age of the LP (1948–90), and radio claimed a national audience only at the end of the 1920s. Thus, orchestras of some size or other were made available as much as possible for those who didn't frequent the concert hall or opera house, in summer park recitals at the bandstand, in restaurants, and in theatres. Even *Lightnin',* driest of comedies, was moistened by an Overture (so the program called it) of a medley of tunes from a recent Jerome Kern show, *Head Over Heels;* by various songs of the day between the acts; and by "You're the Very Girl," from the latest Hippodrome spectacle, for the so-called Exit March. All that remains of this practice is the squad of "walkers," the non-playing musicians that the union requires each playhouse to maintain. As long as they're hired, why not use them?

sixty-three-year-old bull fighters, especially in the kinds of romances that Ibañez was known for. Another failure, *Blood and Sand* made a more appropriate transformation that same year as a film with Rudolph Valentino, a mere stripling of twenty-six; a talkie remake with Tyrone Power, near senility at twenty-eight, followed.

One thing that theatre could do in its own manner was the spectacle. This was playmaking that rose above the concept of a script to the marketing of an eyeful, and it derived its power precisely by defying the natural limits of the stage with colossal sets and hordes of extras. One thinks of the biblical pageants popular around the turn of the century— *Ben-Hur* (1899), complete with the galley ship and even a smidgen of chariot race with the horses on treadmills; or the two versions of *Quo Vadis* that opened on the same night in 1900. Or the Hippodrome, whose Godzilla variety shows held the very center of the meaning of "Broadway" for a generation, from its opening in 1905.

Surely, the Babylonian sequence in D. W. Griffith's *Intolerance* (1916) indicated that here, too, Hollywood would absorb the genre—especially as the stage spectacle insisted on pagan settings and religious subjects, exactly where Griffith's successor Cecil B. De Mille was at his liveliest. In fact, Broadway may have held on to the spectacle into the 1920s merely because New York had two gigantic theatres left over from former lives with nothing in particular to do, the Manhattan Opera House and the New Theatre. The first Oscar Hammerstein—that magnate of cigars, vaudeville, and, his favorite, opera—built the Manhattan Opera House (actually the second and grander of two Hammerstein theatres with this name, both on West Thirty-fourth Street) in 1906 to compete with the Metropolitan Opera Company. He was so good at it that the Met had to buy him out. However, no one had to bribe the troupe at the New Theatre out of competition, for this attempt to create a national repertory theatre, on Central Park West at Sixty-second Street, was a two-season disaster in 1909–11.

One of the New's many problems was terrible acoustics. But dialogue was spectacle's least important feature, and the music, on which spectacle strongly depended, could be heard. Renamed the Century, the former New, open to bookings generally, got first pick of the available attractions, particularly from managers F. Ray Comstock and Morris Gest. They tended to shop Europe for likely exhibits, and the sheer size of the things made them headline news. *Aphrodite* (1919) was French in origin, *Mecca* (1920) English, and *The Miracle* (1924), a Max Reinhardt production, German. *The Miracle* especially kept reporters busy. At a time when a big musical might break the fifty-thousand-dollar mark, *The Miracle* cost six hundred thousand dollars, because the set designer, Norman Bel Geddes, built a cathedral interior into the Century's auditorium, the nave running down into what had been the New's orchestra section. No fewer than three hundred workers built the set's elements, and it took six weeks to put it all together. The *New York Times* ran an article on such details next to the first-night review, as if *The Miracle*'s physical entity was as newsy as the experience: but wasn't it? There were twenty-two assistant directors during rehearsals, forty electricians, fifty stagehands, and a cast—so said the *Times*—of seven hundred.

The Miracle's medieval tale of a nun who forsakes her order to visit the world and finally learns that a statue of Mary has come to life to undertake her duties in her absence got some mileage out of the Virgin's being played by Lady Diana Manners. Still, for all its war of sacred and profane, *The Miracle* was extremely chaste next to the excesses of *Aphrodite*. Both shows were hits, because there was a huge public for this kind of thing— and of course *Aphrodite* was "French" at a time when the word carried connotations of erotic brinkmanship. There was even a nude, though her skin was covered in a film of paint, which seems to have made the difference between outrage and titillation.

When Morris Gest caught *Aphrodite* at the Théâtre de la Renaissance in Paris, it was a showcase for the diverse arts that collaborate in these huge forms. Thus, the abundant musical score was by the well-known (though now forgot) Henri Février and the choreography by the still celebrated Michel Fokine, rather overwhelming the delicate byline of dramatist Pierre Frondaie, working from the novel by the also celebrated Pierre Louÿs.

Indeed, the show's high point was music and dance, in a bacchanalia, but then the entire piece is steamy, as one expects. *The Miracle* has its sensationalistically violent side, especially when the heroine nearly gets her head chopped off in a scene modeled on Breughel at his cruelest; *Aphrodite* has violence and sex. *Bref,* in old Alexandria the sculptor Demetrios (McKay Morris, later of *The Shanghai Gesture,* one may recall) must steal three fabulous treasures to win the love of the courtesan Chrysis (Dorothy Dalton). These are the Rhodopoid Mirror, the three-thousand-year-old ivory comb of Queen Nitocris, and the seven strings of pearls adorning Demetrios' own statue of Aphrodite (impersonated by actress Mildred Walker). The theft of the comb involves a murder, and even to touch the pearls is sacrilege. Worse, the innocent Aphrodasia (dancer Mlle. Dazie) is crucified for allegedly taking the mirror. Aphrodite appears to Demetrios in a vision, inspiring him to repulse Chrysis, and she jumps from the Pharos Lighthouse into the sea.

The Broadway version, translated by George C. Hazelton, introduced yet more music, by Anselm Goetzl, as well as camels and horses and a cast of three hundred. Late in rehearsals, David Belasco (who was Gest's father-in-law) took over the direction. Belasco received no billing, but he made one of his solemn bows on opening night, one of the season's biggest at eleven dollars a seat. (Speculators were said to be getting two hundred a pair.) "Too beautiful, too sensational and too novel to be missed," declared the unsigned review in the *Sun*. The carnal atmosphere certainly helped the 148-performance run along, though Alexander Woollcott thought the show "as pure as a Barnum & Bailey parade." However, Alan Dale wrote a priggishly angry review, accusing *Aphrodite* of hiding sordid lubricity behind a facade of Continental art. "Evil" he called it. Worse, he repeatedly stated his horror at the mingling of black and white among the extras. The past really is another country.

A work such as *Aphrodite* reminds us how common European plays were along The Street—and not just from England but from Italy, France, Hungary, and the newly formed Czechoslovakia. Henri Bataille's *Don Juan* (1921), in a translation by Lawrence Langner, was seen here for only two weeks, probably because the star, Lou Tellegen, was one of the least interesting of matinée idols. In this retelling, everyone mistakenly thinks Don Juan has died and he finds that, shorn of his reputation, he cannot get a date. A note in the Garrick Theatre program observed that while the typical *Don Juan* opus punishes the libertine with death, Bataille decided "to punish him with life."

These Continental works were bombing in unusually high numbers. Another two-week failure was Maurice Maeterlinck's *Pelleas and Melisande* (so billed), which Broadway had seen earlier, in 1902, with Mrs. Patrick Campbell, complete with *accents aigus* as *Pelléas et Mélisande* and an orchestra playing Gabriel Fauré's incidental score. The work did not go over, though New Yorkers had the opportunity to hear virtually the entire original Paris cast of Claude Debussy's operatic adaptation in 1908, when Oscar Hammerstein was still playing host at the Manhattan Opera House. It's a shy and furtive piece, spoken or sung, in English or French, but Jane Cowl thought the time was right for this second viewing of the play, in 1923. Rollo Peters co-starred and also designed the sets.

One senses the influence of the Theatre Guild in these arty endeavors, if only because Lawrence Langner (and *Don Juan*'s set designer, Lee Simonson) were Guild honchos, the Garrick was the Guild's home till 1925, and Rollo Peters, too, was a Guild eminence. But the Guild, as we'll see, counted on a subscription audience as a bank against fast closings, while freelance managements daring the exotic were risking all. It was Russell Janney who produced Melchior Lengyel's *Sancho Panza* (1923), adapted by Sidney Howard, and Janney was not enriched by the show's five-week run (though he did clean up on *The Vagabond King* two years after). *Sancho Panza* gave Otis Skinner another Spanish character, this one more age-appropriate than *Blood and Sand*'s young bullfighter. Moreover, Lengyel's impish notion quite suited Skinner's comic flair: what happens to Don Quixote's assistant after Cervantes? Although the piece played the Hudson, whose tiny stage offers virtually no wing space, the critics all claimed to have seen an extremely elaborate production. Quixote appeared only in a prologue, delivering an oration on chivalry. Then Otis Skinner piped up:

SANCHO: When do we eat?

It sounds like fun, especially because of Sancho's donkey, impersonated by Robert Rosaire, who captivated the reviewers. In view of the capsule history of American acting that will maintain a throughline throughout this book, we should note that *Sancho Panza*'s director was Richard Boleslavsky, one of the first adepts of Stanislafsky to preach the master in the West.

It was an American who wrote the oddest of the "Continental" plays, Michael Strange. *Clair de Lune* (1921), drawn from parts of Victor Hugo's *The Man Who Laughs,* changed the spelling of Hugo's British anti-hero from Gwynplaine to Gwymplane, which perhaps suggests Strange's fastidious approach in general. Apparently, she saw the European play as a place of high romance intensely poeticized. Beyond the byline, Strange was Blanche Barrymore, John's second wife, and le tout New York believed that it was only John's enthusiasm—and his having coerced sister Ethel into signing on for a rare joint appearance—that made *Clair de Lune* possible.

The story itself is extremely rococo: the man who laughs was so mutilated under torture that his mouth is fixed in a hideous grin, and his adventures in the play involve him mainly with a sweet-hearted blind girl and a nymphomaniacal duchess. Ethel played Queen Anne, a kind of referee in Strange's game of crazed passions run amok. One of her speeches ran, "I hate sentimentality. It reminds me of people with colds in their heads who have lost their pocket handkerchiefs." That has the flavor of Oscar Wilde. But too much of *Clair de Lune* has the flavor of Michael Strange, as in "The touch of your lips is like a tide rushing, sucking my wakefulness down into the depths of terrible oblivion."

Even so, the opening brought out a mad crush of event collectors, from the great and the near great to the would bes and the curious. Remember, in those days there were no on-site previews; shows either opened cold or tried out in other cities, almost invariably generating contradictory reports. Also, there were no "critics' dates" just before the premiere, as today; critics attended the premiere only, lending the evening a dangerous excitement. The first night was as well a chance to catch an actor speaking not written lines but in his own style, in the star's curtain speech. Playwrights, too, made remark if called to the stage, or at least took a bow.* Perhaps most important, the first night was when New York officially delivered its verdict on the value of the new piece, the new performer, so many prominent people felt it necessary to defend their prominence by taking part in that process. Indeed, major openings called out a vast number of the unimportant as well; cops held them back as the arriving audience became as much a focus as the play on view. Later on in the history, a revue called *Thumbs Up!* (1934) featured a song by Vernon Duke (words as well as music) called "Autumn in New York."

---

* A venerable tradition that allowed the public its sole "honest" contact with star thespians, the curtain speech fell away in the 1930s as naturalistic acting replaced the personality star. With no permanent character to display in show after show, the actor now became one with his various roles, and thus had no "self" to exhibit at the curtain. As each performance ended, so, in effect, did he.

Extolling and regretting the typifying matters of the timeplace, Duke's lyric troubles to relish "the thrill of first nighting."

So John and Ethel Barrymore in John's wife's demented play was reason to throng the Empire Theatre, and choice pairs of tickets were touted at the door for as much as two hundred fifty dollars. Almost no one liked the piece, but it certainly wasn't boring: it ended with John cutting out his own heart and the duchess lapping up the spilled blood. *Clair de Lune* ran 64 performances.

The romance of the Barrymores is one of the most enduring tropes in American celebrity culture; it is difficult to imagine early-twentieth-century show biz without them. One reason why it took the movies almost two generations to overtake the stage was simply its "illiteracy." But the main reason was that stardom had long been established as a kind of secular Mass celebrating an individual encountered in real time, real life. Even without the opening-night curtain speech, the public enjoyed a relationship with stage players that simply could not be rivaled by the dumb show of silent film. Then, too, the theatre's stars maintained lengthy careers, creating a bond with their public, a mutual support system. Movie fame could be bizarrely transient; we've already noticed that one of the greatest Hollywood reigns, that of Theda Bara, was over in five years.

The Barrymores not only sustained full-length careers but were scions of a dynasty, the Drews. This lent a comforting stability to the very business of theatre, which—especially after 1919—seemed ever crazing into novelties that divided the audience, such as Shakespeare in a unit set, or scripts that baffled genre. Ethel made headliner first, under Charles Frohman's management, as an opera singer marrying into New York society in *Captain Jinks of the Horse Marines* (1901). It was typical Frohman: a brand-name playwright (Clyde Fitch) who knew how to focus attention on a star player while riffing mildly on social antagonisms. Thus Frohman set Ethel upon a course she seldom veered from thereafter, exploring the nuances of charm for an appreciative public, albeit in rather a variety of roles. Still, there were almost always the patented Ethel things—refinements of tone in the husky voice, the gala bearing and sheer class of a woman who wouldn't dream of letting you know that if she isn't among royalty she's slumming. There were more interesting actresses, but no finer company.

The older Lionel actually spent most of his youth making movies; his stage work was so spotty that he never enjoyed an abiding relationship with any management. As anyone familiar with his talkies can attest, he was made for melodrama. His breakthrough part, as Illinois farmer Milt Shanks in Augustus Thomas' Civil War piece *The Copperhead* (1918), was typical of both Lionel and the genre: suspected of Southern sympathies and ostracized by the community, he waits fifty years to disclose that he was working in secret for the North. The scene of revelation—made in a letter of commendation from President Lincoln—was one of those old-fashioned Big Moments that redeem the season and become officially Unforgettable.

Still it was John, the youngest, who occupied the center of the Barrymore romance; who inspired the clucking of tongues and (later) shady gossip-column items; who passed his first fifteen years in the theatre as a light-comic matinée idol only to discover a genuine dramatic gift in first-rate works mounted by top-line managers; and whose defection from the stage for drunken gambols through movieland became a favorite retelling of that great American saga of the doomed beauty.

Make no mistake: everyone was in love with John Barrymore. Lookers are plentiful in the acting trade, but a looker with wit and spirit can be unforgivably magnetic, and while John loathed long runs, he did love assuming new roles, changing his form and magnetism. Another joint Barrymore appearance took the two boys to Medici Florence, in Sem Benelli's *La Cena delle Beffe*, adapted by John's pal Edward Sheldon as *The Jest* (1919). Lionel played a thug and John the mouse who defeats him with guile, and the pair enjoyed a genuine triumph. But note how the *Times'* John Corbin discerned in John "a white flame of beauty, half spiritual, half decadent." The last word was contemporary code for "gay," so what exactly was Corbin discerning? John's role in *The Jest* had been played, in Italy and France, as a trouser part (i.e., by a woman in male drag), and when John left *The Jest* during the New York run, Gilda Varesi, a minor member of the company, took over for him. Is this character less that of a mouse—he does end up sleeping with the thug's mistress—than that of a pansexual? Disciplined in his youth by a strict grandmother, the redoubtable Mrs. John Drew Sr., John would be exiled to the attic for a time-out in the dark. "You can't hurt me!" he would call out, ascending the dreadful stairs to who knew what monstrous beings. "I have a wonderful power!"

They all did, those Barrymores: though John was more fun than Lionel and more tolerant than Ethel. He was infuriatingly undependable, but he had the gift of youthfulness: those who knew him said he never aged in spirit. Better, he kept them young. How much of that did his public sense, and how much drew them to him? Did they *know* these people on some level—or else why did they clap so very warmly when Ethel made her first entrance after the Strike, in *Déclassée* (1920)? The critics ticketed it as thanks for her leadership in the 1919 job action, her sense of responsibility to her community.

Shakespeare was another way to effect that distant intimacy with leading players, for there was always a revival going up, and theatregoers knew their Bard. John donned the mantle of America's Most Promising Actor as Richard III in 1920, under Arthur Hopkins' management (Hopkins not only produced but directed), a well-nigh luminous evil. Then, in 1921, Hopkins starred Lionel in a universally despised *Macbeth* that sounds fascinating, as designer Robert Edmond Jones set the action in front of giant masks in suspended pools of light and as Hopkins directed Lionel and his Lady, Julia Arthur, to create innocent beings in thrall to witchcraft. However, Broadway was not yet ready for this kind of rethinking, and Lionel never got over the humiliation of failure in Shakespeare.

Hopkins and Jones also presented Ethel in *Romeo and Juliet,* in 1922, a month before Jane Cowl and her faithful Rollo Peters (again designing as well) appeared in the same work. Ethel had the busy McKay Morris as Romeo and Basil Sydney as Mercutio (Cowl's was Dennis King) and suffered a kind of qualified disaster. It wasn't terrible; it just had no reason for being there. Worse, for Ethel, Cowl's show was acclaimed. Flopping in a new play meant the playwright had let the star down. Flopping in Shakespeare was *flopping,* the actor's real nightmare. Sheer glamor did not avail, for the most relentless Shakespearean of the day was an actor without a shred of charisma—the opposite of a Barrymore, a Jane Cowl, even, one has to say, a Rollo Peters. This was Walter Hampden, perhaps the least mentioned of all Golden Age names. Though he appeared in a few new works as well as Ibsen and Barrie, he seemed to prefer performing plays that were four hundred years old, keeping an avid public in thrall. In Cole Porter's *Jubilee* (1935), a coterie of Noël Coward fans hails the Master's return from a long absence by reviewing all Broadway with "And as for actors the only one," going on to "was Walter Hampden, and that's no fun." As we'll see, the glittery Porter-Coward axis would challenge plain old actors like Hampden for reign on Broadway. Tradition? Or Sophistication?

Or simply John Barrymore as Hamlet? When Hopkins and Jones got to this event, also in 1922, there was, in John Corbin's words, "an atmosphere of historic happening." I save the word "legendary" for mythical figures; but doesn't John Barrymore now hold mythical status in America's actor culture? Certainly, his Hamlet is legendary, not least for—this is Corbin again—"the hushed murmurs that swept the audience at the most unexpected moments" and "silent crowds that all evening long swarmed about the theatre entrance." That "thrill of first nighting" that Vernon Duke sang of apparently extended even to those who couldn't gain the auditorium. But they could say, "I was there."

Those who actually saw John Barrymore's Hamlet cannot tell us of it, because he gave no one Hamlet. This restless subject of everyone's hopes experimented and improvised and even played jokes to keep from hating the 101-performance run. (This broke by one repetition Edwin Booth's grand old turn of 1864–65 at the old Winter Garden, on Broadway above Houston Street.) Perhaps the true John Barrymore Hamlet was the one he gave the first week or so, the result of painstaking rehearsals surprising in one who so often threw entire performances away.

This of course was the Barrymore Hamlet that the critics saw, and they let loose with near-unanimous praise on the highest level. John Corbin sent another valentine, recalling John's "exotic beauty" bringing "a thrill of admiration that was half pain" in Tolstoy's *Redemption* (1918) and *The Jest,* and seeing now a "slender figure, with its clean limbs, broad shoulders and massive head." Heywood Broun of the *New York Tribune* declared John "the most interesting, intelligent, and exciting Hamlet in this generation," and Kenneth Macgowan called John "truly magnificent." Even the support was thought excellent, with Blanche Yurka as the Queen (though she was John's junior by seven years), Tyrone Power (father of the movie actor) as Claudius, and an unusually sensual Ophelia from Rosalind Fuller.

Corbin did think the set design "trivial and grotesque": a great flight of stairs extending from wing to wing, with a curtailed playing area downstage and an arch at the back. As with the Hopkins-Jones *Macbeth* for Lionel, this was modern thinking, disturbingly ahead of its day on The Street, though it did allow for the novelty of continuous playing through each of

Hopkins' three subdivisions of the text. (His intermissions occurred after the first Players' scene and the murder of Polonius.) We forget now how fitfully Shakespeare played in the age when a change of scene often meant an empty wait while the stagehands struck and reset—and we should note, too, that while audiences of 1922 did rather know their *Hamlet,* Hopkins' cuts sought out untraditional options. This *Hamlet* really was a novelty from every standpoint.

So it wasn't just excellent: it was shocking. After taking it to London, John toured the show at home, making a three-week return to New York in November of 1923 at that cavernous Manhattan Opera House, proving what a phenomenon it was: the John Barrymore Hamlet! For years afterward, people disputed the meaning of that phrase, because it showed that John really was America's great actor, but it showed also that John himself didn't care. He walked. He went Hollywood. How valid was Broadway's cultural self-importance if America's great actor didn't need it?

After the Shakespearean revival—and the classics in general—perhaps the most prestigious theatre genre of the 1920s was the chronicle play. It attracted "serious" writers and a "serious" public, and its subjects were if nothing else prominent. True, Percy MacKaye's *George Washington* (1920) failed to resonate even with that dignified Walter Hampden as the First American, with Martha Washington, Alexander Hamilton, Patrick Henry, and Tom Paine along for a look at thirty years' worth of founding fathers. The problem was MacKaye, always so daintily visionary, so laborious yet so fanciful. A narrator called Quilloquon and two children sang between scenes, and side by side with Hamilton and Paine were such characters as The Comic Mask, The Tragic Mask, and The Presence. A two-week failure, *George Washington* ended the remarkable MacKaye dynasty, for Percy's father, Steele MacKaye, had been a major figure of the late nineteenth century as playwright, manager, and innovator in theatre design.

There was an *Abraham Lincoln* (1919) that same season, and this one was a big success. It had already been a hit in London, at the Lyric, Hammersmith, and was in fact the work of an Englishman, John Drinkwater. Unlike the sprawling *George Washington, Abraham Lincoln* concentrated: the piece began with Lincoln accepting the presidential nomination and ended with the assassination. Again there was a narrator, speaking in verse.

Otherwise the play was almost absurdly simple in diction, with no attempt to pastiche the lingo of Lincoln's day. Heywood Broun thought too much of Lincoln was missing, especially the "crackerbox storyteller." Broun liked the show but felt that a lively character had been turned into a Woodrow Wilson. Still, that all-important first-night audience was moved and even exhilarated, cheering for, of all people, Robert E. Lee. In the house was Robert B. Stanton, son of Lincoln's second secretary of war, Edwin M. Stanton; Junior had known Lincoln and declared the play true to the man.

George Washington had revolved around the colorless grandeur of Walter Hampden, but *Abraham Lincoln* had no stars, and the Lincoln, Frank McGlynn, was an unknown in his fifties, much as Frank Bacon had been when *Lightnin'* opened. McGlynn's playing was as simple and effective as the script, and he certainly looked the part. His was not the last word, however, for there was another Lincoln play the following season. This was the short-lived *A Man Of the People* (1920), by Thomas Dixon, author of the novel and melodrama *The Clansman* (1906), the source of D. W. Griffith's *The Birth of a Nation*.

But meanwhile, the South was displeased with Drinkwater's reading of history, particularly his characterization of Robert E. Lee. In an editorial, the *Richmond News-Leader* got righteous about the matter in somewhat racist tones: "A northern city, with a population half of whose ancestors were in Europe in 1860, may throng a theatre to see a false picture of Lincoln, but an Anglo-Saxon South . . . will never countenance any injustice to the memory of that prince among men [General Lee]."

This referred to the rumor that Drinkwater was contemplating writing a play about Lee: and he did. *Robert E. Lee* (1923) even began its tryout in this same Richmond, the very capital of the Confederacy. Along with Berton Churchill in the lead was Alfred Lunt as one of a quartet of young gentlemen who act as foils to the protagonist throughout the action, devoted to the war years.

Robert E. Lee closed quickly, as did *Voltaire* (1922) and *Pasteur* (1923), though both starred eminences of the pre-1919 era, respectively Arnold Daly and Henry Miller. In whiskers and glasses, Miller disappeared into the lead role of an unexpectedly all-male ensemble, and there was further innovation when *Pasteur*, in the middle of a speech, was heckled by doubters in his audience. These were impersonated by plants in the auditorium of the Empire Theatre, anticipating the vivid dramatic coups of the Federal Theatre's Living Newspapers of the 1930s.

The mystery was a favorite genre, often counting on the mass audience that avoided Shakespeare and chronicle. Rewriting Cora Dick Gantt's original script, George M. Cohan spoofed the form in *The Tavern* (1920), this one, too, with Arnold Daly. It had all the clichés—the dark and stormy night; the mysterious stranger; the unconscious girl carried in from outside; the gun aimed at the hero, who scoffs that it's out of bullets (or is he bluffing?)—and it scored a hit. But the public preferred its thrillers straight. John Willard, who had co-authored Theda Bara's vehicle *The Blue Flame,* wrote *The Cat and the Canary* (1922) around that soon-to-be old standby, the attempt to drive the heroine (Florence Eldridge) insane, to cheat her of a legacy.

A similar plotline ran through Avery Hopwood and Mary Roberts Rinehart's *The Bat* (1920), drawn from Rinehart's story "The Circular Staircase." At 867 performances, *The Bat* was for a few years Broadway's second-longest-running attraction (after *Lightnin'*), but this is to ignore *The Bat*'s national popularity. In the 1920s, successful plays—generally those running between 100 and 150 performances in New York—could then tour the road for one or two years as well. However, *The Bat* didn't wait to tour after the Broadway closing, and instead sent out specially organized touring companies—a total of six by the spring of 1922. Further, the piece was a favorite of high-school and amateur groups for two decades.

Yet *The Bat* is actually rather humdrum, short of the eccentric characters that enliven the genre in its later form. Think of Agatha Christie's *Ten Little Indians* (1944), with its sanctimonious spinster and devious doctor. What holds *The Bat* together is that perennial cartoon relationship of the no-nonsense lady of the manor and her credulous maid. We get the typical isolated house and raging storm right from the start, and within a line or two the maid establishes that all the other servants have run off because of . . . "it."

THE LADY OF THE MANOR: Fiddlesticks!

Suddenly, the mistress veers into nonsense, as the pair consult a Ouija board that spells out B, then A, then T. Returning to no-nonsense mode, the mistress decides to collect some hard news in the evening paper. So of course:

HEADLINE: POLICE AGAIN BAFFLED BY THE BAT

And we're good to go. Others in the cast include a Japanese butler; a hired detective; and a romantic couple, the mistress' niece and the new gardener. One reason why George M. Cohan liked to twit the form was that the serious thrillers depend so much on contrivance, as when the detective blandly defies plausibility with:

THE DETECTIVE: The architect who built this house was an old friend of
    mine. We were together in France. . . . Just an hour or two before a
    shell got him, he told me he had built a *hidden room* in this house.

Did I mention that a fortune is supposed to be concealed on the site? If only they can locate the blueprints . . . Wait, what's that strange rapping noise?

There is at least a fine first-act curtain, when the entire cast is onstage as the telephone rings. This particular outlet connects only with other rooms in the house, so:

THE LADY OF THE MANOR: But we're all here!

As the others look suitably nervous, perplexed, or guilty, the mistress picks up the receiver, listens, gasps, and allows an expression of terror to seize her features. And the curtain falls.

And here's a canny way to launch Act Two: the curtain goes up on *the very next moment*. Then, too, after the bad guy—the detective, as it happens—is outsmarted, the curtain comes down only to rise again on a nineteenth-century device relegated by this age to only the corniest fare, a kind of eleven o'clock pantomime. *The Bat*'s was devoted to May Vokes, an audience favorite as the maid, who was seen poking open a door, looking around in fear, then backing out of sight as the public presumably let out an appreciate chuckle.

———

As we range through the content of Broadway in the early 1920s—searching, especially, for signs of evolution—we must note the surprising staying power of one manager who would appear to represent the most old-fashioned of theatres, David Belasco. However, this former actor who by the late 1890s had established himself as playwright, manager, and director was in fact as inventive as he was conservative. Though he worked in a variety of forms, by the early 1900s he was emphasizing melodrama. Some may call it damning that two of Belasco's offerings turned so easily into Puccini operas; and his *The Darling of the Gods* (1902) is *Tosca* in Japan. Then, too, there is Belasco the fraudulent "realist," rationalizing these melodramas with crudely naturalistic decor. This only stresses the humbug, by looking real in an unreal context. And what of Belasco the starmaker? Isn't the ridiculous Svengali of *Twentieth Century* (1932) inspired in part by Belasco?

Even so, all this ignores Belasco's ability to organize acting ensembles for his shows even while centering those precious stars of his, such as Mrs. Leslie Carter, Blanche Bates, and David Warfield. Other directors treated the extras as if they were bric-à-brac; Belasco individualized them. (No wonder he was called in to unify the sprawling *Aphrodite*.) Further, Belasco rehearsed more meticulously than other directors, searching (and rewriting) the text for characterological honesty in a shockingly modern way. History's verdict is that Belasco was a gifted but antique show-off. Yet critics of his first nights saw it differently: Belasco put on good shows.

The difference in perception lies, obviously, in the ephemeral nature of performance. All that survives of Belasco today is the unimpressive scripts. Of Belasco's collaboration with writer George Scarborough, *The Son-Daughter* (1919), the *Evening Sun* observed "a paste jewel put into a handsome gold setting." Too often, the play wasn't the thing: Belasco's execution of it was. *The Son-Daughter* set forth the latest Belasco discovery, Lenore Ulric, as a young woman of New York's Chinatown who avenges her father's murder and an attempt on her fiancé's life by agreeing to give herself to the bad guy. She despatches him instead in an elaborate murder scene. It's more *Tosca*. There was also the customary Belasco pageantry, in a set-piece wedding in The Chamber of the Smiling Joss.

Ulric is a "son-daughter" because she loves like a woman, with filial respect, but counters outrages with rough justice, like a man. More conventionally, Ulric went on to Belasco's French backstager *Kiki* (1921), as a chorus girl on the rise, thence to Belasco's production of a Hungarian sex comedy, *The Harem* (1924). Returning to the unconventional, Ulric got into blackface for one of Belasco's biggest successes, *Lulu Belle* (1926), written by Edward Sheldon and his nephew Charles MacArthur.*

Lulu Belle is *Carmen,* set in Manhattan and Paris and anticipating more than slightly what Oscar Hammerstein did in *Carmen Jones* (1943). Where *The Son-Daughter's* dramatis personae are entirely Chinese, *Lulu Belle's* are black but for the local cop and, eventually, the heroine's French admirer. All the principals have parallels in Bizet's opera: Don José becomes George (Henry Hull), Escamillo a boxer named Butch Cooper (John Harrington), which precisely looks forward to Hammerstein's Husky Miller, and Micaëla is altered from village sweetheart to moralizing Uncle Gustus (Lawrence Eddinger). Even Zuniga is present, as a doctor whom Lulu Belle knocks unconscious with a hypodermic before rolling him.

No question, Lulu Belle is a user and a cheat. Bizet's heroine is admirable in her independence. She doesn't ruin men; they ruin themselves for her. Lulu Belle, however, is a parasite. She's attracted to George mainly for the sport of stealing him from his wife, and the more he resists the

---

* No American theatre history is complete without a footnote on Ned Sheldon. A stagestruck Ivy Leaguer with a magnetic personality, Sheldon was still in his early twenties when he became Broadway's reigning serious playwright, particularly for *Salvation Nell* (1908), an outstanding title in the evolution of realism. But Sheldon loved more than the truth of theatre: he loved its mad sad glamor, and enjoyed his biggest success with *Romance* (1913), on the doomed relationship between an Italian soprano and a Protestant cleric. Sheldon had his own doomed relationship: he was apparently in love with the homophobic John Barrymore, and this may have been the cause of a hysterical paralysis that gradually crippled and blinded Sheldon. This teaming of the man of ideas with the unavailable beauty is a gay trope, as each builds the other's self-esteem. But this time something else happened, and perhaps the breaking of Sheldon's confidence broke his health. Not yet thirty, he was unable to move about freely, but he was a favorite along The Street and never lacked for social diversion. Spiffily dressed pour le sport, lying down as if to nap after the Harvard-Yale regatta, Sheldon attended shows in his bedroom; the best cast parties climaxed with everyone roaring up to Ned Sheldon's to encore the play for him alone. Reduced to collaborating, he continued to produce his specialty, the woman's star vehicle, writing his last two entries with Margaret Ayer Barnes: Jane Cowl in *Jenny* (1929) and Katharine Cornell in *Dishonored Lady* (1930), in which she gets away with murdering an inconvenient lover. Sheldon had become a living corpse when he learned that John Barrymore was about to die, and entrusted a letter to nephew MacArthur with instructions to travel across the country to deliver it personally. Who but this valiant, wonderful, destroyed Ned Sheldon could have asked for such a favor; and can you guess what was in the letter? When MacArthur got to Los Angeles and handed the letter to John, he tossed it into the fire without reading it. Perhaps he'd guessed.

more she vamps him. His "Git away f'um me" is just so much confetti on her runway:

> LULU BELLE: It's too late now! I'm gonna cook an' carve and chew yo' up and swallow yo'! [Indeed, his grip on her tightens; the script calls him "intoxicated."] Eat me like I wuz a piece o'candy! Drink me like I wuz a glass o' wine! Kiss me! Kiss me till I'm dead and buried!

They get into "a long, wild kiss," and George comes gasping out of it "like a drowning man." No point in wasting time:

> LULU BELLE: Wheah yo' live?

Now we get a sample of the Belasco touch, albeit in a play written by others: a combination of absurdly posing showmanship and casual naturalism at once. The showmanship inheres in what we immediately sense will be the first-act curtain: grabbing George's arm, Lulu Belle cries, "Let's strut!," leading the poor bewildered man off for an exhibition exit. Comes now the naturalization, for as the curtain very slowly starts to fall, two biddies who have spent the act commenting on the doings from their overhead windows reappear for a last shot. Says Mrs. Frisbie in the last seconds before the orchestra strikes up for the intermission, "She's landed him, Mrs. Williams."

This is the paradox of David Belasco, the faker of Big Moments even as he undercuts them with dead-on realism. Belasco played the old with the new at once, for instance in the near-documentary feeling of the first act, a tableau of West Fifty-ninth Street with apartment buildings, movie theatre, De Luxe Café and Bar, a real automobile, and over one hundred actors. This was virtuosity of mimesis: yet all the principals were whites in black makeup, as if in a minstrel show.

Similarly, the last five minutes of the evening comprised a murder out of louche melodrama—played, however, with minute care for the details of how such a murder might actually occur. It was as if Eleonora Duse had found work on a showboat, for the language was pure ten-twent'-thirt' cautionary tale, as the discarded George catches up with Lulu Belle in Paris and tells her she's coming with him . . . or else! "Make your choice, Lulu Belle," he demands. "On one side's heaven. On the other side's Hell!"

The rhyme is distracting, but not to Lulu Belle. "Suits me," she briskly declares. "I'll see all mah frien's!"

George grabs her for a kiss, but she slaps him repeatedly, even spits at him. Then she makes a curious mistake, handing him a gun so he can kill himself. But please do it in the bathroom: "I got a big ma'ble tub yo' kin hol' yo' haid ovah."

The atmosphere has changed, for it occurs to George to kill Lulu Belle instead, and suddenly the nineteenth-century posing and squawking are over. The show's remaining moments are the kind of thing Belasco could rehearse to perfection. Belasco doesn't want *Carmen* now. He wants what happens when a man kills his ex-lover.

Scared at last, Lulu Belle throws pillows and boxes of thing at George, and as he reaches her she actually dives into the bedclothes in sheer panic. As he hauls her up to strangle her, she's laughing and screaming at once—hysterical—and Belasco pulls out one last crazy trick: she will take hold of whatever's within reach and try to beat him off with it. It turns out to be a bunch of flowers; and so she dies. With the gendarmes at the door, George embraces the corpse with agonized cries of "My Lulu Belle!" as the curtain comes down.

Lulu Belle ran 461 performances, the stay of a smash, and while Belasco died in 1931 his continued prominence on The Street in the 1920s marked one of the theatre's most apparent connections with its primitive past. Another connection was the revival, extremely common at this time. In 1921, *Trilby* (1895) came back with its original Svengali, Wilton Lackaye (now nearly sixty), and two of his original colleagues, and five more recent successes returned that same year with the headliners of the premiere: *The Squaw Man* (1905) with William Faversham; *The Easiest Way* (1909) with Frances Starr; *The Return of Peter Grimm* (1911) with David Warfield; *Peg O' My Heart* (1912) with Laurette Taylor; and *Romance* with Doris Keane. (We remember the last as Edward Sheldon's great hit; in the excitement, he proposed marriage to Keane.) These really were revivals of memorable portrayals. Still, Arthur Hopkins brought back his production of *The Jest* seven years after the Barrymore brothers had stunned the town in it with, merely, Basil Sydney and Alphonz Ethier (who had in fact succeeded Lionel as Neri during the original run). Yet it ran ten weeks, impressive for such meager leftovers.

There were some new genres in play along with the familiar ones. The postwar attitudes toward sex, increasingly freer than before, encouraged the development of the so-called bedroom play into what we now term "boudoir farce"—that is, from the flirtatious into the sinful. In the first of the sophisticated musical revues, *The Greenwich Village Follies* (1919), a number called "I Want a Daddy Who Will Rock Me To Sleep" remarked on the growth of sex comedy by working applicable titles punningly into the song's verse—*Up in Mabel's Room, A Sleepless Night, Twin Beds, The Dame in Room Thirteen, Newlyweds,* and *She Walked in Her Sleep* (into the arms of married men, also outside an apartment building along the ledge of the sixteenth floor). These plays really were farces with come-hither titles; after 1919, the program got spicier. Otto Harbach's *No More Blondes* (1920) typified the earlier form, as husband Ernest Truex and someone else's wife Eileen Wilson got trapped together while various strangers intruded, spied, and threatened. But Avery Hopwood and Charlton Andrews' *Ladies Night* (1920) set the whole cast running in and out of rooms in a Turkish bath, the men in drag; and Hopwood's *The Demi-Virgin* (1921)—referring to a bride who abandoned her marriage at some point during her wedding night—so toyed with the cautions of the day that the police shut down the Pittsburgh tryout and there was further legal challenge in New York.

By far the essential early-twenties sex comedy was *The Gold Diggers* (1919), because it saw the world of men and women as a war of dupes versus takers. The men are rich and the women attractive, and the problem with the game they play is that only the women know the rules. Such a typifying entry should be produced by A. H. Woods, written by Avery Hopwood, and headed by Hazel Dawn, the genre's prime practitioners. (It was Dawn, the violin-playing heroine of the 1911 musical *The Pink Lady,* who originated the title role in the best-remembered of the sex comedies, *Getting Gertie's Garter* [1921].) But *The Gold Diggers,* by Hopwood, was produced by David Belasco and starred his latest discovery, Ina Claire.

The Gold Diggers wasn't typical Belasco fare, with the same ordinary set for all three acts, a mere nineteen in the cast, and a narrative almost embarrassingly placid. Society Boy falls for Chorus Girl; his uncle disapproves; her best friend vamps the uncle. Why? Because when uncle sees what a heartless trollop the friend is, the chorus girl will seem ideal by comparison.

What twaddle, of course: but all lies in the execution. Audiences enjoyed learning what a Nice Girl the trollop really was: in the evening's biggest laugh, uncle Bruce McRae poured vamp Ina Claire some champagne and, when he turned away, she emptied her glass onto the carpet. Gold digger? She ended up revealing her scheme and marrying the uncle. She even had a mother, right there on stage; bad girls don't have mothers. In fact, most of this gold digging was just talk and show. A lot of the show's wickedness lay in the dialogue assigned to a pack of these fortune hunters, bragging about the millionaires they were fleecing. But were they truly living the life or striking a pose?

There were such women, of course. Peggy Hopkins Joyce, the forerunner of today's Pointless Celebrities such as Paris Hilton, was the gold digger of the age. But Peggy put out. Sex comedy was really about chastity only appearing to stray.

On the other hand, "society drama" liked its heroines disgraced. This form dealt with people who live in mansions rather than apartments, the social set later popularized by Philip Barry. Barry's favorite question was How much independence is available in a world ruled by convention? Barry's precursor, Zoë Akins, asked rather, How much independence is available to women in a world ruled by men?, and society drama's typical protagonist was a woman, especially Ethel Barrymore in Akins' *Déclassée* (1919). Lady Helen Haden, English by birth and breeding—the goddaughter, indeed, of a queen of England—is simply too principled for a reckless and unscrupulous beau monde.

She is also "the last of the mad Varvicks," but we see no madness: just nobility. Trapped by her own code, Lady Helen must reveal as a cheat someone who will take his revenge by making public her recent . . . indiscretion. He was the man in the case, and he has the letters to prove it. If she exposes him, he'll expose her. Lady Helen's reply—and the first-act finale—was Ethel at her most superb. As one always has a helping of the fashionable world waiting in the wings in plays like this one, Ethel called them in and announced, "I've something to tell you." As she started in on the who, what, and where of the scandal that would destroy her, the curtain blushingly closed down the scene.

So Lady Helen is now déclassée, and Akins' script delineates the stages of degradation till there is no way out but for a taxicab to knock the heroine down just before she is to be reunited with the very man who caused her downfall, now mature and repentant. Too late. Though her final aria, onstage, was remarkably staid for someone dying of internal injuries—Akins permitted a single tasteful convulsion—Ethel made it radiant and thrilling within her narrow range.

Interestingly, Akins' *The Varying Shore* (1921) anticipated Kaufman and Hart's *Merrily We Roll Along* (1934) by telling its tale—of another noble and thus devastated heroine—backward. In fact, she's dead at the start, set in 1921, and "youthens" into her forties in Act Two, her twenties in Act Three, and seventeen at last, in 1847. The critics thought the work needed a stronger actress than the journeyman Elsie Ferguson; these society shows were, after all, star vehicles. Michael Arlen's *The Green Hat* (1925), from his novel, got Katharine Cornell, and it needed her badly. Novelist Arlen was Enjoying a Vogue at the time; it's not clear why. His writing—his playwrighting, anyway—is overwrought and loaded with fifi philosophizing. Let's let Brooks Atkinson describe Arlen's characters: "restless, bored, cynical, worldly, futile." Atkinson said this of another Arlen play that opened but three weeks after *The Green Hat*, *These Charming People*. This was an unproduced old script that Arlen pulled out of the drawer and blithely named after his latest novel despite there being no connection between the book and this play.

The Green Hat—named after the heroine's trademark accessory, a cloche number in felt—begins just after Cornell's Iris March suffers an altogether shatteringly bogus honeymoon: her husband killed himself. Doesn't one hate when that happens? And everybody simply raving at poor Iris, including the man she *really* loves, Napier Harpenden (Leslie Howard). Of course, one never does anything in italics in the world of Michael Arlen, even while suddenly gazing at the moon, wishing it were a pie one could cut up and eat. Then there would be no more sorrow in the world, no more contamination, only the innocence of dear playmates. (Memo to Howard: regard Cornell with a strangely turbulent fondness at this point.) Remember, my dark angel who drives decadently about Europe in a yellow Hispano-Suiza?

Actually, Arlen himself humiliates any imitation:

NAPIER: What's love? Do you know, Iris?
IRIS: Love? Love is a hurricane of pain. That's love.
NAPIER: (intensely) Iris, you do something very strange, very—unholy
    to me.

One of Arlen's stage directions runs, "They speak as in a dream." I'll say. But note that, while raised in England, Arlen shared the growing American disenchantment with social norms—an alienation that, developed by Philip Barry and perfected in Hollywood, would create one of America's most vital inventions, the screwball comedy of bohemian revolt. Ultimately, Iris comes up against Napier's father, "a magnificent exponent of caste," Arlen warns us. "The kind of success you respect," she tells Senior, "is like a murky sponge wiping out the lines of a man's character."

Then Napier, too, defies his father, going on to reveal why Iris' husband killed himself on their wedding night: he "had picked up some beastly woman . . . and caught about the foulest disease a man can have." When he told Iris and "saw the disgust and horror on her face . . . well, he was always an unbalanced devil, and he just chucked himself out [of the window]."

Syphilis. Note the utter callousness of this moral judgment, the eagerness to blame the victim. It reminds us why Henrik Ibsen remained for many in the preceding generation a byword for wanton immorality rather than, as we now see him, a doctor treating society's hypocrisies: because in *Ghosts* (1882) he brought venereal disease onto the stage.

Even in 1925, this was most truly the love that dare not speak its name. Worse, by exposing the secret that Iris had been guarding, Napier has robbed her of her one selfless act. Like *Déclassée*, *The Green Hat* kills a noble heroine by automobile, though Iris March commits suicide, speeding that yellow Hispano-Suiza into a tree. It is left to the ingenue, Napier's wife, to console him with a thing unknown to the play so far, unquestioning love:

VENICE: We must be together now. Or else we may hate each other.
    And, oh dearest, we *mustn't* hate each other.

Ann Harding was Venice during *The Green Hat*'s tryout. Replaced by Margalo Gillmore, Harding left to play the lead in an Italian work called

Stolen Fruit (1925), about a Frenchwoman searching for her long lost infant daughter's grave who learns that the girl is still alive. It was a meaty role in Harding's own vehicle, opposite Rollo Peters, a prima donna's favorite for his ability to grace the stage without taking it. The first thing Jane Cowl asked after accepting a role was "Has Rollo Peters been engaged yet this season?" We've met up with Peters before and we'll be seeing more of him anon.

We'll see even more of Leslie Howard, who along with Harding was indispensable to these society plays, for this pair of quietly restless personalities embodied at once the strength of character and nonconformist individuality that obsessed playwrights in the coming years. Howard especially became the avatar of the new leading man who was not your father's hero. He had ambivalence, Howard, but also had a glow about him: a redeemer.

There was a shortage of charismatic actors in comedy. Is it coincidence that John Barrymore won renown precisely when he was graduated from light-comic roles to serious ones, thence to Shakespeare? There was also the problem that, for all its popularity, comedy wasn't very well written at this time. We find that kind of humor that ages as a pallid charm rather than as laughter, and we find it hard to imagine that anyone ever enjoyed it.

There were five types of comedy, and here are some examples, all hits. First, domestic comedy, centered on marriage or family life, as in Booth Tarkington's *Clarence* (1919) or Frank Craven's *The First Year* (1920). Clarence, the nerd handyman who soothes the testy wife (Mary Boland), straightens out the errant son (Glenn Hunter), and reproves the flapper daughter (Helen Hayes), was the role that launched Alfred Lunt's stardom. It was an exhibition performance, both overstated and nuanced and capped by a solo on the saxophone (which Lunt mastered for the production). *The First Year,* which Craven wrote for himself to star in, is a shyer piece, devoid of flapper and saxophone. It is daily life unadorned: the first twelve months of a middle-class marriage. Boy marries Girl, loses Girl, gets Girl. Nothing else happens, save a second-act set-piece dinner party sabotaged by an inept black maid. "A wooer of the homely chuckle," the *Times* dubbed Craven, which tells us why he was chosen to play the Stage Manager in *Our Town* almost a generation later. As writer or performer, the *Times* went on. Craven was strong in the "humor of recognition."

Topical spoof, however, had the humor of novelty, as in George Kelly's *The Torch-Bearers* (1922), on the "little theatre" movement of small professional or amateur groups dedicated to staging their own Broadway out in the regions (which included Greenwich Village). The Provincetown Players, to select the most immortal example, brought together intellectuals and artists of visionary content; Kelly's people are the competitively pretentious small-town matrons—led here by Mary Boland and Alison Skipworth—who exploit the stage for social prominence. Kelly's tone is contemptuous rather than loving, and it is a historian's choice irony that *The Torch-Bearers* became a staple of amateur groups, who mistook Kelly for a sympathizer.

There were as well romantic comedies, like Arthur Richman's *The Awful Truth* (1922), the source of the Cary Grant–Irene Dunne film, Hollywood's classic Comedy of Remarriage. The play reunited *The Gold Diggers'* Ina Claire and Bruce McRae. There were situation comedies, like *The Whole Town's Talking* (1923), by John Emerson and his wife, Anita Loos, in which a nerdy guy tries to impress his standoffish light of love with pictures of the great beauties he has conquered: Queen Marie of Romania, the Mona Lisa, and Julian Eltinge.* It's not working, so he acquires a fourth picture, of a current movie star, inscribing it to himself in memory of their "happy, hectic Hollywood hours" together. So of course the movie star herself shows up—in Toledo, Ohio—complete with her belligerently protective director. Situation comedy was essentially farce without slamming doors.

More common than one might suspect was stereotypical ethnic comedy, the outstanding instance of course being Anne Nichols' *Abie's Irish Rose* (1922). Setting the new record to beat at 2,327 performances, *Abie* became a national joke, because not only did no one know anyone who'd liked it: no one knew anyone who'd seen it. Writing the squibs for the theatre listings in the *New Yorker,* Robert Benchley kept jabbing at the piece, then, sometime around its fifth year, gave up with "An interesting revival of one of America's old favorites."

---

* Queen Marie was another of the many novelty people who began to turn up in the 1920s as a product of the new style of personality-centered journalism. As visiting royalty, she created a momentary stir, and for years afterward served as an aimless summoning term, in effect a noun without a definition. Julian Eltinge was a musical-comedy star of the first generation of the twentieth century. He played women in drag—not for comic exaggeration but with tasteful aplomb.

These titles have more in common with *Lightnin'* than they do with the comic shows that succeeded them in the late 1920s and after, because of a pokey and even rustic quality that permeates even the titles treating lively urban folk. A good study for us might lie in a huge hit of 1922, George S. Kaufman and Marc Connelly's *Merton of the Movies*. Its public attended it better prepared than we, for apparently the entire American middle class read the *Saturday Evening Post,* in which Harry Leon Wilson's novel of the same name had been serialized. Like Booth Tarkington and George Ade, Wilson was regarded as satirist, sociologist, and joke bag all together and now is so over he can't even be called forgot. But Wilson did latch onto something of note in the appeal of the movies. They don't just turn cynosures into stars: they turn nobodies into fantasies.

Merton of the Movies is a spoof of Hollywood, with its mania for making nothing but love stories. A film based on *Robinson Crusoe* gives Friday a white sister to play opposite Crusoe ("so we can get the sex into it," says a director), and a western original called *The Little Shepherd of the Bar Z* is released as *I Want More Children.* The first act establishes Merton Gill in Simsbury, Illinois, where he clerks in Amos Gashwiler's general store. But comedies of the day often broke into four acts, and *Merton*'s other three find the hero in California, where he seeks cowboy stardom as Clifford Armytage.

It's a lopsided name—the "y" tilts masculinity into the precious—and Merton is a lopsided actor. He turns everything into a joke just by showing up—for instance, in his western drag, correct from Stetson to boots but for chaps made not of leather but rather of what looks like the fluff of New Zealand's entire sheep population. Glenn Hunter (of *Clarence*) played Merton, opposite Florence Nash as his supporter, Miss Montague, who loves him even though she knows he's a fool. For *Merton*'s real subject is not Hollywood but how easily the unequipped fancy themselves potential stars.

In fact, Merton does have potential: as a comic. Unbeknown to him, his first feature is a western *spoof,* and Clifford Armytage is the prize goofball. He learns this at the picture's first screening, and is so crushed by the laughter that he stays out all night—a desperate act from a nice kid from Small Town, Illinois. Kaufman and Connelly were able to produce a movie studio before our eyes, with the fake little set, the lights, camera, and crew, the violinist to soothe and inspire the director. But they couldn't show the all-important screening, leaving a typical early-twenties hole in the show:

some turns of plot weren't technically available for staging till the next decade. Instead, the authors jumped to the aftershock, in which poor Merton confronts himself. He has "a low-comedy face," he tells Miss Montague, his dream crumpling as he speaks. Then, with no more self-esteem to lose, he throws himself at her feet and sobs in her lap. But she puts Humpty together again:

> NASH: There, there. Don't you worry. Did he have his poor old mother going for a minute? Yes, he did. He had her going for a minute all right. But he didn't fool her very long, not very long, because he can't ever fool her very long. And he can bet a lot of money on that.

We are but a moment or two from the happy ending, for Merton comes to see that Hollywood stardoms are interchangeable, and a comic can be as beloved of the public as a cowpoke. In fact, Merton immediately enjoys his first star interview (by telephone), with a fan magazine. He is asked if he has a girl friend, and he suddenly realizes that he does. He is proudly smiling at Miss Montague and praising her nurturing skills as the curtain falls.

So *Merton of the Movies,* though one of the day's outstanding comedies, is really more of a charm show than a comedy as we know the form today. It's not gaggy: it's sweet, with more of those homely chuckles and humor of recognition. Glenn Hunter himself made the silent, for Paramount in 1924, and the talkie Mertons were Stuart Erwin and Red Skelton. Oddly, *Merton* seems not to have gone musical, though surely somebody in the BMI workshop gave it a whirl. A singing Merton would fulfill the destiny of Wilson's creation, for the essential quality of our music theatre is that the main characters want something badly. And nobody wants more than Merton does.

Sifting through the categories, we find one all-important genre missing: the straight play that avoids melodrama's upheavals and Belasco's self-serving naturalistic études, something that doesn't need "society" in order to be literate or a European source for imaginative color. Something, too, without cosmetic novelty. What we're looking for is something basic, a piece about life. Just a *play*. There were a few, more and more as the 1920s wore on, and I hope you're sitting down because the one I want to discuss is *Rain* (1922). You know this one, about the prostitute and the reverend, with the crash-and-burn star who didn't live out the decade and two generations of references throughout the culture. If I told you that Bette Davis once headed a musical revue and that the first-act-finale burlesque spot centered on a famous tart, wouldn't your first guess be "Sadie Thompson"?

W. Somerset Maugham's short story of 1921 called "Miss Thompson" (later retitled "Rain") is really more about the reverend than about the prostitute. The setting is Pago Pago, where the missionaries Reverend and Mrs. Davidson and Dr. and Mrs. Macphail, representing the starchy propriety of civilization, come into contact with Sadie, the avatar of hedonism. Though an American, she has adopted the lifestyle of monsoon Asia, living for the sheer pleasure of it. Reverend Davidson lives "to instil into the natives a sense of sin," and he does this by taking away all their pleasure, using his power and influence to destroy any who thwart his will. He is that singular piece of evil, the control freak using God as a front. Yet we recall the *White Cargo* theme: when Western man ventures too far East, his buttons open. The rain that ceaselessly pounds away symbolizes nature's assault on order, just as Sadie's irritating gramophone symbolizes her spirited independence. Davidson plans to make Sadie his great conversion—but it is nature itself, human nature, that proves to be the reverend's ultimate challenge.

He is as colossally inflexible as John Brown, but he fails his own test, and interrupts his personal-trainer prayer vigil with Sadie for carnal exercise with her. Maugham's story cleverly withholds this all-important twist till its final two lines. At first, all we learn is that the reverend's body has been found with its throat cut. When Dr. Macphail tries to silence Sadie's gramophone out of respect, Sadie—who knows nothing of the reverend's suicide—simply shouts at him. "You men!" she cries. "You filthy, dirty pigs! You're all the same, all of you! Pigs! Pigs!" The doctor lets out a gasp of realization. Says Maugham concisely, "He understood."

The play lingers past this moment, to tell Sadie what happened to Davidson and confront her with his widow, who is too shattered to do anything in the old-fashioned melodramatic style. Five years before this, there might have been fireworks, but *Rain* is at the least a transitional work, looking forward to the naturalistic writing of the 1930s. As the marine sergeant who is more or less Sadie's romantic opposite stands by her side, Sadie expresses hope for a better life in her next port of call, but the words catch in her throat as she utters them. In naturalism, there are no endings; and the curtain falls.

"Missionaries won't like this play" was the merry observation of the *Times'* John Corbin. He thought *Rain* a piece of "extraordinary grip and significance," and I need to underline that last word, because today to mention this play is to conjure up the lurid antiques that tricked our grandfathers. Maugham himself thought little of his tale's potential for the stage—but then, he thought little of any play below the level of Aeschylus or Shakespeare. Theatregoing, to Maugham, was akin to "wood-carving or dancing," whose aim (and he meant this condescendingly) was "to afford delight."

Maugham was an authority in this matter, however. As a playwright himself, he was very much a part of Broadway at this time, like his fellow Brits James M. Barrie and A. A. Milne. It's a loose confederation; Barrie was a Scot and Maugham, few recall, was born in Paris of Irish family. They were agreed on one point, that social-problem plays were for writers working on other stages. Maugham in particular favored light comedies about marriage, set in drawing rooms. Adultery, in Maugham, is quite the fashion, as in *The Circle* (1921) and *The Constant Wife* (1926), another of Ethel Barrymore's outstanding successes. There really can be too much fidelity in this world, as in Maugham's *Home and Beauty,* produced here by A. H. Woods and retitled *Too Many Husbands* (1919), as if it were one of Woods' sex comedies. But there isn't any sex, because Estelle Winwood has simply remarried, thinking her first husband dead. He isn't. Worse, the two husbands are longtime buddies faithful to each other, each of whom insists that his alternate's vows be honored. So Estelle does the only sensible thing and runs off with a war profiteer.

Clearly, Maugham's world was not ready for a Sadie Thompson, even if she was his invention. Note that when Maugham wrote his own South Pacific piece, in *The Letter* (1927), he was still plying such devices as adultery, murder, and blackmail. True, in telling his short story around Reverend Davidson, Maugham might not have noticed that Sadie had the makings of what Brooks Atkinson later called "one of the few bravura parts in the contemporary drama." This brings us to the legend of the show: Jeanne Eagels in *Rain*.

Cited as often as the John Barrymore Hamlet and Laurette Taylor's Amanda Wingfield, Eagels' Sadie encapsulates that favorite American concept of fame, ruin, and early death (at thirty-five). Barrymore and Taylor were brand names—though he was fresh and she a has-been—when they earned their myth, but Eagels was relatively unknown when, on *Rain*'s opening night, the audience in Maxine Elliott's Theatre gave her the ovation of the century. Here, again, is that idyll of the First Night, the reason why people made a point of attending them, fishing for the next heavy catch. In her prostitute's business casual of black-belted white dress, lace mantilla and woolen scarf, five-and-dime beads topped by a feathery hat overlooking high-button spats, sporting an umbrella, and slipping from brusque and feisty to soothed and radiant within ten seconds, Eagels gave Sadie the dizzy magic of the drug addict. No wonder. After the New York run of 648 performances and two and a half years on the road, *Rain* closed, freeing Eagels for a show to be staged by New Top Director George Abbott. He found Eagels maddeningly unreliable, with loopy excuses, such as the "a strange man was following me, so I got on the train to Albany" kind of thing. Abbott hired someone else, and after a few silent films, an anticlimactic minor success in the play *Her Cardboard Lover* (1927) opposite Leslie Howard, and two talkies, Jeanne Eagels was dead, of substance abuse.

While she was with us, she was *Rain* and *Rain* was Jeanne Eagels, as when she danced dirty with another of the marines that Colton and Randolph added to Maugham's scenario. ("Oh, I love that step," she says, bending backward for him to lean over her as the two shimmy on Sunday.) Few high-octane acting parts take in such wanton fun as well, and New Yorkers got a chance to test the uniqueness of the Eagels Sadie when Maria Bazzi brought her Italian production of the piece, *Pioggia*, to the Manhattan Opera House. A classic tragedienne with a gorgeous voice, Bazzi apparently gave a grandly scaled *Rain* where the work is in fact lean and tight, a breakaway piece. *Rain*'s producer, Sam H. Harris, vainly applied for an injunction—but who wanted to see *Rain* without Jeanne Eagels? True, it was filmed without her, with Gloria Swanson, Joan Crawford, and finally Rita Hayworth. There was even a flop Rodgers-and-Hammerstein-style musical, *Sadie Thompson* (1944). With a score by Vernon Duke and Howard Dietz and a miscast Ethel Merman (who left during rehearsals, replaced by June Havoc), *Sadie Thompson* tells how original *Rain* is by the way the musical's authors had to reappoint and rationalize it. Their Sadie becomes a heart-of-gold whore, the kind with a Wanting Song. Davidson is a secret chaos of primitive visions. The marine sergeant is the Boy Who Meets Girl.

The play is better: plainer and truer. Sergeant O'Hara isn't Prince Charming; he's a lug. Davidson is the opposite of chaos: he's Heinrich Himmler, evil in the form of absolute order. And Sadie doesn't know what she wants well enough to sing of it in, for instance, "The Love I Long For."

She doesn't Meet Boy. She meets boys. In the aforementioned climax of the play, when she is free of Davidson's rage but not of the hypocrisy of men, Sadie has an odd line, "Life is a quaint present from somebody." It's the statement of one stuck with the worst character flaw in drama: bad luck. Yet the musical made the moment into the jaunty "Life's a Funny Present From Someone," as wrong as can be. The thought is not the occasion for a list song. It's the stalling act of the butterfly aware of the pin.

Back in 1922, on *Rain*'s opening night, Davidson (Robert Kelly) got booed, and not in high spirits. The public was energized and taking sides. One of the first American plays to dwell entirely outside genre, *Rain* is a piece about life, about how some enjoy it and some try to murder it. Like Davidson using his authority to curtail others' liberty, New York's district attorney, Joab H. Banton, began menacing the theatre two years after *Rain* opened. Sex farces kept playing brinkmanship with the received pieties, language was growing frank, kisses were looking genuine, and the mixed-race marriage in Eugene O'Neill's *All God's Chillun Got Wings* defied standard cautions. In 1924, there was little more than a touch of censorship here and there—for instance deleting a scene in the O'Neill that featured the two leads as children. It hurt the presentation of O'Neill's theme, but the play did go on.

Three years later, however, roused by the religious pulpit, various demagogues, and even New York's governor, Alfred E. Smith, Banton arrested the producers and casts of three plays. One of these was *The Virgin Man,* a sex comedy about three women trying to seduce a Yale student. It had opened but three weeks earlier, while Jane Mast's *Sex* had been playing for nine months, giving theatregoers their first taste of Mae West's act: for Mast was West. She not only wrote but starred in the piece, the second on Banton's list.* The third was a serious work, Arthur Hornblow Jr.'s translation of Edouard Bourdet's *La Prisonnière,* as *The Captive*. The woman protagonist's

---

* West had been knocking around in vaudeville and musicals uneventfully for about fifteen years when she got the idea of remodeling herself in imitation of the drag comic Bert Savoy, who had been killed when struck by lightning, in 1923. Savoy's hourglass figure, antique finery, and catchphrase—"You mussst come over"—had thus passed into the public domain, free for the borrowing. (The catchphrase, of course, became "Come up and see me.") West signaled her homage to Savoy in referring to his famous stack of jokes about his friend Margie and all the trouble she gets into: West's role in *Sex,* that of a sailor-chasing prostitute, was named Margie Lamont.

prison is a love affair with another woman. Helen Menken played her, opposite Basil Rathbone as the well-meaning fellow who marries Menken anyway; the marriage fails.

Surely the play did, too, one thinks: a piece on lesbianism in 1927? On the contrary, *The Captive* was selling out at the Empire and had run over four months when Banton—presumably irked by the very title of *The Virgin Man*—closed these three plays. True, even those who admired Bourdet's piece were quick to condemn the subject matter. The very approving Brooks Atkinson peppered his review with such phrases as "twisted relationship," "loathsome possibility," and "revolting theme." Perhaps Bourdet disarmed some of the homophobia by keeping The Dangerous Woman offstage. Like Bert Savoy's Margie, she was much mentioned but never seen.

Oddly, the sensational publicity of the Banton raids and the three closings—PADLOCK DRAMA, the tabloids cried—did not attract customers. *The Captive* agreed to suspend further performances, and the charges were dropped. *The Virgin Man* and *Sex* took Banton on. Released on bail, their companies reopened, but business stuttered, both shows closed, and their honchos got short jail sentences, West included.

It is regrettable that the theatre community did not organize to fight this development. The state's closing of plays—even of plays by Mae West and maybe even especially plays by Mae West—is like the state's closing of newspapers. However, some managers and playwrights feared to bait the philistines and risk a censorship war. And the actors—so unified by the 1919 strike and a follow-up action in 1924, on the matter of the closed shop—had no power to speak on extramural issues.

Yet Banton *was* defeated. Writers of far greater power than John Colton and Clemence Randolph were moving far beyond *Rain* (if not *The Captive*) in the defiance of bourgeois proprieties. Even as Mae West went off to start her week in the workhouse, there was already too much Broadway for the authorities to control. Davidson ended a suicide; Banton simply evaporated.

One reason why was the changing ethnic makeup of American theatre—really, show biz as a whole. Two generations of European immigrants had by the 1920s produced offspring assimilated enough to communicate with the rest of the nation yet different enough in their attitudes to alter the national style. The Joab Bantons could not have been happy with the prominence of Al Jolson, for example: but what criminal charge could they hang on him? Like Mae West, Jolson was out of control. He incited his public to . . . what? Knowing more about the world? And isn't knowledge perilous to the rule of the Joab Bantons?

Things were so easy for them before. American culture in the 1890s wasn't all that different from what it had been in the 1880s. Nor did all that much happen before our entry into World War I. By the 1920s, however, a great deal was invented, revealed. The people called it "jazz."

Three

The Rise of Wisecrack Comedy

The 1920 census was the first that found more Americans living in urban than rural territory, and the national humor changed accordingly, from what we might simply term "Mark Twain" to the wisenheimer art of the Marx Brothers and Jimmy Durante, of the snazzy know-it-all lyrics we hear in Lorenz Hart and Ira Gershwin, of the new gossip columns, of *Krazy Kat*. It was a mongrel art, the verbal equivalent of the jazz band, and it took hold in the 1920s.

Perhaps George M. Cohan is the theatre's preceding transitional figure, for he was cracking wise avant la lettre; ironically, his first public was that of the middle-class towns on the touring circuit, not of the metropolis. To enlarge the paradox, by the 1920s Cohan had grown reactionarily folksy, emphasizing ideals of flag and mother where the wisecracker was irreverent about everything.

About women, for instance: as in Avery Hopwood's aforementioned *The Gold Diggers*. Simply the concept of a woman who makes a science of exploiting men is a sacrilege fit for a decade like the 1920s, and Hopwood's novelty phrase of a title caught on as a cliché. The culture kept the words "gold digger" in common play into the 1940s. Naturally, much of the show's atmosphere inhered in a pack of the kind, bragging about their millionaires and the activity sheet of wearing furs, clipping on jewelry, and cheating around. In the *Tribune,* Heywood Broun wanted "to rush off to find some woman . . . with whom I could discuss the prose style of Walter Pater."

In fact, Hopwood's gold diggers were snow white next to the Warner Bros. model of a decade or so later. In the talkie of James Cagney, Joan Blondell, Lee Tracy, Glenda Farrell, Warren William, and even William Powell (between Paramount and MGM), a gold digger really knows how to use the wisecrack. Warners had filmed Hopwood's play as a silent in 1923 and as a musical in the first year of sound, 1929, as *The Gold Diggers of Broadway*. The studio's third try, *Gold Diggers of 1933,* offered Ruby Keeler and Dick Powell as the sweetheart couple, Warren William as his interfering uncle opposite Joan Blondell in Ina Claire's old role, and deadpan Ned Sparks as a producer, a character not in Hopwood's play.

Not till now had the wisecrack been perfected in all its tones. The all-purpose smart-alec retort:

> SPARKS: The show is about the Depression.
> BLONDELL: We won't have to rehearse that!

The personal put-down, for use with enemies or, as here, a sort-of friend, as the heroines contemplate dressing up for Sparks:

> GINGER ROGERS: I look so much better in clothes than any of you. If [Sparks] saw me in clothes—
> ALINE MACMAHON: He wouldn't recognize you!

The sarcasm, to create an air of invulnerable cynicism, as when Sparks claims he could chisel a show on for fifteen thousand dollars, if only he had it:

POWELL: (who everyone thought was a penniless nobody) I'll advance
   you fifteen.
MACMAHON: Say, what does he use? I'll smoke it, too.

And, most evolved, the remark of sociopolitical omniscience:

BLONDELL: I can remember, not so long ago, a penthouse on Park
   Avenue . . . and now—stealing milk!
MACMAHON: That's all right. The dairy company stole it from a cow.

These samples, drawn from deep in the Depression, turn a key into the purpose of the wisecrack: to empower the powerless. This is no doubt why this uniquely American form of humor did not quite jell in the more comfortable 1920s, though it was unquestionably in the cooking stage. Guy Bolton's comedy hit *Polly Preferred* (1923), on how Polly Brown becomes Polly Pierpont, movie star, got in some of the new tough talk within the first minutes of the opening scene, in an Automat. Polly's fellow chorus girl Jimmie lets a waiter know that she's up for a revue featuring Ziegfeldian nudity.

WAITER: Say, I'll have to see that!
JIMMIE: Oh, sure! Gee, you men . . . you all know what us girls look
   like but you'll pay good money just to see for sure that they ain't
   started makin' us any different.

Wisecrack comedy's spotty twenties history fills in somewhat in James Gleason and Richard Taber's *Is Zat So?* (1925). This one tickled audiences for eighteen months with its look at a "box fighter" and his manager, orphaned brothers in all but name who never stop sparring. Hap, the manager, is the more aggressive of the pair; Chick, the boxer, is the dumb straight man, always starting but never finishing what amounts to a title song:

CHICK: Is zat so?
HAP: Yes, *zat's* so!

CHICK: *Is zat so?*

HAP: *Yes, zat's so!*

They're a "can't live with him can't live without him" team:

HAP: You fight? Why, you couldn't fight a paralyzed blind man unless they muzzled him for you. A fighter? A fighter? Yeah—a *horizontal* fighter!

The play starts with the two more or less homeless, sitting on a bench on Fifth Avenue, where a society lad takes a liking to them and provides the plot by inviting them to sign on as his butler and second man. *Is Zat So?*'s driveline is Hap and Chick's adventure in Vanity Fair, where they do some romancing and rid their employer of his parasitical brother-in-law. However, the real purpose of the show is the exploration of Hap and Chick's put-down tango. Note that their battles are animated by slang, bad grammar, and Hap's Brooklyn accent. Women are "frails," money is "jack," and to look is "to lamp"—not to mention the irreplaceable *"G'wan!"*

James Gleason in fact became one of the exponential wisecrackers. (In a more serious vein, he delivers the famous last line of Frank Capra's *Meet John Doe* [1941], to foiled plutocrat Edward Arnold: "There you are. The people. Try and lick that.") Gleason and Taber wrote *Is Zat So?* because they weren't getting anywhere as actors and needed a showcase; even so, the script kept being rejected till a Shubert scout attended a staged reading. Gleason played Broadway's Hap (Taber headed the national tour in the part) opposite Robert Armstrong's Chick. In Fox's 1927 *Is Zat So?* film, the prematurely grizzled Gleason was recharacterized in the matinée idol Hap of Edmund Lowe, with the Chick of the outrageously handsome Hunk of the Lot George O'Brien. The latter had been a boxing champ in the navy, so this was authentic casting. However, reducing wisecrack dramaturgy to its lettering on title cards demoralizes its adaptability, its unique reinvention by each performer who uses it. Think of how differently Clark Gable and Robert Montgomery apply the style. Both were MGM stars at the same time, but Montgomery sounds the derisive confidence of the ruling class while Gable's blasts remind us that, if a man of Gable's power is proletarian, society is unstable. The wisecrack is class-oriented, partly the invention of twenties assimilation culture but the weapon (as we'll see) of thirties political culture. Like the improvisations of jazz players, wisecrack comedy cannot be read off cards, only called out and heard live.

And yet it was creeping into twenties lit, perhaps especially in Anita Loos' *Gentlemen Prefer Blondes*. This one had impact. Published in November of 1925, it reached its ninth printing within four months and became one of the decade's prime artifacts. The novel was not yet a year old when Loos and her husband, John Emerson, turned it into a play. Of course, they retained the book's title; that's what sold the tickets. Indeed, the show went on an unusually long tryout tour: not because it needed work but because it didn't. Audiences flocked to this saga of America's greatest gold digger, Lorelei Lee (June Walker), and there was a film in 1928, a musical in 1949, and a movie musical in 1953, with Loreleis Ruth Taylor, Carol Channing, and Marilyn Monroe.

Because Loos' book, subtitled "The Illuminating Diary of a Professional Lady," runs on the voice of the semi-literate Lorelei, Loos pranked in irony: through what Lorelei doesn't realize she is saying, as in "Well Dorothy and I are really on the ship sailing to Europe as anyone could tell by looking at the ocean." The play, however, took advantage of the savvy of Dorothy, Lorelei's sidekick, as in this snippet of their voyage:

DOROTHY: Hope we don't hit an iceberg. I hate ice. Unless it's in a glass.

That is the closest we've yet come to the wisecrack as we use it today; I hear it in the voice of *Will & Grace*'s Megan Mullally. And just as that character more or less uses her facetiae and affronts not only to define her world but to welcome others into it, twenties wisecracking could be used as much to bond with others as to insult them. *Is Zat So?* vanished because it has no grip as a story, just that arresting voice of the contentious working-class New Yorker. But *What Price Glory?* (1924) more successfully takes that voice into an all-American setting of marines in France during World War I.

It's a ghost of a play, if a famous one. *What Price Glory?* might even be the most famous American play that few among the living have seen, partly because its wartime setting all but dates it out of revival, but also because it is a very strange piece of work. It was written by a war veteran amputee and an anarchist who was going to make his mark bringing back the verse play—something like the duo of the "girl tuba player and a one-legged jockey" in that joke in Billy Wilder's film *Some Like It Hot*. It's a campy byline, a mating of uncongenial backgrounds. Nevertheless, Laurence Stallings and Maxwell Anderson shared congruent agendas in their wish to wean the American public away from what the French call *la gloire*. They expose war as neither necessary nor heroic. It's so stupid and evil, in fact, that the only way to take it is by jest.

What Price Glory?, then, is serious comedy, a weird format in 1924. Famous for its bold language, the play utters nothing worse than "God dammit." Still, the authors were adroit in creating the atmosphere of richly blaspheming men simply in their quasi-improvisational riffs on any, on all, topics. It's not the words themselves we hear as much as the libertarian energy. How the authorities longed to close this show! But there was nothing tangible to seize on: *What Price Glory?* defines the word "suggestive." It never teases the Index, yet it acts as if there weren't one, encouraging playgoers to think so as well. After the final curtain, in one of the many versions of the *What Price Glory?* joke of the day, matinée matron Florence asks her seatmate Elvira if she liked the play, and Elvira says, "Cram that. Let's get the hell over to Violet's for her goddamn stinking birthday party."

The rugged language supporting the war-is-hell realism was *What Price Glory?*'s second element. Its *first* element was the hate-to-love-you relationship of Captain Flagg (Louis Wohlheim) and First Sergeant Quirt (William Boyd), another of those romances in which two heteros vie for the same woman, make love to each other in the caress of verbal insult humor, and ultimately abandon the woman because they're already married:

To each other. It's not exactly homoerotic, though it is dick war. We really don't have a term for the feelings that Flagg and Quirt entertain; it's something like "asexual fuck buddies." They dislike each other in a fascinated way, and while the play spends much time developing certain of the other marines—besides the French characters, there are twenty-three American servicemen on hand—Stallings and Anderson keep returning to the two leads and their curious rhetoric of repetition and of top-this putdown, which at times bears a hint of sextalk:

FLAGG: You're talking thick and wild, Quirt, thick and wild. You'd better turn in somewhere and sleep it off.

QUIRT: Me? Sleep off a couple of drinks? I was living on cognac when all your buttons was safety pins.

FLAGG: Yeah, well, you can't carry it the way you used to, then. You're
   getting old, Quirt. Old and feeble. Yeah, you're getting old.
QUIRT: Not me. *You* may be an old man, Flagg. Or an old woman if it
   suits you better, but not me.

Like *Is Zat So?*, *What Price Glory?* was filmed too soon for its dialogue to
be spoken, by Victor McGlaglen and (again) Edmund Lowe. These two
proved so appealing that they made a sequel in the first year of sound, *It's a
Cockeyed World* (1929).* Indeed, the Flagg and Quirt story never does end:
in the play's famous final curtain, Flagg and Quirt decide to settle the question of their girl, Charmaine, once and for all with a hand of blackjack, a gun
on the table between them. The winner of the hand gets the gun; the loser
takes off real quick. Quirt, the loser, flings the table over in Flagg's face, putting out the candles, and Flagg shoots in the darkness. When a lamp is lit,
Quirt is nowhere to be seen and Flagg has Charmaine. Then orders arrive for
the battalion to move, and Flagg wearily kits up and shoves off.

   That could have been the show's ending: the fog of war, the fatigue, the
homicidal improvisations. And, of course, the picturesque sorrow of Charmaine, once the object of a love rush and now left with nothing. It would
make a fine piece of irony for the audience to look at as the curtain drops.
Instead, Quirt returns, kisses the girl, and philosophizes, "What a lot of
God damn fools it takes to make a war!" About to exit, he lets out the immortal line, "Hey, Flagg, wait for baby!" Quirt goes off. And *then* the curtain falls.

   For all its gamy charm, this ending obscures the authors' wish to drive
the glamor of war straight off the pier of infamy; but the middle of their
three acts has already done that. As Act Two nears *its* end, the runt of the
outfit, Private Lewisohn, is carried in wounded, screaming for Flagg to "stop
the blood." It is as if everyone, not just Quirt, sees Flagg as a man of unnat-
ural gifts, superhuman. While Lewisohn continually begs Flagg to save him,
Flagg orders the medic to give the boy morphine. "Oh, Captain Flagg,"
Lewisohn finally whimpers, clutching him, "can't you please, sir, stop the
blood?" As Flagg lowers Lewisohn to the floor, he soothes him with "You'll
be all right, boy. You'll be all right. You'll be all right." The men looking on

---

* Broadway's *Glory* leads, Wohlheim and Boyd, made their own sort of *What Price Glory?*
silent, *Two Arabian Knights* (1927), palling and brawling around in the desert.

are motionless. Lewisohn dies. Nothing happens for six seconds. And the curtain falls.

The use of wisecrack comedy in a serious work helped create a form unique to the late 1920s, satiric melodrama. The "crook play" is a genre we haven't yet considered, because it didn't truly throw off its exhibition pieces till now: *Broadway* (1926), *Chicago* (1926), and *The Front Page* (1928). Each centers on a murder, but in the ordinary crook play good guys face off with bad guys. In these three titles, the concept of guilt is intellectually elaborated to take in not only the actual culprit but his or her media enablers as well. Where does crime end and a crime-obsessed press begin? And why is show biz suddenly so often a partner of crime? Is crime entertainment by other means?

Think, for example, of the last sequence of Warner Bros.' *Little Caesar* (1930), filmed against the backdrop of a billboard announcing the stage musical *Tipsy Topsy Turvy*. This show's stars are the characters portrayed by Douglas Fairbanks Jr. and Glenda Farrell—both former cohorts of Little Caesar himself, Edward G. Robinson. It's that wonderful Warner Bros. irony: Little Caesar is shot by machine guns while hiding behind the billboard, and this vacant show-biz tear sheet is the last thing we see. But why does this film—as do many others—find it logical that a gangster's ex-partner (Fairbanks) and floozy (Farrell) would repent and go straight on the musical stage?

But then, wisecracking had integrated itself most comfortably into musical-comedy books, probably because the comics peppered their parts with their best vaudeville lines, and the book writers duly absorbed the style. Does *Little Caesar* then see it as logical that Fairbanks and Farrell get into a musical because the most cynical voices in American culture are musical-comedy characters and movie gangsters?

At that, why is *Broadway* made entirely of entertainers, criminals, and cops? Remember, the word "Broadway" at that time conjured up everything from Ziegfeld girls to Walter Winchell, from high-stakes gamblers to the Barrymores. There was so much there in "Broadway" that not till the 1960s did the word denote simply a bunch of theatres, mainly because the nation's cultural action had moved to southern California.

So *Broadway* is not a backstager as we think of the form. It concerns performers rehearsing, but it takes place in the private party room of the Paradise Night Club—in the wings of show biz, so to say. Like *Chicago* and

The Front Page, Broadway is loaded with slang and bad grammar: with, really, colloquial urban English of the late 1920s. The wisecracks bite more tensely in *Chicago* and most so in *The Front Page*, but all three plays seem to use offensive sarcasm as the marines do in *What Price Glory?*, to affect a sense of control in an environment that threatens to engulf them. The new metropolitan America has laid aside its Frank Bacons and Mertons of the Movies for lives with more risk in faster tempo. The characters find themselves under siege, and the only defense is to seem stronger than everyone else, unconquerable. *Broadway's* dialogue is written to be shot forth as if weaponized. Let the song-and-dance man edge out an "If you ask me," and his boss—the usual Greek named Nick—cuts in with "Well, I don't ask you. I don't ask nobody." Let the song-and-dance man tell one of the club's showgirls that he and the ingenue are rehearsing an act, and he gets a faceful of street argot: "Aren't you wise that she's given you the bum's rush?" Everything in this cosmos is "baloney," and whether you're a "cabaret spender," a "gorilla," or a "poor nut," the dream is "the big time," with an ad in *Variety* and everyone saying, Hey, I used to know that guy. "God," the song-and-dance man lets out, so rhapsodic that he drops a preposition, "I used to dream about it years."

That was Lee Tracy, who was to become, briefly, as symbolic of the new style of comedy as Lightnin' Bill Jones was of the old. *Brash* was the attitude, getting by on guts and front, finagling with a nervous grin. Topping *Broadway's* Roy Lane with *The Front Page's* star reporter, Hildy Johnson, two years later, Tracy suddenly found himself sliding into second-best stunts, suggesting that the edgy twenties style in wisecrack comedy would suave down in the 1930s. Tracy co-starred above the title with Jean Harlow as a studio PR man in *Bombshell* (1933), a film whose script is a virtually unbroken series of wisecracks—but how many unromantic leading roles are there in the movies? A powerful masculine presence used the wisecrack as an element of his identification. The at best daintily phallic Tracy entirely consisted of the wisecrack; he had nothing else. So Tracy's MGM contract took him from *Bombshell* to a one-scene bit as John Barrymore's abused agent in *Dinner at Eight* and a supporting role in *Viva Villa!*. On location in Mexico, a drunken Tracy whizzed off a balcony on some passing soldiers. It was a definitive stunt, the wisecrack as bodily function; but MGM threw him out. Tracy was reduced to jobs like taking over from Raymond Massey Alfred Lunt's role in the London production of *Idiot's Delight*, though, a generation later, Tracy pulled off an "I'm still here" return from the dead in a short but telling role as a Truman-like ex-president in *The Best Man* (1960).

Broadway's heroine, called Billie Moore, was cast with an anybody, Sylvia Field. She's a Sweet Kid, wildly out of place in the chorus line with slum belles Mazie and Pearl, an anticipation of the real-life Ruby Keeler, who was just about to break into stardom as a Broadway ingenue while being courted by both Al Jolson and a gangster. It's that tango of show biz and crime again—and *Broadway*'s plot leads on to two onstage murders. The first is gangster on gangster, but the second is Pearl on gangster: the first victim was her boy friend.

It's a tough world, *Broadway*. Chicago's protagonist, Roxie Hart (Francine Larrimore), would fit right in, as another murderess—and one with far less motivation than Pearl. It is *Broadway*'s belief that Pearl's vengeance is moral, so while the police detective who haunts the Paradise figures out what happened, he terms the murder a suicide. This lawman even tosses a fast heads-up to the anguished Pearl in fluent Broadway: "Pull yourself together, kid."

Roxie's going to get off, too. But in *Chicago*, crime isn't simply conducted in the vicinity of show biz. Crime *is* show biz, a point made yet more securely in the musical *Chicago* (1975) because the smirk of the Bob Fosse style lifts the action into a vaudeville heaven in which the ectoplasm of Bert Williams, Helen Morgan, Eddie Cantor, and Sophie Tucker keep reminding us that crime sells newspapers the way stars sell tickets. Still, the notion is written into the original work, as when a cynical reporter—the Lee Tracy role, if he hadn't been busy with *Broadway*; Charles Bickford played it—recalls for Roxie the Harlan murder trial:

> JAKE: She fed Lysol to her two step-children and the baby died; and the
> last day of the trial they had the other one run down the aisle cryin'
> "Mamma! Mamma!" and the jury sent her home to her husband
> and the dear little one who needed her.

The Front Page goes yet further in showing how journalism colludes with crime. *Chicago* moves from Roxie's place to jail to courtroom, but *The Front Page* sits entirely in the press room of the Criminal Courts Building, again in Chicago, and virtually all the principals are reporters. Both plays believe that no American court deals in justice because newspapers inform the jury pool and newspapers love crime. Not the commission of it: the selling of it. The reporters in these works are in effect putting on shows starring various killers. In *The Front Page,* the murderer of the moment, a wan little anarchist, is of no interest as an individual to the press until he escapes: because this is more show biz.

Such exaggeration was comic in the 1920s but it's serious today, when Manny Mozart, proprietor of the Fame Shop, decrees which murder cases are to be produced by the media—for instance, the one about the killing of a pregnant housewife? There's the ironically upmarket California setting, the husband's apparent flight in fashionably dyed hair and goatee, the infantile Other Woman, the beguilingly vapid cell-phone dialogues, the bitch lawyer with the eyes that see all men congenitally guilty of rape, the confusing barrage of circumstantial evidence that convicts the husband of capital adultery. Throughout, various relatives, intimates, glancing acquaintances, and television-crazed strangers touted as "spokesmen" assume roles right up into the eulogy at the memorial service, spoken by a pastor unknown to the victim's family who guests on the *Today* show the next morning. In the 1920s, faith was show biz, in the Pentecostal tent shows of such as Aimee Semple McPherson. But now show biz is faith, so the "religious right"— meaning anyone whose contribution to culture consists of spotting the face of Jesus on manhole covers and in cheese sandwiches—tack onto the murder an imaginary crime, the killing of an unborn fetus. The conviction is ultimately for capital abortion.

This is another way of observing that the 1920s was a great time for satire, because one had to exaggerate to observe. Genuine satire—as opposed to spoof—is rare today, because the show biz of crime now outstrips its own implausibility. The current revival of the *Chicago* musical, far more successful than the 1975 original, is less satiric than descriptive. *Broadway,* too, went musical, but as a film (1929) only; a *Front Page* musical turned up in London, as *Windy City* (1982). Interestingly, *Broadway* has vanished in any form, buried by a back-from-the-dead revival on The Street that lasted 4 performances in 1987; and *Chicago* has been absorbed by its musical. But the *Front Page* play is still vital, as the funniest of this trio—the busiest, too, in the suspenseful evolutions of its farcical plot. Then, too, the work boasts a powerful character conflict between, in 1928, Lee Tracy's star reporter and Osgood Perkins' star editor, called Walter Burns and modeled on Walter C. Howey, of the *Chicago Herald & Examiner.* Cleverly, the authors create Burns through other characters' stated views of him, and this goes on so long into the action that the first-time spectator accepts him as an offstage eminence. Finally, near the end of the second act (of three), the story reaches a shocking turn and the stage nearly empties in utter silence . . . and Walter Burns appears. It is as though Godot has entered.

Note that none of these three smash hits of the late middle 1920s had stars the way that *The Jest* or *Lulu Belle* did (though Roxie Hart was the role that Jeanne Eagels lost in the aforementioned episode of her druggy instability). Lee Tracy, again, was only relatively prominent and Osgood Perkins' achievement was siring Anthony Perkins. Even the first *Front Page* film offered the capable yet mere Pat O'Brien and (replacing *What Price Glory?*'s Louis Wohlheim, stricken with cancer) Adolphe Menjou. Howard Hawks' *Front Page* remake, *His Girl Friday* (1940), paired two of Hollywood's most enduringly popular importations from Broadway, Cary Grant and Rosalind Russell. Now it *was* a star show, and jumping off a pun—"Hildy" is short for Hildebrand but also for Hilda—Hawks made of the play's two leads that Hollywood stereotype the "exes who still." But he did this without changing the Hildy-Walter dynamic in the slightest: *The Front Page*'s two male leads love to fight and fight to love. What makes the play eternally fascinating is the love plot by other means that we get in the battle between the reporter who wants out and the editor who has locked the exits. There's nothing homoerotic in it, to be sure. Yet we do hear *What Price Glory!*'s suspiciously intimate verbal shoving match, in "You drooling saphead" and "You got the brains of a pancake" and "Listen, you bastard! I can blow better newspaper stories out of my nose than you can write!" They're not in love, but, like Flagg and Quirt, they're in *something,* and this, along with the dizzy runaround narrative, has made *The Front Page* one of America's classics.

I haven't mentioned any authors yet because, at the time, the names famous for the mounting of the this trio were: last of all, *Chicago*'s producer, Sam H. Harris, and second of all the directors involved, George Abbott of *Broadway* and *Chicago* and George S. Kaufman of *The Front Page*. First of all was the producer of *Broadway* and *The Front Page,* the most hated man in Broadway history, Jed Harris.

The reason why producers had such réclame is that the director, as such, had scarcely been invented. Remember that term "manager"? It means "producer," but most managers also directed, starred, or at least created a style—Charles Frohman, for example. At Frohman's Empire Theatre, at Broadway and Fortieth Street, the subject matter was decorous, the writing was classy, the house staff was spiffy, and the occasion was Ethel Barry-more. Theatregoers of a certain worldview might frequent the Empire without knowing anything about the shows they were to see: because they knew about Frohman.* His style was so consistent, so imitable, that others took over his concern after his death, presenting under the rubrics "Charles Frohman, Incorporated" and "The Charles Frohman Company." (Oddly, the output included one of our padlock dramas, *The Captive*, a play the liv-ing Frohman would not have gone within six degrees of.)

So when the former publicist Jed Harris meteored over The Street as the producer of four smash hits inside of two seasons—*Broadway*, *Coquette* (which gave Helen Hayes her stardom), *The Royal Family* (on the Barry-mores, incogniti), and *The Front Page*—Harris was credited with having his own Touch. Just like Frohman, Belasco, Ziegfeld; and Noël Coward dubbed him "Destiny's tot."

Certainly, the aura that Harris gave off was one of the very latest in the genius business: fast, smart, and no older than last Thursday. A Harris play—remember, they were neither written nor directed but only produced by him—was the very next possible thing, so *Coquette*, for instance, tells of a flapper who sleeps with her boy friend. Booth Tarkington would have found a sweet way out of it, but in the Harris version she finds herself preg-nant and commits suicide. Even *The Royal Family*, with its veneration of dynastic tradition, was perceived as ultra-contemporary, less about the old grande dame than about the star of today and even her dullish daughter.

In fact, the Jed Harris Touch had less to do with putting on plays than with irritating and betraying, with behavior of such pointless, gleeful de-structiveness that when theatre folk said they'd never work for him again they actually meant it. Stories about how vile Harris was fill the Broadway

---

* When he began, as a teenager, in the 1870s, Frohman worked as an advance man for touring companies—that is, the guy who visits the next date to set up the PR and make certain that the theatre is troupe-ready. However, Frohman's acumen in all things theatre was so sharp that he became prominent in his late twenties and magisterial in his thirties. At thirty-three, when he opened the Empire (with a Belasco collaboration called *The Girl I Left Behind Me*, an army-versus-Indians western), Frohman's name was a common noun in the industry, as with "a kleenex" or "a frigidaire." Those touring troupes often spent en-tire seasons on the road without ever hitting a theatre capital like New York or Chicago, very often setting up in two or three playhouses every week. Rather than try to learn each next theatre manager's name, actors and advance man alike simply called him "the frohman."

anecdotes file. Laurence Olivier based his Richard III on Harris, and when someone called Harris his own worst enemy, George S. Kaufman replied, "Not while I'm alive."

But "Every playwright has to have Jed Harris once" was another of Kaufman's remarks: "have" in the sense of a disease to be suffered and overcome for everlasting invulnerability, like the measles. Because, in the long run, exposure to Harris was a strengthening process. He had a broad education and a razory intelligence; above all, he knew theatre, hot or cold. He was supposed as well to have charm—they all said so—but as he was ugly, volatile, and treacherous it's hard for us today to imagine where the charm fit in. George Abbott, the most imperturbable man in the business, said of Harris, "I wanted to smash him in the face."

Abbott, of course, was the co-author of *Broadway* (and of *Coquette,* for that matter) with Philip Dunning, who wrote the original script before Abbott came on for a rewrite. Maurine Watkins wrote *Chicago,* and *The Front Page* was the work of Ben Hecht and Charles MacArthur (whom we met as the co-author of *Lulu Belle*). None of these names controlled the fame that belonged to Harris *at the time:* by now, the credits have sorted themselves out, and we care far more about how these writers commented on contemporary urban culture than about how Harris took the credit for their insights.

The cartoon realism that energizes this trio is hardest to maintain in *Broadway,* because the tension set by the gangsters jars with the feeble talents of the nightclub's performers. How imbued they are with those dreams of the big time! Yet when they get a chance to perform, they go into clunky routines. The dream of Making It is sacred American text—but doesn't it belong to the fringe-on-top talent like Judy Garland or, in the 1920s, Marilyn Miller? Lee Tracy's unfulfillable ambitions are objectified in a sight gag when he doffs his suit jacket, revealing a kind of tank top, his "shirt sleeves" being just a bit of cotton sewed into his coat cuffs. No wonder musicals have titles like *Tipsy Topsy Turvy:* they seem to have everything but content and talent.

Amid all this, the *Broadway* gangsters come off as absurdly competent in their own form of Making It, as when uptown's "Scar" Edwards stands up to midtown's Steve Crandall, who has been encroaching northward. Crandall's henchman makes a grab for Edwards, who turns away from Crandall with a "Take your hands off me or I'll bust your god-damn face!"

And here's the first of those two shootings: Crandall whips out his gun and shoots Edwards dead in the back.

Chicago's character content is more consistent: everyone's a whore. Note that both *Broadway* and *Chicago* pardon their woman killers, for, like *Broadway*'s Pearl, Roxie doesn't pay for her crime. And Earl Williams, *The Front Page*'s murderer, is reprieved from the gibbet, albeit in a work so furiously paced for comic irony that the bearer of his stay of execution very nearly doesn't get through. *Broadway* is continually in motion, but *The Front Page* is like a Feydeau second act that runs three hours. It's a pennywhistle pinwheel of a piece, even more confident of its realism than *Chicago* is, because its moral climate is one big wisecrack.

The morality of *Broadway* brings frontier justice to Times Square. "The last thing you see before you go," Pearl tells the man she's about to kill, "is Jim Edwards' woman." Thus the second of our two *Broadway* shootings. And the morality of *Chicago* is cynical, because justice belongs to money and power: the press. But the morality of *The Front Page* is nihilistic, because justice is tipsy topsy turvy, a shocker of a headline and a snappy opening. *Hook* the public; the rest doesn't matter. As Walter Burns puts it, "Who the hell's going to read the second paragraph?"

Four

Beauty That Springs from Knowledge:

NEW BROADWAY

Among the theatre's experiments in the 1920s, three in particular stand out as antagonistic to what we could call Broadway Before the Strike. Some may see these three experiments as typifying a revolt against naturalism—against, more precisely, the "realism" of David Belasco, in which, many felt, a veneer of innovation was painted over *passéiste* romanticism. Nevertheless, all three of these novelties characterize New Broadway as surely as the many new theatres built north of Fortieth Street made obsolete the older auditoriums farther south. Of the trio, one was ephemeral, one was long-lived and claims a historical contribution that has been in dispute for seventy-five years, and the last one proved enduring right up to the present day.

The ephemeral invention was a style: expressionism. Whether in painting, music, or theatre, expressionism employs fantasy, distortion, and alienation to amplify its power of communication. But it shows up in so many forms that it's easier to cite adherents or examples of the art than to define it. Arnold Schoenberg, Edvard Munch, Franz Kafka. *The Cabinet of Doctor Caligari,* Richard Strauss' *Salome, Berlin Alexanderplatz.*

Or perhaps it's better to isolate the particulars of expressionism on the American stage. There is, for instance, the depiction of a crowd of nobs coming out of church in Eugene O'Neill's *The Hairy Ape* (1922) as, the author directs, "a procession of gaudy marionettes," even "Frankensteins in their detached, mechanical unawareness."

Or consider Woodman Thompson's set designs for John Howard Lawson's *Roger Bloomer* (1923), including a street scene of houses leaning drunkenly on one another under an elevated railway that curves elastically through the sky. This is another element of expressionism's visuals—the deformation or enlargement of ordinary things. A sight of the age is the gigantic mechanical calculator that Mr. Zero climbs around on in Elmer Rice's *The Adding Machine.* Music and noises—rackets, especially—are also a feature of the style, as in the steady *incalzando* drumming that begins after the first scene of O'Neill's *The Emperor Jones* (1920) and continues through the penultimate scene.

Expressionism's fantastical surprises may inspire dream sequences or rudely cut themselves into "real" life. In George S. Kaufman and Marc Connelly's *Beggar On Horseback* (1924), reality is a somewhat skinny frame surrounding a vast surreal enactment on expressionism's favorite theme, the corruption of human existence by the parochial intolerance of lowbrows. *Beggar*'s protagonist, a fellow of artistic bent, is so rattled by his future in-laws' Main Street emptiness that he kills the lot.

Murder is almost de rigueur in expressionism, a kind of poetic Scream in which every man is his own Caligari. *The Adding Machine* thus treats not an artist but a nerd—our Mr. Zero, an accountant—as a psychosis waiting to happen. Dehumanized by a life as dreary as his job, then told he is to lose even that, and to a machine, Mr. Zero snaps, murders his boss, and is executed, to sample various afterlives till he is sent back to earth for more of the life that is nothing. However, in another John Howard Lawson title, *Processional* (1925), yet another murdering protagonist busts out of jail in the literal sense, simply breaking his cage apart despite *his* story's more or less naturalistic atmosphere.

What we find most elemental about expressionism is the oddly skewed nature of its hyperspace dialogue, that quality of characters not so much conversing as confessing, or sharing drastic poetry with the audience, or simply free-associating. Sophie Treadwell's *Machinal* (1928) presents a heroine as alienated as Mr. Zero. But he speaks in ordinary urban English, while Treadwell's protagonist spends a monologue letting her mind go for a walk. Then, too, there are the famous asides in O'Neill's *Strange Interlude* (1928) and *Dynamo* (1929) and Elmer Rice's *The Subway* (1929). *Strange Interlude* uses its asides most variously, sometimes as lengthy monologues and sometimes as momentary observations or skinny little reveries:

PROFESSOR LEEDS: (greeting his former student) So glad to see you, Charlie! A surprise, too! We didn't expect you back so soon!

Fortunate, his coming back . . . always calming influence on Nina . . .

MARSDEN: And I never dreamed of returning so soon. But Europe, Professor, is the big casualty they were afraid to set down on the list.

PROFESSOR LEEDS: Yes, I suppose you found everything completely changed since before the war.

The war . . . Gordon! . . .

Above, I have named all the major American expressionist plays, to emphasize that the movement—if such it was in the first place—began in 1920 and was over by 1930, counting a mere handful of titles. The extent of expressionism's influence is not clear, though the style has resurfaced from time to time, as in the fantastical non sequiturs and avowals in the dialogue of the musical *Follies* (1971). Though revisions have naturalized it, the original show was virtually an evening-long expressionist dream sequence like the one in *Beggar on Horseback*.*

* The title recollects a phrase used more than once in English lit. Isn't the most famous one "Set a beggar on horseback and he will ride a gallop"? That's from Robert Burton's seventeenth-century *Anatomy of Melancholy*; but what does it mean and how does it relate to Kaufman and Connelly's play? While we're chatting, *Beggar on Horseback* is based

Note, too, that *Beggar on Horseback* was the work of deacons of The Street, not iconoclasts like O'Neill, Lawson, and Treadwell. True, the show is far less dangerous than *The Hairy Ape, Roger Bloomer,* or *Machinal,* because its distaste for boobois America was one that educated folk were happy to share. "All right we are two nations," John Dos Passos wrote at the time, and we seem even more so today in a red-and blue-state America. One wonders, though, if any of the audience wondered why the authors felt the Cady family deserved to die. Yes, Mr. Cady is a sanctimonious money-grubber, his wife a simpering nincompoop, their son a slimy conniver, and their daughter—the protagonist's romance—a stupid flirtbag. Still, their only real offense is that they're boring and thus like boring things.

The protagonist (Roland Young, much later Hollywood's Topper) is a penniless classical composer with a doting neighbor (Kay Johnson) who is his real love—as he finally realizes. This pair further isolates the Cadys as American types: Young has talent and Johnson's a pistol. In fact, the authors never give the Cadys a chance; several times the four of them speak over each other for long passages, and we aren't supposed to discern what they're saying because they aren't saying anything. For life. The real point of the show is to reveal what Cadys mean by the word "culture," for the big dream sequence includes a visit to the Cady Consolidated Art Factory, where everything is mass-produced. A novelist dictates to a stenographer, and when he dries up in mid-cliché she goes right on for him. A tour group passes:

VISITOR: Say, will you show us how the artist works?
GUIDE: Certainly. What will you have—a cover or an advertisement?
VISITOR: What's the difference?
GUIDE: There isn't any.

Coincidentally, though *Beggar on Horseback* preceded *Broadway, Chicago,* and *The Front Page,* it already saw how a murder trial might be "produced" as a show-biz event. Indeed, Manny Mozart must have put on this show,

on Paul Apel's play *Hans Sonnenstössers Höllenfahrt* (Jack Sun-Basher's Journey To Hell, 1912). Kaufman and Connelly worked from an outline only. Their producer, Winthrop Ames, wanted nothing derivatively German but a native American piece, to bite into Babbitt and not Biedermeier. Perhaps the phrase "beggar on horseback" wants to reflect the oxymoron of Apel's original title: if a sun-basher is thrown down to hell, a beggar may at least ride.

too, for no sooner had Roland Young killed the Cadys ("Now you've done it," says Mrs. Cady, after he stabs her daughter) than newsboys came running into the Broadhurst Theatre's auditorium. "Extra! Extra!" they shouted. "All about the murders!" This was a clever piece of showmanship: as the public turned to take in the action in the aisles, the curtain sneakily came down, ending the first act without the standard punctuation.

There's a noisy newsboy in *Processional*, too, getting the play off to the fastest exposition in theatre history: "Extry! Soldiers and miners clash! Threats! Thrills! Throngs!" That's the plot premise—events surrounding a labor action. Plot is the least of *Processional*, however, for it was Lawson's ambition to leap beyond what he called "the facile mood of Expressionism"—really, the verbose monologues and visual exaggerations. Lawson wanted to abstract something of "America's character and rhythm," using "vaudeville patter and jazz noises." He even employed an onstage band, in the deliberately peculiar grouping of flute, bassoon, trumpet, trombone, French horn, banjo, accordion, harmonica, and Jew's harp; the players maintained speaking parts but mostly accompanied the action using pop tunes of the day. Like the paperboys of *Beggar on Horseback*—which opened exactly eleven months earlier—*Processional*'s band marched in right up the theatre aisle.

While Lawson's dialogue is seasoned with a touch of the customary expressionist raving, he strove to concoct his own blend of the vernacular and the poetic, albeit using little punctuation. His protagonist, Dynamite Jim (George Abbott, climaxing his early acting career to concentrate on writing and directing), the aforementioned jailbreaker, is here entertaining a visit in his cell by his mother and grandmother, the latter called Old Maggie:

OLD MAGGIE: I can see in the dark. Monkeydoin's Sin an' capers . . . why ain't men got nuthin' better to do but kill an' drink an' chase womenfolk? . . . What makes 'em do it?
JIM'S MOTHER: I dunno the moon, I guess.
JIM: Yes, and corn liquor.

Processional is filled with "characters" and reprobates of all kinds, from the Chamber of Commerce to the Klan, and while Jim's killing of a soldier in a fight is not something we sympathize with, *Processional* is meant more as a crazy vaudeville than as persuasive narrative. Indeed, the show ends as

Jim marries Sadie Cohen (June Walker) in "The Jazz Wedding," bringing back *Processional*'s own newsboy, one Boob Elkins (Ben Grauer) to cry "Extry! Extry! All about the big peace!" as the entire company marches up the aisle to the hot-rodding of the band. This is the "processional" of the title: the parade of American culture that—so we are told once again—becomes its own show biz because that's all that Americans believe in.

Clearly, Lawson planned to seize his public with something clamorous, weird, and exultant. *Processional* is something like a concept musical without a score, yet another piece of New Broadway. The critics weren't ready for it. Percy Hammond of the *Herald-Tribune* thought it "suffers from convulsions," and the *American*'s Alan Dale called it "pointless, witless, opaque, ill-written, and abjectly foolish." Keep in mind, though, that both men held reactionary views. (Remember Dale fulminating about the racial integration in *Aphrodite*'s ensemble?) The more curious Heywood Broun, of the *World,* thought *Processional* in need of revision. But, for now, it was "the scratch paper of a great American play." That's actually quite a compliment, and audiences kept *Processional* running for three months.

If Kaufman (yet not Connelly) remains one of Broadway's golden names and Lawson is forgotten, Sophie Treadwell came out of obscurity for a nice little huzzah when *Machinal* made a return at the Public Theater, in 1990. Expressionism has been extinct for so long that, back in the 1930s, when someone would say to George S. Kaufman, "You know what play of yours should be revived?," Kaufman would snap back, "It's dated," having assumed the allusion was heading for *Beggar on Horseback*. Yet Treadwell apparently tapped into something timeless in *Machinal*. Again, we have a murder case, this time a real one. Here's how reporter Damon Runyon described guilty accomplices Ruth Snyder and Judd Gray: "A chilly looking blonde with frosty eyes and one of those marble, you-bet-you-will chins, and an inert, scare-drunk fellow that you couldn't miss among any hundred men as a dead set-up for the blonde, or the shell game, or maybe a gold brick." It was, said Runyon, "the Dumbbell Murder" because of the pair's inept killing of Snyder's husband and their inability to keep their stories straight. As *Broadway* has been telling us, murder was a headliner's act; if the world was a vaudeville bill, a capital-punishment trial was the coveted next-to-closing spot. Jolson wasn't bigger. Among those sent to report on the Snyder-Gray days in court were D. W. Griffith (presumably to discern the hidden allegory), Peggy Hopkins Joyce (for the gold-digger angle), Mary Roberts Rinehart (who, we recall, co-wrote *The Bat* and thus knew crime), and the Reverends Billy Sunday and John Roach Stratton. A *Daily News* photographer with a camera concealed in his pant leg caught a cloudy view of Snyder dying in the electric chair, and it greeted the city on the front page the following day.

Treadwell's take was not prurient but artistic: why did she do it and what kind of story does it tell? An expressionist one, of course, so Snyder has become, as the form prefers, symbolic and somewhat dehumanized as simply the Young Woman (Zita Johann). We eventually learn her name: Helen Jones. But expressionism really likes names like Mr. Zero or Boob Elkins, or simply job designations, so the rest of *Machinal* takes in the Husband, the Mother, the Judge, the Priest, and the sole character who actually listens to what the Young Woman is saying, the Man (Clark Gable, a couple of years ahead of the movies). The nine scenes bear titles—another expressionist exercise—such as "At Home," "Prohibited," "The Law," and "A Machine": the execution, of course. The Young Woman's final words are "Somebody! Somebod—." Snyder's were "Forgive them, Father."

Treadwell avoided *Beggar on Horseback*'s fantasy and *Processional*'s gallimaufry of theatricalities, inventing instead a kind of expressionist naturalism—to heighten the experience without wallowing in The Experimentalism Of It All, and to explore her protagonist's feelings as an individual. The other two plays do that at times, but are also eager to kick away convention for the threats! thrills! and throngs! that so much of Broadway's twenties experiments depended on. Treadwell's approach is stylized, true—but her storytelling is person-scaled. In *The Adding Machine* or *The Hairy Ape*, the alienation of modern life is an institution, a monster, virtually a character in the play. This is because expressionism generally was about the playwright: about his ingenuity in dramatizing his cross-section of society. Treadwell wanted to be ingenious, too: but she needed even more to show how a woman denied any happiness in her working, social, or romantic life chances upon someone loving and appreciative—the Clark Gable figure—and more or less loses her reason in trying to find her way back to that brief happiness. Yes, through murder.

Thus, the title of the "Prohibited" scene is a loaded pun: combining Prohibition (the setting is a speakeasy) and the forbidden love of adultery (Clark Gable comes into the Young Woman's life at this point) but also the feeling that anything gentle, pretty, or caring is banned in the Young

Woman's life. More: the even more forbidden love of the homosexual world gets what may be its first honest presentation in Broadway history in this scene. True, *The Captive* had come and gone two seasons previously. However, *The Captive* kept its Captor—the other woman in the lesbian affair—offstage. The fearless Treadwell shows us an older gay man picking up a chicken, and her stage directions tolerate no ambiguity. She calls one "a middle-aged fairy" and the other "young, untouched." They are last seen leaving the club together, supposedly to view the older man's rare-book collection. "I have a first edition of Verlaine," he says, "that will simply make your mouth water."

This subversive honesty is very much a part of twenties Broadway. It's why the authorities pounced with legal penalty but also why they finally gave up: there was too much of it. The Charles Frohman theory of playgoing held that the theatre is a place of beauty. The generation of managers that succeeded Frohman's, led by Winthrop Ames, Arthur Hopkins, and Gilbert Miller (son of the star actor Henry Miller, whose theatre still stands on West Forty-third Street), held that theatre is a place of surprise. Not a plot twist: an insight.

This introduces the second of the great twenties novelties, the long-lived one: the Theatre Guild. Indeed, it endured for fifty years, though its days of greatest influence did not outlast its first decade or so, after which it became, increasingly, a producing organization like most others, eventually taking on conventional comedies like *The Tunnel of Love* (1957) and *A Majority of One* (1959) and conventional musical comedies like *Bells Are Ringing* (1956) and *Darling of the Day* (1968), the final Theatre Guild presentation.

Yet in its heyday, its admirers claim, the Guild specialized in surprise, in the utopian philosophy that worthy plays should be produced even if they are too special to succeed. Imagine going into business to lose money. Actually, the Guild didn't expect to fail, but rather to develop an adventurous audience with a string of what we can call "prestige successes." It's a euphemism, of course. Long after all this, thinking of her own lean years with Kurt Weill when they first came to America, that symbol of twentieth-century Western-civ show biz Lotte Lenya dismissed the concept of prestige successes. "You can starve on them," she said.

The Guild didn't starve—but then those who scorn it believe it imposed an embourgeoisement upon nonconformist theatre. Yes, it made available work that was unproduceable before 1919: but to a public that expected to be reverent and even awed but protected from having to think, because to subscribe to the Guild was already an intellectual act, complete in itself. One didn't have to attend in any deep sense, simply to go, sit, and bring home the program. The Guild, say doubters, was not revolutionary. It was fat and happy.

There was a Board of Managers, and the managers *were* the Guild: phlegmatic maestro Lawrence Langner, chic designer Lee Simonson, chief stage director Philip Moeller, character actress and professional eccentric Helen Westley, moneybags Maurice Wertheim (historian Barbara Tuchman's father, by the way), and all-around directrix Theresa Helburn. Broadway needed and resented them. The problem was the obvious one: how can six people, especially six as cantankerously discrepant as these, ever agree on anything? They can't. They didn't. Many a future hit for other producers was turned down by the Guild because half the committee scorned the script. Then there were the Sunday-night run-throughs for the committee, with six wildly different opinions bearing down on playwright, director, and cast. One of the Guild's most eminent offshoots was the Playwrights' Company, a management founded by major dramatists who couldn't stand dealing with the Gang of Six any more.

The Guild itself was an offshoot, of an earlier group called the Washington Square Players, founded in 1914 and somewhat recherché in its emphasis on one-acters, especially by European writers. America's entry into the Great War broke up the organization, but in 1919 it came back together, this time for full-length outings on The Street. All but penniless—the coffers held about two thousand dollars—the Guild had to oblige itself to philanthropy for its home. That ubiquitous Maecenas Otto Kahn lent them the Garrick Theatre, which he held under lease, and which we know was to see the Guild triumphing with the only non-musical play to run through the Actors' Strike, *John Ferguson.*

Ironically, while the Guild saw itself as New Broadway, destined to repave The Street with Art, the Garrick was Old Broadway, down on Thirty-fifth Street just east of Sixth Avenue, where nothing mattered. Opened in 1890 as Harrigan's Theatre after Ned Harrigan broke up his act with Tony Hart, the playhouse was managed by Richard Mansfield and saw one of the classic performances of the age in William Gillette's assumption of the title role in his own adaptation of *Sherlock Holmes* (1899). Charles Frohman produced it, as he produced also at the Garrick the emergence of Ethel Barrymore in Clyde Fitch's *Captain Jinks of the Horse Marines* (1901). Gad, what great names of Old Broadway!—even if Barrymore was by 1919 in mid-career and Gillette still turned up as Holmes from time to time.

Thus, to enter the Garrick was not unlike stepping into a Great Pyramid. Worse, the Herald Square location did not encourage walk-in business, at a time when improvisatory theatregoing provided the bulk of a show's audience at most evening performances.* Nevertheless, the Guild prevailed. It so energized a New Public to match its New Broadway that the Guild was able to build its own theatre in 1925, six years after it had opened shop at the Garrick. The new house, the Guild (today the Virginia), was consecrated with a revival of George Bernard Shaw's *Caesar and Cleopatra,* with Lionel Atwill and Helen Hayes. (Helen Westley played Ftatateeta.) And here's another irony: to raise funds for tapestries to dress either side of the new auditorium, the Guild gave Richard Rodgers and Lorenz Hart their Big Break with a revue opportunity. The result rocked the town with delight at our old friend the Garrick, now within a decade of demolition yet immortalized in the revue's title: *The Garrick Gaieties.* The show began with a spoofy quartet called "Soliciting Subscriptions" that rhymed a knock on culture vultures (as "people on Fifth Avenue") with "We bring out the aesthetic soul you didn't know you have in you." This is where the Guild's supporters and critics come together: was this a breakthrough in theatre culture or mass-market snob appeal?

Take the Guild's views on casting. Running annual, full-scale seasons without at least a star or two would have been unthinkable, and the Guild did use stars—Ina Claire, George M. Cohan, Katharine Hepburn, and, above all, the Lunts. However, for its first decade or so the Guild banned star billing by policy: the *play* was the thing. Is this idealism, or the flattery of Guild subscribers, who have thus been distinguished from the mob of star chasers? Indeed, was the Guild trying to imply that it had been graduated from the Old Broadway of the hokum queen and the matinée idol with an integrated acting ensemble? *That's* why the hoardings never mentioned the players? At times, the Guild would rotate productions in repertory at a single house with a kind of stock company. There was Helen Westley as the

---

* Matinées in general and special holiday afternoons in particular tended to attract family groups. Special occasions, they were booked in advance and often sold to the last seat.

Old Dame, Dudley Digges' Heavy Father, George Gaul for the Romantic-Heroic roles, Margalo Gillmore's Chirpy Ingenue, and Utility Juvenile Earle Larimore. It had consistency, if nothing else: but it had nothing else, because the Guild's sense of "ensemble" simply meant The Same People in Every Play.

On the other hand, twenties theatregoers would not have known how to respond to stagings that were not star-centered. In *Caesar and Cleopatra*, for instance, one followed the action through the confrontations of Atwill, Hayes, and Westley: the "spotlight" aroused concentration. Yes, the Moscow Art Theatre made its famous visit in 1923; but they were acting in Russian, out of the loop. Not till the 1930s, when the Group Theatre was formed—paradoxically, by restless Guild underlings—was Broadway to have its own acting ensemble with a philosophy of aesthetics to match a philosophy of subject matter.

The Guild's subject matter, following the Washington Square Players' penchant, was Europe. There were scarcely any Americans—and none of note—in the Guild's first four seasons. Rather, there was Jacinto Benavente, St. John Ervine, August Strindberg, Leonid Andreyef, and Georg Kaiser, whose *Von Morgens bis Mitternachts* (1917), given as *From Morn to Midnight* in 1922, is sometimes considered the first work of classic (i.e., European) expressionism seen on Broadway.

Elmer Rice turned up in the Guild's fifth season. Still, Europeans overwhelmed local talent till the tenth season, and not till the fifteenth season did Americans predominate. Of course, there had to be a little something by Luigi Chiarelli slotted in with the natives, of course in the Somerset Maugham translation.

And there was Shaw. A great deal of the Guild's reputation depended on Shaw's giving it world-premiere rights to his newest pieces when he was the most imposing playwright in the English-speaking world. *Heartbreak House* (1920), *Back to Methuselah* (1922), in three nights, and *Saint Joan* (1923) were thus launched under Guild auspices; between them, older Shaw was revived to assert Guild interest. Yet no one spoke of a Guild playing style in Shaw: or, to repeat for emphasis, a Guild playing style at all.

Yes, the constant use of director Philip Moeller suggested a wish to harmonize Guild actors' self-presentation; and Moeller employed exercises to test and expand his troupe's abilities, much as the Group was to. However, the Group's Lee Strasberg worked from a program of thespian preparation.

Moeller was a showboater, making it up as he went along; he often began re-hearsals without having read the script.

As for designer Simonson—who often planned costumes and lighting as well as sets—here at least was a unifying contribution. He helped pio-neer the use of a permanent structure against which inserts and drops could be flown for fast changes of scene. Alternatively, Simonson kept the playing area all but empty against a great simple backdrop. He put this ef-fect to spectacular use in that *Caesar and Cleopatra,* in the fourth-act ban-quet scene: the back half of the stage was cut off by what looked like a silken nothingness, hung from wing to wing. Before it, Simonson set a sim-ple dining table and a wooden lounge chair, with the stage apron cut open for the entrance of slaves from below bearing trays, urns, and exotic carv-ings. It was an eyeful fit for the opening of the Guild's own theatre, even if the drop was so sensitive that if someone in the last row of the balcony fid-geted with his program, the entire back of the stage billowed like an ocean. Still, it must be said that, in design at least, the Guild was often bold, com-missioning sets and costumes from Miguel Covarrubias for *Androcles and the Lion* (1925) that created a children's-book atmosphere for this most gentle of plays.

Was this constant presence of Shaw the Guild's unifying element? No: because it put on anything else. The Guild's historical reputation is based ex-clusively on its famous shows, its prominent authors such as S. N. Behrman or Ferenc Molnár, its Paul Robeson *Othello*. But, in between, the Guild sim-ply took a smash at a piñata of theatre work, staging whatever could—however dimly—be called "artistic" rather than "commercial." Including musicals. Including even an opera—but that was *Porgy and Bess*.

Let's get our bearings with a few more or less descriptive titles, for if no single idea or person essentialized the Theatre Guild, certainly the organi-zation created a body of work that *seemed* to amount to something. First of all, we should cite the Bizarre European Piece—such as a tale of poor folk in Budapest, with a tremulous heroine who falls for a thuggish merry-go-round barker who abuses her and kills himself after a botched robbery. With its somber background and drably eccentric characters, it's a flea market of a play, suddenly moving into fantasy late in the evening, to show that even Heaven cannot redeem its anti-hero. It's like *Carousel* without the music. It *is Carousel* without the music: Ferenc Molnár's *Liliom,* "a leg-end in seven scenes and a prologue," put into English by Benjamin F.

Glazer for the Guild's 1920–21 season.* *Liliom* was a surprise hit, moving from the Garrick up to the Fulton (later the Helen Hayes, now demolished) and even the oversized Forty-fourth Street, for a total of 311 performances.

We might also consider the first play about robots—the work, in fact, in which the word "robot" was coined, from the Czech *robota* ("work"). In Karel Čapek's *R.U.R.* (for Rossum's Universal Robots, the company that manufactures them), robots are workers, slaves of mankind till they rebel. Clad in leather helmets, metallic tunics (bearing serial numbers) with flaring shoulders, and knee-length boots with pointed tops, they looked fit for a fifties kiddie matinée, even a film by Ed Wood. But then, *R.U.R.* generally has a horror-film feeling, though in the end a male and female robot develop feelings for each other and look to be the Adam and Eve of a new race. This show, too, was a hit.

While the Guild doted on those Bizarre European Pieces, there was nothing like the Absolutely Guaranteed Classic for inspiring the troops. Ibsen's *Peer Gynt* (1923), an adaptation of *The Brothers Karamazov* (1927), and the First Part of Goethe's *Faust* (1928) were useful here. Fidelity to text was a Guild hallmark at a time when producers routinely put on adaptations rather than straight translations of foreign-language writing. However, if *Peer Gynt* is long, even the first half of *Faust* is endless. Shaw held the Guild to word-complete performances of his plays—and he kept watch through a confederate living in New York. But Goethe was dead, so the Guild borrowed a translation by Graham and Tristan Rawson, used in 1924 at London's Old Vic, that cut whole scenes (including the Prologue in the Theatre, Goethe's timeless excoriation of moneybags show biz). Further, the Rawsons made combinings and tucks all along the way; one has to, just to get this show onstage. Perhaps out of guilt, the Guild imported Friedrich Holl, director of the Berlin Volksbühne, to direct: an authentic *Faust*, or at any rate a German one. The casting drew heavily on the Guild stock company, with George Gaul's Faust, Dudley Digges' Mephistopheles, and Helen Westley's Martha, though the Chirpy Ingenue, Goethe's Margaret (so called in the Guild's program), was Helen Chandler.

---

* "Liliom," Hungarian for "Lily," is the tough-guy hero's ironic nickname. Note how Rodgers and Hammerstein used both the Hungarian and its translation in renaming the character. "Lily" became "Billy," and the scan and general sound of "Liliom" created his last name, "Bigelow": Lily Liliom.

Faust was one of the Guild's debacles. Apart from the ingeniousness of Lee Simonson's set changes, nothing was praised. Worse, each critic found this *Faust* ridiculous in a different way: too perfunctory, too driven, too silly, too studied. Come to think of it, why was a German who couldn't speak English hired to direct an English-speaking cast, at that in poetry? And isn't this masterpiece at long last a poem that its author never meant to see performed?

Another Guild genre was the Inexplicable Novelty, put on as if defining the Guild with indefinability, in a string of objets trouvés. As I've said, what identifies the Guild *today* is the *E*xplicable Novelty, something unusual yet artistically so righteous that it needs no excuse. DuBose and Dorothy Heyward's *Porgy* (1927), which we all "know" from the extraordinarily faithful Gershwin version, is an ideal example, for it centered the black folk play movement with such disarming sincerity that one can date the decline and eventual death of stereotype entertainment from *Porgy*'s premiere.

However, when the Guild was young many theatregoers associated the organization with the Inexplicable Novelty. This would be something like *Red Rust* (1929), given by the experimental Theatre Guild Studio, albeit in a full-scale staging at the Guild's "other" Broadway house, the Martin Beck. A Soviet play, introduced in Moscow in 1927, *Red Rust* was a melodrama of the kind that later Soviet censorship would outlaw: the good guy was a bourgeois and the bad guy was a commissar. Some of the cast (Franchot Tone, Luther Adler, Lee Strasberg) would prove to be stalwarts of the Guild's breakaway cell, the Group Theatre, warning us that those committed to social drama thought the Guild dispiritingly apolitical. Certainly, *Red Rust* was "Soviet" in little more than its setting; the *Times* called it "*The Front Page* crossed with Channing Pollock." (The latter was a successful journeyman playwright who made a turnaround in the 1920s and went preachy.)

Another typifying Guild genre—but only from the late 1920s on—was the all-American piece by a pet writer. These were, first, Sidney Howard, then, chronologically, S. N. Behrman, Eugene O'Neill, Philip Barry, Maxwell Anderson, and Robert E. Sherwood, four of them founders of the Playwrights' Company; and we know why. Yes, the Guild Board of Managers was rough on writers. Still, once the Guild got going, those six did prove loyal to the more apparent dramatists, at least some of whose prestige had been borrowed from the Guild's.

The organization's treatment of Sidney Howard is instructive, for the six became interested in him only after he had worked his way through a youthful output of fantasies and derivative European romances, including his translation of the Hungarian *Sancho Panza* for Otis Skinner that we glanced at a bit ago. When he found his métier, Howard excelled at edgy American stories about charismatic but somewhat unlikable people. He seemed to enjoy testing his public; or perhaps he simply saw the world as being filled with rogues and squishes. Interestingly, Howard's most enduring work is his screenplay for *Gone With the Wind*—and while he didn't invent its characters, note that each of the four leads is in one way or another unsympathetic, two of them squishes and the other two fascinating rogues.

The Guild embraced Howard in the mid-1920s with three works, *They Knew What They Wanted* (1924), *Ned McCobb's Daughter* (1926), and, scarcely a month after, *The Silver Cord* (1926). Each is a variation on a format of the day—respectively, melodrama, crook play, and domestic drama—and Howard filled each tale with those characters we find engrossing and disagreeable. In *Ned McCobb's Daughter,* it's Alfred Lunt—or, really, it's everybody, in a kind of bootleggers' backstager about evading the feds, embezzling, and doing time. But it was Lunt who caught the eye, as Babe Callahan, speaking an underworld argot that was all the more flashy in the Maine seashore setting and getting into physical combat with his brother (Earle Larimore) and sister-in-law, the title role (Claire Eames). It is a picturesque irony of theatre history that some of our greatest actors couldn't begin work on a portrayal till they physicalized it in some way. Olivier always started with the nose, and for Lunt's Babe Callahan it was a gold tooth, so obnoxiously shiny that it blinded the balcony. This was a Howard family show, by the way: Eames was Mrs. Howard, and her baby girl was played by the Howards' own daughter.

In *The Silver Cord,* Howard brought his unpleasant people into the American middle-class parlor: two schmengie sons and their manipulative and grasping mother. This character, Mrs. Phelps, is a classic, very Jazz Age in Howard's debunking of sentimental piety. But Howard is subtle. Other writers simply made mothers into heaving monsters; Mrs. Phelps is almost comical in her petty gameplaying. One striking scene finds her greeting son David, just back from Europe. Mrs. Phelps busily pets and fusses at him, all the while pretending that she hasn't noticed that David has brought home his new bride, Christina: who is standing next to him. It's the kind of thing Carol Burnett might have done, or perhaps Doris Roberts in a revue sketch (that is, if there still were variety revues). David keeps trying to introduce Christina, and Christina keeps trying to speak—yet Mrs. Phelps is all but annulling the marriage by instituting a village shunning. Finally, Christina gets out a sentence, and Mrs. Phelps now has to deal with her:

> MRS. PHELPS: (affecting surprise) Eh? (Noticing Christina as if for the first time, with a dead, flat tone) Oh.

A lot of content lay in that "Oh," for Laura Hope Crews—later, by coincidence, the Aunt Pittypat of *Gone With the Wind*—played Mrs. Phelps as a kind of evil Billie Burke. "Sometimes she goes over to farce too generously," Brooks Atkinson thought. No: the lady has charm and humor; that's how she gets away with it. It's a great role, but the play is unrevivable because of a stagnant ending: Christina analyzes Mrs. Phelps' flaws like a detective summing up the case at the close of a whodunit.

They Knew What They Wanted is not unrevivable, though its musical version, Frank Loesser's *The Most Happy Fella,* all but subsumes it with more agreeable principals. It's a triangle, centering on a young woman in a spot beloved by thirties Hollywood: caught between the hot man and the good man. The former, Howard tells us, is "dark, sloppy, beautiful, and young," all appetite and no intellect, despite left-wing political interests. The good man, an Italian immigrant with a heavy accent, is "stout, floridly bronzed, sixty years old, vigorous, jovial, simple, and excitable." That's no fun, either.

The girl, at least, is a looker, originally played by Pauline Lord, one of the most mannered actresses of the day, though descriptions of her style suggest that she might have been a pioneer in a highly inflected naturalism. She was gifted, by all accounts: her Great Role was Anna Christie, in 1921. Tiny and fearful, hesitant of speech and forever keening and cringing, Lord was the ultimate *pathétique*. Yet she had stamina, and a strange ability to fill auditoriums with those moony quadrilles. Only the strongest actresses could be trusted with the decathlon part of Nina Leeds, in *Strange Interlude*. Lynn Fontanne created it, and a future Medea, Judith Anderson, replaced Fontanne and toured the show. But the first national company was headed by Pauline Lord.

O'Neill himself introduces another Guild sub-repertory, for he became a Guild partisan in 1928 with *Marco Millions* and *Strange Interlude,* assigning to the Guild all his New York premieres until his death. One cannot understand theatre in the 1920s without seeing O'Neill and the Guild as a correct mating. Inevitable, even—or simply as symmetrical as the last-minute pairing off of a Gilbert and Sullivan chorus. For O'Neill was by 1928 the Great American Playwright and the Guild was Broadway's most prestigious management.* Moreover, *Marco Millions* and *Strange Interlude* in particular proved irresistible to the Guild: because the first presented a challenge to the designer in its kaleidoscope of exotic places, and the Guild pioneered in design; and because the second's nine acts and strange Dinner Intermission spoke to the self-sacrificial attitude of the Guild devotee.

For its part, *Marco Millions* is one of O'Neill's more enjoyable pieces—a comedy, in fact, on the adventures of Marco Polo. The show is as well a spectacle, turning that kaleidoscope so generously that O'Neill had wanted Max Reinhardt to stage the piece. Indeed, Reinhardt brought his Berlin production of *A Midsummer Night's Dream* to Broadway scarcely two months before *Marco Millions* opened. But Reinhardt's New York reputation rested not just on spectacle but on the colossal—remember Reinhardt and Norman Bel Geddes turning the Century Theatre into a Gothic cathedral for *The Miracle*? The Guild's experiments in staging technology, on the contrary, lay in getting the most out of the least, "tricking" rather than filling the eye.

That approach suggests not Reinhardt but David Belasco. We remember him at the Century, too, helping out on *Aphrodite*. Still, Belasco's art—that is, when he wasn't setting a real-life Child's pancake house on stage, complete to the coffee steam—was the art of illusion. However, Belasco was Uptown Establishment as much as anyone. It tells us how determined O'Neill was to get out of Little Theatre—or to bring it to Broadway—that he actually gave the *Marco Millions* script to Belasco. How did Old Broadway feel when the author of *The Emperor Jones* offered him his latest work? Astonished, surely. Flattered? Flabbergasted? Belasco even took an option,

* While the Guild had turned down earlier O'Neill, including *Anna Christie*, the Guild's aforementioned antecedent the Washington Square Players staged an O'Neill title, the one-act *In the Zone,* in 1917, at the Comedy Theatre on West Forty-first Street, just west of Bryant Park. There's an irony in this, for at that time O'Neill was wholly involved in the Washington Square group's only real rival, the Provincetown Players. The latter were bohemian and revolutionary, strictly Downtown even when moving a surprise hit from the Village to Broadway. But the Guild, from the start, had an Uptown agenda. So, when O'Neill finally signed on with the Guild, was he going Establishment, or was the Establishment incorporating the revolution?

if perhaps only out of politeness. In the end, Belasco declined, and O'Neill presented *Marco Millions* to the Guild and launched their partnership.

Rouben Mamoulian directed, following up on his Broadway debut directing the Guild's *Porgy* the previous year. Mamoulian had distinguished himself especially in the use of music and in his deftly detailed crowd scenes, and *Marco Millions* is filled with crowds and music. The latter comprised new material by Emerson Whithorne and also Rudolf Friml's *Chinese Suite,* borrowed for the occasion. Unfortunately, O'Neill's wide-ranging scene plot outwitted Lee Simonson so consistently that the public's enjoyment was compromised by long waits between each sequence.*
Nevertheless, both the Guild and Mamoulian extended themselves in giving *Marco* the color and activity that O'Neill asked for. Those two nouns are not typically associated with O'Neill—but he is not as monolithic as his popular profile suggests. There are plenty of aberrant O'Neill plays, especially in the 1920s and especially *Marco Millions*.

For one thing, it has almost as much plot as a farce. The Prologue, though relatively short, is crowded with event. It is set in the middle of a great empty space in the Persian wasteland, marked by a single tree of sacramental importance. There, three commercial travelers—Christian, Magian, and Buddhist, to establish the play's war of West and East—take rest from the heat. While sharing news, they argue over legends of the tree's origin. The Buddha picked his teeth with a twig that grew into this very—No! Here was found the wood that made the True Cross! Nay, you fools, it was planted by Zoroaster!

As the dispute continues, we learn that the Christian is an agent of the Venetian trading house of Polo Brothers and Son, and that the Prologue occurs not before but *after* the action of the play proper: an introductory epilogue. Meanwhile, thirty Chinese extras drag in a wagon bearing a coffin covered in white cloth; a Chinese captain is escorting the body of Princess Kukachin to her burial. It's an arresting coincidence, for the Venetian has

---

* Musicals covered set changes with short scenes "in one" (that is, downstage, before the so-termed traveler curtain), often resorting to a musical number to cover stagehand noise. However, straight plays with more than one set per act and no revolve could keep an audience waiting for as much as five or six minutes between scenes. Stagecraft did not fully catch up to authors' imagination till 1960. For example, *Auntie Mame* (1956), with a vast array of sets ever switching from and back to the elaborate living room that centered the action, was reduced to projecting corkscrews of light on the traveler while the next visual was prepared.

already implied that Marco Polo and the princess may have been intimately involved, in a kind of peace of West and East. Uncovered, the coffin is revealed to be glass, Kukachin's lovely face glows, and music plays—as if, O'Neill directs, "the leaves [of the tree] were tiny harps strummed by the wind." The captain and the three merchants fall to their knees in alarmed prayer, and the dead Kukachin speaks, apparently to the Polos' deputy:

> KUKACHIN: Say this, I loved and died. Now I am love, and live. And living, have forgotten. And loving, can forgive. (Here her lips part in a smile of beautiful pity) Say this for me in Venice!

I ask you, does this suit that popular idyll of O'Neill the mournful autobiographer, thrilled with his own incoherence and mythic to a fault? Remember, his blood ran with the zest of Old Broadway from his actor father, the Count of Monte Cristo. Eugene was even born on The Street, at Forty-third and Broadway, on October 16, 1888. And note the black humor with which he closes the Prologue: as three of the bearers have died from the labor of racing across the plain with their burden, the Captain decides to enslave the three traders in their place. Frantically, the Venetian shows the Captain a letter of introduction to the Chinese court, which the Captain promptly tears up. "And now," he concludes, "forward march!" With the three traders bound to the others, the Captain whips the wagon off to wails of despair, leaving behind the three dead coolies and a reminiscence of Kukachin's tiny harps. The Prologue is over.

Wow. If *Mourning Becomes Electra* (1931) had as much sheer story, the premiere wouldn't have let out yet. Then, too, O'Neill's Marco is no avatar of legend but, quite simply, a babbitt among sophisticates. The court of Kublai Khan treats of nuance and wisdom, while Marco communicates in clichés and chamber-of-commerce good-guy routines. He likes to repeat the joke that "an Armenian doily-dealer told me down in Baghdad," the kind that begins "An old Jew named Ikey," and it seems that our Marco can handle anything except honest feeling. In fact, he writes poetry—but furtively, lest anyone suspect him of effeminacy. So Mamoulian timed his drums, gongs, and choruses to visual coups, working with Simonson on the lighting to be certain that the audience saw the East that Mamoulian saw; but Marco toured it all without ever taking it in. Here's why: he doesn't listen. No matter where he is, he might as well never have left the city of Zenith in the state of Winnemac. It's what Italians call "campanilismo" (literally, "church-belltowerism"): knowing only what everyone else in the parish knows, ignorant of all else. In a way, O'Neill might have designed this eye candy of a play precisely to characterize his unappreciative hero. The audience, taking in scene after scene of luxury and worldliness, could thus watch in real time as Marco endlessly fails to get it.

Margalo Gillmore might have lacked the soaring wonder with which Kukachin is ideally invested, though Baliol Holloway's Khan and Dudley Digges' Chu-Yen, the court sage, apparently gave weight to the Chinese scenes. Alfred Lunt was Marco—surely one of Lunt's tours de force, as he hints of the potentially expansive personality that the nitwit deliberately limits in himself. Indeed, he must if he is to succeed, for—as other titles have already warned us—American business culture creates mediocrity. Its salesmen purvey it; its customers demand it.

No one seems to have liked *Marco Millions,* though all agreed that Mamoulian and Simonson had given O'Neill his spectacle. In 1964, José Quintero and his designers, David Hays and Beni Montresor, tried a spare *Marco* for the first season of the Repertory Theatre of Lincoln Center, in its temporary home in Washington Square. Hal Holbrook, Zohra Lampert, and David Wayne (as Kublai Khan) led a cast all but excoriated as unworthy, and the play again impressed no one.

Yet the O'Neill *classics* hold the stage. *Strange Interlude,* which the Guild unveiled only three weeks after *Marco,* brings us to the more familiar O'Neill, depicting a contemporary American world in which nobody really gets what he wants and what little one does get costs more than the ego can afford. Because Lunt and Fontanne had not yet teamed conclusively, he was playing *Marco Millions* at the Guild while she played *Strange Interlude* at the John Golden; and she wasn't happy. Much later, she claimed to have instituted cuts in the script, apparently unbeknown to O'Neill; it was an open secret on Broadway that the ninety-minute dinner intermission started a good twenty minutes early. One wonders if Fontanne ever heard the joke in *Auntie Mame,* when sidekick Vera fusses over being late for an audition at the Guild. She can't quite recall the title of "this lovely, lovely play where everybody thinks out loud and it runs four and a half hours":

VERA: It's called *Strange . . . Strange Inter . . . Inter . . . Inter . . .*
MAME: *. . . course?*

O'Neill probed the psychosexual nature of humankind in *Strange Interlude* especially in that his protagonist, Nina Leeds, is surrounded by men who find her overwhelming or simply aren't "man" enough to match up to her. These are, for starters, her professor father (Philip Leigh), described in one character's aside with "condescending affection":

> Good little man . . . he looks worried . . . always fussing about something . . . he must get on Nina's nerves . . .

That speaker himself, Charles Marsden (Tom Powers), comes off no better in one of Nina's asides:

> Nice Charlie doggy . . . faithful . . . fetch and carry . . . bark softly in books at the deep night . . .

Meanwhile, Sam Evans (Earle Larimore) is there "to mother and boss and keep [Nina] occupied," in the opinion of Edmund Darrell (Glenn Anders), the only male lead who isn't a girly man. Darrell is the Clark Gable role in the 1932 film, and it is Darrell who, at least, can sire upon Nina a bastard who grows up eagerly joining in the wars for possession of one another's soul that obsessed his elders. "The sons of the Father have all been failures!" Nina cries near the play's end.

It's a Strindbergian notion: all O'Neill studies refer to the Swedish dramatist first and anyone else after, and following O'Neill's death the right of premiere passed from the Guild to the Royal Dramatic Theatre in Stockholm. But didn't Strindberg like a real battle? His most enduring work (at least arguably so) is called *The Dance of Death,* the murderous tango of a married couple. *Strange Interlude* never shows us Nina's interaction with her sole magnetic opposite, a sublime hunk with the sublime-hunk name of Gordon Shaw, an aviator killed in the war. As many have pointed out, *Strange Interlude* is really a novel that for some unexplained reason is being performed on a stage. True, the asides are in effect a dramatization of what a garrulous novelist might have stated as "explanations." Yet the piece is some four hours of asides; worse, everyone is so *dreary.*

Not Nina, perhaps—or not entirely. But after such twisty O'Neill inventions as Brutus Jones and *The Hairy Ape*'s Yank, after the grimy wistfulness of the one-act sea plays, after even the deadpan listing of the extras in the racially explosive *All God's Chillun Got Wings* (1924) as "Whites and

Negroes," *Strange Interlude*'s presentation of library, dining room, sitting room, and terrace as a set of Freudian mosaics finds O'Neill horribly lacking in Old Broadway panache. True, Act Eight (and how many other plays even have one?), set on the afterdeck of a cruiser, features an offstage boat race and a fatal heart attack; but it's too little, too late, as one says. Is there a single moment in all these nine acts as instantly inductive of character as Anna Christie's entrance into Johnny-the-Priest's saloon? She drags her suitcase to a table, plops down, and orders the first of the evening:

ANNA: Gimme a whiskey—ginger ale on the side . . . And don't be stingy, baby.

Immortalized in the 1930 talkie as the first words heard from Garbo's lips on a movie screen, the bit might be O'Neill at his most quotable, challenging Mary Tyrone's "I fell in love with James Tyrone and was so happy for a time." The last note sounded in the resonant echo texture of *Long Day's Journey Into Night*, it is a curtain line of superb and conclusive irony. It truly *finishes* the play.

Is there any such writing in *Strange Interlude*? Beyond the interplay of all those asides, there's little in it at all that is truly theatrical, except for a boat race and a heart attack. Yet the show played 426 performances, the mark of a smash in the 1920s. And it sent out those two road companies, won the Pulitzer Prize, and sold one hundred thousand copies of the text in cloth.

"The *Abie's Irish Rose* of the pseudo-intelligentsia," Alexander Woollcott called it. Worse, Lynn Fontanne had sent Woollcott the script while the play was in rehearsal, and *Vanity Fair* published his scornful response a few days *before* the opening, creating a scandal. But then, by this time O'Neill was already becoming what he has been ever after—the disputed genius, undeniably ambitious yet *at times* stubbornly deficient in talent. Or was he too full of content ever to edit it down to fair portion? For all his flaws, he was *the* hot-date playwright of New Broadway, just as expressionism was New Broadway's finery and the Theatre Guild its tailor. O'Neill is the third of our twenties innovations—and see how interlocked the three are. The Theatre Guild produced *The Adding Machine* and *Processional* as well as O'Neill, and O'Neill drew heavily on expressionism in his early years.

O'Neill was, if nothing else, the great breakaway playwright, in length, in his physical demands on design technology, in subject matter, in his reclamation of the Classical monologue. And O'Neill was something else in any case: the writer who reinstructed the stage on its ancient role of interpreter of myth. *Desire Under the Elms* (1924) retells Phaedra's love for Hippolytus, son of her husband, Theseus, setting the tale on a New England farm in 1850. And note that O'Neill did not leave the look of the piece to the designer's imagination but specified—indeed, characterized—the visual environment in two huge elm trees that loom over the farmhouse with an aspect of sinister maternity, a crushing, jealous absorption. O'Neill actually drew matrices for set designer Robert Edmond Jones (who also directed) to work from. O'Neill's use of masks, in *The Great God Brown* (1926), unites ancient Greek usage with Freudian concepts. The actors raised or lowered the masks according to the narrative context, developing an arresting (and troubling) visual conceit of the kind favored by such Little Theatre progressives as Jones and another O'Neill collaborator, producer and dramaturg Kenneth Macgowan. O'Neill tried Christian myth as well in *Lazarus Laughed* (1928), a pageant that the Guild simply couldn't afford; it came forth at the Pasadena Playhouse. O'Neill even explored twentieth-century myths, not only using Freud but trying to combine Oedipus and electricity into a parable of the New God in *Dynamo*.

And what of O'Neill's sheer love of the different forms of theatre? His output is vivaciously diverse, more so even than that of Maxwell Anderson, who could mystify you with a verse play one season and then write book and lyrics to a musical. The average theatregoer may not be aware of how many kinds of O'Neill there are because of the emphasis on the famous later titles, all dire and long in the *Mourning Becomes Electra* (1931) manner—though *Ah, Wilderness!* (1933) falls into that group as well.*

---

* A nostalgic domestic comedy about the coming of age of a romantic young man (Elisha Cook Jr.) on one very busy small-town Fourth of July, *Ah, Wilderness!* cast George M. Cohan as the protagonist's father. It was a stunning coup; Cohan was almost inarguably the outstanding American thespian, the most famous, the biggest. Besides, the Guild didn't work with performers like Cohan. The Guild worked with . . . you know, Dudley Digges or the Lunts. Actors, not national institutions. An adjustment in policy was necessary, for while Cohan could go on without makeup, as always before, and persist in his seething refusal to join Equity, the Guild could not present the greatest of headliners without name billing. The *Ah, Wilderness!* poster showed a young couple side by side in a rowboat under a full moon, and Cohan's name was spelled out, albeit in smallish type below the title. Thereafter, the Guild retired its "no stars" policy, and important players were heralded on the Guild's showcards, though almost invariably under the title.

Of course, when they haul out O'Neill's less celebrated twenties titles for a fresh look—the more picturesque items such as *The Great God Brown*—they can seem finicky and affected, vaingloriously determined to dare. Then, too, after the excruciating dialect used in the early 1920s (as in this snippet of *Desire Under the Elms*: "Sun's a-rizin'. Purty, hain't it?"), suddenly O'Neill goes into Standard English, with little of the poetry we expect of a great playwright.

That's the half-empty. The half-full gives us the real-life coming of age of a romantic young man. He is not an arresting wordsmith, but something larger: a great carpenter of theatre, building on, first, his father's grand old stage ("Mine, the treasure of Monte Cristo! The world is mine!"); second, on the Little Theatre's wish to remake the stage into a religion of ceremony and terror somewhat in anticipation of the theories of Antonin Artaud; and, third, as the handsome yet resentful guy who was either the victim of one of those Great American Destinies or the inventor and master of a new kind of destiny.

For instance, O'Neill's career proves that there *are* second acts in American lives. The writing kept improving—and yet that very early *Anna Christie* is as hardy as any later O'Neill title. It is his least experimental piece, though it does bear an extremely O'Neillian symbolization of the sea as a fate: "Dat ole davil" is how Anna's seaman father, Chris, refers to it. The first version of the play closed out of town in 1920. Oddly, though it turned on a triangle of father, daughter, and her suitor, with a single appearance for a hokum queen as the father's on-and-off girl friend, Marthy, the original script was otherwise very different from the final version we know today. For one thing, Anna was originally a refined young lady with an English accent. In *Anna Christie,* she's a prostitute.*

Well, of course: possibly the most famous prostitute of the American stage. (This is not implied; the text places her former employment in a

* There is some confusion about this work's titles. The first script was called *Chris Christophersen,* and so it was named when finally published, in 1982. However, the 1920 tryout, in Atlantic City and Philadelphia, billed the piece as *Chris.* When O'Neill revised the text, now called *The Ole Davil,* he learned that the Swedish father's name is correctly spelled "Christopherson," and so it is spelled in the final version as well, the *Anna Christie* that finally reached Broadway. All this fuss over the father only reminds us that O'Neill's interest in the big figure of the sailor who hates the sea led him into the blunder of writing, at first, the wrong play. Chris has no story. The action treats his daughter and her touchy relationship with the world of men. Lynn Fontanne played Anna in *Chris.*

brothel in Minnesota.) Her romantic opposite also gave O'Neill trouble. In *Chris,* as Paul Andersen, he's a pallid Prince Charming. Dumbed down to the oddly spelled Mat Burke in *Anna Christie,* he stands far from O'Neill's tortured young men, so often in love with their mothers or obsessed by manias. Mat seems so good for Anna, so much the cure for what vexes her, that audiences kept thinking that *Anna Christie* ended happily ever after when O'Neill purposefully left Anna's future ambiguous. In O'Neill, it's Once vexed, always vexed, and Anna may be beyond cure. Ironically, public satisfaction and the second of O'Neill's three Pulitzer Prizes (*Beyond the Horizon* won the first) told O'Neill that he must have accidentally written a bagatelle. It turned him against the work forever.

Everyone else likes it. It's especially good for actors, even if that wonderful jalopy of a Marthy disappears early on. Broadway has seen Celeste Holm and Kevin McCarthy in a 1952 City Center revival, briefly moved to the Lyceum; the musical version, *New Girl in Town,* for Gwen Verdon and Thelma Ritter's expanded Marthy, in 1957; Liv Ullmann and John Lithgow in 1977; and, for the Roundabout in 1993, Natasha Richardson and Liam Neeson, conveying great erotic juju, to the town's acclaim. Adding Garbo and Pauline Lord, already mentioned as the first Anna Broadway saw,* we might now ask why so many actors have exalted themselves in O'Neill if the charge is true that he's talky in clumsy language. There have been failures—Claudette Colbert baffled by *Dynamo,* James Barton fumbling the first Hickey. Yet the merely capable Fredric March made a stunning James Tyrone, as if the role itself, the *writing* of it, gave him stature; and Jason Robards Jr.'s reputation is based almost wholly on his ease in O'Neill. His *ease!* So O'Neill is a naturalistic writer, after all?

He thought so, though his naturalism was in effect a "higher" realism—"to probe," he said, "in the shadows of the soul of man." O'Neill wasn't trying to write what his characters say: he was writing what they are. Yet he

---

* In the late 1950s, *Theatre Arts,* a magazine addressing middle-class theatregoing culture, ran a series called "My Ten Favorite Plays," in which luminaries from Otto Harbach and Katharine Cornell to John O'Hara and Ruth Gordon took part. Some cited works because of a particular star's performance; others listed works by title alone. (Shirley Booth included *Come Back, Little Sheba.*) Eventually, a pattern of appreciation for certain portrayals emerged. Along with a sentimental nod at Maude Adams' Peter Pan and a surprising number of mentions for John Gielgud's Hamlet, three assumptions reigned: John Barrymore's Hamlet, Laurette Taylor's Amanda Wingfield . . . and Pauline Lord's Anna Christie.

felt betrayed by his players. He actually told Lawrence Langner that he filled *Strange Interlude* (and *Dynamo*) with those asides because actors were too one-dimensional to play a subtext.

But "It is a great mistake to suppose that they don't know good actors here," an important visitor wrote in a letter to a friend back home. The writer was a thespian himself, one of the twentieth century's most influential theorists on acting, and he went on to praise David Warfield's Shylock in David Belasco's *Merchant of Venice* as being beyond the talent at home. John Barrymore's Hamlet was hailed with qualification—"far from ideal but very charming"—and "such a Peer Gynt as [Joseph] Schildkraut we have not got in Russia."

Thus spake Stanislafsky (who by the way went on to compare our opera and symphony orchestras favorably to those in Europe). So we had, indeed, the acting pool to accommodate the twenties revolutions. Stanislafsky's appreciation of Warfield suggests that Belasco's reputation really does need revising, and Barrymore as a "charming" Hamlet puzzles, especially because Barrymore famously overplayed on the night the Moscow Art players came by.

The blurb for Schildkraut's Ibsen is worth investigating, however, for while considering the discoveries of twenties playmaking we should consider its outstanding stars as well. Schildkraut presents an odd case, not least because by genetic rules he should have made his career in Europe, not here. Born in Vienna, the son of the distinguished actor Rudolf Schildkraut, Joseph learned enough English to get through the American Academy of Dramatic Arts, in New York. He was "discovered" by O'Neill's collaborator Kenneth Macgowan, who took him to the Theatre Guild. They were interested in this magnetic young man, especially when Macgowan raved over the actor's work in Vienna: the Gang of Six was contemplating its third season and thus still in its period of European infatuation. It was Schildkraut who suggested *Liliom* (and Eva Le Gallienne, whom he rather fancied) to the Guild, and in his striped tank top over checked pants and baroque socks "Pepi" Schildkraut embodied Molnár's anti-hero, a sensual piece of real estate but a disaster in the moralities of life. The actor seems to have been another of those accidentally transitional figures, schooled in old fashion yet new wave in his lack of mannerism. He was exciting and unpredictable on stage, but casual, natural. "I start with all the tricks, props, and technical things," he once said, "and then discard the props, discard this, discard that, more essence, more essence, more extract, until I have it." As we'll see, this is not unlike the approach of some adherents of The Method.

Because of his German accent, Schildkraut specialized in foreign roles. The Peer Gynt that Stanislafsky admired appeared in the Guild production already mentioned, with Helen Westley and Dudley Digges as the trolls' royal family, Edward G. Robinson as the Button-Moulder, and Lillebil Ibsen, granddaughter of the author, dancing Anitra. Grieg's music was used, and while the Guild broke its rule against cutting, the show still ran three and a half hours. "The American theatre's rejoinder to the Moscow Art Theatre" is how the *Evening Mail*'s James Craig saw it, affirming Stanislafsky himself. Note, too, that Craig thought only the Theatre Guild could have mounted Ibsen's gorgeous monster "on anything like such a scale"—and the run of 120 performances suggests a hit. Remember that the roles listed above (along with the two secondary leads, Ase and Solveig) are little more than glorified bits; *Peer Gynt* is built around its protagonist as few plays are.

So Schildkraut was either one of our important actors or extremely sharp in his timing. Breaking with the Guild for commercial management, Schildkraut tried an American play on a European subject, featuring another super-lover, Benvenuto Cellini. In Edwin Justus Mayer's *The Firebrand* (1924), Schildkraut did all the things that guys do when they go around in tights, such as dueling and passing sarcastic remarks at aristocrats. It's a mannered role in a mannered play, yet Schildkraut seems to have brought it off with his typical "extracted" exuberance, never giving the same performance twice.

Mayer was disappointed that Schildkraut didn't look more like Cellini, who sported one of those Father Time beards. At the dress rehearsal before the usual in-crowd guests, Schildkraut concocted a verisimilitude of a beard in the Cellini style; and now we meet Schildkraut Sr. Young Joseph had no more than entered in his Renaissance muff than his father rose up in the Garrick Theatre orchestra with "Beard! Beard! Where are you running with my boy?"

To the thrill of the house, Rudolf actually gained the stage, tore off the bad hair, and sent his son back to his dressing room to clean off the remnants and recommence. According to Pepi, the show's director was so offended that he departed and Rudolf took over, changing not only the title (from *The Golden Key*) but the very style of the production "into a naughty French bedroom farce." Just like that?

While Joseph Schildkraut had a father, Richard Bennett had daughters. Three got into acting, and Constance and Joan became movie stars. Bennett père made his debut in 1891 in Chicago as Tombstone Jake in something called *The Limited Mail* and came to New York with it that same year. So Bennett was Old Broadway, on the scene early enough to play romantic leads in important titles before 1910; by the 1920s, Bennett was in his fifties and playing Heavy Fathers. Yet he had one romantic lead left in him, if only a *kind* of romantic lead, because the play was one of O'Neill's, *Beyond the Horizon* (1920).

This was the first full-length O'Neill to play Broadway, and it was Bennett who got it on. Producer John D. Williams had optioned the piece and then got nervous, because like so much of O'Neill it is wishful and angry at once, a heady combination for theatregoers of 1920. Bennett urged Williams to spring for a few trial matinées, with Bennett and Edward Arnold as brothers who tragically trade dreams. Bennett's is to travel, but Arnold goes seafaring while Bennett stays home to dwindle into the worst thing an O'Neill character can become: starved out of his fantasy. Bennett and the play were a smash in a regular run; the success of Eugene O'Neill was under way.

Actor and playwright both moved on to the Theatre Guild, which shows us once more how collaborative the forces of New Broadway were. In Leonid Andryeyef's *He Who Gets Slapped* in 1922, Bennett was so perplexed by his title role that the play's translator, Gregory Zilboorg—later famed as Broadway's Psychiatrist To the Stars—explained the character as if to a patient on the couch. Still perplexed, Bennett sought a solution in the terminology of the stage, asking Lawrence Langner, "Is this a Bassanio part or a Mercutio part?" That is: romantic or comic?

It's not that simple any more. Like many of O'Neill's characters, the role of He didn't answer to any of The Street's traditional skills sets. Nor, for that matter, did Tony, Bennett's role in *They Knew What They Wanted*; it's vivaciously stolid, a combination of Bassanio and Mercutio parts. Oddly, Bennett's later credits suggest the interesting actor rather than the great one. Though he rose to the King Learish role of the haunted judge in Maxwell Anderson's *Winterset* (1935), Bennett was fired out of town on his last job, as Gramps in Paul Osborn's *On Borrowed Time* (1938). For that matter, Joseph Schildkraut's power waned with his youth (though we'll see him again, most prominently, much later on).

Who was the outstanding Broadway actor at this time, the one taking over for John Barrymore after he moved to Hollywood? But who could? Barrymore had more than talent: that Name. Glenn Anders couldn't compete in sheer household recognition; but producers did seem to call on Anders first of all when casting charismatic leads. Anders faced down even the redoubtable George Abbott, as opposites in a dynastic feud in the Blue Ridge Mountains in Hatcher Hughes' *Hell-Bent Fer Heaven* (1924). To make it interesting, Hughes arranged for Abbott, of the Hunt family, to love Anders' sister, of the Lowrys. Even more interesting, *Hell-Bent Fer Heaven* disgraced the Pulitzer Prize by winning it, for the prize jury had chosen George Kelly's domestic comedy *The Show-Off* that year. The prize's administrator, Columbia University, overruled the jury in favor of Hughes, a Columbia professor. One of the jury alerted the media, and there was quite a noise on The Street.

Anders projected well in male ego war: later that same year, he fenced with Richard Bennett for Pauline Lord in *They Knew What They Wanted*. You remember—"dark, sloppy, beautiful, and young." That was Anders. But he had the range and traction for O'Neill, as that wary top man in *Strange Interlude* and then the obsessed acolyte of techno-God in *Dynamo*, the latter a truly heroic role, intense and exhausting.

So Anders was far more than a matinée idol—and he could play in boulevard* style, too: chic, soigné, cocasse. Anders did little in Hollywood, but he was on Broadway from the age of nineteen till a City Center return engagement of *The Visit,* when Anders was seventy. Balancing those boulevard roles with more experimental work, Anders entered upon an amazing period of flops, including Philip Barry's evening-length one-act of psychoanalytical exorcism, *Hotel Universe* (1930); one more romantic hero in Laurence Stallings' adaptation of *A Farewell To Arms* (1930); *False Dreams, Farewell* (1934), a spectacular version of the *Titanic* tragedy with even more scenery than the

---

* "Boulevard" as a genre refers historically to the chain of boulevards (St. Martin, Bonne Nouvelle, Poisonnière, and so on) running through Paris' Right Bank from the Place de la République in the east to the church of La Madeleine in the west. Created by Baron Haussmann's mid-nineteenth-century redevelopment, these streets hosted theatres (the Ambigu, the Renaissance, the Gymnase) catering to guiltless bourgeois attractions. In later eras and other places, such fare was Noël Coward or Terence Rattigan in the West End and Kaufman and Hart or, say, *I Remember Mama* on Broadway. The last major American boulevardier writer was Neil Simon.

later musical; and William Saroyan's *Get Away, Old Man* (1943), as that quintessential Saroyan figure the drunken syllogist. Could Anders have been too versatile for his good? Seldom unemployed, he nevertheless failed to carve out that niche that stardom thrives in, and, like "Joseph Schildkraut" and "Richard Bennett," his name means nothing today.

But then, it is the English who run a stable of major male actors, from the ruling triumvirate of Olivier-Gielgud-Richardson to such as Alec Guinness, Michael Redgrave, Anthony Quayle, and many another working today. Broadway was the place of the Big Lady, and this brings me to one of the personal stories with which I punctuate these volumes. After college, new in New York, I made the acquaintance of unsung former Broadwayites— usually chorus men who hit thirty-five and turned to stage managing—glad of the chance to try their anecdotes on a fresh ear. I thus learned a great deal of lore not otherwise taken down, such as exactly how *Lady in the Dark* changed décor from "real life" into dream, or how Laurette Taylor could enjoy thirty years of stardom without showing any sign of the coming brilliance of her Amanda Wingfield.*

Of course, these veterans of Broadway past had seen all the actresses who dominated The Street, and one of my informants gave me an odd précis of the one I was least acquainted with. This was Katharine Cornell: because she left the least behind, mainly ambiguous critics' reports, two TV shows, and the of course touching cameo in the film *Stage Door Canteen* (1943), in which she plays *Romeo and Juliet*'s Balcony Scene with an infatuated young soldier.

---

* *Lady in the Dark*'s designer, Harry Horner, cut two large turntables into the deck, with a smaller turntable inside each one. At the cue for the start of each dream, the heavy real-life set broke apart during a blackout, sliding offstage as the revolves brought separate pieces of the dream locale into view. Furthering the illusion, director Hassard Short, a lighting expert, used spots to guide the public's eye while the pieces were joined into a new set; upstage, a fifth turntable changed the background. As for Laurette Taylor, her extraordinary talent may have been hobbled by her adoring second husband, playwright and director J. Hartley Manners. He produced Taylor as a stage version of Mary Pickford: the eternal maiden with a love-me style that blew more kisses than Yasir Arafat arriving at a Hezbollah luau. Manners died in 1928, freeing Taylor to express herself, most notably as the fluttery older woman of the pathetic kind. A drinking problem made her virtually unemployable, but she pulled herself together for a 1938 revival of *Outward Bound* that gave Taylor perhaps the most ecstatic notices of the century. So Taylor did warn of her brilliance to come; one doesn't, however, create a legend in a revival unless it's Shakespeare, Chekhof, or Ibsen. Wasting her genius on Sutton Vane, Taylor turned to new work seven years later in Tennessee Williams' perfect play with a perfect Taylor part; the rest, finally, *is* legend.

My adviser recalled Cornell as the best actress of her day. He called her "exotic, mercurial in a slow-motion way, and stagy yet not old-fashioned." She had, he concluded, a kind of "new-wave staginess."

This confused me; couldn't one say something of the like of all the divas of Cornell's day? No, and he ticked them off: Ethel Barrymore was the very voice of aristocratic elegy. Helen Hayes was lovable, cute. Jane Cowl was daffy. Lynn Fontanne was a quibbling enigma but a superb technician. Had Kabuki allowed women, she would command the longest-lived myth in Japanese culture.

"Then what was left for Cornell to be?" I asked.

"Implausible," he replied. "The others were marvelous, but you always knew that they came from somewhere or other. Cornell was placeless. They were actresses—she was a fantasy."

Bizarrely beautiful and possessed of the rounded vocal tone of the finishing-school girl taking the lead in the class play, Cornell set herself apart from the stars named just above as the last of the actor-managers, often her own producer, in collaboration with her husband, director Guthrie McClintic. She was unusual, too, in having prima donna glamor without the egomania. She believed a challenge improved her game, and loved working with Laurence Olivier on S. N. Behrman's *No Time For Comedy* (1939) even though Olivier was stealing everything but the furniture while Cornell could never seem to satisfy her ambitions for her own portrayal. It's almost shocking to report that when Olivier bowed out of the post-Broadway tour to rejoin his lover, Vivien Leigh, in Hollywood, Cornell was heartbroken.

Yet Cornell's theatre was Old Broadway. She loved The Entrance—even better, The Exit. When Katharine Cornell came onstage, she brought with her a somber beauty, a dedication to the text, and a rapt intimacy of character to mesmerize the entire house. And when Katharine Cornell left the stage, she took everything with her, including the grand piano.

Cornell was born in 1898, so the 1920s and Cornell's twenties almost exactly coincided. It was a wonderful time in which to earn stardom: a time very under the spell that youth and beauty cast when talent tells the charm. As film was still silent, Cornell would not consider preserving her roles, and by the time sound came in Cornell was resolute. Thus that snippet of *Stage Door Canteen* comprises her entire Hollywood output. It was left to others to film Cornell's stage roles. Katharine Hepburn got *A Bill of Divorcement* (on Broadway in 1921); Dorothy McGuire *The Enchanted Cottage* (1923);

Garbo *The Green Hat,* filmed as *A Woman of Affairs* because the Hays Office feared the novel's notoriety; Jeanne Eagels and, in remake, Bette Davis *The Letter* (1927). All four are of English origin, but Cornell tried as well Edith Wharton, adapted by others, in *The Age of Innocence* (1928), filmed sixty-five years later with Michelle Pfeiffer in Cornell's part. Cornell played Shakespeare and Chekhof (though not Ibsen), but her Great Roles found her in two Shaws, *Saint Joan* and *Candida,* and Rudolph Besier's *The Barretts of Wimpole Street.*

Cornell's Joan became so famous a portrayal—for once the character was as implausible as the actress—that it is a theatrical factoid that Cornell created the role. No: Winifred Lenihan, the one Guild contractee at the time who was even vaguely right for it. Cornell assumed the part in a 1936 revival, putting foremost her salient quality in tragedy, an insanely deep projection of womanhood refusing to let men's treachery distress her. Whether as Joan the Maid, as Oparre (in Maxwell Anderson's version of Medea, *The Wingless Victory* [1936]), or as Anouilh's Antigone, Cornell mixed a solution of equal parts of patience and divine inspiration, with a dash of the imperious. McClintic directed and Jo Mielziner designed *Saint Joan* with wit: the Gentleman of 1920, who interrupts the Epilogue to brief the principals on Joan's twentieth-century canonization, was made up to resemble Shaw himself. Paradoxically, Cornell's comic style had the dashing clarity of a pebble skipping across the surface of a pond. Sheer charm. She revived *Candida* many a time—and note, once again, her love of strong partnerships: one of her Marchbankses was the twenty-two-year-old Marlon Brando.

Was Cornell the outstanding actress of the group? It's interesting to observe that there was yet another great talent who seldom makes the short list—Eva Le Gallienne. I think I know why: Le Gallienne's more or less career-long obsession with the creation of a repertory company of classic titles is a concept that lacks glamor. Defies glamor, even. One reason why is that one somehow never gets a *Candida* with Marlon Brando that way; one gets *Rosmersholm* and *John Gabriel Borkman.* It's not good Broadway, and that unfortunately is the point: it's not supposed to be Broadway at all. Though Le Gallienne appeared opposite Joseph Schildkraut in that Theatre Guild *Liliom,* she nourished ambitions that would take her far from not only The Street but even the Guild, which was already off The Street. Those show shops and their browsing public! the Guild might say. That Theatre Guild and its pathetic starter kit in cultural pretension! was Le

Gallienne's response, we presume. Something like *Liliom* was worthy art, but wasn't most of a Guild season *fill?* Weren't those Lunts boulevardiers at heart? Of cultivated European upbringing, Le Gallienne was a princely character, noble and conservative. One of the few to regard the usual Otto Kahn contribution as a short-term loan, she astonished Maecenas by paying him back—in cash!—and she worked into the 1980s (and lived till 1991) still speaking in the old tongue. Actors were "engaged," not hired. They didn't act: they "played." And the play itself was "the bill."

But could one base a career exclusively on the most stimulating assignments? Even Alla Nazimova, eventually a member of Le Gallienne's company, had once appeared in such show-shop ware as *That Sort* (1914) and *'Ception Shoals,* both with her husband in polyandrous union, Charles Bryant, and the latter play calling for Nazimova to make one entrance dripping wet in a bathing suit.

Husbands and bathing suits! Le Gallienne would have none of this. Her stage must present texts of the highest literary order, combining new work with the classics. Most important, she wanted to draw her public not from the intelligentsia but from . . . well, the neighborhood. Though Le Gallienne was to pursue the dream of her own repertory company in the 1940s and 1960s, her memory as actor-manager rests on her Civic Repertory Theatre, which lasted from 1926 to 1933, and took "Broadway" down to the border between Chelsea and Greenwich Village. Indeed, Le Gallienne had not specifically intended to set up shop away from The Street. However, a disused playhouse at the northwest corner of Fourteenth Street and Sixth Avenue* turned out to contain a scene dock reaching all the way back to Fifteenth Street. This would allow production décor to be stored on site as the bill changed from day to day, an economic boon considering that Le Gallienne intended to hold to a $1.50 top. It was her dream to make theatre as available as sunlight, to popularize while adhering rigidly to the highest standards in that golden trio of Shakespeare, Chekhof, and Ibsen, along

---

* Opened as the Théâtre Français in 1866, the house first offered seasons of French-language work, and was later the home of Haverly's Minstrels. It had long been called the Fourteenth Street Theatre by the time Le Gallienne moved in, and had seen a little of everything over the years in which "Broadway" steadily traveled north of Twenty-third Street, Thirty-fourth, Forty-second. (To accommodate walk-in business from uptown, the Civic maintained a supplementary box office in Town Hall, on Forty-third and Sixth.) Le Gallienne's house was demolished in 1938.

with Molière, Goldoni, Rostand, *Camille* (as we popularly term *La Dame aux Caméllias*), *Peter Pan,* and Le Gallienne's own adaptation of *Alice in Wonderland*. Le Gallienne looked forward to a day when her concept would be acculturated nationally, and in a speech first delivered in 1928 and kept in use for long afterward, she spoke of the special gift that theatregoing can present to the young especially as "the beauty that springs from knowledge."

It is difficult to speak of Le Gallienne's acting style, because, while praising her, critics offer little information of the precise kind, even when she gave her reading of standard roles, ones they had knowledge of. Le Gallienne was certainly the most remarkable woman of her phylum, not least in living openly as a lesbian at a time when Cornell, for instance, entered into a mariage blanc with a gay man.

As producer, director, and star, Le Gallienne made a great success of her Civic Rep, foiled at the last only by Depression economics. However, she did have a problem attracting top talent. True, Nazimova signed on, but she did little more than "her" Madame Ranyefsky (to Le Gallienne's Varya). No one else of Le Gallienne's standing shared the Civic stage, and she too often had to go on with makeweights. Dumpy little J. Edward Bromberg may have been fine as *Peter Pan's* Nana, but he was an odd choice as Mercutio. Even the Romeo, Donald Cameron, only looked the role; Brooks Atkinson called him "a dull swain" in "monotonous recitation." And Jacob Ben-Ami, the Escalus, made slush of the poetry with his European accent. When Katharine Cornell staged her *Romeo,* in 1934, Brian Aherne made a glittery Mercutio and Basil Rathbone a correct Romeo—and the Escalus, Reynolds Evans, spoke English.

Naturally, Le Gallienne was no more attracted to the movies than Cornell was. Nevertheless, Le Gallienne ended up in three, in onstage scenes in the Edwin Booth bio, *Prince of Players* (1955), as Kirk Douglas' mother in *The Devil's Disciple* (1959), and, getting a supporting Oscar nomination, in *Resurrection* (1980). At least Le Gallienne's gala Fanny Cavendish in the 1975 revival of *The Royal Family* was preserved in a TV taping. Simply by default, it is now Le Gallienne's Great Role, we can only imagine Le Gallienne as a matchlessly destructive Hedda Gabler, with the delicately feral beauty that the actress had in youth, a blond doll who could change personality as others changed gloves. But anyone today can revisit Fanny, beautifully turned out of Louisa Drew by Mrs. Fiske, archon and devotee at once. Le Gallienne knew the traditions of the stage even if she couldn't use them in her style, which like that of her Liliom, Joseph Schildkraut, restlessly anticipated the naturalism that Lee Strasberg and Elia Kazan were to unleash. And yet Le Gallienne knew also that one mustn't frustrate all of the public's expectations, that now and again one is less the Servant of the Art and more the Star. Helen Sheehey's biography of Le Gallienne includes lighting designer Tharon Musser's recollection of working for the actress' last try at a permanent company, the National Repertory Theatre. Musser apparently seemed to be arranging far too much apparatus for Le Gallienne's entrance into *The Seagull*: all those gels and tech for a performer who carried her apparatus with her as surely as Cornell ever did. They called it "glamor" then. "I'll light a cigarette," Le Gallienne told Musser. "They'll know who it is."

They knew who Lynn Fontanne was, too; but I'm saving her for the next chapter because her partnership with Alfred Lunt puts her into a unique category among Broadway's divas. Note that the Lunts, too, interconnect with our three twenties innovations, for Lynn played in expressionism (in *Strange Interlude*), both played O'Neill, and the pair were Theatre Guild mainstays right to the end of the 1949–50 season. For some, the Guild *was* the Lunts: or even all Broadway was. In what the couple represented to the nation, the Lunts occupy the center of this book, and we can date precisely when "the Lunts" incorporated as a concept. It wasn't when they met, backstage at the New Amsterdam Theatre, when Lunt came in through the street door, lost his footing on the stairs, and crashed to the floor at Fontanne's feet. Nor was it when they married, in 1922, at New York's City Hall, after she had closed *Dulcy* and he was supporting star Billie Burke in Booth Tarkington's *The Intimate Strangers*.

It began, rather, when Joseph Schildkraut broke his contract with the Guild because instead of letting him play Shakespeare's Richard II, as promised, they wanted him to do more Molnár. It was *The Guardsman*, which Schildkraut regarded as "witty" but "phony." Who would believe that a husband, even a husband who was an actor—even a madly jealous one— would play a role in real life in order to test his wife's fidelity? He can disguise himself so well that we think she might be fooled? By her *own husband*? And then she says she knew it was he all along? So *she's* playacting, too? We are to accept that a married acting team never get out of the theatre—that all their world really is a stage?

Said Schildkraut, "I have never been able to stomach [*The Guardsman's*] preposterous premise." That's gentler than some comments about the new material that was passing for entertainment in this decade of national change. Many were feeling what O'Neill wrote for the Senior Tyrone's dismissal of his younger son's library of Baudelaire, Schopenhauer, Ibsen, Wilde: "atheists, fools, and madmen!" Even "whoremongers!" Old Broadway gazes upon New Broadway, and completely misses the point.

Five

Sophisticated

he Guardsman might have been written for
the Lunts, for their world really was a stage.
S. N. Behrman said, "You couldn't *be* with
the Lunts without rehearsing." They were the ultimate theatricals: they never lit. It wasn't so much
that they were always rehearsing as that they were
always performing—enjoying their trademark over-
lapping dialogue not only in the theatre but everywhere else in their peculiar version of real life;
balancing his sulky boy with her teasing mother
all the more easily because she was (secretly) five
years his senior; and playing the most provocative

love scenes onstage while fooling everyone about the asexual nature of their marriage. Or *were* they fooling?

At once the best known and most mysterious of the show-biz acts of the age, the Lunts distinguished themselves above all in the stupendously nuanced blend of loving and fighting, luring and rejecting, that they brought to each new work. The first thing you noticed about them was that, in each new show, she made the entrance of the most glamorous woman on Broadway while he would so alter his appearance that you'd wonder who it was. But the second thing was the way they skewed their portrayals to change all the emphases, to fight and love in some novel way. Other great duos teamed for life; the Lunts teamed only for a particular work, then broke up the act and reteamed anew, rediscovering each other in new characters. Through it all, they were always in love and always suspicious, and they presented it as the height of logic to part after making sure that neither would survive without the other.

They brought such sensation to what they did that their solo work before their definitive teaming seems a sheer waste of Lunts. And yet the piece that solemnized their decision to play as a unit is Sil-Vara's *Caprice* (1928). This was another of the ephemeral titles turned out by the Budapest-Prague-Vienna boulevard wheel, and so was the *first* outstanding event of Luntplay, *The Guardsman,* for it gave Broadway a preview of what Alfred and Lynn were going to excell at: boulevardier masque.* Typical Alfred: his disguise with which to test his wife's fidelity is not that of the erotic icon but a monster, a Slavic *thing* suggesting a blend of Rasputin and the Emperor Jones. Is it because he actually wants her to be able to pass the test or because he thinks women are crazy? Or is *he* the crazy one? Typical Lunts—they raise more questions than they answer. And now comes The Confrontation: as she reclines on a couch with a book while he throws open a costume trunk just behind her head and, inches away from her unseeing eyes, feverishly yet fastidiously makes up in a hand mirror as the Guardsman. Then he stands before her, himself the evidence of her treachery.

---

* *The Guardsman* was not the Lunts' first teaming, nor even their first on Broadway. When she was still under contract to George Tyler, they made a few joint appearances with the Tyler stock company in Washington, D.C., and bowed on Broadway in one of J. Hartley Manners' Laurette Taylor showcases, *Sweet Nell of Old Drury,* in 1922. A revival of Paul Kester's play of 1900, it placed Lunt opposite Taylor rather than Fontanne, and in any case was too treacly to introduce the tart flirtation that the Lunts were to maintain.

Billed in the program as The Actor and The Actress, the two might be in their own place on their own time, not on the stage of the Garrick Theatre, speaking lines written by Ferenc Molnár:

> THE ACTRESS: You came in at that door yesterday at exactly sixteen minutes past six. At seventeen minutes past six, I had recognized you. At eighteen minutes past six, I was wondering whether I should laugh in your face—and at nineteen minutes past six I had decided to play the comedy to the end.

Playing comedy to the end was another of the Lunts' trademark approaches. Not merely to the end, but past it to every permutational riddle. *Had* The Actress recognized him? The Lunts also gave of their utmost in the physical sense: they did their own stunts. Not only would they never fake a fight, but they looked upon every instance of knockabout abuse as a chance to shatter theatrical precedent. Not till management had to distribute plastic protection to the folks in the front row at *The Miracle Worker* (1959)* did Broadway see the like of the brouhaha that Alfred and Lynn arranged for C. K. Munro's *At Mrs. Beam's* (1926). An English comedy about boarding-house tenants suspicious of That New Couple, the piece was a showcase for Jean Cadell, who had introduced her role of a twee busybody in London. The Lunts, however, totally took over her show with a fight scene that started with the hurling of objects and escalated into a smashing battle across the furniture and onto the floor.

Even the relatively sedate *Reunion in Vienna* (1931), a comedy in the Molnár fashion by Robert E. Sherwood, offered up the defining Lunt Moment of sex and violence in a scene carefully delayed till the second act. Former lovers, the pair were to have parted forever, she now married to a Viennese psychiatrist and he, a Hapsburg prince, driving a cab in Nice. A political exile, he has to sneak back into Austria disguised as a Tyrolean peasant. This provisions another quasi-incognito Alfred entrance, into the

---

* Schmengie Footnote Number One: For those who genuinely don't catch this reference—all tourists will immediately return to the text, please—*The Miracle Worker* featured a scene early on in which Anne Bancroft and little Patty Duke had a food fight. Not a fraternity-house caper: a violent clash of egos around the dinner table, as Duke fought to resist Bancroft's regime and Bancroft fought to instate it. Wary theatregoers sat in the rear of the orchestra, or New Jersey.

utterly Molnáresque setting of the sitting room of the Imperial Suite of the Hotel Lucher. "Good evening, venerable strumpet" is Alfred's greeting of the hotelière, Frau Lucher (the indefatigable Helen Westley). "Still wearing the red flannel drawers?"

Watch how Sherwood, though a socially committed dramatist (and later one of Franklin Delano Roosevelt's speechwriters), slips with sheerest self-effacement into the rococo eros of Alfred and Lynn enjoying another Caprice. First, he demands like some pasha that *she* be brought to him, all but threatening the impedient Frau Lucher. The latter makes herself scarce, Alfred resentfully throws himself into a chair facing away from the door, and we wait—because of course this is the Moment. After four, maybe five, beats, Lynn enters. No: Lynn comes into the room in a backless silver-white gown with a high-waisted, pleated front and an absolutely unreadable expression on her face. Alfred stares at her in the mirror. The call is coming from inside the house; now let Sherwood take over:

> (Rudolf starts toward her, pauses, then walks around her. Elena does not move, but her eyes follow him. . . . He is behind her. He reaches out to touch her, but doesn't touch her. He walks around, in front of her, stares at her, then slaps her face. He seizes her in his arms and kisses her, fiercely.)

Follows then a very long duet, not unlike that of Tristan and Isolde in *their* second act. Toward the end, she is slapping and kissing him till:

> RUDOLF: My God, Elena, there is such a thing as going too far.
> ELENA: No, there isn't.

That's part of their style: they went too far as a rule. The *World-Telegram*'s review of *Reunion in Vienna* called the Lunts "actors who love their job"—and that's the other part. They were not only the deftest technicians around, but people so born to play make-believe that real life was a dress rehearsal for the stage. This is why S. N. Behrman found them relentlessly discussing the play they were in the middle of. Other actors discussed the news or fashion or other people's plays. The Lunts had a single subject. Not themselves: their work. They never stopped going over that scene, that line, that half-turned gesture, so subtle it wouldn't play past the fifth row. And this conversation could occur as late as the last day of the run.

It would have taken a Kenneth Tynan to describe exactly what the Lunts actually did in *Reunion in Vienna,* or another Sherwood, *Idiot's Delight* (1936), or Chekhof's *The Sea Gull* (1938), for critics of the 1930s weren't apt at such analysis. They could type the traditional approaches, but the Lunts were Different in an innovative way that defied elucidation. Still, critics and public greatly enjoyed Different when the Lunts did it. And it wasn't called Different then. It was called Sophistication.

Like the Lunts themselves, the word was loaded with meanings. It denoted "smart and worldly," of course, and also "complex" in the sense of being made of many parts, "impure." It also meant "liberated from bourgeois morality," in the sense of "tolerant." And it also meant "gay," as when, say, Milly asks Cynara about the dating possibilities in an attractive man, and Cynara replies, "Well, he's . . . sophisticated, you know." The word implied that there were things in human nature that many people knew nothing of; but the Sophisticated knew. When a song in Rodgers and Hart's *On Your Toes* (1936) called "Too Good For the Average Man" spoofed the craze for going into Freudian analysis with a line about a male patient "waking up to find that he's a girl," only a portion of the audience laughed. They were Sophisticated: they understood the world.*

Those who weren't Sophisticated longed to be. This was an age that wanted its leadership class not only educated and intelligent but Aware. Sophistication was the condition to attain in the 1930s as surely as cool is the modern counterpart, with a defining antithesis in that the Sophisticated were curious about the world and the cool are solipsistically closed off. The Sophisticated made judgments about the relative value of things—crossword puzzles and *The New Yorker,* Father Coughlin and Walter Lippman, Debussy

---

* Those tolerant of gays had their euphemism, too: "broad-minded." Like "sophisticated," the term meant many things, among them the equivalent of our modern "gay-friendly." The truly evolved personality, most up-to-date and civilized, not only knew who was gay but tolerated and at times welcomed it. In Dorothy Parker's "From the Diary of a New York Lady," the diarist introduces a character named Ollie Martin, the kind of man who, when he escorts a woman home at night, falls asleep in the cab. She does, too: because she's safe. "What do I care if he *is* one?" she asks. The Love That Dare Not Speak Its Name didn't have to in the company of the enlightened.

and swing. The cool make no judgments. Everything is equal because nothing is considered. The difference between Sophistication and cool is the difference between an age of theatregoing and an age of—no, not moviegoing, for, as we'll see, Hollywood and Broadway were intricately intertwined in the 1930s, to their mutual benefit. It's hard to know what the age of cool is, for while it has its roots in the beats of the 1950s and in such avatars as Marlon Brando, James Dean, and Paul Newman—as we'll see—its present-day exponents are rather miscellaneously derived, from David Letterman to Sean Combs.

The cult of Sophistication reached its apex in the success of Cole Porter and Noël Coward, because both were not only smart, complicated, liberated, and gay, but more or less openly so. Porter entered into one of those Lunt-like no-fly-zone marriages, but it wasn't intended to fool anyone. In Porter's world, one did What Was Done in public and what one pleased in private; Porter married for form and money.

Coward was bolder—or was it just that beards are so much trouble to maintain? Lying drains one's creative energy, and while Porter was prolific once he got going, Coward gushed: with comedies and dramas, yes, but also musicals as well as fiction and movie work. And he acted. Like the Lunts, he acted wherever he went; but that was a style of the time. What was that relentlessly legendary Algonquin Round Table if not a scene of posing and line-reading? The midcult audience was ever reminded—by the Round Tablers especially—that their luncheons were the height of wit. And true enough, many of the regulars, such as George S. Kaufman or Dorothy Parker, were exponents of wisecrack humor at its sharpest; it's impossible to imagine an Algonquin Round Table populated by people like Frank Bacon, Raymond Hitchcock, or Charles Lindbergh. But then, this is another way of saying that New Broadway, Sophistication, and the melting-pot culture of post-1919 urbanized America coincided just when certain of our more apparent people introduced the concept of Playing Oneself: of making one's life part of one's art.

The Sophisticated styled themselves in the standard cautions of the day, but they could be strikingly honest. That, too, was part of the style. Of all the writers, Cole Porter was the nearest to a performer; he did make a few commercial recordings, and of course he was a renowned party entertainer. It was really his creation of the list song that rivaled the Lunts' love scenes for personal revelation. Porter's parade of the great and near great combined historical figures and people of myth with celebs of the time, all in such gossipy glee that he might be singing out the names of his sex partners. "Let's do it," Porter urged.

He even slipped past the euphemisms commonly used for "gay." As far back as *Hitchy-Koo 1919,* Porter used "queens" in a context between ambiguous and explicit. And for Ethel Merman in *Anything Goes* (1934) he wrote "Kate the Great," playing on the sexual omnibus that Catherine of Russia legendarily rode. In Porter's version, this queen made not only the butler and the groom: "she made the maid who made the room." Ironically, Merman, who swore like a groom, suddenly got dainty and the number was cut.

So the Sophisticated were a race apart—even from their confederates. True, Merman's beginnings as a stenographer from Queens are so devoid of glamor myth that they constitute the most famous one-line bio in showbiz annals, as far from Porter's wealth and Yale as one gets. But the Sophisticated really did stand apart: as teachers, snitches, exotic birds. Not one's own kind. Part of the fun of *The Man Who Came To Dinner*—by two of the leading Sophisticates, Moss Hart and George S. Kaufman*—is the fantasy of what happens when one of the Sophisticates invades your life, your home, even your Family Secret. After all, Sophistication held power in American culture by that very apartness, by keeping its distance. It made worldly knowledge available to what we might loosely call the straight world on the understanding that straights might become smarter but never, themselves, Sophisticates. As with the sorcerer's apprentice of Goethe's poem, the magic is dangerous in the amateur's hands.

Instead, the amateur is permitted to attend classes in Sophistication, such as Noël Coward's ménage-à-trois comedy *Design For Living* (1933); the title alone is such a Sophisticated concept that Margot Peters used it for her Lunts biography. Coward could have called his show *Design For Playwriting,* for it was eleven years in the making because of The Plan. Coward himself unveils it, looking back to the days when he and the Lunts, already set to be lifelong confidants, were utterly unconnected as public

---

* Though commonly referred to as "Kaufman and Hart," the two in fact varied their byline according to which of the two made the more substantial contribution—usually in conceiving the premise. *Once in a Lifetime* (1930), which Hart first wrote by himself before the pair launched their collaboration with a *Lifetime* rewrite, was obviously a Hart and Kaufman work. Interestingly, Hart also took first credit on their most enduring titles, this same *Man Who Came To Dinner* and *You Can't Take It With You.*

figures: "Lynn and Alfred were to [become] idols of the public. . . . They were to act exclusively [as a duo, and] when all three of us had become stars . . . we would meet and act triumphantly together."

The Plan was made in the very early 1920s, which attests to Coward's prescience, for each of the three had by then made a start, no more. As we know, the Lunts did unite their headlines; and Coward punched out with *The Vortex, Hay Fever,* and *Easy Virtue,* West End sensations brought to New York within a few months of each other in 1925. After a few years of ever greater renown for all three, Coward got a cable from the Lunts: "Contract with the Guild up in June—we shall be free—what about it?"

"A satyr comedy" is how Brooks Atkinson described *Design For Living,* using the historical term for the fourth and final play in the ancient Greek tetralogy, the bawdy afterpiece that tops off the three tragedies and sweeps the public out in jubilation. John Mason Brown of the *Evening Post* posted an "adults only" blurb: "Cannot be warmly recommended to deaconesses." This is because the climax of The Plan discovered Otto (Alfred), Leo (Noël), and Gilda (Lynn) in a new kind of love triangle. It is not the "eternal" one in which one of the men must step aside. Rather, it is a circular triangle, in which each of the three loves the other two. An eleven-character action allows for one other lead, Ernest, the dreary husband that Gilda at one point collects—a Walter Hampden, one might say—and John Mason Brown, flashing on Lynn's Nina Leeds in *Strange Interlude,* observed that once again she has three men. But Ernest (Campbell Gullan) doesn't count in a play that is essentially about a gay threesome.

Oh yes, it is; what else is Gilda saying to Ernest early in Act One?:

> GILDA: The only reasons for me to marry would be these: To have children; to have a home; to have a background for social activities, and to be provided for. Well, I don't like children; I don't wish for a home; I can't bear social activities, and I have a small but adequate income of my own.

Isn't that Gay Theory 101? And isn't this next quotation the reasoning behind the theory, as Gilda announces her intention to be "my unadulterated self"?:

> GILDA: Myself, without hangings, without trimmings, unencumbered by the winding tendrils of other people's demands.

And try this snippet after Gilda has wheeled about and married Ernest:

OTTO: Ernest hasn't got a penis.
GILDA: Yes, he has: but only a little one, gentle and prim.

I'm a sneak, boys and girls. Here's what Coward really wrote—but doesn't it mean the above on the metaphorical level? That is, could Coward be remarking on the sheer sexuality of Sophistication?:

OTTO: Ernest hasn't got a personality.
GILDA: Yes, he has: but only a little one, gentle and prim.

"The fluff of worldly success and the vaudeville of telephone conversations," said Atkinson, "suit Mr. Coward's skimming pen exactly." However, Sophistication often looked frivolous to those not living within its state of absolute independence. Atkinson had a boss, a marriage, and a rota of social and family obligations. Coward was picturing three people who don't and much of Sophistication in fact consisted of these hints about how life might otherwise be lived, with the heavy dick of genuine liberty. Not just sexual liberty: *liberty,* period.

That wasn't abundantly clear at the time, because so much of Sophistication relied on top choice in fashion, on the flaunting of wit, on the delicate shudder when anything democratically popular was mentioned. All the same, at its core Sophistication told of the isolation of the independent, and we note that thirties social drama, the very opposite of Coward in every respect—a *Waiting For Lefty* or *Dead End*—was invariably about folk whose helpless position in society compromised their independence absolutely. To the casual observer, *Design for Living* appears to be fluff because it behaves . . . well, yes: fluffily. But fluff is its style, not its content.

Interestingly, the show's tryout took it from Cleveland through Pittsburgh to Washington, D.C., before New York—not exactly American cultural capitals. But they were avid for the Lunts. Sophistication was something many people did not entirely approve of yet were eager to know about simply because of the charm of its exponents.* Naturally, the New

---

* Further charm went into the mix when *Design for Living* was filmed, during the very year of the New York run, with Gary Cooper, Miriam Hopkins, and even Fredric March, not all that charming but at least sturdy, or something. True, Ben Hecht gave director

York premiere was, as Gilbert W. Gabriel wrote, "one of the storied first nights . . . which keen the pencils of the society editors, give the autograph hunters St. Vitus dance and lay a stair carpet of ermine from Longacre Square to Seventh Heaven." Gabriel didn't mention the guests at the feast—Laurette Taylor, Irving Berlin, Amelia Earhart, Philip Barry, Lillian Gish, Jerome Kern, George S. Kaufman, most of Broadway's major producers from Guthrie McClintic to Mr. J. J. Shubert, and a special detachment of cops to handle the overflow outside.

Obviously, the Lunts *and* Noël Coward in a romp that had the town mongering report from the first day of rehearsals would tantalize to the utmost. We have to admire Coward for fearlessness in co-starmanship, sharing the stage with the monarchs of Sophistication. There was none of that Jane Cowl "Has Rollo Peters been engaged for the season yet?" stuff about Coward, even though he must have been aware that no one thought of him as a deep or brilliant actor. He was, though, a brilliant Sophisticate. Perhaps that gave him the confidence to take on Lunt,* an amazing talent whose true range was never to be revealed because his career was married to his wife's. Sometimes Lunt spoke of trying Macbeth; but then he would have had to have married Judith Anderson.

Note, by the way, that while Lunt was the most versatile performer of his day, Coward was the least. He could venture no further beyond his lightly truffled self-portrait than S. N. Behrman or the lightest Shaw. (Coward did their *Second Man* and *The Apple Cart,* respectively, in London.) Indeed, this limited—or, let us say, consistent with public expectation—Coward is how theatregoers seemed to like him. He was so What He Was that jesters found

---

Ernst Lubitsch a new script substituting wisecrack humor for Coward's more insinuatingly subversive coquetry. Note, too, that *Design for Living* was conceived for Americans' notion of the enlightenment hiding within taboo. Coward never expected to repeat his stunt with his two co-stars in England: for there taboo was still unapproachable. The Lord Chamberlain thought it over for six years before allowing a production. German emigré Anton Walbrook and Rex Harrison boyed around with Diana Wynyard, and The Master did not even trouble to stage the piece himself, as he was in New York at exactly the same time, putting on his revue *Set To Music.*

* Some readers may recall Coward's casting Laurence Olivier in the London *Private Lives* (1930), which Coward wrote for himself and another Sophisticate, Gertrude Lawrence. But Olivier's was a little nothing of a role, and the actor himself was at that point in his career merely surviving in a stream of failures. No one in the West End could have anticipated what he would become.

him an irresistible subject. Moss Hart and Cole Porter *Jubilee*'d Coward as a character called Eric Dare; they were respectful. And Hart again—now with George S. Kaufman—spoofed Coward in *The Man Who Came To Dinner,* as Beverly Carlton. Once more, the riff was fond. But some of the other Coward takeoffs were frumps with the names of pixies, as in the Beverly Waverly of the Rodgers and Hart college show *Too Many Girls* (1939). Yet didn't Coward start it off with his *own* characters and their pixie names— Sholto Brent, Nicky Lancaster, Elyot Chase, Charles Condomine, Garry Essendine, Hugo Latymer: all written by Coward for Coward to play? And in *Design For Living,* Coward's surname is Mercuré. Yes, with that gallant little quartering of the *accent aigu.*

And that's a paradox of Sophistication. If it was essentially precious and limited, it was necessary to the culture of theatregoing. Western Civilization would be unthinkable without Noël Coward. Worse: uneducated. Gay sensibility is honed to a sharp sense of observation at an early age, because gay adolescents have to watch The Others very carefully, to be able to imitate them and pass. It's a form of creativity, and tells us why so many gays are artists. But it's also why gay writers tend to favor list songs or, later on, concept musicals: because as outsiders they can place the content of culture in perspective for The Others to study. That really is what Sophistication was in the 1930s: something as basic as the title song of *Anything Goes* (1934), in which gay King Cole lists the items that make up Modern Times so the average person can catch up.

So the often explicit *Design For Living,* with Coward and his fellow travelers the Lunts, is the key show in this arena. At the time, it was simply the key hit of a disappointing season; the critics spoke of "impeccable," "delicious," "audacious," as if seeing no more than the technical precision of fluff. So expert were these players that one night Alfred and Noël found themselves speaking each other's lines during the duet drunk scene that closes Act Two. Coward's stage directions call for the pair to get close on a couch and all but launch a mutual seduction. Were even they aware of how much Sophistication lay behind the comedy, or were they simply enjoying that technical precision? Because, midway through the scene, Otto must hiccup, and Alfred feared that this was too much tech for Noël to finesse his way through. Adroitly sliding from Leo back into his accustomed Otto, Alfred reclaimed the hiccup. Is that all the scene is about?

Among native-born American playwrights, the two prime Sophisticates were Philip Barry and S. N. Behrman. They were born three years apart in the 1890s, but Barry, the younger of the two, died in 1949 while Behrman plays were still being premiered in the 1960s, and he lived till 1973. By now, like that other brand-name playwright of the 1930s Maxwell Anderson, Barry and Behrman have lost much of their respect, though the former at least left a classic behind in *The Philadelphia Story* (1939), and the Barry name itself still denotes something among the literate. Behrman never won a space in the immortals' parking lot, mainly because he was one of those plotless story-tellers who left much of the heavy lifting to charmers such as Ina Claire, Jane Cowl, Katharine Cornell, and Edna Best. The Lunts played for him regularly. Behrman was conversation pieces, but he did have the wit that was Sophistication's central quality. That and Behrman's charm divas won him a following.

Barry, on the other hand, ever tested his following by surprising them. Barry's hits were high comedy: in between, he wrote really quite strange pieces, usually with a religious or symbolic patterning and often suffering failure. *John* (1927), amazingly enough, tells of the Baptist (Jacob Ben-Ami) in the year A.D. 30, resisting the temptings of Herodias (Constance Collier) and, at last, facing death under the inspiration of the Gospel. It was perhaps just a few years too late for this kind of thing, so successful in the spectacle format, though Barry's set designer was that wizard of spectacle Norman Bel Geddes.

Barry's *Tomorrow and Tomorrow* (1931) is more implictly derived. The title of course evokes *Macbeth,* but Barry drew his treatment from the fourth chapter of the Second Book of the Kings, on the tale of Elisha and the barren Shunammite Woman. Discussing the difference between facts (sheer physical data) and the truth (as a humanistic emotional understanding that defies facts), Barry found modern-day equivalents for Elisha's ability to give life, even to a corpse, though the reviving of the young boy omitted the Bible's picturesque resuscitation: "and the child sneezed seven times, and the child opened his eyes." *Tomorrow and Tomorrow,* exceptionally, was a hit, at 206 performances.

More religion: *The Joyous Season* (1934) deals with a nun's visit to her Boston relatives. Barry wrote it with Maude Adams in mind, in hopes of scoring the coup of the season by luring Peter Pan out of retirement. It was actually a genre of the day—the Booth Tarkington play that Alfred Lunt was in when he married Lynn Fontanne was another would-be Adams vehicle—but in the end Lillian Gish played Sister Christina.* Barry's most spiritual piece of all might be *Here Come the Clowns* (1938), set in Ma Speedy's Café des Artistes, an adjunct to James Concannon's Globe Theatre. One may already pick up a taste of Barry's symbols, and he assured us that he meant them as such. Mystified by doings even more bizarre than those in Barry's *Hotel Universe*—more of those symbols!—the critics actually revisited *Here Come the Clowns* during its eleven-week run. Lo, the mystery remained veiled: so Barry *himself* reviewed the piece, in the *World-Telegram*. His blurb was ready: "an extremely simple play, as easy to understand and as clear in its meaning as any fable might be."

So Barry felt most cogent when others found him obscure. Ironically, his most original work lay in those high-comedy hits that no one had any trouble understanding—original because there Barry invented a figure unique in American narrative art. We might call him the Bohemian Aristocrat, a male or female of the leadership class unwilling to live within the class rules. The most memorable example must be Johnny Case of *Holiday* (1928), who confounds his fiancée and prospective father-in-law by proposing to live in wastrel ease on the fortune that he has amassed through lawyering, though he is only thirty years old. To the girl and her father, unorthodox behavior is objectionable *because it is unorthodox*. Persistent rumors about Barry's sexuality—though he married and raised a family—suggest that he had something in common with Noël Coward: a love of those born Different. *Holiday's* dramatic interest lies in its typical Barry premise: the guy we like is going to wed a woman we don't. She doesn't appreciate the "holiday" in him, his free spirit. Moreover, New York's favorite real-life debutante actress, Hope Williams, was on the scene—and *she* loved Johnny *because* of what he is.

Less well known than *Holiday* but even more essential Barry on the same theme is *The Animal Kingdom* (1932). Lucky for us, the original production lives on after its 183-performance run in a very faithful screen version, a record of how high comedy played in the early 1930s. The protagonist, Leslie Howard, repeats his stage role of Tom Collier, caught between two women

---

* Adams made a few appearances here and there in the early 1930s, but *A Kiss For Cinderella* (1916), when she was forty-four, marked her last New York engagement. The author was James M. Barrie, the management was Charles Frohman's (though he himself had died the year before), and the house was Frohman's Empire: an authentic Maude Adams package. She went into teaching and then departed in 1953, having disappointed a generation of playwrights who couldn't get her unique delicacy and tendency to sell out even during Holy Week out of their heads.

in the usual Barry choice of the social Cecilia Henry (Lora Baxter on stage) and the Bohemian Aristocrat Daisy Sage (Frances Fuller). Note the names— the neutral yet somehow basic and noble Tom Collier. Cecilia Henry is . . . what? Proud and beautiful, surely. Tom calls her "C.": "a marvelous object," "cunningly contrived," "artful child." It's Myrna Loy in the film; she has the looks and she knows the kind, manipulative and without intellect. And who but the radiant Ann Harding as Daisy Sage, too beautiful for what Barry has in mind—a pal, really—but projecting that nobility of soul that in Barry is as necessary as independence in the hero's makeup? The "Sage" is a tell: she has the wisdom to take on life.

In *Design For Living*, the three leads are innovatively balanced, but in Barry's world, only two may play. On the other hand, *The Animal Kingdom* isn't the usual drawing-room thriller in which we watch to see which woman prevails. Something more important is happening: Barry says sex doesn't matter. He makes it explicit that, after a mad affair, Tom and Daisy ceased to relate erotically while Tom's attraction to Cecilia is droolingly phys-ical. Indeed, Barry sees sex as the ruination of marriage. The Barry paragon must *admire* his wife; when in rut, he takes a mistress.

Stop the music! Our classic conservative boulevardier sees adultery as an essential ingredient in a good marriage? *Yes!* And note that Barry is at his most Sophisticated here in siding with the nonconformist (Daisy) against the conventional beauty (Cecilia). Complicating the scene is of course the usual Barry Father—Tom's—who sides with Cecilia, because they share an obsession about knowing the Right People and doing the Right Things and an utter lack of tolerance for all other people and things.

We want to strangle them—but weren't many in the audience of 1932 sympathetic to their attitude? Wasn't Sophistication partly an unpleasant education for the upper middle class, an imparting of revisionist values by one of their own, the "conservative" Barry? Even today, the words "Philip Barry" are a summoning term for that all but vanished American character the well-off WASP. And, yes, Barry wrote of him: but for wistfully revolu-tionary purposes. Listen as Father Collier reduces his humorous, quizzical, tolerant, and sex-driven son to the two most clueless sentences of the de-cade. It is the character who is clueless, not Barry:

THE SENIOR COLLIER: I send him to Oxford, and he commutes from Paris. I put him in the bank and he . . . (sigh).

Man, you have *Leslie Howard* for a son; don't you get it? True, men like the Barry Father always respond to power, and Barry sees nature's best men as somewhat helpless: it's the women who reign. One wonders what kind of sex a Barry hero and heroine would have, because Barry clearly has given it some thought. He's not as shy as folks like to believe he is—don't forget that ambiguous midnight swim that Katharine Hepburn and a reporter (Van Heflin on stage; James Stewart in the film) take in *The Philadelphia Story*. And listen to Daisy Sage when she thinks she has lost Tom forever, in a description that has all the comprehension and savor that Father Collier's lacks:

> DAISY: He's so young! All slim and brown and sandy! He'll always be
> like that, even when he's old.

It has the effect of celebrating Howard as boyish delight in tweeds, and reminds us that in Barry—as in almost all of Sophistication—the subject is sex even when it isn't.

The other two *Animal Kingdom* stage players who made the RKO film with Howard were subsidiary yet interesting. William Gargan plays Red the butler, a former boxer who acts more like a best buddy than a servant. This helps to define Howard's ease around eccentricity: his nonconformism. It defines Cecilia, too: when she makes Tom fire Red. But Barry twists the plot—it turns out that Red wants to quit, because Tom's affiliation with intolerance grieves him. The scene in which Red and Tom unhappily dance around the truth while getting drunk is Barry at his best: sharply dressed and good theatrical stuff, but above all honest and touching.

Ilka Chase, the third of *The Animal Kingdom*'s three stage players thought indispensable for the film, presents that ubiquitous thirties character The Unmarried Sarcastic Woman. Here, too, Barry tweaks convention, creating a type half in Cecilia's world and half in Tom's. Usually, this character took sides absolutely, as in the Helen Broderick sidekick role; Ilka Chase, as Grace Macomber, is unquestionably Cecilia's ally but cultivates a penchant for knowing the famous. That attracts her to Tom, a book publisher whose list includes prominent bylines. However, the famous were by this time tending toward independence of cultural conformity. Famous people used to be Mark Twain and William James; now they were the Marx Brothers. One feels that Barry likes Grace and wishes that she had a bit more adventure in her.

Tom will leave Cecilia for Daisy. He must: if he didn't, *The Animal Kingdom* would be Barry's comic tragedy. The playwright doesn't bring his curtain down on the reconciliation, however. As in *Brigadoon* (at least, as it was originally played), we don't have to see the Girl to know that Boy gets her. More important to Barry is the break with the wrong girl—how it comes about and what it looks like. The senior Collier has attempted to control his son with a check of such vast amount that to let us in on the exact sum would be vulgar. After a bit of drinking before sex, Tom lets Cecilia slink off to the bedchamber (which, by the way, is how she controls Tom: when he thwarts her will she locks the door). But the drinking has cleared Tom's head. He doesn't want sex: he wants Daisy. Endorsing the check over to wife Cecilia (who is really his "mistress" of sex), Tom offers Red a ride to town (New York, of course, the world capital of Sophistication) as Tom returns to his mistress Daisy, who of course is really his "wife." That is, to emphasize this crazy perception, Daisy is Tom's heroine and idol, the woman he loves rather than the woman he scores.

Now for a star exit. The show's director (and co-producer, with Howard himself), Gilbert Miller, was so fond of this last bit that when he caught Percy Hammond slipping up the aisle to get a head start on his review, Miller sent Hammond back to his seat. As they staged it, Red leaves first, and Tom pauses to take a final look at the place of his "marriage" to an erotic fribble. Everybody smoked in those days, especially the Sophisticated, so Tom takes a heavy drag, blows out the puff, and walks out. The empty stage is haunted by the character we don't see—not Daisy, who has her (happy) ending all set. No, it's Cecilia, waiting in bed for Tom. The endorsed check, sitting on the mantel under a vase, is what we see; it's what Cecilia is. The library of Tom Collier's converted farmhouse in Connecticut sits empty for five or six seconds. And the curtain falls.

For his part, S. N. Behrman never attempted anything as meaty as *Here Come the Clowns* or even, really, *The Animal Kingdom*. Behrman's Sophistication resides entirely in wordplay arising from a conflict of etiquettes—between a society scion and a woman from Downtown, say, or between the honest artist and the prevaricating politician. To the extent that anything of Behrman's has lasted, *Biography* (1932) is his most lasting title. Or is it *End of Summer* (1936)? Both Theatre Guild offerings for the end-of-summer tantalizer Ina Claire, these plays observe artists and their supporters trying to survive while fascists of the left and right struggle for world control. It sounds like the work of a political writer, perhaps a Robert E. Sherwood. Indeed, it sounds exactly like Sherwood's Lunts show *Idiot's Delight*. But Behrman never thought of himself as a political writer. The political like politics; Behrman liked Ina Claire.

In *Biography,* she is a painter commissioned to write her memoirs. This puts her in the center of a struggle between her frantically leftist publisher and her former amour, about to become a National Figure and obviously anxious about what she may say. As always in Behrman, the plot thickens because his men are always falling in love with his star. Philip Barry separates the erotic woman from the brilliant woman, with the intention of complimenting the latter. Behrman, however, combines the erotic with the brilliant. That in itself provides his content, along with the usual epigrammatic observations that typify Sophistication at its least dangerous. For example, Claire and an old European friend haven't seen each other for many years now. Not since . . .

THE PUBLISHER: Vienna!

CLAIRE: (astonished) Yes. How did you know?

THE PUBLISHER: It's always since Vienna that Bohemians haven't seen each other, isn't it?

Behrman sometimes uses the erotic as a shocker, particularly just before the second intermission, as when the publisher suddenly drops his professional non-fraternization rule and more or less throws himself at Claire's feet:

THE PUBLISHER: Marion, my angel!

CLAIRE: (infinitely compassionate, stroking his hair) Dickie—Dickie— Dickie . . . Why have you been afraid to love me?

It's always about love, not politics, whereas Barry thinks it's about independence (and, sometimes, justifying God's ways to man). Behrman had an odd explanation for his lack of weighty subject matter. In fact, he had several. *No Time For Comedy*—the one that Laurence Olivier stole from Katharine Cornell—is ironically titled. Set in 1938, the piece argues that a dangerous age is *precisely* the time for comedy. Olivier is a playwright, drawn from his actress wife, Cornell, into the arms and under the influence of Margalo Gillmore, who wants Olivier to Rise to Tragedy. The result, *Dilemma,* is terrible—though of course Behrman wants him to fail. "We are living in an era of death" is his defense, but "Don't spin me fantasias of death," Cornell begs. "Imagine for me variations of life." Of course, Behrman makes as much of the Olivier-Gillmore adultery as of Olivier's doomed attempt to switch modes. "Sleep with him if you must," Cornell tells her rival, Gillmore. "But don't spoil his style."

Another of Behrman's apologias was more philosophical. In a symposium on "the propaganda play" in *The Stage* magazine in 1934, Behrman quoted Heywood Broun: "The drama which fails to convey a moral or to preach a sermon is generally a feeble thing." To which Behrman replied, "From Shakespeare to Galsworthy the enduring playwrights have been neutrals." And so, he thought, it should be: "The artist, like the scientist, should have no prejudices."

It seems strange to liken the attitudes of two Englishmen to Americans, especially when one precedes the Depression by over three hundred years. At that, don't some of the surviving works of the Athenian Dionysia bear strong political subtexts relating to contemporary events?

Worse, by 1934 the term "propaganda play" meant different things to different folks. Propaganda is essentially a commercial for a point of view, sometimes a dishonest marshalling of arguments and invariably representing an argument impervious to contradicting proofs. But some people lumped all plays of social inquiry into the umbrella stand of "propaganda." By that definition, *Pygmalion* (on class), *You Can't Take It With You* (on the work ethic), and—hold on to your hat—*Brigadoon* (on the lack of spiritual meaning in modern life) are propaganda. And if artists are to work like scientists—a risible concept to begin with—even scientists eventually draw some conclusion. Of *End of Summer,* Brooks Atkinson complained, "You scarcely know what side [Behrman] is taking." Yes, you do: Ina Claire's side. Or, in *Rain From Heaven* (1934), he's on Jane Cowl's. Presiding over an English house party, Cowl is caught between the usual Behrman twosome, here an American crypto-fascist adventurer (Ben Smith) with Charles Lindbergh's heroic profile and a Hitler refugee (John Halliday), both Cowl admirers. Behrman makes a great deal of the refugee's Jewish identity, though he actually has only a single Jewish great-grandfather (and will thus not be classified as Jewish even under the Nuremberg Laws of the following year).

Halliday got into trouble in Germany for writing . . . well, a piece of propaganda, a pamphlet called "The Last Jew," which anticipates the Nazi annihilation of European Jewry. The very word "extermination" is used, at a time—again, this is 1934—when few outside the very highest levels of Nazi government could even have imagined what lay in store. The eponymous last Jew is about to commit suicide when "an excited deputation from the All-Highest" offer to protect the propagation of his kind. For with the Last Jew gone, "their policy is bankrupt." The episode, as Halliday recounted it, includes a personal repudiation from a character unmistakably modeled on the writer Gerhart Hauptmann, a former liberal who accommodated the Nazis.

So Behrman is at pains to ground his piece in real-time naturalism while opening his theatre to politics. This is indeed no time for comedy, and Behrman is no one's idea of neutral. Yet note how a powerful revelation of American anti-Semitism immediately jumps into another of those Behrman frisson curtains at the end of the second act. The Lindberghian character wants to marry Jane Cowl; it suddenly appears that she prefers the refugee and has even granted him access to her boudoir:

SMITH: You dirty Jew!

COWL: (horrified) Rand!

HALLIDAY: It's all right, Vi. This makes me feel quite at home.

SMITH'S OLDER BROTHER: You swine! Maybe those people over there [in Germany] are right.

COWL: Hobart, please remember—Herr Willen is not only my lover, he is also my guest. (With a smile) But we mustn't disappoint [the help]. Let us go in to dinner.

And with the audience looking, I'd guess, rather like the one in the movie of *The Producers* during the "Springtime For Hitler" number, the curtain falls.

As if admitting that he himself had no stories to tell, Behrman took to making adaptations of foreign-language plays for much of the rest of his career. In fact, a citation of lasting Behrman titles should possibly center on *Amphitryon 38* (1937), more apparently because it was one of the Lunts' most celebrated duets, but more truly because the text was originally set down (in 1929) by Jean Giraudoux, one of France's most playful wits. It was Giraudoux's impishly exaggerated contention that his was the thirty-eighth retelling of the Greek tale of yet another Olympian dalliance with a mortal; this time, the king of the gods takes the form of the lady's husband. But Giraudoux has a twist: the all-powerful wants to be loved for himself by a willing partner—Alcmena, most faithful of wives! With their peculiar gift for making infidelity into a sort of fidelity in code, the Lunts were perfectly cast. When the god seeks admittance to Alcmena's palace, Lynn catechized Alfred with the questions that all the women out front love to hear and that all the men find bewildering: "Are you he by whose side I wake every morning and for whom I cut from the margin of my own day an extra ten minutes of sleep?" and "Are you the one whose least footfall is so familiar to me that I can tell whether he is shaving or dressing?"

"They wrap a play around them like a costume," said Brooks Atkinson. As we already know, the Lunts wrapped life around them like a play, especially this play. It is Behrman's best work, which is obviously not a compliment, but at least the translation is quite stylish. "Adaptation by S. N. Behrman," the official billing, suggests creative retooling, but Behrman stuck relatively closely to Giraudoux in a kind of freely literal rendering. When Alcmena's predecessor Leda (Edith King) shows up to advise and consult and reveals that the god bestows no material reward, Alcmena is deflated. "Not even a little colored egg?" she asks—and we hear Giraudoux in the line. It's whimsey *à la Franco-Française*. Then Behrman slips into what is surely his own Broadwayspeak when Alcmena sizes Leda up with "He didn't even make an honest legend of you." In fact, the first of these two lines is Behrman's addition to the text, and the second, however extravagated, originates in Giraudoux.

Sophisticated writers enjoyed amplifying Americans' sensual experience, not only in verbal but in visual teases, and Behrman rang one change on Giraudoux by moving the original work's first dialogue scene from a terrace outside Amphitryon's palace to the heavens. So the public's first sight was of Jupiter and Mercury (Richard Whorf)* perched on a cloud looking down at the earth, heads resting on their hands, their legs thrust up behind

---

* Note that, like most Europeans, Giraudoux used the gods' Roman names despite the Greek setting; Molière did the same thing in *his* version of *Amphitryon* (1668). They should, of course, be Zeus and Hermes.

them, their perfectly molded buttocks and Phidean thighs and calves clear to the view. The audience gasped, then realized that the physiques were built into Lee Simonson's set of airy fleece: Lunt and Whorf were actually standing upright below the construction, all but their heads hidden under the sightline. We are told that the house continued to giggle at this coup de crypto-boylesque throughout the scene, not settling down again till the traveler curtain closed.

Of course, the Lunts were expected to be ever edging Broadway over the cliff of what was permitted, because they were lovably dangerous. No one thought of them as revolutionaries—especially because, in other parts of the forest, the Lunts' colleagues were effecting comparable transformations, with popular success. Who could have predicted a smash run for a work 2,500 years old?—Aristophanes' *Lysistrata,* in its first local professional production in English. The bawdy look at a feminist sex strike to impose peace on the warrior gender includes a few scenes that would startle today. The recruiting of Lampito, during which Lysistrata inspects the comely tenderfoot with erotic abandon, may be the great lesbian moment in Western Theatre. The Moscow Art players had offered the piece in 1925—in Russian, of course—but not till 1930 was Broadway to hear it in the vernacular, translated by Gilbert Seldes and directed and designed by Norman Bel Geddes.

A combination of slapstick, lewd costuming, and the original's racy jests made *Lysistrata* a surprise hit for the Philadelphia Theatre Association, and it was decided to take it to The Street. Fay Bainter, the Lysistrata, was replaced by Violet Kemble Cooper, with Miriam Hopkins and Hortense Alden as two of her subordinates, Sydney Greenstreet leading the men, and short and squishy Ernest Truex as Kinesias. (Lampito was not the rack diva one hopes for, but rather the hulking Hope Emerson, a comic monster.) The authorities were wary enough to assign cops to listening posts in the auditorium just in case; but the time when theatre could be silenced was over. Sophistication was a major reason why: because it was suggestive rather than defiant. They could close Mae West down—but the Lunts? Noël Coward? Aristophanes? Sophisticated wasn't seditious: it was naughty. *Lysistrata* seduced—better, neutralized—even suspicious cops. Entranced by the opportunity to Get One's Culture In while enjoying a burlesque show, the public kept *Lysistrata* running for seven months in the cavernous Forty-fourth Street Theatre at a $5.50 top, high for the day.

There was more Greek gender war in Julian Thompson's *The Warrior's Husband* (1932), a spoof of myth in which Hercules is a coward, Homer a kind of press agent, and the Amazons' husbands are bearded ladies, talking fashion and cuisine. Note the title's hazardous fun; not till one knows that the Warrior is a woman is one, so to say, free to enter. She is Hippolyta (Irby Marshall), and her husband is Sapiens (Romney Brent), with Dorothy Parker's future second and third husband, Alan Campbell, as Achilles. However, attention was focused on the second couple, Antiope (Katharine Hepburn) and Theseus (Colin Keith-Johnston), because the others were funny but these two were beautiful. He was a natural-born hero, much admired as the nobly weary Captain Stanhope of *Journey's End*—and she was already Katharine Hepburn. She made her entrance carrying a slain stag on her back as she vaulted down a flight of stairs, eventually kicked that Achilles right in his heel, and wooed her man with war. In their matching breastplate and greaves, Hepburn and Keith-Johnston got into what appeared to be genuine physical combat, and while Romney Brent walked off with the notices, the town was talking about that crazy girl in the armor.

As a script, *The Warrior's Husband* is witless; Gilbert W. Gabriel thought the show should have been a musical by Jacques Offenbach. And a musical it became, though it was by Rodgers and Hart (book as well as score), with Brent's role centering the action as a vehicle for Ray Bolger: *By Jupiter* (1942). Clearly, this material is Sophistication in its crude form. With the Lunts and Barry and Behrman, Sophistication is elegant and droll. Thompson's play is a rough-hewn sitcom and the musical downright lewd, wartime escapism played down to servicemen and their dates. All the same, Thompson's notion contributed to an important aspect of Sophistication: a widening of our humanistic frame of reference by turning received opinion (i.e., men are strong and women silly) on its head.

The Lunts themselves did much the same in Alfred's staging of *The Taming of the Shrew*, in 1935. To be archival about it, we should note that Harry Wagstaff Gribble was the credited director; the Luntian byline ran "Scheme of production devised by," and both Alfred and Lynn were thus appreciated, along with star billing larger than the title. In fact, Alfred ran the show, throwing it at the public with the coarse and crazy energy of an improvisational troupe in a medieval fairground while controlling it with the tautness of a lute string.

Granted, the *Shrew* is not the Shakespeare of lilting monologues and subtextual undertow. Still, it had never been this racy; nothing had. Despite the Lunts' reputation—today, at least—for spending their lives in boulevard sex comedy, these two really liked to shock, and this was not your father's *Shrew,* such as the 1887 Augustin Daly staging with John Drew and Ada Rehan. "Tumbling and revelry," Brooks Atkinson reported, were mixed in with "a cluster of midgets, a pair of comic horses and some fine songs set to good beer-garden music." Sydney Greenstreet was in this, too, as Baptista—"corpulent, frightened, bewildered, hopeful" was Atkinson's impression of the portrayal—but the cast really was less portraying than dancing around like loons, treating the audience to insolent commentary, and making spectacularly timed accidents with the props look serendipitous. It was one of the decade's outstanding stagings, something doing every moment, and its fanatically professional director tamed his entire company before the last day of the run by calling for a full-dress runthrough: because Friday night had been sloppy.

Above all, Lynn and Alfred brought out the sex in Shakespeare; they made him Sophisticated. Ironically, another of the movement's guardians made a connection with this *Shrew* when the Lunts revived it for a tour in 1940. Arnold Saint-Subber, their stage manager, gaped in fascination at the way the roaring terror of a courtship onstage went right on when the two passed into the wings and reassumed their life roles as devoted sparring partners. Years later, as producer Saint Subber, he commissioned with partner Lemuel Ayers a musical version of that *Shrew* as *Kiss Me, Kate* (1948), which of course brings Cole Porter back into view.* Porter's Sophistication is extremely paradoxical, for while he lived among the droll and elegant, he wrote of life among the rough-hewn and lewd. A Cole Porter show was a dirty show—not just risqué or suggestive, but low-down, coarse, and itchy. However, much of that was locked into the book material

---

* Bella Spewack, co-author with her husband, Samuel, of *Kiss Me, Kate*'s book, disputed Subber's version of the show's conception. Broadway's two earlier Shakespeare musicals, *The Boys From Syracuse* (1938) and *Swingin' the Dream* (1939), each found a different way to encompass Elizabethan theatre, the first in standard "musical comedy" and the second in a mixed-race jazz raveup. Neither stunt was repeatable; Bella says she suggested the backstager approach, in effect writing a new story around the one in the *Shrew*—and this entirely innocent of any knowledge of Luntian life practice.

and the way the Porter creeps, molls, and stooges carried themselves. The Porter songs themselves found an esoteric poetry in these people; when Ethel Merman sings "I Get a Kick Out Of You" or "Down in the Depths (on the Ninetieth Floor)" or "Do I Love You (Do I?)," we momentarily forget that her characters are a notch above being actively employed in a brothel.

Another notable quality of Sophistication is its Continental or English flavor. Those European writers that the Theatre Guild made into Broadway regulars were regarded as oracular in the style—who was more Sophisticated than Ferenc Molnár? We've encountered him thus far in the capriciously intense Luntfun of *The Guardsman* and the doleful fantasy of *Liliom;* like Walt Whitman, Molnár contains multitudes. The language barrier that has kept Hungarian culture the Western World's biggest secret held Molnár back from the status he deserves, leaving him as a kind of delicatessen theatre, not least because he draws on the frivolous for his subjects and mans a shell game for his conclusions.

Still, of all our Sophisticates, Molnár tells the best stories. *The Good Fairy* (1931), in Jane Hinton's translation, presents a cinema usherette (Helen Hayes) whose exposure to the sublimating narratives of the movies leads her to become all things to as many men as possible. Molnár gives us three in particular: a lascivious businessman, a middle-aged lawyer, and a charming writer. Let Brooks Atkinson once again fix the style of the piece for us: "a matchless facility for humor, sin and fancy." Molnár was Budapest's chief boulevardier, and he became Broadway's chief central European, as chic as Coward and the Lunts. Robert Garland of the *World-Telegram* noted a preponderance of "the top hat-and-ermine crowd," at *The Good Fairy*'s premiere, and Percy Hammond emphasized a favorite theme of mine in his phrase "The First Audience." Important playwright bylines brought out Important Theatregoers, who doubtless felt well paid for their trouble when *The Good Fairy*'s producer-director himself, Gilbert Miller, came before the curtain after the last act to introduce a change in the text. Miller could not abide Molnár's unresolved conclusion, he explained, and he had dared to ask our Hungarian master to write an epilogue finishing off the story: which of those three men does Helen Hayes end up with? Hungarian by choice as well biologically, Molnár drew on his native culture's love of surprise in giving Hayes to a fourth man, a minor character who was the last person one expected to see onstage at the end of the piece. The audience said, "That's the ending?" And the curtain fell.*

We begin to notice that Sophistication favors unusual woman leads—not just Lynn Fontanne and Katharine Hepburn, but also Helen Hayes as a naive kid who emerges from male entanglements stronger and even purer. On one level, Sophistication simply recommends that one take a broad view of life with all the tolerance that society frowns on and none of the hypocrisy that it can't seem to live without. The opposite of Molnár would be the exploitation of the Sophisticated woman in a cheap sex comedy, such as John Larkin Jr.'s short-lived *Society Girl* (1931). It's Debutante Meets Boxer, with the novelty that the deb is aggressive, cute but tough. The role was assigned to Claire Luce, Fred Astaire's last stage dancing partner (after Adele Astaire, Marilyn Miller, and Tilly Losch) and a prime exponent of the new thirties lady. Playing opposite Fred Astaire—at that in a Cole Porter musical, *Gay Divorce* (1932)—gave Luce a very diploma in Sophistication. But *Society Girl* had her throwing her weight around the boxer (Russell Hardie, a specialist in such roles) and pointlessly provoking the boxer's manager (Brian Donlevy). Dealing in mean stereotype, Larkin contrived an ending rather less subtly than Molnár in *The Good Fairy*: Hardie pasted Luce one in the mouth and made her repent of her arrogant—or was it independent?—ways. In the hands of Noël Coward and especially Ferenc Molnár and most of all Philip Barry, the Sophisticated Woman sparred on equal terms with men. In a sleazy pop piece like *Society Girl,* a Sophisticated woman was too big for her britches. Not independent: spoiled.

Without question, the most extreme of the Sophisticated plays was the one about the older gay man who keeps Laurence Olivier as a boy toy, thwarts Olivier's attempts to break away heterosexually, and is shot dead by Olivier's father.

What? On Broadway? Yes: but Englishman Mordaunt Shairp's *The Green Bay Tree* (1933) is written in a code at once clear and ambiguous, so one could just as well have seen it as the tale of a pampered young man

---

* It was a double surprise, for not till later on did anyone learn that Molnár had written it all out in the original, announcement from the stage, "new" epilogue, and all. After the premiere, a stage manager spoke for Miller.

who wants to stay pampered. But why would a young man *be* pampered unless . . . especially if the older man doing the pampering is a certain Mr. Dulcimer, known to the young man as "Dulcie"?* Shairp defines the pair's relationship by not defining it. Having cut himself off from his biological father, young Julian is Mr. Dulcimer's "son and companion" by a procedure innocent of bureaucratic seal. Of course, any spectator in the house who needed to believe that these two really are a sort of father and son could take heart in the appearance of Leonora Yale, the one character whose type the audience was already conversant with: a level-headed young woman in love.

We should pause here, for a paradox. The sensible ingenue—in Shairp's *Green Bay* description "clean-cut, charming, strong-willed, decisive, quite free from pose"—turned up in all sorts of plays without really claiming her share of Broadway history. These are not famous or memorable roles: because important women didn't play sensible. The stars were quixotic, mercurial, pathetically lost, or radiantly redemptive, and in any case were constantly putting the public in touch with their inner goddess. We've seen the Cornells and Le Galliennes at work: they play *unique*. Leonora is by profession a veterinarian—*there's* a role for Cornell! It is no coincidence that the outstanding female portrayal of the century was— here's that cliché once again—an old drunk doing a turn as a destructive southern mother, bound in lacy nostalgia and naggy protectiveness. Those who spent their careers in the sensible portrayals never made it to stardom— Ann Andrews, say, or Patricia Collinge, so obscurely prominent in their day, or even Margalo Gillmore, a name we've encountered several times thus far and who at least left a bit behind as Mrs. Darling in the television broadcasts of the Mary Martin *Peter Pan*.

Olivier's real-life spouse before Vivien Leigh, Jill Esmond, played Leonora, as if providing Julian with an offstage beard. Esmond also gave the show its dramatic energy as the only major principal who is not a member of the tribe—for of course Mr. Dulcimer (James Dale) employs a butler, Trump (Leo G. Carroll, later television's Topper), who gives his notice when Julian becomes engaged to Leonora. "A married establishment," he explains, "means women servants." Then there's the Coward-like dialogue,

---

* What a choice of word! "Dulcimer" is even worse than "Dulcie," for the dulcimer is a thin stringed instrument played with tiny hammers, a kind of faggy little piano.

as in this couplet, cued in because Julian has been helping Leonora with her veterinarian work:

JULIAN: (ruefully) How would *you* like to give some dog an emetic?
MR. DULCIMER: I should hate to give anyone an emetic.

Let us note as well Mr. Dulcimer's lack of a first name, as if hiding in plain sight—the typical existence of a gay man in this era—or even his insistence on skipping the first act of *Tristan und Isolde,* on stylistic grounds. It's the rigor of caprice.

"One may read anything one chooses, or very little," wrote Brooks Atkinson of Mr. Dulcimer's relationship with Julian. It sounds naive, but then *The Green Bay Tree* isn't about sexuality. It's about luxury. So, of course, was Sophistication in general, and part of its attraction lay in its re-fusal to state precisely what it was. In both London and New York, *The Green Bay Tree* ran five months on Shairp's ability to treat a "difficult" theme in a way that presented no difficulty. Mr. Dulcimer is so exquisite that he has virtually no reality even though he is the defining figure in a play that is even more essential to the history of gay theatre than *The Captive* is. Bour-det's play, remember, never produced its lesbian; Shairp revels in Mr. Dul-cimer. This character's power is such that he controls Julian even in death. Art was the key, music and sculpture. Mr. Dulcimer discovered Julian as a boy soprano in Wales, bought him off his biological father, and coddled him with the sensualist's virtues of the epigram and showing up at public events later than everyone else. After his murder, Mr. Dulcimer retains stage control as a death mask hanging on the wall, and after Julian rejects Leonora and the butler retracts his resignation, the lights dim on a beaten Julian in a chair, smoking. We see only the light at the tip of his cigarette and a glow on the mask, as if the two men were communicating; and the curtain falls.

Clearly, this was an age in which gay life was, as Bourdet says, "captiv-ity." In Lillian Hellman's *The Children's Hour* (1934), a lesbian kills herself when outed, stating, shortly before her last exit, "I feel so God damned sick and dirty." Chester Erskin's *The Good* (1938) pictured a tyrannically self-righteous mother driving her son into an affair with a church choirmaster, as if one went gay only in despair; and we know from chronicle what happens in Leslie Sewell Stokes' *Oscar Wilde* (1938). The English Robert Morley took the title role in this English import—which, unlike *The Green Bay Tree,* played London in a private club because the Lord Chamberlain refused it a license. Was this because Wilde never thought of his sexuality as captivity? Staying in New York for 247 performances, *Oscar Wilde* was a hit, but behind the celebrity protagonist was, really, just another piece in which the homosexual comes to a bad end. What was missing from the catalogue of plays with gay characters was someone who was neither a swish nor a mess, because with Real Men in it, Sophistication becomes Corruption. Let me address this problem with another of my personal notes.

This concerns the Burns Mantle *Best Plays* annuals—probably the last place one would expect to find evidence of the gay life that was quietly and happily going on separately from the theatre's captives, suicides, and vindictive affairs with choirmasters. As the most reliable source of Broadway data from the 1899–1900 season forward, these volumes form the foundation of one's library, and I had been catching up on the older entries in the series in the antiquarian shops. Some of these used books carried bookplates or handwritten names. The front flyleaf of 1922–23 bore the idiosyncratic ownership claim of a fifties revue funster in a heavy ink of block letters as "SIGYN RONNY GRAHAM," and Mantle's first successor, John Chapman, personalized copies for friends with innocuous messages. Most interesting is the inscription in 1944–45, which I quote in full:

Christmas '45
These [plays] we didn't see. You did, naturally, but not I—not me. Still, they did all right and so, within limitations, did we. We probably always will, you know.

To Nelson from his favorite naval officer—a.

There were no roles for Nelson and his buddy on Broadway in the 1930s, because sexual anomaly could be treated only through Sophistication, and Sophistication didn't recognize ordinary people. Sophistication was worldly, funny, and smart, as we have seen; it also had its wicked side: sin as a fashion statement. Above all, however, Sophistication counted on a steamy sense of style, whether in the name of Mr. Dulcimer, in Katharine Hepburn's wrestling with Colin Keith-Johnston, or even in the too-too diction heard in Philip Barry, where the sex drive is sublimated in conversation so tender that we wonder exactly how close Leslie Howard is to that ex-boxer butler. Sophistication included such disparate elements as a Cole Porter double meaning and a country house party in S. N. Behrman, yet on one level all of it contrived to inform and fool the public at once. It was revelation but also a pose. The notion of a gay naval officer serving his country in wartime in the next decade disrupts the affectation, cleans away the steam. At heart, Sophistication was like an evening with the Algonquin wits, so original and stimulating, so well-read, -heard, -lived. They had much to tell that you hadn't known before, and it was all so entertaining, surprising, educational. Captivity? Call it liberation: and some of it was even true.

Six

The Celebrity of Eccentricity

isten to the first paragraph of Damon Runyon's story of 1929, "Romance in the Roaring Forties":

> *Only a rank sucker will think of taking two peeks at Dave the Dude's doll, because while Dave may stand for the first peek, figuring it is a mistake, it is a sure thing he will get sored up at the second peek, and Dave the Dude is certainly not a man to have sored up at you.*

Of course, the story revolves around a sucker, and he is one Waldo Winchester, "a nice-looking young guy who writes pieces about Broadway for the *Morning Item*." Also on hand is Dave the Dude's doll, Miss Billy Perry; and Waldo's confidante, speakeasy proprietor Missouri Martin, who "tells everything she knows as soon as she knows it, which is very often before it happens."

In that little dramatis personae, we read the content of what the word "Broadway" had come to mean by the 1930s: gossip. A few chapters ago, we saw "Broadway" take in nightclubs and Prohibition crime as well as theatregoing; now Broadway was the beat of the men who tattled, who created the myth of Broadway by reporting, snitching, and inventing.

Waldo Winchester is of course Walter Winchell, of the *New York Graphic* in 1929 but soon to settle in at William Randolph Heart's more imposing *New York Mirror,* with a syndication deal that promised a readership in the millions. (Soon enough, Winchell would add radio and, later, television to his domain.) Missouri Martin is Texas Guinan of the "Hello, sucker!" with which she greeted patrons of her various clubs, and Billy Perry is any of the thousands of young women of the kind we met in *Broadway,* cuties dancing in places like Guinan's. The successful ones were the gold diggers, the unsuccessful ones dwindled into cold-water-flat marriages back in the neighborhood, and the most famous of them was Ruby Keeler, who had to fend off the courtship of gangster Johnny "Irish" Costello to marry Al Jolson. Winchell redrafted the story into treatment for a film of 1933, *Broadway Thru a Keyhole,* with Constance Cummings, Paul Kelly (who had actually done time for murder), and Russ Columbo as the singer Cummings prefers to gangster Kelly. And here's tattle: Jolson flew at Winchell the next time their paths crossed, at a prizefight in Los Angeles, and Jolson had to be pulled off Winchell mid-fight. Guinan got into the film, too, playing herself for authenticity of personnel. A figure based far more in the pay-no-price 1920s than in the repentant Depression, Guinan died before the end of 1933; but Winchell was essential. In all show biz, only Al Jolson was big enough to take a swing at the National Columnist who controlled the matter of Rise and Fall in the day-to-day of the entertainment world till his own downfall in the 1950s.

"Gotta get in the column!" sing Manhattan's guys and dolls in the recent musical based on a novella and film on the world of Winchell, *Sweet Smell of Success.* A mixture of plugs and attacks, social and political opinion, and random jottings, The Column was above all a feast of scandal, Broadway thru a keyhole. And of course that "Broadway" was by now expression by synecdoche, referring less to theatregoing than first-nighting and not so much to playhouses as to high-status nightspots such as the Colony (for bluebloods) and, more famously, the Stork (where Winchell hung out) and El Morocco (less racy, and, some said, strictly for those who couldn't get into the Stork). "We've been seen around New York," runs a line of Oscar Hammerstein, "El Morocco and the Stork"—and we immediately place the voice as that of a Ranking New Yorker, on first-name terms with its arts, money, and fame.

In The Column, all three were one, as if adulterous exposé were Kaufman and Hart by different means. Didn't *Chicago* and *The Front Page*—not to mention De Tocqueville—warn us that market-driven democracy causes everything to conduce to show biz, to ticket-selling and role-playing? Winchell was the barker of this carnival. Yet for all his scandalmongering, editorializing, and slandering any who challenged his worldview, he made the theatre—the real meaning of "Broadway"—elemental in The Column. This man was so relentlessly narcissistic that actually attending a play—that is, sitting in a dark hall with a thousand others, none of whom was paying the slightest attention to him—must have driven him crazy. Yet he never missed an important opening, and he tossed off his theatregoing recommendations as energetically as he unveiled broken romances. There were plenty of other gossip columns, but only Winchell's could break a new performer into prominence, fill an empty club—or guarantee a weak play's success.

Why did Winchell's readers obey these summonses? Because his judgments were so ubiquitous in conversation that geeks in search of content wanted to see what he saw and go where he went. Thirties movies were obsessed with the word "Winchell": it meant something, perhaps the difference between famous and Famous. Winchell's Broadway was a freak show, but then so was the Broadway of the beloved Runyon's guys and dolls, in his unvaryingly present-tense narration of the underworld of Hymie Banjo Eyes, Frying Pan Joe, Baseball Hattie, Mrs. Colonel Samuel B. Venus, the late Cockeyed Corrigan, or Obadiah Masterson. (Readers may place the last named in *Guys and Dolls,* as Sky Masterson. Runyon in fact refers to him only as The Sky, so called "because he goes so high when it comes to betting on any proposition whatever.")

What inventions! And Winchell's entire world was an invention, really. He dealt in a kind of iconoclastic idolatry, shattering the totems during the very worship service in a breathless ratatat of made-up phrases: "phfft" (the end of a relationship) and "infanticipating" (expecting a child) were perhaps the best known. It was a national joke that Winchell could predict to the day the "blessed event" (another of his terms), before even the parents had the information. In that Warner Bros. musical that helped wipe *Lightnin'* away, *42nd Street,* a honeymooning couple devotes the release of "Shuffle Off To Buffalo" to this concept. Looking forward to the purchase of baby clothes, the male admits, "We don't know when to expect it," closing the couplet with "But it's a cinch Winchell knows."

Symmetrically enough, Runyon was to become one of Winchell's few genuine friends; a book about them, by John Mosedale, is entitled *The Men Who Invented Broadway.* What they invented was the celebrity as an eccentric, both as lawless as Runyon's folk and as unpredictable as Winchell's: the famous are crazy. And like Winchell—the most famous of them all because he *controlled* famous—they all spoke fluent wisecrack. One night at the Stork, someone said something about women being the profession of idle men, and Winchell began jotting it down to use in The Column. Warned that the line was a quotation of George Bernard Shaw, Winchell replied, "I'll give it some circulation."

That's a wisecrack. It's cynical and funny but, mainly, it seizes power, taking over the moment with a comeback that, like The Column, is bigger than you. We have seen wisecrack comedy enter the vernacular through its use on Broadway in the 1920s and its wider dissemination in the first talkies. Now is when we see it spread throughout American life through many models but, above all, in the New York that Winchell and Runyon claimed as their patch.

If *The Front Page* is the first of the enduring wisecrack comedies (*Chicago* endures only as a musical), the next title, at that a marginally enduring one, is Samuel and Bella Spewack's *Boy Meets Girl* (1935). Ironically, the Spewacks wrote the piece as a look at how *The Front Page's* authors, Hecht and MacArthur, fared in Hollywood. They were turned into Benson (Jerome Cowan) and Law (Allyn Joslyn), who spend their studio time clowning around and uttering one-liners, which are the comebacks that don't wait for their cue, as in:

LAW: I can't dictate to a stenographer who won't wear tights.

For a hobby, Benson and Law pass scornful remarks at the cowboy star (Charles McClelland) they're supposed to be writing for and vexing their producer (Royal Beal). The latter, named C. Elliott Friday and known as C. F., is of a type we might in modern parlance call the Clueless Hetero. This character typically knows a few things about his line of work but seems to know absolutely nothing else; think of Trent Lott without the wit and sparkle. Representative of C. F.'s schemes for "the picture of the year" is "a sort of Bengal Lancer, but as Kipling would have done it."

A great deal of *Boy Meets Girl*'s fun lies in watching Benson and Law outwit the selfish and talentless western star and the idiotic authority figure; and the rest of the fun lies in the way the Spewacks fondly develop the title's concept (BENSON: Boy meets girl. Boy loses girl. Boy gets girl.) as they introduce an impoverished Brit (James MacColl) to a pregnant, unmarried commissary waitress (Joyce Arling), dash them apart, then reunite them. This subplot cuts into the driveline in that Peggy's baby becomes the cowboy's co-star, as Happy, "America's Crown Prince." By the way, the Brit turns out to be an aristocrat.

George Abbott's customary sleek pacing and sharp advice to his players on how to land the jokes put *Boy Meets Girl* over for a run of 669 performances. But the show is more important for its use of the wisecrack as an embodiment of power. The Clueless Hetero can hire and fire and even create stardom. Yet ultimately he has no power because he has no wisecrack: that humor belongs to those with intelligence and judgment. Interestingly, the Spewacks purged the wisecrack style of the slang and bad grammar that saw it through the 1920s; now the wisecrackers might be drawn not only from the working class but from the intelligentsia as well. Rather, it is the cowboy, enemy of wisecrack, who can't get his verbs to agree with his subjects; and for all his actory popularity he is unable to regulate his movie career because, living on the Planet Me, he has never taken notice of anything he can't exploit and is thus floundering in a kind of all-purpose ignorance.

That is why *Boy Meets Girl* marks a significant breakaway. From now on, the wisecracker has, above all else, perspective. He has been looking at life and learning from it; this makes every wisecracker his own Walter Winchell. Not the Winchell spying thru a keyhole, but the perceived Winchell who seemed to know everything, a sage in a fedora. *This* is power: a worldly grasp of the realities of human existence and the ability to read the patterns in culture, to put names to concepts. When the cowboy star tries to marry the Girl to stabilize his career, Law exposes the cowboy's dying box office in wisecracker terms—and note the use of the jejune in both geography and celebrity:

LAW: Even Wilkes-Barre doesn't want him and they're still calling for Theda Bara.

Oddly, Damon Runyon's presumably stage-ready rogues' gallery did not draw him to much theatre work. With Irving Caesar he wrote the unpro-duced *Saratoga Chips,* which became a movie for Ethel Merman and the Ritz Brothers, *Straight Place and Show* (1938), and with Howard Lindsay he wrote *A Slight Case of Murder* (1935), a two-month flop. However, nu-merous minor films were made off Runyon characters, and of course after Runyon's death, in 1946, material from two stories was combined to make *Guys and Dolls* (1950).

The director of that musical's original production is one of this era's most prolific creators and a central wisecracker, George S. Kaufman. He was steeped in theatre, serving as the drama editor of the *New York Times* from 1917, when its theatre coverage was vast. There was of course far more theatrical activity then than now; there was also more public interest in it. A small band of reviewers covered the openings, the featured critic to reevaluate the major titles in a longish Sunday piece. Further, out-of-town openings and European productions of American plays caught the *Times'* attention.

No one seems to have remarked a conflict of interest in a drama editor's being as well a working playwright (on Broadway from 1918), probably be-cause Kaufman's integrity was famously unimpeachable. Still, one wonders how Kaufman could run his office while attending rehearsals and tryouts. For reasons apparently unknown even to his family, Kaufman kept his day job right through the 1920s, when *Dulcy, Merton of the Movies, The Butter and Egg Man* (1925; the only major title that Kaufman wrote without a col-laborator), *The Royal Family,* and *June Moon* (1929), a Tin Pan Alley spoof written with Ring Lardner, had made him wealthy. Indeed, Kaufman did not leave the *Times* till just before the start of the 1930–31 season.

That was when Kaufman launched his partnership with Moss Hart, on the Hollywood satire *Once in a Lifetime* (1930). By then, Kaufman had honed his wisecracking skills on two musicals with the Marx Brothers, *The Cocoanuts* (1925) and *Animal Crackers* (1928), for Groucho and to some extent Chico speak nothing but wisecracks. (Chico's secondary mode is lovably breezy chiseling. No sooner has he sauntered into Mrs. Ritten-house's A-list *Animal Crackers* house party than he utters the immortal line "Where's the dining room?") We presume that Kaufman (and Morrie Ryskind, his co–book writer on *Animal Crackers* only) were simply adapt-ing to the Marxes' style, already placed in time for their Broadway debut in the revue *I'll Say She Is* (1924). In fact, when away from the Brothers, Kaufman seemed more in harmony with the gentle laughter of *Merton of the Movies* than with the uprising urban inflection of the wisecrack.

On the other hand, when away from the stage, Kaufman the person ap-peared to have wisecrack hardwired in his system; along with Dorothy Parker, he is the most quotable of the era's sarcastic wits. We have already logged a pair of Kaufman's Jed Harris quips; and when Groucho defended ad-libbing on a weekday afternoon during the run of *Animal Crackers* with "They laughed at Edison, didn't they?," Kaufman jumped in with "Not at the Wednesday matinée, they didn't."*

Perhaps it was Moss Hart—fifteen years younger than Kaufman and a born lover of musical comedy while Kaufman couldn't wait for the music to end—who rejuvenated his partner with an infusion of stage wisecrack, the signature tone of the 1930s. Certainly, *Once in a Lifetime* reverberated with it, not least when Kaufman himself took the stage as an exasperated screen-writer. But now for a paradox: the third and arguably most impressive Kaufman-Hart title, *You Can't Take It With You* (1936), looks back to out-dated tradition by setting a kind of Frank Bacon into the wisecrack format. Grandpa Vanderhof (Henry Travers) has the folksy tang of *Lightnin'* and even that character's view of life as a condition one strolls through at leisure.

There the resemblance ends. *Lightnin'* amuses itself by pitting its star player against a bunch of dopes and cheats. *You Can't Take It With You* has

---

* Unlike Dorothy Parker, who would say anything to execute a jest (e.g., when Harold Ross asked why she hadn't visited the *New Yorker* office to make a contribution: "Some-one was using the pencil"), Kaufman's gags were usually very seriously meant, however witty. In the mid-1950s, Kaufman was involved in *Silk Stockings*, a Cole Porter musical based on the Lubitsch-Garbo film *Ninotchka*. Kaufman, directing and co-writing the show till he was fired out of town, favorably impressed Hildegarde Knef (billed as "Neff"), in the Garbo role, and she beseeched Kaufman on behalf of a German colleague, a director. He wanted to stage one of Kaufman's plays in Germany; the Jewish Kaufman forbade all such production. Defending the director, Knef said, "This man emigrated dur-ing the Hitler period." "The audience didn't," Kaufman replied.

no star, but Grandpa is at least the patriarch of its family setting, and he presides over a houseful of zanies. Grandpa's daughter (Josephine Hull) writes plays—a war play, a religious play, a sex play. Her husband (Frank Wilcox) makes fireworks. One of their daughters studies ballet to the coaching of a wild Russian expatriate and her husband's xylophone playing. None of these is a wisecracker, however. It is rather the authors themselves who make the acerbic commentary, by juxtaposing the loony with the sensible, as when Grandpa meets a drunk actress (musical-comedy veteran Mitzi Hajos):

> GRANDPA: Have you been on the stage a long time, Miss Wellington?
> GAY: All my life. I've played everything. Ever see *Peg O' My Heart?*
> GRANDPA: Yes, indeed.
> GAY: (with that fine logic for which the inebriated brain is celebrated) I saw it, too. Great show.

or by reality-testing the farcical doings with some old-fashioned common sense, when the actress passes out:

> PENNY [THE PLAYWRIGHT]: Do you think she'll be all right?
> GRANDPA: Yes, but I wouldn't cast her in the religious play.

or by showing us how merrily disorganized the Vanderhof household is:

> ALICE: What time is it?
> PENNY [HER MOTHER]: I don't know. Anybody know what time it is?
> PAUL [HER FATHER]: Mr. De Pinna might know.
> ED [HER BROTHER-IN-LAW]: It was about five o'clock a couple of hours ago.
> ALICE: Oh, I ought to know better than to ask you people.

Indeed she ought to: because Alice (Margot Stevenson) is the one family member besides Grandpa who is not a screwball. She's the Girl who Meets Boy. He's the boss' son Tony (Jess Barker), and of course the play's famous set piece finds Tony's Social Register parents spending an uncomfortable evening with the Vanderhofs.

It's a classic setup for farce: the tycoon obsessed with money and his

Haughty Lady wife facing off with picturesque wastrels. Typically, neither side comprehends the other; and the boss and his wife are snobs. However, something pointed runs through the culture-shock fun: the wastrels lead happy lives and the snobs are so locked up in behavioral codes that they've never noticed how miserable they are. Worse: like Philip Barry villains, they go on this way only because they think One Is Supposed To. Barry would have treated them to an uncomfortable evening with the characters of *Design For Living,* or at least Leslie Howard and his uppity butler. What Kaufman and Hart produce instead is the very opposite of Sophistication: uncultivated bohemians, hoi polloi as Algonquin stars.

That's one reason why *You Can't Take It With You* is more often revived than the Sophisticated titles: its language hasn't dated. Another reason is abundance of content. There are fifteen principals and many small parts balancing an unusual number of throughlines that all tie up beautifully at the end. The writing mixes the cockeyed with the homespun—the Vander-hofs actually say grace before dinner, Grandpa extemporizing his thanks to heaven. And there's a lovely notion behind the industrious storytelling: with but one life apiece, why not enjoy ourselves?

You Can't Take It With You also underscores the thirties observation that all the interesting Americans are screwballs or screwball-friendly. That is, intelligence and imagination alone are not enough: one must have independence as well, a tolerance not only of others but of oneself. Those who are Different are the referees of democratic liberty—Alexander Woollcott, for instance, or Bette Davis. Eleanor Roosevelt or Orson Welles. Fiorello La Guardia or Gypsy Rose Lee.

Or Clare Boothe. One of the last of the adventuresses, a modern Becky Sharp or Lola Montez, Boothe collected her detractors almost exclusively among women, for she was a born enchanter of men. It is said that men don't like smart girls. No: they don't like the smart girls who make them feel stupid. Clare Boothe made them feel exciting. Better, her ability to capitalize on and even develop her strengths made her one of the most successful women of her day, one that so limited possibilities for her gender that she was bound to turn to writing. Not the novel, though: Boothe wanted to connect with the more public world of journalism and theatre. Her magazine was *Vanity Fair,* with its love of the accomplished celebrity, the deserving famous. And her play was *The Women* (1936). Boothe wrote other plays and eventually served in Congress and as ambassador to Italy;

and she made one of the most prominent marriages of the day, as we shall see. But *The Women* is why Clare Boothe is an interesting American yet today. A look at the mores of New Yorkers, the piece counts thirty-five speaking parts, not a one of them male. Though Boothe troubled to bring in a few working-class characters, all her leads belong to the rich wives' club. One of the play's early working titles was *Park Avenue*.

Is it a hateful play—as some said, including, for the first time, a few male Boothe detractors? More to the point, is it accurate? It is, above all, hard-boiled, a quality the 1930s loved in its art. A diverse group of principals varying from likable to despicable shares a cynical view of the world, spoiled though they are: "Practically nobody ever misses a clever woman," for example, or "Where would any of us get if we played fair?" True, Boothe's central woman, Mary Haines (the ever-ready Margalo Gillmore), starts out with a generally rosy worldview. But Boothe's driveline is the Wising Up of Mary Haines, as her husband leaves her for Crystal Allen (Betty Lawford), one of those mean-streets gold diggers, and not the lovable Warner Bros. kind. Worse, one of Mary's best friends, Sylvia Fowler (Ilka Chase), champions the intruder, forcing Mary to learn how to fight another woman for her man. In the excitement, class war wins out as Sylvia abandons Crystal to side with Mary, who, Crystal snidely remarks, is "welcome to my leftovers." Has Mary no pride?

MARY: No, no pride, that's a luxury a woman in love can't afford.

Touring the ladies' sphere of operations, Boothe took her public from living room to bathroom (where Lawford lolled in a sudsy tub, an arresting novelty), from hospital to gym, and even to Reno. The first coup de théâtre occurs at the hairdresser's, where a gossipy manicurist unknowingly tells Mary that her marriage has become New York's latest phht. (Sylvia has set it up, the beast.) But the scène à faire is Mary's confrontation with Crystal at the dressmaker's, where a group of the women gather outside the door to eavesdrop as the audience gapes in pity and terror.

Well, *is* it hateful? Accurate? Some were unhappy at seeing third-rail issues so unapologetically contacted. Were these gleefully idle people representative of a culture, a social order, a gender? The unseen men of *The Women* seem to be nothing but stooges—accessories, mainly, like those madcap hats or that nail polish that all the girls go for, the revealingly named

Sophie Treadwell's *Machinal* is notable for a recent Public Theatre revival that revealed twenties' expressionism as fresh and vital; overtly gay characters (at left table) on the make; and Clark Gable (at right table) smiling at heroine Zita Johann.

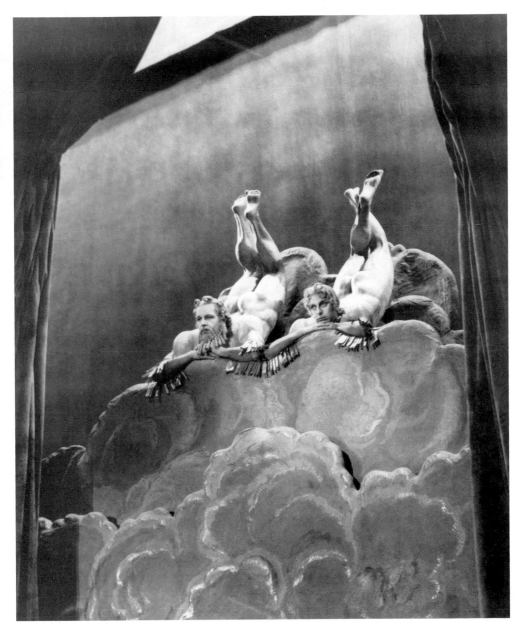

To many, the Golden Age is a concept known as "the Lunts" (on left page) in another shot of their *Taming of the Shrew,* a madcap Baroque raveup in the middle of the 1930s. (Above) Lunt and Richard Whorf in the opening scenelet of *Amphitryon 38* that had the public giggling for ten minutes.

Thornton Wilder's *Our Town* is the Great American Play (above), a somber sampler, or a disquisition on the meaning of "is." In its simple decor (that's the real back wall of Henry Miller's Theatre), the original irritated some as pretentiously plain. Yet its simplicity is what finally endeared it: the bare stage and easy-to-play script appealed to high school drama clubs, and thus popularized the show. We see the third-act funeral, as Emily Webb Gibbs (Martha Scott) takes her place with the dead. Katharine Cornell (right page), arguably our greatest actress, in what was arguably her greatest role, as Shaw's St. Joan.

Sophistication. (Above) The Master, Noel Coward. (Left) An uncharacteristically dressy Bert Lahr. Two opposites, you say? Yet Lahr often laid aside his brawling-gink persona to satirize Sophistication's minty moue. Those who think they have entirely collected these two giants of twentieth-century theatre should know that Coward played Shaw and Arnold Wesker (in a one-minute mime specialty in a revival of *The Kitchen*; and he brought down the house) and Lahr introduced *Waiting for Godot* to Broadway.

A view of the Golden Age would not be complete without at least a token musical. Here's the first moment of *Carousel*'s second act. The curtain has gone up on a brass fanfare quoting Act One's "June Is Bustin' Out All Over." Then, over the vamp to the second act opening, "A Real Nice Clambake," one girl cries, "Look here, Orrin Peaseley! You jest keep yer hands in yer pockets if they're so cold!" All six of *Carousel*'s principals can be seen: Jean Darling and Eric Mattson at far left, Christine Johnson on rock (in black), John Raitt and Jan Clayton at far right, with villain Murvyn Vye (in black T-shirt) on the end.

Carousel brought us into the 1940s, and in the 1950s we reach *Auntie Mame*. (Above) It's Staircase Entrance, a diva's perk since the nineteenth century. Note Jan Handzlik (as Young Patrick) and Beulah Garrick (his nurse) at center and close friends John O'Hare, Polly Rowles (as Vera Charles), and Grant Sullivan in front of the landscape. (Right) Diva perks also include Vamping a Hunk. Katharine Cornell had Marlon Brando; and here's James Monks (as Brian O'Bannion) luncheoning with "Roz."

Jungle Red. Worse, while marriage is everything to the women, if only as a mark of caste, Reno is their Rome, the place all roads lead to. Yet this was an era in which divorced women—and not divorced men—were an oppressed minority group. Boothe's lesson in womancraft was the harder to bear when Mary's mother (Jessie Busley), the most sensible character in sight, strongly advised her daughter to ignore Mr. Haines' infidelity:

> MARY'S MOTHER: Fifty years ago, when women couldn't get divorces, they made the best of situations like this. And sometimes, out of situations like this they made very good things indeed!

The Women was a smash, lasting 657 performances and going Hollywood in 1939 in the MGM ultra treatment (complete with a fashion show in Technicolor), starring goodwife Norma Shearer, false friend Rosalind Russell, and gold digger Joan Crawford, not to mention Mary Boland as Boothe's most arresting novelty yet, a professional divorcée who talks exactly like an old queen. A 1956 musical remake entitled The Opposite Sex, with the men on site, offered June Allyson, Dolores Gray, and Joan Collins in the pivotal roles, along with Ann Miller, Ann Sheridan, Joan Blondell, and Charlotte Greenwood. The 1950s saw a proliferation of summer tours cast with has-beens and getting-theres—Kay Francis Meets Elaine Stritch—and such a congestion of colorful principal roles had to promote at least one all-star revival. In 1973, Broadway saw Kim Hunter, Alexis Smith, Dorothy Loudon, Rhonda Fleming, and (as Mary's mother) Myrna Loy head the marquee. The gold digger was an unknown, Marie Wallace, perhaps to emphasize the social gulf between her and the others; but such moderately notable names as Mary Louise Wilson, Claudette Sutherland (the original Smitty in How To Succeed in Business Without Really Trying), Polly Rowles, Leora Dana, and Jan Miner filled out the playbill. For some reason, The Women baffled London, running only 66 performances. (Boy Meets Girl logged 65 and You Can't Take It With You just 10, though that forerunner of wisecrack comedy, Is Zat So?, ran 234 performances in the West End, a longer stay than on Broadway.)

One might imagine The Women too antique to play today, at least in its subject matter. There still are such people, but nowadays they are little more than a reference point for "The Ladies Who Lunch." However, there was a Roundabout staging in 2001; it showed how poorly today's directors understand the mores that inform thirties social drama. In Mary's duel with Crystal at the dresssmaker's, director Scott Elliott froze Cynthia Nixon with her coat half off her shoulders as the fight with Jennifer Tilly began, to leave it hanging thus for the entire scene. No: the women Boothe wrote of let nothing distract them from their sense of style, and a lady never allows a homewrecker to catch her in disarray.

One odd note in all this helps characterize how wisecrack comedy was perceived at the time: some assummed that Clare Boothe hadn't written *The Women* herself. George S. Kaufman was given credit for heavy doctoring if not wholesale creation. Remember, wisecrack comedy is how strong personalities defend themselves from fools and bullies. The wisecrack putdown is an aggressive—a phallic—act, and as no woman had ever written so well in the style before, it was logical to question the byline. Then, too, Boothe's only previous Broadway entry, *Abide With Me* (1935), was an utter failure. Kaufman was king of wisecrack—but wasn't Dorothy Parker its queen? If Parker could work in wisecrack, why not Boothe as well?

However, Parker had no plays to her credit at that time; Parker worked in short forms. Poems, stories, feuilletons. You know: ladies' pieces. It was Kaufman (and his collaborators) who built wisecrack into sizable constructions. What's more, everyone on The Street knew that Kaufman had been involved to an unknown extent in *The Women*'s Philadelphia tryout.

In fact, Boothe was simply writing ahead of the curve. Controversial by nature and as heedless of detractors as any woman has ever managed to be, Boothe was Different. It's that simple; the play is hers. True, it was a bit vexed in Philadelphia, and both Kaufman and Hart were handy, having tinkered on their own tryout, of *You Can't Take It With You*, for perhaps two days at the most. They found themselves with a little free time, and as both had worked, separately, for *The Women*'s producer, Max Gordon, it was doubtless Gordon who brought the boys in for help. Kaufman was happy to oblige, because like all straight men he had a thing for Clare Boothe. But he didn't add much to the piece. There were only two problems, anyway: a dull scene in the Haines kitchen and a third act that wasn't playing well. Kaufman thought the kitchen scene too thematically intrinsic to cut (though revivals skip it), so he apparently blessed it with a new blackout line. His and Hart's plans for redoing the third act struck Boothe as a dizzying round of fast-food playacting that lost sight of her characters' (which is to say her gender's) agenda. So Boothe simply tackled the job herself. The play, again, is hers.

Boothe's first, brief marriage was for money; her second, the lasting one, was for content, with Henry R. Luce. A Nutty Superachiever in the line of Henry Ford, Howard Hughes, and Ted Turner, Luce was one of the century's most influential Americans, as a creator of, mainly, *Time* (in 1923) and, a year after his and Clare's 1935 wedding and shortly before *The Women* opened, *Life*. In an age when the public was beginning to desert the newspaper for the magazine, Luce combined the two formats, in *Time*'s digests of stories in the dailies and *Life*'s photographic journalism. It was Luce's Yale classmate and *Yale Daily News* colleague Briton Hadden who devised *Time*'s punchy, adjective-heavy style, but it was Luce who thought of arranging doodads of news observed from various points of view into one crisp little compilation. Thus, in historian J. C. Furnas' words, a piece on a coal strike came off "as if by an omniscient reporter who had simultaneously been on the picket line and attended [one] meeting of President Coolidge's cabinet and [another meeting] of John L. Lewis' high command of the United Mine Workers."

Eventually, *Time* accumulated its own reporters and made the subject of each weekly cover story an initiate into history, focusing yet more attention on the matter of fame and how one deserves it—and *Life*'s picture essays, covering everything from natural catastrophe to politics, reveled in human interest. What concerns us here is Luce's emphasis on the arts in both publications, the theatre especially. It reflected the respectful attitudes of his class, but it is remarkable that, for decades, both *Life* and *Time* monitored Broadway as if insisting that America's growing treasury of notables included, among the statesman, the athlete, and the movie star, the people of the stage. Broadway folk knew that they mattered not when their name went up in lights but when they made the cover of *Time*. And *Life* might spread its color over the emergence of a new volcano or dictator—then turn the page upon a house party in Bucks County just at the moment of bridge and croquet with Kaufman and Hart, the Lunts, Harpo Marx, Thornton Wilder, Alexander Woollcott, Lillian Hellman, and others of this great world of the accomplished.

That little picture essay of leisure among the gifted was as close as the ungifted curious might get in those days, except in à clef theatre. This form was Broadway's version of celebrity journalism, making plays out of the famous while veiling them in pseudonyms. *Revelry* (1927), by *Chicago*'s author, Maurine Watkins, dealt with the oil-land swindles that created

President Warren G. Harding's Watergate, "Teapot Dome" (after one of the grifted sites, in Wyoming; the other two were Elk Hills and Buena Vista, both in California). *Spellbound* (1927), an English play banned in England, recalled the sensational trial of a woman and her young lover, who killed her old dud of a husband; and *The Song Writer* (1928) was Irving Berlin, courting his debutante, Ellin Mackay.

There were other such titles; we have toured a few already. Though not as precisely delineated as a scandal bomb detonated in Winchell, the à clef piece functioned rather like celebrity appearances on television talk shows today. The behavior may be scripted and even wholly misleading: but it *is* contact. Certainly, the Spewacks might have written *Boy Meets Girl* as another Hollywood spoof without heaving heard of Hecht and MacArthur. But who would have conceived of *The Royal Family* if the Drews and Barrymores hadn't already existed? That play is *made of* Drews and Barrymores.

Was it a breakthrough of some kind when boxer Jack Dempsey himself appeared in *The Big Fight* (1928)? Vaudeville had long been a stopover for notables of various kinds trying show biz, usually on their way down. *The Big Fight,* however, was Big Broadway, a David Belasco staging at the vast Majestic that climaxed with a bout at Madison Square Garden. The champ was no actor, though as pugilist "Tiger" Dillon he could not be called miscast. But what role would be right for Alexander Woollcott? None: and that didn't stop producer-director Guthrie McClintic from putting Woollcott into S. N. Behrman's *Brief Moment* (1931). In this typical Behrman farrago, socialite (Robert Douglas) marries nightclub singer (Francine Larrimore), provisioning a disquisition upon class as it obtains among the *gratin* of New York's cultural scene—Arthur Miller's "talent and the interesting rich" at its most basic.

Behrman's script description of the Woollcott character, Harold Sigrift, specifically describes Woollcott and even says—no doubt waggishly—that Woollcott "conceivably might play him." But it is inconceivable. Woollcott an actor? On the contrary, Behrman later called him "one of the busiest non-actors in the country," what with his *New Yorker* column, various freelance one-offs, and his radio show as the Town Crier. Note that title, comparable to the post that Winchell held, for on one level gossip about celebrities made the national public into a sort of media village in which, instead of everyone's knowing everyone else, everyone knew *about* everyone else. About, that is, everyone else who mattered.

Brief Moment was another à clef piece, "suggested," Brooks Atkinson thought, "by a recent episode in New York life" involving Otto Kahn's son Roger Wolfe Kahn. As always with Behrman, there was something to praise and something to deplore. The same old things, really: "the subtlety of [his] intellect, the freshness of his wit" drew praise from the *Sun*'s Richard Lockridge, who went on to deplore Behrman's "almost complete lack of any real dramatiic sense."

In fact, *Brief Moment* squeaked into the black only because people came to see Woollcott. Not only a nonactor but a terrible one, he lolled about, waved a pudgy arm, and spoke to the audience rather than to his fellow players. Arthur Pollock thought him "a fat Greek chorus." It didn't matter: he was Alexander Woollcott, on display in full true—for of course Behrman knew his star well enough to unveil him just as he was. Note how closely Behrman's Harold Sigrift anticipates Kaufman and Hart's Sheridan Whiteside, also modeled on the real-life noise of Woollcott. Hero Roderick Deane claims to have found in his club singer an energizing force, a palliative to his round of personal failures in the field of music, aviation, fine art:

SIGRIFT: Will the prima donna of the Hotsy Totsy change all that?
RODERICK: I don't say she will. . . . She may turn me down flat. (Sigrift just whistles) Well, she may!
SIGRIFT: If she turns you down, my blossom—then I'm Skippy.
RODERICK: She's lovely. . . . She's unspoiled by civilization.
SIGRIFT: Unspoiled by it? She hasn't encountered it yet.

Brief Moment undoubtedly would have failed without its virtual thespian, but Behrman waited six seasons before inviting Woollcott back to the stage—this time *expecting* his guest to accept—for *Wine of Choice* (1938). Woollcott duly appeared. Such stunts rarely support sequels, however, and this time fewer ticketbuyers responded.

Anyway, the à clef piece is supposed to present copies of its subjects. It doesn't do to have the subjects themselves breaking through the fourth wall from that Neverland they call reality. Copies are reassuring; copies can act. Better, copies don't suddenly decide, right in the middle of the run, when director Guthrie McClintic is otherwise engaged, to emulate their dear friends the Lunts by throwing lines away to achieve the Higher Sophistication, unfortunately without the Lunts' expertise in vocal projection.

Even if the subject has presence, isn't the point of these charades to *game* with the truth? They're variations on a theme. What if Walter Winchell played himself on stage—as he did in a few movies? Hollywood can handle Winchell; movies are made in Neverland. But a theatrical Winchell was far more welcome digested, dramatized, and impersonated: in *Blessed Event* (1932). This comedy told of Alvin Roberts (Roger Pryor), a gossip columnist who invents slang and foretells to the day when prominent women will give birth. "Blessed event" was a Winchell idiom, and some of the critics called him the play's real star. One review thought Pryor made Winchell "both believable and likable," going on to "And that, if you know your Alvin Roberts, is no mean achievement."

The play's two unknown authors were not presumed to have had the exposure to their model that Behrman had to Woollcott. But everyone in America knew what Winchell sounded like: a raspy voice barking out The Column. In short: Lee Tracy, show biz's official brash newspaperman. Playing Alvin Roberts in Warner Bros.' *Blessed Event* movie, rushed out within months of the play's closing, Tracy warns a hospital nurse, "I want the names the very minute they book the room!"

Surely the real Winchell worked through subordinates. What's authentic about the various versions of Winchell that decorate theatre, film, and lit in the 1930s especially is the atmosphere of New York one-upmanship. Where Winchell goes, wisecrack follows, not only from the master but from all around him, for in a Winchell world everyone wants to be Winchell:

> ALVIN: Do you know how many Jews there *are* in New York?
> HIS SECRETARY: (dryly) There must be dozens.

Doesn't that remind us exactly of the byplay between columnist John Lithgow and *his* secretary (Joanna Glushak) in the aforementioned musical *Sweet Smell of Success*—another study of Winchell?

We should note as well *Shooting Star* (1933), the life of Jeanne Eagels, though management denied it. Another pair of unknown writers told of Julie Leander (Francine Larrimore), who, inspired by Duse's Camille, deserts husband and child and sleeps with a producer not unlike Sam H. Harris to win the role of Carrie Smith in one of those East of Suez jobs, *Port of Call*. That is: the role of Sadie Thompson in the Sam H. Harris production of *Rain*—and Larrimore's *Port of Call* costume in a dressing-room scene re-created Eagels' *Rain* getup. The new star wows Broadway and the road in *Port of Call* for four years, just as Eagels did in *Rain*. The twisty plot veers from the Eagels saga to pair Larrimore with a *Brief Moment*esque socialite for whom she gives up the stage; but he deserts her and she dies the customary death.

Shooting Star was something of an epic, with a huge cast, plenty of scenery, and a plot so busy that the critics generally admitted to having missed the last two or three twists to go off and write it all up, filled with misgivings. In fact, the show followed Eagels' true tale so closely that the reviewers confidently guessed that Larrimore reached a finale of devolution on booze and drugs. Thus the title contains an unforgivably sordid pun; but there was a sunny bit in that Larrimore's own children Tyke and Tuppence alternated in a touching cameo as Leander's offspring.

The work that put the most celebrities on view was a musical, *Jubilee* (1935): what if the king, queen, prince, and princess of a place not unlike England ran off with, respectively, Elsa Maxwell, Johnny Weissmuller, Noël Coward, and, say, Ginger Rogers? That last character is indistinctly inscribed, but Maxwell, Weissmuller (at first in a wolfskin loincloth), and Coward are unmistakably on hand, characterized—once again, for this is crucial—by writers who partied with them.

Jubilee was a sort of musical-comedy version of The Column, an exposé of the celebs who attend eccentrically themed balls and sleep around and conquer the dance floor during the beguine (who but a celeb even knew how to dance it?) and get into mischief on a public beach. *Jubilee*'s authors, Cole Porter and Moss Hart, agreed with Walter Winchell on one thing if no other: even celebs want to know other celebs. "I've *turned* on singers," the Porter-Hart Elsa Maxwell avers, dismissing the very notion of Grace Moore. But she hasn't, really: no celeb turns on another without some intense personal reason, because American fame is a zany heaven where the only morality is the act of what we might call celebrifying: whereby fame creates more fame, inducting new recruits and toning up the veterans. Winchell and his fellow columnists celebrified in scandal and the discovery of talent, *Life* magazine in showing the faces, and Porter in the list song. Hart celebrified by concocting stories about the joyous perquisites of fame but also about the depression that seizes those denied them. Hart's most typical writing is carefree *Jubilee*; his most important writing is *Lady in the Dark* (1941), a musical about a magazine editor suffering a nervous breakdown who thinks her problem is a lack of glamor. It isn't. Her problem is the only problem anyone has: one parent disdained her and the other parent enabled the disdain. The Lady's problem is thus a lack of self-belief. But in American culture, fame *is* self-belief; one doesn't need anything else, not even supportive parents. To be able to celebrify is power. To be celebrified is to be loved: to enter the light.

Moss Hart was perhaps even more the Town Crier than Alexander Woollcott, for it was Hart who made American art out of American celebrity. Most of his work is haunted by these characters who show us what the famous do, how they feel, and—most important—how we feel when they like us. We are celebrified, like the lady in the dark whose dream of love is marriage to a movie star. All looks and no content, this Hollywood fantasy has a fantasy name, Randy Curtis, and was originally played by Victor Mature, whom David Thomson has described as "simple, crude and heady." Yet the era-defining celeb was usually complex, polished, and of a direct appeal—not a Hollywood fantasy but a real-life one. Someone whose restless attention spans and urgent caprices explain the superiority of being Different. One of the reason the 1930s is filled with screwballs as well as wisecrackers is that both types Get Away With It. *The Women*'s Mary Haines has to give up her pride to win back her husband; had Clare Boothe made Mary a wisecracker, she wouldn't have lost him in the first place.

Moss Hart thus doesn't waste our time with "normal" celebs, second of all because he only invented Randy Curtis to demonstrate the irony of the lady in the dark's romantic longings, and first of all because there were no normal celebs. (Indeed, the lady finally realizes that the man she loves isn't prominent or glamorous at all, but simply her irritatingly masculine managing editor, a rufftuff in a suit.) When men other than Moss Hart wrote musical revues, they homed in on human foible or the news of the day. When Moss Hart wrote *As Thousands Cheer* (1933), he filled it with notables to be impersonated by the show's stars, Marilyn Miller, Clifton Webb, Helen Broderick, and Ethel Waters. These four (and a few featured players) presented Joan Crawford, Douglas Fairbanks Jr., the Rockefellers, Mahatma Gandhi, Aimee Semple McPherson, Josephine Baker, Herbert and Lou Hoover (on White House moving-out day), and even King George V and Queen Mary, who confront the Prince of Wales after reading that he's engaged . . . in Walter Winchell's column!

Americans can be defined as a people who idolize nonconformist behavior in public figures while hating it in their neighbors. We applaud, say, an Alexander Woollcott, with his la-di-da arrogance, flowery effusions, and ruthless put-downs; but we don't want him doing it in our living room. So, muses Moss Hart, what happens when Alexander Woollcott actually *gets into your living room*? We know it was Hart's idea because he got first billing in his and Kaufman's *The Man Who Came To Dinner* (1939), in which Woollcott, as the great and terrible Sheridan Whiteside (Monty Woolley), terrorizes the Stanley family and various other citizens of Mesalia, Ohio. It's a classic premise for farce, as a constant series of irruptions into the action by major and minor characters maintains a Feydeauvien energy. Any good writing team could get a play out of it, framed by Whiteside's being cooped up with the Stanleys because he broke his hip on their icy doorstep and, in the show's final seconds, does so again and is carried back inside amid the customary bedlam as the curtain falls.

But this team wants a really fine play, it seems, for the authors swell their scene with two abetting throughlines, either of which is a story in itself. One is a sweet little romance tucked into the uproar, between Whiteside's secretary (Edith Atwater) and Mesalia's newspaper editor (Theodore Newton). It's particularly sweet because we sense that the secretary, Maggie, isn't really enjoying her invitation to the Mad Hatter's tea party of the famous. Whiteside knows them all, so Maggie knows them all. Yet all she wants to be is Mrs. Stephen Haines. Unable to replace this managerial gem who keeps his chaos functional, Whiteside tries to bust up the romance, and the pain and despair that she feels when he seems to be succeeding gives the Maggie of any revival something solid to bite into. Her counterpart in *You Can't Take It With You* has no such opportunity, for she's an ingenue with her whole life ahead of her. She can lose a boss' son or two. Maggie, older and less adorable ("business-like-looking" is her faint praise in the authors' stage directions), may have only this chance, and we truly worry for her.

That is, we would worry if we didn't already know the piece, as they say, cold. What American theatregoer doesn't? Simply to quote its exhibition lines ("Go in and read the life of Florence Nightingale and learn how unfitted you are for your chosen profession") is to play chicken with cliché. Yet the returning veteran may be surprised to note how many Names the authors invoke to establish Whiteside's seat at the head of the fabulous table. A partial listing: H. G. Wells, Felix Frankfurter, Jascha Heifetz, Katharine Cornell, Elsa Schiaparelli, Anthony Eden, Arturo Toscanini, Kirsten Flagstad, Sacha Guitry, Hattie Carnegie, Louella Parsons, Gertrude Stein, Aldous Huxley, Salvador Dali, Shirley Temple, Ethel Waters, and, sine qua non, the Lunts.

Thus, like *Jubilee, The Man Who Came To Dinner* spins a loopy yarn about celebs getting into mischief while its true intention is to give the public a taste of the celebrity lifestyle in "virtual" close-up. It's not What if Alexander Woollcott got into your living room as much as What if you got into his?

This brings us to *The Man's* second throughline, which physically produces three of the most important people in show biz, all bizarre figures in one way or another: Gertrude Lawrence, Harpo Marx, and—as we already know—Noël Coward. Of course, they are (very thinly) disguised. As stated earlier, Coward shows up in one of his "Beverly" *noms de pièce*. Gertie retains her real-life scan as Lorraine Sheldon, and Harpo becomes Banjo (with unseen brothers Wacko and Sloppo). Because the shock of a very king of wisecrack let loose in the Midwest keeps the action robust, the authors can delay the first of these guest-star visits till midway in the second act, when Lorraine (Carol Goodner) parades in to Whiteside's "Take that skunk off and tell me everything." Beverly (John Hoysradt) actually performs a Noël Coward number at the Stanleys' piano, a flawlessly observed piece of pastiche called "What Am I To Do?," by Hart's *Jubilee* pal, Cole Porter.*

Kaufman and Hart were prescient in their choice of à clef models, using not the ephemeral grandee but those who would prove classic. One reason why *The Man* is still vital today is that its neon twilight of star impersonations keeps alive the essential nature of the day's nobility: their quirkiness. Imagine if Whiteside's visitors were based on the likes of Grover Whalen or H. V. Kaltenborn. You can't—not because these once go-everywhere names mean nothing today, but because they lack the thirties personality. We think of Clark Gable's maverick authority, by which his behavioral code outcocks yours; or Claudette Colbert's endless wonder at the sheer vanity of men. Or,

---

* It's turnabout, for Coward wrote his own set of lyrics to Porter's "Let's Do It," and a few of the usurping couplets outshine the originals. One of Coward's inspirations *begins* with a punchline, "Snow White felt she must do it," then tops itself with "Seven dwarfs together just do it."

as here, Noël Coward's suave allegiance to the most original of sins or Gertrude Lawrence's ability to enchant the house while cheating and slutting her way through real life. This is even to admit that Kaufman and Hart's Harpo (David Burns) is extremely approximate. When he makes his entrance (in the *third* act!), his first good line, to Whiteside's nurse, is pure Groucho: "Come to my room in half an hour and bring some rye bread." And much of the rest of his part sounds like Jimmy Durante, who ended up playing it in the extremely faithful Warner Bros. version.

Banjo is nonetheless an astonishing invention, not only the shortest lead in any title in the American repertory but a mating of whirlwind and deus ex machina. The usual convoluted farce plotting has led Whiteside to use Lorraine as a siren to woo the newspaperman away from Maggie; but now Whiteside suffers a change of heart. Even a sense of guilt, possibly for the first time in his life. It is Banjo who facilitates the removal of Lorraine, in a mummy case, a Christmas present from yet another VIP, the Khedive of Egypt. ("What did you send *him*?" asks Banjo. "Grant's Tomb?") Note that this absurd fantasy brings all four of the à clef figures into the love plot: Woollcott and Gertrude Lawrence to menace it, Noël Coward to make the first failed attempt to save it, then a Marx Brother to succeed. In effect, the authors have *humanized* their celebs, quite an achievement, as Woollcott was one of the most improbable humans ever to walk the planet.

Then, too, the masterstroke of introducing a new principal in the last fifteen minutes of the running time renovates a form that congenitally suffers from feeble third acts. Traditional farce loads the gun in the first act, fires in the second, and has little more to do in the third than clean, oil, and store. It's limited fun. *The Man Who Came To Dinner,* however, is an evening-length turkey shoot, a fireworks of wisecrack that almost succeeds in concealing a terrible secret: the screwball has feelings.

He has to: because the play would be unbearable without this happy ending. Perhaps we need to see, for once, the wisecracker rendered powerless by the Clueless Hetero. Mr. Stanley has a warrant for Whiteside's eviction and two deputy sheriffs to execute it—but Whiteside has yet to get rid of Lorraine to redeem his betrayal of Maggie. This is genuinely expert plotting, because thus far *The Man Who Came To Dinner* has been little more than a charade made on the title: a Whiteside vaudeville of his baroque quibbles and hurdy-gurdy tantrums, with no more story than that unexpected romance for Maggie. Now, suddenly, the narrative is as suspenseful as that of a whodunit, all the more amusing in that Whiteside is now Lorraine's worst enemy while she has no idea what's going on:

> STANLEY: *Five* minutes, Mr. Whiteside! (He indicates the mummy case) Including *that*. (He leaves)
> LORRAINE: Why, what was all that about? Who is that man?
> WHITESIDE: He announces the time every few minutes. I pay him a small sum.

Getting Lorraine into the mummy case is one of the funniest bits in American comedy, for she herself steps into it. Seized by the historical grandeur of the woman who once occupied this coffin—who "lived and loved, full of the same passions, fears, jealousies, hates" as Lorraine—she crosses her arms in faithful mummy style. Then, just as Whiteside and Banjo simultaneously realize that they hold the key to the show's climax, Lorraine steps out.

Of course, by now the entire audience is involved in the plot, and no sooner is Lorraine cajoled back inside and secured therein than the authors spring a last surprise: Stanley's loony sister, one of the many subaltern characters who have been wandering into and out of the action, turns out to be a former ax murderer. (Whiteside, an aficionado of violent crime, has finally recognized her.) With the wisecracker thus restored to power, the reconquered Stanley must serve at Whiteside's pleasure in helping Banjo carry off mummy Lorraine; and the way is clear for the final curtain of wonder, panic, and comic despair.

The Man Who Came To Dinner does not travel well. At least it isn't difficult to cast, once one has the proper Whiteside. *Jubilee* calls for stars, but the Bucks County Playhouse gave *The Man* in 1941 with Kaufman as Whiteside, Hart as Beverly Carlton, and Harpo Marx as himself. *Harpo speaks!* (Edith Atwater repeated her Maggie, lending the production professional confidence.) Even with extra matinées, the Playhouse did turnaway business. Yet in 1988, England's Royal Shakespeare Company, led by John Wood, got fewer laughs out of the show than Judith Anderson did in *Medea*. Do the English simply not get wisecrack comedy, or do they dislike its anarchy? English comedy tends to treat the pacification of disorder—*The Taming of the Shrew, A Midsummer Night's Dream, The School For*

Scandal, Blithe Spirit. Wisecrack comedy creates disorder, which is arguably another word for classless democracy.

Gentle Philip Barry is the last writer one would associate with wisecrack; his people are more arch than sarcastic. Yet he absorbed the style, and a mild version of its disorder, in *The Philadelphia Story* (1939). One of our classic comedies, it is nonetheless vexed by chaotic plotting, and as late as the day of the New York premiere, the person around whom the whole thing revolved feared that it would be a vast flop.

That was Katharine Hepburn, arguably the epitome of the eccentric celeb that dominated American culture in the early middle of the twentieth century. Because Donald Ogden Stewart's screenplay for MGM's *Philadelphia Story* movie (1940) straightened out Barry's coiled storytelling, we think of the play as a look at the heroine's growth from an overly judgmental goddess into a compassionate human being. In fact, the play's original premise was a look at an invasion of privacy, as reporters from *Destiny* magazine—apparently a merging of Henry Luce's *Time, Fortune,* and *Life*—threaten to "expose" a Main Line family. Hence the play's title: the journalist pair, a writer and a photographer, are to turn in The Philadelphia Story by getting the dope on the Lord family, newsworthy because of the remarriage of debutante Tracy Lord.

That's the Hepburn role, and it's worth remembering that Hepburn's mystique drew partly on the arrogance that is Tracy Lord's salient quality. So *The Philadelphia Story* is as much "made on" Hepburn as *The Man Who Came To Dinner* is made on Alexander Woollcott. That's all they have in common, for *The Man* is an absolutely frivolous work. It never asks dangerous questions, such as What did Woollcott do for sex? *The Philadelphia Story,* however, scrutinizes Tracy Hepburn—at the commission of Hepburn herself. After the merry gender-punning of *The Warrior's Husband,* not to mention such film roles as a faith healer in the Ozark Mountains, an adulterous aviatrix in a bumblebee suit, Mary of Scotland, and a boy, Hepburn apparently wanted to play what she was: fiercely appealing but difficult.

Here, as never before, we come up close to the à clef subject. The charm of Barry's play lies largely in Hepburn's relationship with four very different men—her former husband (Joseph Cotten), her stuffy husband-to-be (Frank Fenton), her errant father (Nicholas Joy), and the male of the two reporters (Van Heflin). These bonds are mercurial, ever shifting, as suits the heroine's restless intensity; she is, in the best *and* the worst sense, unpredictable. For example, she ends in trading in her fiancé for her ex-husband—but Barry's producers, the Theatre Guild, thought Hepburn better matched with the rough-edged Heflin than with the suave Cotten, and asked Barry to change the ending. He didn't; and MGM took out love-plot-logic insurance by gentling the reporter down to James Stewart and casting irresistible Cary Grant as the ex-husband. Now Hepburn *had* to remarry her ex, who bears a name only Philip Barry could get away with: C. K. Dexter Haven.

Heflin and his reporter partner (Shirley Booth) are wisecrackers set into the usual Barry troupe of perfectly spoken aristos who are never rude by accident. If twenties wisecrack style gave the powerless some traction in his dealings with the powerful (from the cultured elite to gangsters), the more articulate thirties wisecrack reinforms the battle, which now pits the liberal against the conservative. To make it interesting, Barry tips the leftist Heflin into the same self-righteousness that afflicts Hepburn. But she melts him: because he melts her.

The mistress of the cut direct, the snub nuancé, and the rebuff *a mezzo forte*, Tracy Lord is surely the greatest role that Barry ever wrote; and this was not the first time that Hepburn inspired him. Some portion of celeb culture was created by its promoters—Winchell, Luce, Hollywood publicists. But some other portion was created in the sheer freaky charm of the celebs themselves. It's a truism, of course—yet when Hepburn first showed up, no one got her. She seemed less special than ungainly.

It's worth a pause to inspect the rise of Hepburn, as an introduction to the broader consideration of the Broadway-Hollywood connection coming up in the next chapter and also because much of what happened to Hepburn typifies the opportunities open to actors at this time. For instance, Hepburn's first performing job, after work with the Bryn Mawr drama club, took her to Baltimore and one of the last of the stock companies, run by Edwin Knopf. This was 1928, and there was so much theatre going on that an attractive young woman could get an engagement simply by planting herself in a manager's path with a letter of introduction (which, in the event, Knopf didn't even read). This was not a fly-by-night company, or so comfortably "regional" that it lacked standards. Mary Boland's New York hit *Women Go On Forever* (1927) had just closed, and now Boland was gracing Knopf's marquee; Hepburn appeared with her in two titles, a superb way for an amateur to scope out star style. Kenneth MacKenna (Jo Mielziner's brother and the original lead in *Merrily We Roll Along*) was also in the troupe, and he sent the as yet awkward Hepburn to Frances Robinson-Duff, doyenne of New York's acting coaches.

By her own admission, Hepburn completely lacked confidence, yet, paradoxically, was shameless in putting herself forward. Here was one woman who never even considered accepting the destiny of a Mary Haines. Hepburn did marry at this time, but very obscurely, and unlike most wives she lived not through her husband's life but through hers. (Not till later, in an unvowed liaison with Spencer Tracy, did Hepburn "wed"—at that, to one who would share but not lead her life.)

Hepburn now went through an astonishing series of upsets and victories: from understudying the lead to going on and being fired after the first performance of Knopf's production of *The Big Pond* (1928); nonetheless impressing first-nighter Mr. J. J. Shubert but turning down his offer of a five-year contract; finally making it to Broadway in a one-week flop called *These Days* (1928); understudying Hope Williams in Philip Barry's *Holiday* and going on but once, on the post-Broadway tour; accepting and then rejecting a lead in a Theatre Guild offering, S. N. Behrman's *Meteor* (1929), to play the heroine of *Death Takes a Holiday* (1929), getting fired during the tryout; winning the lead in *The Animal Kingdom* and learning that, indeed, Barry had modeled the inspiringly independent Daisy Sage on Hepburn herself, then to discover that Leslie Howard didn't like her. He, too, dealt in the rebuff *a mezzo forte:* trying to oblige the star, Hepburn asked Howard, about a line of script, "What would you like me to do here, Mr. Howard?" He replied, in an eerie anticipation of someone else's words in *Gone With the Wind,* "I really don't give a damn what you do, my dear." Hepburn was fired before rehearsals had finished—fired from a role that Barry made on her!—and when she called Barry he told her, "To be brutally frank, you weren't very good."

Did he mean she was Different? Or was she still too raw, unable to metabolize her many warring instincts into a finished portrayal? "Spark the part" was her motto. "Strike it. Light it." Yet it didn't come together thus till they gave her the role she was uniquely qualified for in looks and temperament, that of the Amazon princess we met in *The Warrior's Husband.* Hepburn was Hepburn-ready at last.

She was, even so, on the Different side, even at RKO, the Different studio in its unusually Sophisticated style. Paramount, too, was Sophisticated, but above all elegant. RKO was edgy.* In fact, RKO was the most New York–oriented of Hollywood outfits, most determined to dress up in the glamor of New York. Not Walter Winchell's New York: Hepburn's. Notice, then, how quickly this Different Hepburn got to Broadway, but also how logical it seemed that she bring Broadway to Hollywood. For when Hollywood brought together Philip Barry's ritzy wastrels with the coarse world of the proletarian striver, wrapping them in Hepburn's wish for freedom from authority and adding a purification process in which the rich learn to walk in the proletariat's shoes, the result was that Great American Genre, screwball comedy.

Why didn't Broadway's playwrights invent it first? Because the geography wasn't available on stage. Not till the camera could show us precisely where in real life the Maverick Newspaperman takes the Runaway Heiress—you know: Clark Gable and Claudette Colbert on a road trip in *It Happened One Night* (1934)—could the sociopolitical transaction of screwball comedy be realized. Then, to top off, doesn't the form reach its apex in *Bringing Up Baby* (1938), with *It Happened One Night*'s gender plot reversed so that Maverick Heiress Hepburn takes Academic Plop Cary Grant into Hepburn's wonderland version of real life? Another piece of Broadway that Hollywood utilized in formulating the screwball genre was the disguise that Sophistication doted on, and at one point Grant is detoured into a frilly peignoir. Commentators have spent three generations reckoning exactly what Grant means when he says, "I just went gay all of a sudden"; more explicitly informative are the getups that he and Hepburn don when they run around Hepburn's aunt's estate looking for a lost dinosaur bone. Grant is ready for the baronial hunt and Hepburn appears to have mugged Luise Rainer on the set of *The Good Earth* and stolen her clothes. Thus, Grant and Hepburn dress as the opposite of what they are: the commanding hero and the Chinese bride. On the contrary, it's Hepburn who wears the pants in this story, a not wholly unexpected conceit from producer-director Howard Hawks but unthinkable on Broadway at the time. Isn't *The Philadelphia Story* a kind of *Taming of the Shrew*, essentially conservative even with Van Heflin's Maverick Newspaperman?

---

* The typical Paramount director was Ernst Lubitsch, suave to a fault. RKO was too rich a place to have a typical director, but it did have the greatest of the uncelebrated Golden Age directors, John Cromwell. He was in charge of one of Hepburn's most bizarre and fascinating thirties flops, *Spitfire* (1934), the one about the Ozark Mountains faith healer.

Barry had his nonconformist side, we know; but he didn't like to mix his classes. Screwball comedy is subversively egalitarian.

One odd note in all this is that the screwball films were largely built around movie stars—people like Grant, Gable, Colbert, Irene Dunne, and Melvyn Douglas who began in the theatre then abandoned it or, like Douglas, returned only after their film career sagged. Hepburn, perhaps the outstanding screwball because of her merrily reuthless wrecking in *Bringing Up Baby,* maintained a lifelong affair with the stage, even at the height of her reign with Tracy at MGM. She never stopped visiting Broadway: in more Barry, in Shakespeare, in boulevardier comedy, in a musical. And Hepburn herself uttered (about Fred Astaire and Ginger Rogers) the line that, if twisted, explains the matter: Broadway gave stars class and Hollywood gave them sex.

Hepburn was short of sex. Not till *The Philadelphia Story* did she even know how her public liked her, especially the moviegoers. Hepburn's most bizarrely mannered portrayal, in *Morning Glory* (1933), actually won her an Oscar, and her hits were as unalike as the bluestocking melodrama *Little Women* (1935) and the very nearly tragic comedy *Alice Adams* (1935). Who was she?

A return to the class of Broadway was Hepburn's Austerlitz, because she had bought the screen rights from Barry before Hollywood could Jean Arthur it. So, as the play took off on its tryout, Hepburn was already California-bound. But she wasn't confident even now, or especially now, for she had toured in Helen Jerome's adaptation of *Jane Eyre,* also for the Guild, during the 1936–37 season, and though it did terrific business it didn't dare come in.

Why? Because everyone wanted Katharine Hepburn to fail? Was she simply too Different, even too rebellious against the rule of men? Other strong women of Broadway made some obeisance to the cautions. Fontanne and Cornell married; Hepburn married but not really. She married so she wouldn't have to marry. Remember, the Nineteenth Amendment to the Constitution, giving women the vote, was barely a generation old when Hepburn and *The Philadelphia Story* arrived in New York. Everyone got ready while she kept murmuring to herself the fantasy that this wasn't The Street but a mere tryout town, where no one hoped you'd fail. In Baltimore and such places, they clapped when the star entered, but Tracy Lord has no star entrance. She is to be not celebrified but humbled, democratized the better to be relished for being special. To put it bluntly, she has to become a little less Different. No more *Spitfire*—come now *State of the Union, Pat and Mike, Summertime*.

So *The Philadelphia Story*'s curtain rose on the sitting room of the Lord mansion, with Hepburn in view, sitting in an armchair with a leather writing kit on her lap, turning out thank-yous for her wedding gifts. The first nighters didn't give her a warm welcome, but after three hours of fun they were licked. The show was raved and Hepburn's career secured. No one had wanted her to fail, after all.

Seven

Having Wonderful Time:

THE POPULAR STAGE

In the 1930s, Broadway and Hollywood enjoyed a unique cultural and economic synchronization. Earlier, film was silent and thus unacquainted with the sheer verbal communication of the stage; by the 1940s, the movies were made of forms and personnel with little or no theatrical roots. Thus, Orson Welles and his Mercury Theatre troupe made their name in the 1930s on The Street; but their work on *Citizen Kane* (1941) marks an ideal demarcation point in the separation of screen from stage in the history of American narrative art. The film is not only an original—it was *conceived* so kinetically that even its key line, "Rosebud!," is really a key shot: the child's sole enabling innocent memory is tossed into the furnace as the man himself goes to hell.

So it is the 1930s when theatre and film share history; one cannot recount the one's without the other's. The first reason why is the most obvious: suddenly talking, Hollywood needed scripts to film and actors with viva voce command. Also obviously, Broadway in its Depression desperately needed Hollywood money. And note that the movie studios didn't buy just hits: the studios bought *plays*. Sometimes it seemed as though they'd take anything that opened; a manager could actually sell a ten-thousand-dollar flop to the movies for two or three times that amount. A crime drama by the unknown Marie Baumer called *Penny Arcade* (1930) ran three weeks but had caught the eye of Al Jolson. He snapped up the movie rights for more than the production had lost and resold them to his studio, Warner Bros., for a profit, recommending that the Bros. take along two promising players from the stage cast. In the retitled *Sinner's Holiday,* James Cagney and Joan Blondell made their screen debuts.

The second reason why the 1930s saw a fusion of theatre and film is that theatregoers who had scorned the movies were now becoming moviegoers. It took a generation for "the flickers" to emerge as an alternative art, though opinionmakers still disdained cinema as ignorant and silly. Not till James Agee in the 1940s did a respected writer take film seriously, preceding Pauline Kael in the expansion of a personal response to movies into a series of position papers on the working of the universe. In a kind of intellectuals' back formation, various thirties movie critics have lately been reclaimed from oblivion to function as prophets; back in the day, however, they had no discernible effect on the box office.

The attraction of the movies to theatregoers in the 1930s was simply the movies themselves. Part of it was the spendthrift casting; Broadway was base camp to Hollywood's peak. When the obscure producer Hugo W. Romberg put on the busy but unimportant Wilson Collison's East of Suez melodrama *Red Dust* (1928) in a pitiably out-of-the-way booking at Daly's on Sixty-third Street, the stage didn't teem with headliners: Curtis Cooksey, Jerome Collamore, Lenore Meyrick-Sorsby, and Sydney Shields. *Red Dust* posted its casting call at the height of the biggest season in theatre history, so all the stars, journeymen, and promising newcomers were working: and not in *Red Dust.* Still, this is a penetratingly dreary quartet, and the play closed in a week.

What would have been the best cast that a neophyte manager could assemble in 1928 for a show set on a rubber plantation in French Indo-China? Positions available: the alpha male who runs the place; the new hireling from Europe; his wife, secretly in love with the alpha male; and the femme fatale who thickens the plot. Perhaps Henry Hull, Russell Hardie, Helen Gahagan, and the as yet inexperienced Barbara Stanwyck? It has the depth of ability without the height of charisma, especially when compared with MGM's version of 1932, retaining the setting but Americanizing the characters as Clark Gable, Gene Raymond, Mary Astor, and Jean Harlow.

In supporting players as well, Hollywood cast distinctively, for instance assigning the *Boy Meets Girl* producer in the film adaptation to the amiably uninflected Ralph Bellamy. This performance brings the Clueless Hetero to a completion so absolute that Bellamy creates something never before thought possible or even necessary: the opposite of Kabuki.

We have already seen how Hollywood's "opening up" of stagebound storylines created screwball comedy by supplying the essential thematic element of The Adventure—the "kidnapping" of the Runaway Heiress in *It Happened One Night*; or the "bringing up" of Baby the leopard; or even one Adventure that isn't shown, the "shipwrecked on a desert island" sojourn in *My Favorite Wife*.

But in fact virtually any play could be improved on at least one level through simple landscaping—telling stories within the infinite space of film. This was not simply a matter of enacting narrative in realistic locations: that narrative could now include scenes that stage scripts surely would have included had set-change technology been more flexible. Was there really a presentation of *The Good Earth* (1932) on Broadway, in the genre of the literary adaptation, a Theatre Guild offering by the father-and-son team of Owen and Donald Davis? Pearl Buck's sprawling tale of Chinese farming life in times of famine and revolution had been a bestseller the previous year, and many theatregoers were avid readers who would enjoy collecting Buck anew in lively form. All declared the makeup jobs on Claude Rains, Alla Nazimova, Sydney Greenstreet, Henry Travers, and the rest of a big cast were astonishingly effective, and the typical Guild team of director Philip Moeller and set designer Lee Simonson functioned well. True, the Davises did not vastly honor Buck: George Jean Nathan likened their work to making a novel out of an Earl Carroll *Vanities* revue. Then, too, Nazimova utilized that deadpan singsong we recall from Florence

Reed's Mother Goddam and, on opening night, slowed up out of nervousness and drove the critics crazy.

Anyway, how does one *stage* Buck's sprawling story? It takes more than coolie hats: it takes a movie, which of course it got, from MGM, in 1937, a year before Buck copped her Nobel Prize. Closer to home, doesn't Owen Davis' southern romance *Jezebel* (1933) need a grander field of play than the Ethel Barrymore Theatre? Tallulah Bankhead rehearsed the diva lead of the usual headstrong belle, then went ailing and ceded it to Miriam Hopkins for a two-week run in a role that won Bette Davis her second Oscar *in the film version.*

Playwrights were discovering that, even as Hollywood treated them as contemptible subordinates, it had effected a kind of technical revolution in the presentation of plays: one filmed them. Consider *The Postman Always Rings Twice* (1936), another bestseller, this time a crime thriller adapted by the novelist himself, James M. Cain. The classic setup of the hot drifter and the young wife with the problem husband—also the basis of Emile Zola's much-adapted *Thérèse Raquin*—turns on murder by automobile crash, as the two adulterers stuff her unconscious husband into his car and, simulating an "accident," run it off a cliff. Acquitted of murder, they are apprehended by Cain's moralistic twist: later they have a genuine car accident. She dies; he looks guilty; they hang him for it. The postman cometh.

How is this to be staged? Jo Mielziner, always ingenious in keeping a set-heavy production in motion, took the public to nine locations along the way of the story, including the second car crash (albeit after it had occurred). Still, this is surely another staged movie, with a story so temptingly cinematic that it has been filmed four times: as *Le Dernier Tournant,* then by Luchino Visconti as *Ossessione,* and twice in Hollywood. Ironically, a movie star, Richard Barthelmess, led the Broadway cast. More frequently, Broadway sent *its* people to the coast for The Movie, as when Robert E. Sherwood's *Abe Lincoln in Illinois* (1938) opened up beautifully around Raymond Massey's Lincoln (with Howard Da Silva as well from the stage troupe).

Could Hollywood be seen as, in part, an archive for certain important portrayals? Jumping over to musical comedy, the number of stars who filmed at least one of their stage roles is thrillingly replete—Marilyn Miller (both Sally and Sunny), Fred Astaire, Eddie Cantor and Ethel Shutta (in an astonishingly faithful preservation of a Ziegfeld stage hit, *Whoopee*), Bert Lahr, Dennis King, Ethel Merman, Ed Wynn, Joe Cook and his stooge

Dave Chasen, Irene Bordoni, Jack Haley and Zelma O'Neal (in *Follow Thru*), and June Knight among others in only the first five years of sound. True, song-and-dance talents are specialized, harder to replace. But many speaking actors as well were thought too "right" to be improved upon; who'd want to see a *Guardsman* film without the Lunts in the roles that inspired their myth? And the arguably less dazzling Otis Skinner's unnamed Poet in *Kismet*, Bela Lugosi's Dracula, and Walter Huston's Dodsworth live on in film, Skinner in both silent and talkie. Even Laura Hope Crews—whose assumption of Mary Boland's role in *Jubilee* so desolated theatregoers' interest that the show abruptly closed—commanded prestige in Hollywood. When RKO shot *The Silver Cord*, it invited Crews to repeat her grasping mother and then kept her on as a contractee for dowager roles.

Or wait. Did RKO simply fear compromising one of its more important artists with so ghastly a part? RKO's *Little Women* came out the same year as *The Silver Cord*, 1933, with Broadway's greatest gift to the movies, Katharine Hepburn, as tomboy Jo. But in casting *Little Women*'s mother, that walking valentine known as "Marmee," RKO called in Spring Byington, not Laura Hope Crews.

For that matter, did RKO import young heroes Burgess Meredith and Margo and gangster Eduardo Cianelli for its version of Maxwell Anderson's *Winterset* (1935) in 1936 because the whole show was so nutty to begin with? In other words, hire the play's three most photogenic leads and fill out the company with character actors? The play's fourth lead, the by then somewhat crazy Richard Bennett, appeared as, more or less, the judge of the Sacco and Vanzetti trial, nagging on about his rulings like Coleridge's Ancient Mariner.

It sounds Shakespearean, not least because it's in blank verse. *Winterset* even *looks* poetic, opening and closing in a dank Hooverville cowering under the Brooklyn Bridge, so star-struck that it seems headed for Judgment instead of Manhattan. And the judge is Lear, surely, in a young-love tragedy merged with cops and robbers on a newfangled sort of blasted heath. That RKO wanted to film *Winterset* at all shows us how pertinent the prestige of The Theatre was to the movies' self-interest—really, to the moguls' need to strengthen their cultural profile in defense against punitive legislation or boycott by the intolerant right. And *Winterset* was a prize winner, taking the first Drama Critics Circle Award for Best Play.

Of course, when signing Broadway actors to repeat their stage roles,

Hollywood preferred a commercial project, something no more prestigious, say, than the latest hit by Robert E. Sherwood—who took the Pulitzer Prize for *Idiot's Delight* when *Winterset* charmed the Critics Circle. Sherwood's cops-and-robbers show was *The Petrified Forest,* far more movie-friendly than anything by Anderson, though here again was a trio of young lovers (Leslie Howard, Peggy Conklin) and gangster (Humphrey Bogart). Warner Bros. picked up Howard and Bogart, both film veterans by then, and passed up Conklin for its own Bette Davis. Bogart used to joke that his early acting career consisted mainly of his appearing in sporting whites to call out a toothy "Tennis, anyone?" But the indelible Bogart is the gangster, and he faced off with another pair of young lovers in Joel McCrea and Sylvia Sydney in Samuel Goldwyn's version of Sidney Kingsley's *Dead End* (1935).

None of the three had played the show. In fact, McCrea's role, on stage, was that of a cripple called Gimpty, in some sympathy with the heroine but no romantic foil. Kingsley isn't interested in the Hollywood symmetry of the love plot; his *Dead End* is literally the utmost eastern yardage "of a New York street" as viewed from the river and, thematically, the crushing destiny of the urban poor. As Kingsley writes it, their code of survival comprises crime leading to incarceration, which creates a confirmed and lifelong lawbreaker.

It's a Warner Bros. film, clearly—but Goldwyn was always trying to outdo his competition in *their* genres. Goldwyn had his Paramount Lubitsch Chevalier-MacDonald operetta (*One Heavenly Night,* directed by George Fitzmaurice and starring Evelyn Laye and John Boles), his "three fortune-hunting dames" comedy (*The Greeks Had a Word For Them*), his Classy Brit (Ronald Colman), his Garbo (Anna Sten). *Dead End* was his comic tragedy of the mean streets, in which wisecracks season the Greek doom that Kingsley lays out. For his part, the producer and set designer of the Broadway production, Norman Bel Geddes, laid out an exhibit to outdo David Belasco, at that in the Belasco Theatre, where Bel Geddes could help himself to the deep stage that The Master had ordered up for his show-off realism, with the back of a fancy apartment building overlooking wharfside tenements bestrewn with junk and laundry—"solid," said Brooks Atkinson, "down to the ring of shoes on asphalt pavement." The orchestra pit was the East River, where a teenage gang went swimming; Billy Halop, Huntz Hall, Bobby Jordan, Gabriel Dell, and the others shocked critics and public with the shameless naturalism of their language and behavior. It was feared that the boys might be authentic street trash, imported from the slums to be exploited; they were in fact professional children, playing their parts with unusual tang.

Goldwyn couldn't resist, and the "*Dead End* kids" (swelled by Leo Gorcey, who was in the show in a small part) enjoyed a minor vogue, making two A features for the Warners with the likes of James Cagney and Ronald Reagan, then moving on to a series of kiddy-matinée programmers. Of all Kingsley's huge stage cast, the only other player Goldwyn found irresistible was on stage for about ninety seconds. Yet her contribution to the whole was so acute—so definitive of the despair of those born to nothing who achieve nothing and die like nothing that led Kingsley to the work in the first place—that Goldwyn snapped this actor up. And there's an intriguing and little known tale that goes with the matter.

Like many playwrights of this time, Kingsley staged his scripts himself, and among those who auditioned for *Dead End* was a woman who made no attempt to light up the moment with the usual "choose me!" radiance. But neither did she appear to have styled herself down for the part she was up for, that of the gangster's mother. Unwashed, carelessly dressed, and scarcely listening to Kingsley, she was beyond reach in distraction. Any other author-director might have shrugged her off, but Kingsley was too compassionate to make no attempt to help someone so obviously in distress. Somehow or other, Kingsley traced the actress to her home and gave her the part—which, despite its brevity, holds *Dead End*'s very center. For the poverty that Kingsley investigates is not inert, not scenery of life: it is an energy of destruction, and the mother of Baby-face Martin is quite simply destroyed. Looking at her son "out of dull, horrible eyes," cracking him across the face, calling him "Yuh stinkin' yellow dog yuh!," Mrs. Martin is as "dull" as she is "hostile," to quote Kingsley's stage directions. She's dead in all but dictionary technicality, and one wonders if Belasco ever got as realistic a performance out of an actor as Kingsley got out of Marjorie Main. We of today can watch her in Goldwyn's film, thinking about her dreary audition with a piece of privileged information: the death of her husband and the collapse of her career had taken a terrible bite out of her life force. She still found jobs—when she read for Kingsley she had just returned from bit work in Hollywood—but the loss of her lifemate, a psychologist who gave what we now call Motivation Lectures, was proving unbearable. The reason she was so unresponsive to Kingsley during her reading was that she had decided to commit suicide.

Main played *Dead End*'s entire nineteen-month run in New York, then relaunched a Hollywood career that would make her one of America's best-known personalities. Paradoxically, the Main identity changed from the devastated urban slattern to a vivacious rural sassafrass, whether in apron and boots or tanktown finery for the Saturday sociable. Like the *Dead End* kids, Main got a B series, with former stage bumpkin Percy Kilbride, as Ma and Pa Kettle, but Main is most famous as a sage maid, in *The Women, Honky Tonk, Meet Me in St. Louis*.

That was a close call, though. Meanwhile, Goldwyn imported another helping of Broadway, bringing in five of the original leads in *The Little Foxes* to join Bette Davis (in Tallulah Bankhead's role) for the film. These two Goldwyn straight-from-Broadway specials, both directed by William Wyler, are not only faithful souvenirs of commercial Broadway's concept of social drama but together make a statement about American society. In Kingsley, too little money—that is, too little socialization—impedes the individual's self-fulfillment. In Hellman, too much money—too much power—impedes everyone else's self-fulfillment.

Yet what different plays. *Dead End* is rude cinematic naturalism, shoving rich right up against poor and not excluding a killing (by the Feds, of Baby-face Martin) in public. *The Little Foxes* is the well-made "society" play, and its killing is the kind that the public doesn't see and that doesn't even get reported: as Regina Hubbard Giddens presides over her husband's fatal seizure, withholding from him the pills that can save him, watching his failure to survive, cheering it on as the death that she and her brothers have longed for, to clear the way for their rape of opportunity. "I'm lucky," she tells her dying husband. "I've always been lucky." *Dead End*'s shooting of Martin is a messy affair: he wounds one G-man before two others cut Martin down in a storm of lead, one of them, avenging his comrade, pumping Martin full of extra death, "literally nailing him to the ground," Kingsley demands. But the *Little Foxes* murder is quiet, a chamber killing. The victim does shout for help, but it comes out as the tiniest sliver of a whisper, and now he's very frightened because he knows he won't make it. "I'll be lucky again," Regina predicts, already thinking of how she'll out-Enron her brothers over who has the Power Among Thieves, as her husband dies.

This is of course the famously political 1930s with its stage militant, and although we'll take on most of it in the following chapter, we should sample it here, for it aligns with the Broadway-Hollywood partnership. In buying up hit plays like *Dead End* and *The Little Foxes,* the movies were disseminating their sociopolitical instruction—sharing throughout the movie business what in sound's early years seemed too often to be a Warner Bros. monopoly. Oddly, what *The Little Foxes* mainly represents today is another of those legendary performances. Too much a looker and a scandal and, some thought, a cosmetic rather than genuine talent, Bankhead had washed out at Paramount at decade's start, and Goldwyn could not have considered her. Davis of course was known for the fascination she could bring to wayward ladies, but when she saw Bankhead's Regina in New York she reluctantly concluded that Bankhead's was the only possible approach: bright and hard as a diamond. The key to the role is turned in the play's very last line, when Regina asks her daughter to stay with her that night. This young Hubbard-Giddens is one of the good guys, and she replies, "Are you afraid, Mama?" She is: but has not realized it till that moment. One could play Regina as afraid from the start, but then this merrily ruthless character makes no sense. Fear must be Regina's discovery, her realization that in fact she isn't as purely rapacious as her brothers. They are relentless hunter-gatherers who only take. Regina suddenly senses in herself a need to give, and Bankhead's portrayal was preserved for us, after all: by Bette Davis, fearful at the close.*

Considering all the parts of Broadway's relationship with Hollywood, we note one that is scarcely ever remarked: the influence of the microphone on performing style. Introduced into the recording industry in 1925 and, obviously, the means by which the sound of talkies was channeled, the mike almost instantly brought all of show biz down from 10 to 6: from Al Jolson to Bing Crosby. We've heard those legends about silent-screen stars destroyed by their voices in 1929, but their problem was more usually

---

* A tiny history of the American musical can be discerned in Goldwyn's *Little Foxes* credits. Hellman adapted her stage script; and Hellman wrote the original book to *Candide* (1956). But Goldwyn called in Arthur Kober for a script tweaking, and Kober, author of a play about a Jewish holiday camp, *Having Wonderful Time* (1937), co-wrote its musical adaptation, *Wish You Were Here* (1952). Kober's tweaking was retweaked by Dorothy Parker and Alan Campbell; Parker wrote the lyrics to *Candide*'s "Venice Gavotte." And the *Little Foxes* film score was by Meredith Willson, author of *The Music Man, The Unsinkable Molly Brown,* and other titles too few to mention. Kober was Hellman's first husband.

an operatic persona, a visual grandeur too fantastical for the wisecrackling talkie.

Those working in musical forms could pursue eccentric presentations because the musical is eccentric. However, Eddie Cantor couldn't clap and prance quite so much when his sound had to feed a mike in a fixed location. Cantor was still Cantor, but his act perforce underwent a certain physical refining; and those in the succeeding generation didn't clap and prance at all.

Actors of the speaking stage had a different problem, for they work within a real-life mimesis that no one expects of the people whooping it up in musicals. Most important, talkie naturalism demanded a comparable naturalism in theatre: Broadway must give up its grand manner or risk alienating the growing ranks of theatregoers who went to movies. At the same time—as we'll see in the next chapter—the Group Theatre's experiments with Stanislafskyan honesty furthered the revolution in American acting. From the overblown style of the turn of the century (or so we believe, on limited evidence), the actor was learning intimacy. Going by the most genuine evidence we do have—film—we discern a statement on thespian evolution from the Best Actor Oscar winner of 1929–30, the sumptuous George Arliss (for *Disraeli*) to the Best Actor of 1938, Spencer Tracy (for *Boys Town*), perhaps the most compellingly prosaic actor Hollywood ever developed. Kiss takes off the makeup.

And is it possible that Hollywood's traveling camera forced Broadway to stampede its crawling technical advances in set design—specifically, in the ease with which one location could cede the stage to the next? In the 1920s, when film was silent, the stage did not greatly fear competition, and while visionary artists like Robert Edmond Jones and Norman Bel Geddes experimented with the relationship of the visuals to the narrative, virtually no work was done, by them or others, on set change per se. Waiting in semi-darkness for the stagehands to get done with it was part of theatregoing; talk quietly among yourselves.

However, in the 1930s, movies really were stealing Broadway's public, and *suddenly*—because now it had to—the theatre devised a host of ingenious new ways to keep a story flowing from place to place. The revolving stage, apparently invented in Japan in the seventeenth century, was introduced on Broadway in the 1920s but not exploited till the following decade. It was especially popular in the revue because the cascade of acts required speedy changes of decor;* but Broadway in general took up the revolve. Note, however, that there was no correlation between this relatively avant-garde technology and the avant-garde creators. The revolve was neither ambitious nor artistic: it was efficient. Whether one singles out Eugene O'Neill, Clifford Odets, or Philip Barry, the major playwrights were comfortable in their accustomed single-set formats.

But Mae West wasn't. Her *The Constant Sinner* (1931), from West's own novel, called for sixteen different settings, mostly the bars and boudoirs in which West did her finest work. Thus, *The Constant Sinner* needed a revolve just to keep up with the adventures of one Babe Gordon (la West), involved with a boxer (the ever happily shirtless Russell Hardie), a Harlem gangster (George Givot, in blackface), and a millionaire (Walter Petrie). As often before, West's milieu was the underworld. The neighborhood is veritably hanging with crooks:

BABE: When I opened my door this morning, five of them fell in. I
     wouldn't have minded, but two of them was dead.

The critics slaughtered the piece, and it lasted only two months. "Mae West's latest personally conducted slumming party," cried the *New York American*. It "smells of depravity and degradation." Percy Hammond thought West "the world's worst actress," failing to understand that West's gig wasn't acting but an Act, probably the greatest nonstop ragging of authority known to the twentieth century. "As a show-woman she is crafty," Hammond allowed, and she "knows as much about life as Balzac, Dreiser, Victor Hugo, Samuel Shipman, or Eugene O'Neill."†

Shows utilizing a relatively simple scene plot of, say, three or four different locations and only two per act could adopt the "jackknife" format. By

---

* A clarification: it was the new-style ensemble revue of the 1930s such as *The Band Wagon* (1931) that maintained an unbroken energy level on the revolve. The older revue format, typified in the *Ziegfeld Follies,* functioned not in ensemble but as assemblies of largely unintegrated excursions, allowing one-off talent to divert the house before the traveler curtain while the set was changed behind.

† This is a freighted compliment. Obviously, Hugo and O'Neill were top names, though the former's plays were not Broadway fare. Hugo was performed only in adaptation from his fiction; we have tarried with Michael Strange's version of *L'Homme Qui Rit,* and there had been stagings of *Notre-Dame de Paris* as *Notre Dame* (1902) and of *Les Misérables* as *The Law and the Man* (1906), written and directed by and starring noted Heavy Father

this plan, each of the two sets to be employed in a given act was laid out on a platform, each platform to be swiveled on an angle into the public's eyeline or back out of sight into the wings. While one set was in use, anchored behind the proscenium, the other was resting offstage, for example at left. Then the first set, on its platform, could be moved off at stage right and the second set hauled into view (all this, of course, behind the house curtain), in a "house lights at half" interval of a minute or so. Any other sets used in the production could await use in a later act way upstage, partly dismantled, then set onto one of the jackknife platforms in their turn during intermission.

Jackknifing was ideal for a work such as John Cecil Holm and George Abbott's *Three Men on a Horse* (1935), which moves back and forth among a suburban living room, a hotel bar, and a hotel room. The tale of a meek greeting-card poet who, infallibly picking horse-race winners, gets involved with low lives, *Three Men On a Horse* would, just a few years before, have had to be written for one set. Thus the authors would have been forced to compromise their narration by locking the action into one place where all the characters—both middle-class and demimondain—could plausibly meet. And that's implausible.*

Obviously, certain plays didn't need to travel the landscape to tell their stories. *Dead End* unveils a social problem in its contrasts of class; and the fun of *The Man Who Came To Dinner* lies partly in seeing how many cra-

---

Wilton Lackaye. Novelists Balzac and Dreiser presumably represent the sexual honesty with which they and West were famously associated—but who was Samuel Shipman? The most forgotten mass-market playwright in American theatre history, Shipman was prominent in the 1910s and '20s, mostly for collaborations, at that in cheap crook plays. With John B. Hymer, Shipman made his name with the comedy *East Is West* (1918), on interracial romance in San Francisco's Chinatown. A vast hit, it featured stereotyping and old-time construction that doomed it to the tiniest of heydays. Meanwhile, *Show Boat* buffs will be glad to learn that "dicty" (meaning "dress-up glam"), Oscar Hammerstein's outstanding touch of ghetto slang, in Queenie's "C'mon Folks," turns up in West's script as well.

* The following anecdote, a dinner-party piece for playwright Howard Teichmann, shows how closely Broadway audiences follow a play's action. In the original *Three Men on a Horse,* Shirley Booth played the girl friend of one of the low lives, Sam Levene. One day, Booth's husband came visiting backstage with their little dog, which somehow got off its lead and ran onstage during the performance. Levene helped it to a practical door and gave it an exit—handed it, in fact, to the assistant stage manager, who happened to be future playwright and director Garson Kanin. *He* promptly sent dog and master out through the stage door. Now, back to our play: except the audience, wondering what that dog business was about, stopped listening to the show and began to worry about the dog. Was it

zies and patsies the authors can stuff into what we had supposed to be the most tranquil spot on earth: a midwestern living room.

But how could Clare Boothe have written *The Women* thus? The piece is not much less than a saga, with as many as five different sets per act. There was no way to play all that in jackknife style, and a revolve tends to curtail the size of the acting space, a logistical nightmare for a script with thirty-five characters. But Boothe genuinely needed a lot of "place" in her show, for one of her observations is that while the ladies of the great world have no legal or political power, they are astonishingly mobile. There's virtually nowhere they cannot go. Boothe doesn't take them to the opera or a Winchellian first night, however. She gives us the *rooms* of the women. Not where they are Seen: where they talk, from Manhattan parlor to the divorcée's day room on a Nevada dude ranch. That is, the decor is not necessarily lavish—but there is a travelogue's worth of it.

Designer Jo Mielziner's solution to this problem was the third major possibility for multi-set shows, the two-platform system. One needs a lot of wing space for this: the playing area hosts one set (on a platform to be rolled on and off stage as needed) while stagehands ready the next set on the platform that is resting offstage. For the change, behind a lowered curtain or in blackout, the onstage platform is wheeled off and the just-prepared one wheeled on. The crew then get started striking the previous set, freeing that platform for its next burden.

With all this new freedom of action, one expects to find few one-set plays at all; on the contrary, producers were attracted to them because they were so much less trouble to capitalize. One thinks of the television mogul played by Gary Marshall in the film *Soap Dish* reminding his staff that his two favorite words are "peppy" and "cheap." Those two adjectives would fairly describe the most unremembered comedy smash of the 1930s, a

---

Shirley's? Was it hungry? Wouldn't it be lonely on the other side of that door? The house went absolutely dead—at one of the decade's most popular comedies, mind you. Come back, little Sheba; and the frantic Kanin went hurtling outside to find the dog. In those days, the West Forties were dotted with bars (*Three Men On a Horse* was at the Playhouse, now demolished, on the north side of Forty-eighth Street just west of Sixth Avenue), and Kanin finally located Mr. Booth and canine in one of them. Kanin rushed them back to the Playhouse and signaled Levene: open the door and retrieve the dog. Levene did so, presumably with some ad lib such as "Had a nice walk, Kaltenborn?," and the audience, reassured, began to follow the action again.

George Abbott production written by Clifford Goldsmith, *What A Life* (1938). Set entirely in the principal's office of an Anytown, U.S.A.'s Central High, *What A Life* introduced a character who would symbolize a generation of American teens, Henry Aldrich. Ezra Stone played him on Broadway, opposite Betty Field as his girl friend and with Vaughan Glaser as the humorlessly impatient principal. (One rather expects a comically hyper principal in the manner of *Our Miss Brooks'* Mr. Conklin.) Stone went on to a *Henry Aldrich* series on radio; then Paramount built some films around Jackie Cooper's Henry, retaining Field and Glaser and also Eddie Bracken, promoted from a bit in the play to a featured part as Henry's sidekick, Dizzy. Others took over the kid leads as the series went on through the war years, and in fact the movies are, however modestly pleasing, more fun than the play.

At least *What A Life* is peppy, because George Abbott was its producer-director; and the dreary set and the costume plot of ordinary people in their go-to-school clothes guaranteed cheap. A kind of teenage Good Soldier Svejk, Henry is well-intentioned but born for trouble and situation comedy. There's not a single wisecrack in the entire script, because the grown-ups and teens of Central High aren't undergoing any real struggle for authority and the setting doesn't welcome the screwball. This is a series of stately entrances and exits rather than a tumble of zanies bashing into view through the traditional slamming doors of farce. In fact, *What A Life* is exceptional to the thirties comic style, that zippy chaos of know-it-alls; instead, it treats such plain old things as making excuses to irritated adults, unmasking the hypocrite who *really* stole the school band instruments, and asking Betty Field to the prom. *What A Life* is the opposite of *You Can't Take It With You,* which is why it is now as forgot as the nation's other plain old things, such as *Lightnin'.* Comedy without wisecracks could still play at this time, but would not outlast it.

So *What A Life* seems somewhat twenties in its derivation; much of thirties fare was similarly long established. The literary adaptation was if anything even bigger now. Edith Wharton's *Ethan Frome* had a solid success in 1936, with Raymond Massey and the original Anna Christie, Pauline Lord, as the married couple and Ruth Gordon as the life-force that breaks them all apart. The father-and-son writing team of Owen and Donald Davis made the adaptation, and Guthrie McClintic directed, reminding us that he was far more than Katharine Cornell's husband. George S. Kaufman directed John Steinbeck's adaptation of his own *Of Mice and Men* the following year, so he, too, was far more than a purveyor of wisecrack wit in comedy and musical. Enjoying one of those exciting first nights that reminded some of the revelation of Jeanne Eagels in *Rain, Of Mice and Men* offered as its leads the less than legendary Wallace Ford, Broderick Crawford (as Lennie), and Claire Luce—so surely the triumph was Kaufman's. Why did he never acquire an extramural reputation as Master Showman in the line of David Belasco, Jed Harris, and George Abbott? Yes, Kaufman was Master Jokester, one of those Algonquin *salonnards* without whom no Broadway bash was complete. But note that Belasco, Harris, and Abbott were subjects of many a tasty anecdote. Kaufman wasn't in anecdotes: Kaufman *created* anecdotes. He even created one around Jed Harris, when Harris was producing the Atlantic City tryout of *The Front Page* and called a meeting with its authors and director—Kaufman, in his first such assignment for Broadway. For some reason, possibly to express his rage at the world by subjecting associates to a physical objectification of his own self-hatred, Harris held the conference naked. Also for some reason (here I draw a blank), the other three put up with it passively. But as they left, Kaufman said, "Jed, your fly is open."

The chronicle play, so vast and impressive in the twenties, was getting more creative. Writer Arthur Goodman veered into what is now called the "counter-factual" in *If Booth Had Missed* (1932), a failure despite excellent reviews. Indeed, Booth's shot is deflected (by a black servant), but the coalition of so-called fire-eaters in Lincoln's own party work for Lincoln's destruction, and his impeachment is defeated by a single vote (as, in real life, was that of Lincoln's successor after the assassination, Andrew Johnson). Ironically, Lincoln is murdered all the same in Goodman's version, by a vindictive newspaper editor.

As in the 1920s, chronicle plays came over from London—for instance *St. Helena* (1936), with Maurice Evans taking over the role that Kenneth Kent played at the Old Vic: Napoleon. But how does someone so inspiring and appalling at once—the Corsican Bandit as Emperor of Europe—reach the stage persuasively? At that, consider *St. Helena*'s strange byline, a joining of R. C. Sherriff (author of that doughty old war play *Journey's End*) and a polyglot actress of mixed family, Jeanne de Casalis, who somehow managed to study with adepts of both Stanislafsky and the Comédie-Française.

Obviously, *St. Helena* deals with the last years of Napoleon's life, in his second exile, this one in the South Atlantic on a barren rock so unused to communication with the known world that one had to make special arrangements to get there (such as plunging Europe into yet another absolutely unnecessary war). Adhering closely to the record, the authors made history available to ticketbuyers, not only in the touching adoration of Napoleon's satellites but also in the almost pixieish megalomania of this second *roi soleil*. Here, General Gourgaud asks Napoleon to check over Gourgaud's account of Waterloo:

> NAPOLEON: Your account? You mean my account?
>
> GOURGAUD: I thought you meant me to write it, sir.
>
> NAPOLEON: (impatiently) We will see. A comma or full stop by me changes everything.

America's chronicler-in-chief was Maxwell Anderson, whose output took him from *Elizabeth the Queen* (1930) to our colonization of northern Mexico in *Night Over Taos* (1932), from *Mary of Scotland* (1933) to *Valley Forge* (1934), and even to the Mayerling incident, in *The Masque of Kings* (1937). All were verse plays—but, as well, star vehicles for the Lunts and Helen Hayes and also Theatre Guild productions or, in the case of *Night Over Taos*, a contribution to the Group Theatre in its first season. That is, Anderson was at once the professional nonconformist, the honcho of the snob hit, and the supporter of the idealistic liberal stage, which is about as many different people as one playwright can hope to be within a single decade.

Anderson was also a figure of fun among some of the New York intelligentsia, partly because verse theatre seems vainglorious in an age that takes its romance in prose and partly because verse theatre makes pretentious opinionmakers nervous. Plays written in poetry are comparable to our modern-day pop operas in that the characters' feelings are so intensely expressed that the good shows are not all that different from the bad ones. So it becomes easy to dash one's reputation with the gaffe of enthusiasm. Of course, if one must write a verse play, *Elizabeth the Queen* is at least scenically hospitable: everyone's already dressed for Shakespeare. But the aforementioned *Winterset,* in which Anderson's typical speechifying treats contemporary concerns, bemused the nonbeliever. In *The New Yorker,* wicked Wolcott Gibbs proposed the Maxwell Anderson version of Little Eva's death scene in *Uncle Tom's Cabin:*

LITTLE EVA: What says it by the clock, by that shrewd handyman of
    Time there on the wall?
HER FATHER, ST. CLARE: Four-forty-one. Four-forty-one or two.

. . .

LITTLE EVA: I'm going home. To God!
ST. CLARE: To God? And where is God, or what?
LITTLE EVA: (with tender amusement) He is no thing, I think, that you
    would know. No wheel, no gear, no formula, no strict pragmatic
    pattern or design that you can study from a book.

. . .

ST. CLARE: She's dying, Tom!
UNCLE TOM: Dyin'? Whut is death? De faulty chemistry ob our po' flesh
    may melt. De atoms change aroun'. De earth git back to earth. De
    soul don' nebba die!

Eventually, Little Eva floats away, to be heard offstage, "explaining something to God." Tom shoots St. Clare in revolt against their very style of speech—"al dem purty words dat don' quite rhyme, but run in neat and calculated rhythm."

At least everyone agreed on the continued advantage of revisiting classic titles. Another of the great evenings still recalled at thespian dinner parties right into the 1960s was the 1930 *Uncle Vanya* directed (as well as produced) by Jed Harris, almost certainly because the Age of the Producer had begun to cede prestige to the Age of the Director, and Harris wanted top rating. The event centered on Lillian Gish's return to the stage after a generation in film, and she soon added Marguerite Gauthier and Ophelia to her résumé. The latter occurred during the dueling *Hamlet*s of the 1936–37 season; Gish played in John Gielgud's entry, universally preferred to Leslie Howard's. Interestingly, the rest of that *Uncle Vanya*—Walter Connolly, Osgood Perkins, Eugene Powers, Joanna Roos—suggests no more than sound support for Gish's star magnetism. Yet the production was hailed as an outstanding instance of ensemble playing, more evidence that, whatever else Jed Harris was, he certainly knew how to run a good show.

If Leslie Howard's Hamlet merely failed to impress, Tallulah Bankhead's 1937 Shakespearean Cleopatra opposite the Antony of Conway Tearle (and with Mr. Bankhead, John Emery, as Octavius Caesar) lasted 5 performances after a sirocco of contempt from the critics. This was a sumptuous *Antony and Cleopatra,* designed by Jo Mielziner with music by Virgil Thomson. Reginald Bach, the director, apparently sought to recapture the spirit of turn-of-the-century Shakespeare, picturesque and hieratic—but Bankhead gave a post-flapper Cleopatra, as if one of Clare Boothe's schemy women trapped in the WAYBAC machine. As John Mason Brown famously put it, Bankhead "barged down the Nile . . . and sank."

Two of the outstanding Shakespearean outings of the decade were updatings. Enfant terrible and Wunderkind Orson Welles, just barely in his twenties, staged an all-black *Macbeth* (1936) for the Federal Theatre in an ambience of Caribbean voodoo, and then played Brutus in his own Mercury Theatre's *Julius Caesar* (1937). Set in the Rome of Mussolini, the production utilized modern-day street clothes and military uniforms, stripping the stage right to the bricks and steam pipes on the back wall. Quite aside from the novelty of playing Shakespeare simultaneously in two different fascisms, Welles' staging looked like nothing seen before, live theatre in black and white: for Jean Rosenthal's lighting, now opening up acting spaces and now closing them down to pinpoints, was the sole visual element in a tumultuously drab presentation.

On the other hand, *The Importance of Being Earnest* can only be done one way, even if, after local appearances in 1895, 1910, and 1926, it went over to musical comedy as *Oh, Ernest!,* in 1927. For its next visit, in 1939, the Wilde reverted to form, though traces of musical-comedy casting may be discerned in the two male leads, Clifton Webb and Derek Williams (who played the Noël Coward figure in *Jubilee*), and also in Hope Williams (who played the heroine of another Cole Porter show, *The New Yorkers*). The Lady Bracknell of this *Earnest,* Estelle Winwood, served also as its director, a rare instance of a woman's taking charge when she was neither playwright nor actor-manager.*

---

* Winwood underwent a remarkable journey, starting as an ingenue in her native England and coming to the U.S. in her early thirties to play the Pretty Little Thing in a wide variety of shows. These ranged from the first play to win the Pulitzer Prize, *Why Marry?* (1917), to Maugham and Coward; from chronicle, as the protagonist's unfaithful wife in

One of Broadway's last East of Suez pieces was Robert Keith's *Singapore* (1932), which the reviewers chose as that season's joke title, the notices to comprise non-stop sassing and larking about. At that, *Singapore* offered an opportunity to second-stringers to show off, for there were two other openings on the night the show baited its satirists; most of the critics attended a passion play at the New Amsterdam, *The Dark Hours*. Oddly, it was the work of Don Marquis, a humorist remembered today for *archy and mehitabel.*

So while the *New York Sun*'s Richard Lockridge took in *The Dark Hours* or the other first night, that of *Dear Jane,* at Le Gallienne's Civic downtown, someone else at the *Sun* signing as W. B. noted how obediently *Singapore* bowed to the clichés of its kind: "The faithful little native girl, the comedy Chinese houseboy, the wise Englishman [who] warns you what to expect, the nice young Englishman." It sounds like *White Cargo* with a sweet instead of scoundrelly Tondelayo. *Singapore* brought forth also a mean young Englishwoman—the nice one's wife—who takes an interest in the local sultan, tries to lose her husband through snakebite, and meets her own doom thus instead. In short, to return to W. B., the show had "all the properties that make a big hit when an Ohio River showboat comes to town on Saturday night."

It was not only corny but messily so, because on its tryout a completely different author, Harold Woolf, had been credited. The climactic scene with the snake, a cobra, also involved a great deal of suspense and a taste of the classy New Dance laid out by Ruth St. Denis. (A few of les girls were topless, though way upstage in darkness.) "The snake," said W. B., "was swell."

The mystery play seemed to fare best in English hands. A West End hit by Edgar Wallace called *The Case of the Frightened Lady* came over in 1932 as *Criminal At Large* complete with shady footmen, a comic sergeant, poisoned drinks, a telltale scarf, a sleepwalker, a woman in the audience who

---

Molière (1919), to period adventure as arrogant Lady Elizabeth Neville, in love with Morgan the Pirate, in *The Buccaneer* (1925). As she aged, Winwood began to capitalize on an eccentric streak that made her helpfully creepy in Agatha Christie's *Ten Little Indians* (1944) and an outright hag as one of the associate crazies in Jean Giraudoux's *The Madwoman of Chaillot* (1948). In her last Broadway outing, a comedy called *Nathan Weinstein, Mystic, Connecticut* (1966), Winwood was a bit girlish for the part of a centenarian bootlegger at a mere eighty-three. The curious can catch Winwood between her enchantress and beldam phases in the Katharine Hepburn RKO of *Quality Street,* made two years before the *Earnest* revival.

screamed on opening night, and a program note asking the public to keep the ending secret. Emlyn Williams repeated his London role of a kind of Lord Verisopht, then finessed this into the charming psychopath in his own *Night Must Fall* (1937), a two-month disappointment here after 435 performances in London. But MGM got a hit out of it, with Robert Montgomery breaking free of his debonair merrymaker Fach in Williams' role, Rosalind Russell as her then usual Haughty Miss, and a handful of the stage support. The movie reestablished the piece in the U.S., and it became a favorite of amateur groups looking for something twisty with which to enliven their season of *Merton of the Movies* and *The Torch-Bearers*.

If not in mystery, the American playwright's strength lay in farce, especially in the wisecrack mode populated by eccentrics. Skipping a bit into the next decade, we note Joseph A. Fields and Jerome Chodorov's *My Sister Eileen* (1940), drawn from Ruth McKenny's *New Yorker* stories; or Joseph Kesselring's *Arsenic and Old Lace*. These were huge successes in the new style of the really long run, 864 and 1,444 showings respectively. Earlier, *Lightnin'* and *Abie's Irish Rose* derived their fame mainly because they played more than a season; this was very rare in the 1920s. But by the late 1930s, in the ebb of Depression, a hit routinely ran a year and a smash considerably longer.

My Sister Eileen and *Arsenic and Old Lace* are both farces set in New York, but they delineate their fun very differently. McKenny's eccentrics are Village bohemians: the flamboyant painter-landlord Mr. Appopolous (another dazzling tour de force for Morris Carnovsky), the out-of-season athlete known as The Wreck, the brash newspaperman trying to make the pretty sister, and also a non-Village character, the dorky manager of a drugstore.

Arsenic and Old Lace, on the other hand, tells of genuinely crazy folk, not just scenic local types strolling around. These people are either housebound (Mortimer's aunts, who poison friendless old men out of sympathy; Mortimer's brother, who thinks he's Teddy Roosevelt) or fugitives (Mortimer's other brother and his partner in crime, the brother played by Boris Karloff as a kind of lively Frankenstein's Monster). More important, *Arsenic and Old Lace* has no core of reality to it, no emotional foundation; the romance between Mortimer and a local girl is so perfunctory that the movie version had to build it up even while keeping it secondary. *My Sister Eileen,* however, gets a lot of feeling out of its two young Ohio women (Shirley Booth, Jo Ann

Sayers) trying to make something of themselves in the metropolis, which is why the play translated into a classic musical, *Wonderful Town* (1953), while *Arsenic and Old Lace* has nothing to sing about. Musicals give us people with needs and plans. The only character in *Arsenic and Old Lace* with a need is the serial-killer brother, whose professional pride is mortified that his aunts have murdered as often as he: twelve times.

Nevertheless, the two shows are equally expert in finding the fun latent in their drivelines—conquering New York (to borrow a title from *Wonderful Town*) and neutralizing one's homicidal clan. More important, the two shows *played* extremely well: because wisecrack comedy became acculturated just when the mastermind director of comedies materialized. Comedy wasn't only funnier than it used to be; it was now composed of writing and performing in a tight unit.

Historians call this the George Abbott Style, though it may well be as much the School of George S. Kaufman. Both men moved into directing and writing (from writing only) at about the same time, and both shared a skills set based on pacing and clarity, with superb instincts about where to cut a lame quart d'heure. Oddly, both worked frequently in the musical despite tin ears and, in Abbott's case, a lack of consistency in character development that never affected his work in the straight play.

It was Kaufman who staged *My Sister Eileen* (and Abbott, in a nice parity, who staged *Wonderful Town*), and we can get a taste of the Kaufman-Abbott mode in *My Sister Eileen*'s three act finales, each a sort of spoken musical number made of a crescendo of jests leading to a cymbal crash of a tonic close. One of *Eileen*'s running gags is the girls' Village basement apartment itself, because of the constant blasting for a subway line and formerly the haunt of a prostitute named Violet and thus the bane of the beat cop. It is he who launches the show's most Feydeauvien moment when he encounters The Wreck, who runs around in tank top and shorts and is obviously "a sex nut," as the cop puts it. The two leading men interested in Eileen are also present, and as the cop gets nosy one of them tries to reason with him while the other runs into a closet—and suddenly a gigantic Cossack bursts in, carrying in his arms the limp form of . . . well, who else? It's Violet, and the Cossack is the doorman of a Russian nightspot. As he deposits Violet on the bed—"She's early tonight!" the cop notes, checking his watch—Ruth brings down the first-act curtain. Try to hear the line in that incomparable blend of smart alec and baby doll that Shirley Booth brought to her comic roles:

> RUTH: Well, for a place with a bad location and no neon sign, we're do-
> ing a hell of a business!

The second act ends with the entire Village erupting in an epic conga line, and the third with a driller pushing up through the girls' apartment floor: "Hey, Pete, it looks like we didn't judge the distance right!"

The domestic play, on American family life, may have been the hardiest genre of all at this time, and it produced two titles that shattered the concept of the popular success with unprecedented eight-year runs. No two families could be less alike than the Lesters of *Tobacco Road* (1933) and the Days of *Life With Father* (1939), but then most of my readers know how unalike are the works themselves, the one a mess of sensationalism appealing to the prurient and the other a gingerbread house of quaint nostalgia.

Or so everyone assumes—and this is easy to do, as *Tobacco Road* and *Life With Father* are two more of those famous titles that we never actually experience, like *What Price Glory?*. In fact, the pair accumulated those gigantic performance tallies because they are quite capable examples of that essential thirties genre, the folk play: in which language and mores define a culture and that culture defines its subjects, who foolishly believe themselves to be living in a state of liberty.

True, no one ever thinks of *Tobacco Road* or *Life With Father* as a folk play. The form's standard titles—*The Green Pastures* and *Green Grow the Lilacs*—reveal its assigned venues, black America and cowboyland. But aren't *Tobacco Road*'s rednecks and *Life With Father*'s Knickerbocker WASPs "folk" in the sense of a *kind* of people different from those in the auditorium?

Certainly, *Tobacco Road*'s folk are different. They revolted the critics in exactly the way that some of Edward Albee's characters would do in the 1960s: too much honesty too vividly presented, too many pieties blasphemed. Most often, it was the outspoken political plays, all from the left, that would rile the critics in the 1930s. But *Tobacco Road* offended in a more basic way. Its people of the Georgia back country around Augusta are so poor they're classless, so stupid they use language less to communicate than to kill time, and so wicked they don't know the difference between religion and sex. Brooks Atkinson claimed that the piece "reels around the stage like a drunken stranger to the theatre." Yes—and yet. Perhaps despite himself, Atkinson had to cite as well "spasmodic moments of merciless power when truth is flung into your face with all the slime that truth contains."

Based on Erskine Caldwell's novel, Jack Kirkland's plotless script quite simply sets the Lesters before us in their day to day of going hungry, as father Jeeter (Henry Hull) lazily schemes to turn a dollar out of various daffy notions and mother Ada (Margaret Wycherly, the only other established actor in the original company) humphs and nags and cultivates a soft spot for only one of their seventeen children, the unhappily married Pearl. Another daughter, the harelipped Ellie Mae, flies into giggles and rubs up against available men. A son, the callous Dude, ends up married to Sister Bessie, a preacher of no known religion. ("I generally just call it 'Holy,'" she explains.) In case the critics hadn't already been alienated to the utmost, Dude is a mere sixteen when Bessie takes him; she has to throw a scene in the license bureau to make it legal.

Life With Father is also an adaptation, from Clarence Day Jr.'s *New Yorker* stories about his childhood. These were so autobiographical that after securing the rights to Day's writing producer Oscar Serlin and his authors, Howard Lindsay and Russel Crouse, had to sign separate agreements with Day's widowed mother and his three brothers for the use of their characters. (Day himself, the oldest of the brood, had died in 1935.) These tales look back to an authentic nineteenth-century upbringing—not just amid horsecars and icemen but in a house at Forty-eighth Street and Madison Avenue when the location was suburban. They moved there, says mother Vinnie, "to get out of the city!"

Employing little more plot than *Tobacco Road, Life With Father* runs on two throughlines: Mother's wish to correct an oversight in Father's background and get him baptized, and Jr.'s courtship of a visitor from the Midwest.* The throughlines mirror each other, for just as Father sees men as

---

* The baptism storyline comes from the five stories collected in cloth as *God and My Father;* choice bits were pulled from other titles, including "Father Opens My Mail" and "Father's Old Trousers." Even so, Lindsay and Crouse had to do a great deal more inventing than Jack Kirkland did on *Tobacco Road,* in effect using Day's characters and setting and the baptism sequence but otherwise making a play from scratch.

reasonable and women as flighty, Jr.'s experience with his light of love, Mary, actually bears this out.

In fact, *Life With Father*'s worldview, unshockingly amusing when the play was new, now seems downright genderist. We are supposed to see Father as tyrannical and insensitive, true. But we are supposed to notice as well that he is generally sensible and fair, capable of warmth in emergencies, and, most important, nonconformistically ahead of his time. It turns out that it was no oversight that Father was never baptized: his freethinking parents deferred the sacrament till their offspring were grown and could accept or reject it as they chose; Father thinks it's unneccesary, even silly. In our own age of ever wilder encroachments on democracy by religion fascists, it's refreshing to hear someone of the 1880s treating the spiritual as a part of life for the individual to control, not be controlled by, even if we hear it in a line of comic irony:

> FATHER: Vinnie, if there's one place the church should leave alone, it's a man's soul!

Father is just as independent and "modern" on biblical teaching:

> FATHER: You'd be in a pretty fix if I gave all my money to the poor.

Mother is not generally sensible. Father is dogmatic, but it's really Vinnie who carts all the righteousness around. Third son Whitney is struggling to prepare for his catechism, and Vinnie truly believes that if he fails, Whitney will be denied his final Reward. Father knows best:

> FATHER: I'll be there before you are, Whitney. I'll see that you get in.

The play all but stinks of incense. Leaving Jr. alone with Mary, Vinnie tells them, "Remember, it's Sunday": as if these two teenagers even know how to sin in a living room.

It is Mother, ironically, who controls the family. Father only rules it, a show Windsor. Let him utter a thousand commands: it is Mother who gets her way. Opposite to her is Ada Lester back in *Tobacco Road*, because in a propertyless culture in which religion is opportunism rather than manners, there's nothing to run, nothing at stake. In the propertied culture of the Days, there's power in ownership: and Father owns everything but, again,

Mother reigns over its disposition. She owns Father, too, so of course the play must end with Father getting baptized.

Given the two plays' phenomenal runs—they are still Broadway's straight-play record holders, at over 3,000 showings each—it is odd to learn that they were anything but shoo-ins. *Tobacco Road* was iffy because one could never tell when such a work might triumph on its notoriety or fail to become notorious. But *Life With Father* calls for one set and only sixteen players and is extremely enjoyable. Why did producer Serlin have the devil's own time getting his capitalization? Why did every actor turn it down?: Walter Huston, Walter Connolly, Alfred Lunt (with Lynn, naturally, as Mother), Roland Young, John Halliday. Finally, co-author Lindsay stepped in, opposite his wife, Dorothy Stickney. Still, this play is larger than its actors, in its intimate panorama of a place where even the wholly independent man must accommodate the prevailing cautions or see his culture break apart. It's a premise for Ibsen or Shaw, yet we find it here, in the second most taken-for-granted play in Broadway history.

Tobacco Road is if anything smaller than its actors. Nor is it extremely enjoyable, though it is fascinating—that merciless power that Atkinson had to acknowledge. So little happens in it that the stingy little plot action in its final scene comes off as a chapter of Dickens. At that, the interesting part occurs offstage: reckless driver Dude runs over his mother in preacher Bessie's new automobile. Dying, *Tobacco Road*'s matriarch finally commits an existential act, crawling into view to save daughter Pearl. *This* Father is planning to hand the helpless runaway over to her hideous husband; there's a dollar or two in it, perhaps a sack of turnips. Ada is to say goodbye to Pearl, but when Jeeter drags the struggling girl near, Ada bites his hand and Pearl skedaddles. No turnips for Father. Alone on stage in the show's last moment, he contemplates his nothing of a life as its objective correlative, a loose shingle, falls off the roof. It would raise a laugh today, but in the 1930s it was sound dramatic punctuation to three hours of the existence without content. And there the curtain fell.

Over at *Life With Father,* the final curtain dotes on the Days even while reinforcing the woman conqueror Mother. There's certainly content in *this* existence: amid an unseen entourage of cultural controls and cautions, Mother escorts Father off to his humiliation:

FATHER: I'm going to be baptized, damn it!

Off they go—but note a last statement of the theme of the woman in charge of the men. As Father stomps out of the house followed by the mistress of all she surveys, the curtain starts down slowly enough to allow Jr. to rush in to kneel at Mary's feet in our last point of contact with the story. So the species will survive as this new young Mother learns in her turn the art of control; and by now the curtain is down.*

Opening at the Masque (today the John Golden), *Tobacco Road* moved in its tenth month to the larger Forrest (today the Eugene O'Neill) to accommodate the ticketbuyer storm that lasted long after the average hit would have played its entire run. *Life With Father* was even more popular, and sold out for weeks in advance during some early portion of its six years at the Empire. Then it, too, moved, to the smaller Bijou (now demolished), to make way for Mary Chase's dire "you can't outwit fate" melodrama *The Next Half Hour* (1945), which lasted a week.

Our Town did, too: in Boston. Following a reasonably successful one-night stand in Princeton, New Jersey, the piece so offended New Englanders that the wife of the governor of Massachusetts led a resistance of walkouts on opening night, and *Our Town*'s producer-director, Jed Harris, had to close down with no viable Broadway house in the offing. Desperate, Harris phoned Gilbert Miller, who was out of town with an Ina Claire comedy, Frederick Lonsdale's *Once Is Enough*. This was to open at Miller's own theatre, temporarily dark in waiting for Claire. Miller let Harris bring *Our Town* in for a week's showcase, and while the critics gave it a mixed greeting, Brooks Atkinson was so partial that the Morosco, till then mysteriously unavailable, took *Our Town* for a New York total of 336 performances.

---

* The importance of play over players in *Life With Father* is revealed in Lindsay and Stickney's many replacements, mostly names of note only to indexers: Wallis Clark and Lily Cahill; Arthur Margetson (who with Irene Bordoni introduced Cole Porter's "Let's Do It" in *Paris* [1928]) and Nydia Westman; obscure Percy Waram with the redoubtable Lillian Gish; and the somewhat obscure Stanley Ridges with Lillian's sister Dorothy, the Gishes hitting New York after heading touring companies. Lillian's broke Chicago's long-run record: sixty-six weeks at the Blackstone. *Tobacco Road,* on the other hand, boasted one very prominent replacement when James Barton took over Henry Hull's Jeeter Lester for four and a half years—astonishing when one considers that Jeeter is the longest but by far the least interesting of *Tobacco Road*'s seven main roles. A sharp actor dwindles into cliché in such a part. But then, Jeeter marked a career transition for Barton, from hoofing and a drunk act into straight acting; after *Tobacco Road,* Barton played O'Neill. Barton's uncle John played Jeeter on tour for well over eleven years.

One wonders why this play so angered Boston; it is, after all, set in New England, in Grover's Corners, New Hampshire. It is also set in—to quote one of its lines—"the mind of God." Perhaps that peeved the mind of Boston, where church is an experience not of spirit but of class. Then, too, *Our Town*'s extravagantly basic presentation, with its bare stage, address of the audience, and dead men walking, was a beloved element of American theatre history only after audiences got used to it. In 1938, the plainness of the staging and the fancy ring in the writing struck some as bewildering or even irritating, cheap and grandiose at once. Why bring God into it, and why no sets? Because *Our Town*'s author, Thornton Wilder, wanted to strip away all life's decoration to reveal what life is: which, apparently, is nothing plus God. That awesome notion is why *Our Town* is the *first* most taken-for-granted play in Broadway history.

This misapprehension mistakes the show's simple look for a simplicity of theme. Wilder views a cross-section of small-town life to reveal people with just enough property and social culture to be free. But, says Wilder, they can't use their freedom, because it's such a big idea that we can't comprehend it till we've lost it. Clarence Day's Father knows what freedom is, because marriage, church, and etiquette fetter him. Jeeter Lester is too stupid to contemplate an abstraction like "freedom." It's worse, though, for the folk of Grover's Corners, because they live in a useless freedom, having it without knowing they have it: they are born, they mate, and they die not out of individual lives individually created, but because He wills it so without ever explaining why.

This is a demoralizing lesson even for the believer, and may be why this classic of classics bothered some critics and theatregoers in its first years. Even the casting of the longtime favorite playwright, actor, and Boston native Frank Craven as Wilder's Stage Manager—obviously designed to welcome us into unfamiliar theatre with an intimately familiar figure—did not avail. People who didn't like *Our Town* didn't just not like it. This play was hated.

Actually, Wilder himself thought Craven too folksy and gentle, very sympathetic to Grover's Corners where Wilder had conceived of the Stage Manager as neutral, a tour guide or so. Yet it must be difficult to play the role thus, for it is written as a kind of philosopher's pastoral, doting upon the innocence of the living and then harrowing the spectator with the news of his own death. Indeed, it may be Craven's moist approach that protected *Our Town* when it was vulnerable, tempering Wilder's brutal neutrality with the warmth of a sampler.

For *Our Town* is one of those rare plays that has the power to dwarf its audience, most uplifting if one doesn't follow it closely and most appalling if one does. "They don't understand very much, do they?" asks one of those buried in the town churchyard of another, about those still living. It's sympathetic in a callous way: because the speaker is Emily (Martha Scott), who died young, in childbirth, and she is referring to her husband, George (Frank Craven's real-life son John). Worse, Emily asks this question of Mrs. Gibbs—George's mother—and *she* replies, "No, dear, not very much." Worst, the two are more or less gazing upon the one's son and the other's widower, who is so stricken with grief that he has thrown himself on Emily's grave.

If Wilder's artfully artless visuals sparked one of *Our Town*'s controversies, and if his dimensions, in which a small town represents life on earth, sparked another, the play is newly controversial. In an age when such words as "family," "faith," "Christian," and even "atheist" have been hijacked by bigots of one kind or another, Wilder's play now feels acutely critical of American life. *Our Town* was once a fond picture of it, even given the troubling vastness of Wilder's use of the cycle of life and death. Yet the work finds itself suddenly caught up in the "values" war of present-day America.

Of course, when Wilder wrote, his terminology was, in effect, valueless. In the world Wilder conjured up, "family" isn't a euphemism denoting a homophobic agenda: it's something one is born into, with parents and siblings. "Faith" is a private matter, not something to be vulgarized for political advancement. A "Christian" isn't someone with an enemies list, and "atheist" means the guy who skips the church picnic, not the one who initiates litigation at the sight of a Nativity Scene.

For decades, *Our Town* was a nostalgic classic on the Great American level, the kind of thing that, say, Richard Nixon might happily attend and completely misunderstand. Now it's a rebuke of our bickering "culture of complaint" (in Robert Hughes' phrase), less a sampler than a fantasy. We might even ask if there ever was a Grover's Corners or even a Thornton Wilder. A gay man wrote our National Play, because in his day Americans regarded themselves as citizens of a nation. Today, many regard themselves as members of special-interest groups with a wrecking agenda. Romance usually ages better than satire, but *Our Town* is in danger of becoming an implausible curiosity. Its future public will be like the governor's wife, walking out in Boston, baffled and angry.

Eight

We Are Not Here To Rehearse Your Play:

THE POLITICAL STAGE

I. J. Golden's *Precedent* (1931) dramatized the Tom Mooney–Warren Billings case, in which the two men were convicted of throwing a bomb into a Preparedness Parade in San Francisco in 1916. To center his argument that, as some believed, the defendants were framed, Golden deleted Billings in favor of the more famous Mooney, but otherwise hewed closely to the original story, reset in fictional Queen City.

In Golden's retelling, Mooney (renamed Delaney) is targeted because he tried to foment a strike of railroad workers. The bad guys are the railroad president and the district attorney, and the good guys are, mainly, a newspaper editor who reveals that Delaney was nowhere near the parade when the crime was committed. So, for once, an à clef piece was devoted not to the doings of Jeanne Eagels, Noël Coward, or Alexander Woollcott, but to a sociopolitical figure. Despite a cast of unknowns, the show moved from the Provincetown Playhouse to Broadway, ran 184 performances, and managed a respectable tour.

This is notable, for critics were not generally supportive of shows with left-wing politics, especially this early in the 1930s. John Wexley's *Steel* (1931) ran two weeks after perhaps the worst reviews of its season—"so overwrought," said Robert Garland of the *World-Telegram,* "so overwritten"; and John Mason Brown thought Wexley's concept of Steel the Enemy of Man as irritating as O'Neill's obsession with the "ole davil" sea in *Anna Christie*. Another unheralded cast (including future Hollywood heavy Barton MacLane and *Precedent*'s Delaney, Royal Dana Tracy) enacted the tale of another labor agitator, this one in "The Milltown of Ironton, U.S.A." A *Sweeney Todd* factory whistle punctuated the action, and while Wexley troubled to avoid the propagandist's easy diagnosis with a warts-and-all hero (who at one point seduces his sister-in-law), he capped his piece with an easy remedy: the hero's sister shoots one of the cops who has come to arrest him. On opening night, someone in the balcony responded with "Bravo! Kill 'em all!"

Or consider Albert Maltz and George Sklar's *Merry-Go-Round* (1932), on municipal corruption in a place that the public understood to be New York. Elisha Cook Jr., one year before he played the flaming youth of *Ah, Wilderness!* and later to be immortalized as the jittery "gunsel" Wilmer in John Huston's *The Maltese Falcon,* appeared as a hotel bellboy who witnesses a gangland murder and ends up hanged in his cell. The "suicide" had been drawing attention to ties between crime and law enforcement.

Was *Merry-Go-Round*'s Mayor Manning an à clef portrayal of Mayor James J. Walker? Is this what goaded the city to treat the production to a real-life merry-go-round of harassment? Like *Precedent,* the play moved from the Provincetown to The Street, to the Avon (now demolished) on West Forty-fifth Street, one door west of the Imperial. On opening night, shortly before curtain time, the fire department arrived to padlock the house for an out-of-date license. This created a scandal, not least because plenty of theatres stayed open while waiting for license renewals; the Imperial was doing just that at the time. When the Producing Managers Association and the Dramatists Guild took on the case, *Merry-Go-Round* reopened, though the authorities vindictively insisted on enforcing another legal technicality, demanding pointless structural alterations to the auditorium. Oddly, all this publicity did not generate public interest in attending the play, and it lasted only six weeks.

Still, Maltz and Sklar, like Golden and Wexley, were heralds of a genre that could not in the long run be discouraged: the political play. Few established writers were keen; this was to be a young man's métier. True, Elmer Rice moved from the compassionate *Street Scene* (1929), twenty-four hours in the life of a tenement, to the more imploringly progressive *We, the People* (1933), which expanded from *Street Scene*'s single outdoor set to twenty-one locales involving forty-four speaking roles. Both plays are humanistic "cross-sections," but *Street Scene* has melodramatic tang while *We, the People* is a civics lesson. *Street Scene* played eighteen months, *We, the People* six weeks.

Of the fresh talent introduced in the political play, the most enduring yet underrated is Clifford Odets. (Others endure with a high rating, such as Lillian Hellman; others are underrated but cannot truly be called enduring, such as Irwin Shaw.) Odets' very name is a summoning term for rather a lot of things, but the main one is Depression Drama. This medium is as essential as O'Neill's experiments in the 1920s or the lyrical outpouring of Tennessee Williams in the 1940s and '50s, and Odets left three major titles of the type: in agitprop (*Waiting For Lefty*, 1935), in domestic social drama (*Awake and Sing!*, 1935), and in tragedy (*Golden Boy*, 1937).

Edna Ferber didn't like him. With collaborator George S. Kaufman's indulgence, Ferber wrote Odets into *Stage Door* (1936) as playwright Keith Burgess. Even as he enters the setting, a New York hotel for actresses, Ferber is damning him in the stage directions as "the kind of young man who never wears a hat." You know, one of those who-cares-what-*you*-think? idealists:

> KEITH: Romance is for babies! I write about *today*! I want to tear the heart out of the rotten carcass they call life, and hold it up bleeding for all the world to see!

A year later, however, when he is on the rise through the heroine's support, Burgess sells his next play—and "her" starring role—to a producer who wants a Name. Worse, Burgess is going Hollywood.

Indeed, *Stage Door* opened eight months after Odets left New York for his first of many trips to California, and one of the other things that Odets personifies is the Sellout. A wish for success, legend tells us, was Odets' fatal flaw. Moneyfame, not social progress, was his god. Odets even married a movie star, that MGM Oscar-taker Luise Rainer, with her heartbreaking Telephone Scene, her delicately squashed peasant in Pearl Buck coolie-hat chic, her Great Waltz!

On the other hand, what's wrong with a wish for success? Is writing for film automatically a sign that one has no interest in social progress? If one will marry, why not Luise Rainer? Another of the Depression Dramatists, John Howard Lawson, told one of the major Depression Producers, Harold Clurman, that Lawson found writing for the movies to be no more limiting and compromising than writing for Broadway: that "selling out," in effect, meant doing the same thing for more money.

More important, why does Odets suffer this pile-on when no one blames all the other playwrights who at various times worked for the studios? Odets' fatal flaw, in fact, was his lack of interest in narrative, the very machinery of playwrighting: plot. Odets worked entirely in character: dialogue without events. Another writer, an artistic relation of Odets, Arthur Miller, once summed up the plays that preceded Odets—the theatre of the 1920s—as a "happy deference to talent and the interesting rich." This type of theatre was still vital in the 1930s, alongside Odets. It's screwball comedy, *Jubilee,* S. N. Behrman, something with the Lunts or about Noël Coward, and if Gertrude Lawrence and the other celebrity eccentrics don't attend opening night, they'll entertain at the Party.

That's lovely theatregoing, and while the school of Odets didn't sweep it all away, it did successfully propose as subjects those without talent or money: without veneer. Without, even, the Stage English of the Barrymores or the colorful patois of twenties wisecrackers or of the dialect comics. Even musical-comedy heroines gave elocution lessons; Marilyn Miller looked for the silver lining "whene'er a cloud appears in the blyoo."

Odets breaks with all this by writing the dialect of real life, as chewy as penny candy yet poetic because the challenge of capturing reality inspires Odets, exalts him. Playwrights from the Greeks on have asked what life is made of; Odets asks what it sounds like. His words are an actor's delight. "There's a snap! crackle! pop! to them," Jack Klugman recalled, many years later. It was "wonderful to roll them around in your mouth." Here's a sample of *Awake and Sing!,* as the Berger family of the Bronx finishes dinner:

RALPH: Where's advancement down the place? Work like crazy! Think
    they see it? You'd drop dead first.

. . .

    Just look at Eddie. I'm as good as he is—pulling in two-fifty a week
for forty-eight minutes a day. A headliner, his name in all the papers.

. . .

    Didn't I want to take up tap dancing, too?
BESSIE: So take lessons. Who stopped you?
RALPH: On what?
BESSIE: On what? Save money.
RALPH: Sure, five dollars a week for expenses and the rest in the house.
    I can't save even for shoe laces.
BESSIE: You mean we shouldn't have food in the house, but you'll make
    a jig on the street corner?

. . .

RALPH: I don't know. . . . Every other day to sit around with the blues
    and mud in your mouth.

This is the very opposite of the celebrity of eccentricity, what Italians refer to as "i soliti ignoti," generally meaning "the usual suspects" but literally "the usual unknowns": traditionally unsuitable as subjects for art. *Awake and Sing!,* finds no adventure in the Bergers, but rather presents them in the middle of their real lives, as young Ralph seeks more *something* than subsistence, and his unmarried sister Hennie deals with pregnancy and an impossible future. Their grandfather Jacob provides what little event the play has by playing God, arranging his suicide to look like an accident so he can create that *something* for the idealistic Ralph. "Let me die like a dog," Ralph cries out, about fifty seconds before the final curtain, "if I can't get more from life." Having made a voyage of self-discovery, he now wants to get into not show biz like the hoofing Eddie but progressive politics. Isaiah 26:19: "Thy dead *men* shall live, *together with* my dead body shall they arise. Awake and sing, ye that dwell in dust."

Authenticating the Berger family through the documentary imagination of his dialogue, Odets gives them stature. The intricate character interplay in a show without a plot reminded some of Chekhof; Harold Clurman thought Sean O'Casey a fitter comparison for the Irishman's "tenement tenderness" and a vigorous treatment of everyday matters, till it is "almost impossible to differentiate between 'high' and 'low,' 'important' and 'trivial,' 'essential' and 'incidental.'"

True, the politically energized Odets was bound to compose fanfares for the common man. In effect, he spent the 1930s touring the building Elmer Rice invented for *Street Scene,* getting a play out of each apartment. There's little joy in this world; *Awake and Sing!*'s original title was *I Got the Blues*. This sounds like the Bergers, perhaps too much so: honest and unpromising. But *Waiting For Lefty* sounds like *action;* the class that a Lefty hails from doesn't wait patiently.

So *Waiting For Lefty* would be Odets' first produced work. It uses Berger-like people in a completely different form, a frame of flashbacks, raw and tense, with a good-versus-evil throughline. We actually see the bad guys, and the evening ends as no American play ever did before, with virtually everyone in the theatre on his feet, shouting. Yes, the audience, too.

Agitprop. Coined from "agitation" and "propaganda," agitprop was the ultimate political theatre, an attempt to rouse its public to, if not outright revolution, at least a revolutionary point of view: a pep rally. Yet from the start, even the most primitive examples of agitprop borrowed techniques from the experimental stage. The classic agitprop sketch—the form worked best in short bursts—was a piece of mass authorship called *Newsboy,* based on a poem by V. J. Jerome. All that happens is the exposure of the title character as a stooge of capitalism, with his "Love nest raided on Park Avenue!" and "Yanks take Dodgers 3–0!" Soon enough, we learn the only source of genuine news: *The Daily Worker.* "Time to revolt!" cries one chorister.

The chanting by solos and groups thanks the European avant-garde, and the pattern of simple words repeated in near-hypnotic emphasis suggests Gertrude Stein. By a historical irony, this approach strays from Soviet-approved "socialist realism" into Soviet-banned "formalism," meaning "artistic experimentation."

Lefty's experimental quality lies in Odets' re-creation of a taxi drivers' union meeting—the very theatre itself becomes the meeting hall—as pools of light allow the actors to portray various union members. Watched by their corrupt officials, including union president Harry Fatt, the rank and file enact playlets as if on a workers' organization's skit night, theatre within theatre. A third level is introduced in Odets' "Notes For Production": he based his dramaturgy on the minstrel show, with its suite of chairs and yes-men, its merry leaders Mr. Tambo and Mr. Bones, its specialty acts. These Odets transformed from amiable stereotypes into individuals learning to stand up to the vicious "leaders" who betray them.

How far from *Design For Living* can one get? As *Lefty* nears its finale, Agate, a union militant exhorting the members to walk out, is threatened by Fatt and his henchmen; other drivers have to stand around Agate to protect him. And now somebody runs up the theatre aisle to explain why the faithful Lefty isn't present: he has been murdered. "Christ, cut us up to little pieces!" Agate cries. "We'll die for what is right! put fruit trees where our ashes are!"

Then he turns to the rest of the workers—to *us*—and asks, "Well, what's the answer?" And audiences of 1935 shouted "*Strike! Strike! Strike!*" right along with the players.

Odets released *Waiting For Lefty* nationally for free use by amateur groups and low fees to others, and it swept the land, winning prizes and getting banned from Boston to Los Angeles. Odets was famous in that overnight way that happens in America, and of course now *Awake and Sing!* was eminently produceable. But note that *Awake and Sing!* not only was written before *Waiting For Lefty,* but does not follow upon the belligerent and sloganizing *Lefty* stylistically. Having given agitprop its masterpiece, Odets now wanted to devote himself to "literary" theatre.

However, the hard left saw the political stage as its property. Though *Waiting For Lefty* treats workers fed up with not Amerika but their own corrupt oligarchs, Odets had become the most apparent of the young leftist playwrights, like his fellows to be sternly monitored by Party honchos and their avid stooges, such as the *Daily Worker*'s theatre critics. What they wanted was more good-versus-evil sagas, more villains like Harry Fatt, not to mention those gleeful capitalist enablers Cole Porter and the Lunts.

But the best writers don't get told how to write; hacks do. Hacks enjoy following directions; it makes everything so much easier. Anyway, Stalin doesn't like surprises. Is it possible that John Howard Lawson abandoned Broadway not for Hollywood's financial security but because in New York he felt torn between Party obedience and the wish to create the unusual? Writing movie scripts cleared his mind of the conflict, though he ended as one of the Hollywood Ten all the same.

Odets had no such conflict. As soon as the Party tried to commandeer his art, he—as they liked to put it then—"drifted away." And he drew further yet from Party theatre in *Golden Boy*, a modern tragedy in classic proportions and politically almost useless: the rise and fall of a young man cursed with fathers. It sounds sappy, like a B movie: Joe Bonaparte can be a violinist or a boxer—that is, he can use his hands for art or war. Still undecided, he breaks his hand in the ring, and opts for war. Then he takes his manager's lover for his own, accidentally kills an opponent, then rides off in his gala new automobile with the lover and murders them both in a crash.

Of course, the Odetsian idiom of, here, immigrants and the rough crowd of the boxing racket distinguishes *Golden Boy* beyond the confines of its plot. But note that this time Odets actually constructs one, ever more tightly wound up against itself over the course of sixteen months in twelve scenes as Joe trades his natural father (music) for, first, a manager father (boxing) and then an eerie gun-toting promoter father (crime). And the eerie promoter, Eddie Fuseli, is Broadway's only gay character in the whole Depression who isn't a friend of Noël Coward; and the manager's lover, Lorna Moon, is one of the decade's most interesting heroines. Uneducated but intelligent, nurturing as well as tough, she transcends type. It's Barbara Stanwyck, isn't it? (And Stanwyck played the role in the film version.) A typical moment:

EDDIE: (To Joe's manager, of Lorna) This your girl?
LORNA: I'm my mother's girl.

Odets directs her to deliver the line "pertly," but that can't be right. Lorna isn't "impudent" or "saucy": she's informing a man that women aren't men's possessions. (Stanwyck speaks the words in a "you aren't worth loathing" drawl.) In a way, all of *Golden Boy* is about the taking and giving of souls, and, being the only sensitive soul in the collection, Joe dooms himself ever more strongly with each personal transaction. No wonder the Party could not make use of Odets: he saw too rich a world to reduce it to stick-figure harangues.

Those willing to work in cartoon drama usually attached themselves to the hard-left theatre collectives that sprang up in the 1930s, though their low profile and limited audience made them little more than aggrandized skit nights. Indeed, a typical organization, the Workers Lab Theatre, made its name entirely on producing the most famous version of *Newsboy*, the very essence of the word "skit."

The most prominent of the collectives was the Theatre Union, founded by an amateur, Charles R. Walker, in 1932. The plan was to graduate agit-prop from *Newsboy* and its fellows to full-length plays in a Broadway-sized house, with tickets priced to accommodate a proletarian clientele. George Sklar and Albert Maltz, the authors of *Merry-Go-Round,* gave the Theatre Union its opening work, *Peace on Earth,* in 1933. It played the Civic Repertory Theatre, and when the company "put in" it found sets and costumes left over from Eva Le Gallienne's last season. After that head start, however, there was nothing but bad press till the Union gave up in 1937, though it did enjoy a semi-hit in Sklar and Paul Peters' *Stevedore* (1934). Here was a piece of pure socialist realism, presenting the problem (white racism, on the docks of New Orleans, where a union agitator is singled out by the money bosses for a lynching) and the solution (whites and blacks unite against the System). Though the protagonist (Jack Carter, the original Crown in the Heywards' play *Porgy*) is killed even so, the working class has discovered a heroic if implausible color-blind bond.

There was a small but eager public for this genre of blunt melodrama, even now when the economy had so dissolved that a balcony ticket meant skipping a meal. But there was no public as yet for the primary author of twentieth-century leftist theatre when the Union programmed Bertolt Brecht's *Mother,* in 1935. Actually, Brecht entitled it *The Mother* (*Die Mutter*) on its Berlin premiere, in 1932, one year before Brecht, Weill, Lenya, Lang, Mann, Grosz, and the rest of the jazzband had to run for cover. Why Paul Peters' translation deleted the article is anyone's guess, for the noun by itself is meaningless. Brecht wrote a parable, universal and symbolic, about *the* apolitical mother of *the* political son. When the son is killed by the police, she is inspired to take up *the* revolutionary banner. The tale of *the* Mother.

It was not only the public but the Theatre Union itself that was unprepared for Brecht, because unlike the others named above, who were still in Europe, Brecht had got to America. He stank of bad hygiene, screamed at the slightest thwarting of his ego drive, and—surely to his hosts' bemusement—dressed in a uniform of worker's drag *tailored in leather and silk*. Though Brecht did everything he could to sabotage the production (as he always did when someone else was directing), *Mother* opened and ran a month, not a bad stay for a piece that is at once dreary and hysterical.

The Theatre Union's use of Le Gallienne's place recalls to us the matter of a national theatre, so often discussed at the time. It sounds prestigious, but a national theatre is simply a grandiose version of the nineteenth-century stock company, based on a permanent ensemble in rotating repertory: Monday's Hamlet plays *Peer Gynt*'s Button Moulder on Tuesday (perhaps completely nude but for a white bedsheet held about himself), defies Fach as a bravely miscast Sir Lucius O'Trigger on Wednesday, goes Albee on Thursday, pastels into one of Anouilh's *pièces roses* on Friday, tries Laërtes on Saturday, and so on.

I'm glad he's having fun, but some ticketbuyers find it frustrating to need to consult a schedule to see a play. Yes, yes, it isn't *that* hard—but, really, isn't repertory prestigious simply because it's so difficult for us to get it right? It works in Europe, where tradition makes perfect: the civic *nomyenklatura* held court in the local theatre, and it wouldn't sit still for the same program night after night. Europeans have had a lot of practice in National Theatre; the Comédie-Française has been playing for 325 years.

Repertory is expensive. Who pays for it? The first time it was tried, rich people supported it—the aforementioned New Theatre. The second time, Eva Le Gallienne struggled with her Civic Repertory Theatre for six seasons before folding it. As we know, she was to try and try again—literally, with two more tries—but our third national theatre is what concerns us here.

This one lasted four seasons, from 1935 to 1939. Taxpayers supported it, and where the New had tone and the Civic dedication, this national theatre put on anything: classics and new work; experimental shows and ancient melodrama; musicals; puppet shows; shows in languages recent immigrants spoke; Shakespeare and Gilbert and Sullivan fiddled and straight; the simultaneous opening in twenty-one cities of an adaptation of Sinclair Lewis' vision of a fascist America, *It Can't Happen Here*; propaganda for the youngsters on a Marxist uprising in Beaverland, *Revolt of the Beavers*; Orson Welles unleashed; T. S. Eliot's *Murder in the Cathedral*; "dance dramas" based on *Candide* and *The Trojan Women* (with Helen Tamiris as Cassandra and music by Wallingford Riegger); revivals of everything from *Captain Jinks of the Horse Marines* to *Processional*; and a hit children's musical based on *Pinocchio*. President Roosevelt ran three relief programs—for writers, for painters and sculptors, and this one: the Federal Theatre Project.

The program's virtues are obvious: if hard times contract the theatre industry, it might not spring back to its former size later, because veterans will have found other work and potential newcomers will have been shy of the risk. Then, too, throwing literally every imaginable kind of theatre at the population all over the place at universally low prices might actually expand theatregoing, thus enriching the culture. As well, the Federal Theatre naturally created some "Negro Units," which guaranteed a steady wage in the precarious employment schedule of the black performer—and, lo, Federal Theatre audiences were racially desegregated, a rare occurrence at the time.

So who would be against the Federal Theatre, besides the customary anti-intellectual politicians, who loathe all arts as tending to promote independent thought? Oddly, there was deeply felt (though largely unspoken) resentment among theatre pros, who had to soldier on in a Depression without governmental subsidy while, in New York for instance, the Craig, the Ritz, and Maxine Elliott's Theatre* were handed over to . . . well, freeloaders. Still, the Federal Theatre's chief, Hallie Flanagan, thought she had the job of the century: making every kind of theatre possible on a heretofore unthinkable scale, even inventing new kinds of theatre with which to invent a new audience.

Alas, Flanagan's job really consisted of a constant diplomatic shuttle between D.C. and the controversies invented in the project's very center, the New York chapter. It was a fight a day, not least because of the Living Newspaper, epic-theatre documentaries put together as journalism is: by editors, writers, and fact-checkers. The Living Newspaper was like a revue without music, a guided tour in the form of a harangue, *Waiting For Lefty* as a science project. It drew on a broad miscellany of theatre forms from monologue to mime, now recalling the intensity of the workers' skits and now the grandeur of Elizabethan chronicle plays. It was a genre of data and passion: how was one to know fact from opinion in such entries as *Ethiopia* (1936), on Italy's African invasion, cancelled before the opening at the State Department's insistence, which led directly to the resignation of Elmer Rice, head of the New York Unit? No less confusing was *1935* (1936), looking back on the Lindbergh kidnapping trial, Dutch Schultz, Barbara Hutton, Huey Long, and the rest of the American crime-and-show-biz grab bag; and *Injunction Granted* (1936), on the bosses' war on unions; and *Spirochete* (1938), on medicine's war on venereal disease; and *". . . one-third of a*

---

* The Negro Unit played the Lafayette in Harlem, and other stages across the city were utilized for less newsworthy offerings.

Nation . . ." (1938), on the housing crisis, the title quoting one of the President's fireside chats on radio.

The Living Newspaper's mass authorship was a novelty, and while established names toiled away as before on their Broadway, the Living Newspaper's credits were introductions. Who were director H. Gordon Graham, designer Hjalmar Hermanson, composer Lee Wainer? Unfortunately, as many in D.C. saw it, the Living Newspaper's true authors were éminences grises: Stalin was the editor, Brecht the writer, and La Pasionaria the factchecker. However stridently so, the Living Newspaper actually favored FDR's policies—but that was issue enough for Washington Republicans; and it was an open secret that the typical liberal indulgence of Communists had allowed the Federal Theatre generally to swell with them. Flanagan simply would not keep a clean house.

One wonders what would have happened if Eva Le Gallienne had been put in charge instead. FDR considered it. But Le Gallienne offered to found an elite company to match the Comédie-Française or the German state theatres. The *best* of a culture. Roosevelt wanted the *most* of a culture, a relief program that—Le Gallienne must have realized—would serve as a safety net for the least capable people in the business. What Le Gallienne envisioned was a perfect *Hedda Gabler*. What Roosevelt envisioned was a poor family treated to a matinée of *Lightnin'* that would open their horizons. Theatre makes you smart.

The Federal Theatre's four years seems small until one remembers what a sprawling beehive it was. A joke in George M. Cohan's star turn as FDR, *I'd Rather Be Right* (1937), found Federal Theatre Unit no. 864 barging in to perform their production number "Spring in Vienna." As the unit director explained, "Whenever we see three people together, we're supposed to give a show."

But it wasn't a joke; there were plays going on all over the place. There was even a sudden flowering of an independent little theatre movement in New York during the 1938–39 season. Congress finally crushed the Federal Theatre on June 30, 1939—the program was shut down starting at midnight on the very day of the vote, the equivalent of a Renaissance Italian poisoning party—but Roosevelt's national theatre never did close, in a way. Because one of its most notable innovations eventually became theatre law: color-blind casting. While the Federal Theatre's Negro Units would have been happy to put on black plays, there was a shortage of the software; and such new items as William Du Bois' *Haiti* (1938) were used up quickly. So why not do . . . oh, *The [Swing] Mikado? Macbeth? The Show Off?* There was even a black staging of the Nativity (to balance a white one) during the Christmas season of 1938 that toured the city in a literal sense, playing on street corners, in front of the *Daily News* building, and on the steps of the Forty-second Street Library.

Here we must backtrack a little, to see how black theatre emerged in the Golden Age, both as a separate entity and, after the late 1930s, more integrated into the mainstream. Historians have a treasury of landmarks to cite, but an often overlooked one concerns a piece of casting in *Abraham Lincoln*, the chronicle play by the English John Drinkwater that we took note of on its appearance here in 1919. In one scene, Lincoln tells a black preacher—a freedman—of the presidential intent to proclaim Emancipation as, outside, men march off to battle to "John Brown's Body." The servant, one William Custis (apparently modeled on Frederick Douglass), was played by Charles S. Gilpin, a black man. Now, this was emancipated casting, for in 1919 custom requested all-white troupes (except for the extras) with black speaking roles played by whites in blackface.* If this was not the first such occurrence, it was the first important one, for one year later Gilpin burst into fame for his convulsive grandeur in the title role of *The Emperor Jones*.

White musicals incorporated separate black ensembles on rare occasions, and Florenz Ziegfeld definitively integrated Broadway in 1910 in hiring Bert Williams for the *Follies*, the first black *headliner* in a white show. In spoken drama, the first citation is the performance by an all-black cast of three one-acts by Ridgely Torrence for two weeks in 1917 at small, out-of-the-way theatres, first the Garden (across the street from Madison Square) and then the Garrick. Gilpin's turn in *Abraham Lincoln* is more

---

* Blackface today is commentative, reflecting critically on the characters who appear in it, such as Mandy Patinkin's scary clown monster in Michael John LaChiusa's *The Wild Party* (2000). In the 1920s, however, blackface was no more than makeup that had inhered in American performance practice for a century. Cartoonishly inflected features and white gloves comprised the look deemed appropriate for Mammy or Dixie songs, and an alternative "natural" blackface darkened white skin in straight plays, such as *Uncle Tom's Cabin* (1853). Curiously, most of the leading blackface singers of the early 1900s, such as Al Jolson, Eddie Cantor, and Tess Gardella, were Jewish or Italian, suggesting a kind of minority-group solidarity in preparation for an informal takeover of show biz in the post-*Lightnin'* world.

significant, right up on The Street at the Cort in an otherwise white troupe. The third breakthrough, most significant of all, is *The Emperor Jones*. Launched by the Provincetown Players on off-Broadway, play and staging alike aroused such interest that the show was taken uptown, in makeshift matinées here and there but then for an open run at the Princess Theatre for a total of 204 performances. Note that in the mixed-race *Jones*, the ringer was now white. (He was Jasper Deeter, soon to found the famous Hedgerow Repertory Theatre, in southeast Pennsylvania.) This led on to more expansively mixed-race productions and, as well, prominent black plays (by whites) such as Paul Green's *In Abraham's Bosom* (1926) and Marc Connelly's Bible retellings, *The Green Pastures* (1930).

The 1930s saw more black drama but fewer landmarks. (One odd statistic: the 1930–31 season was the first in almost eighty years in which there was no major tour of *Uncle Tom's Cabin*.) The Scottsboro case inspired two plays, which opened within the same week in 1934, the little-known *Legal Murder* and John Wexley's famous *They Shall Not Die,* with Claude Rains as the crusading defense attorney fighting a legal lynching. These plays continued to be the work of white writers, but now Langston Hughes entered the lists with a genuine hit, *Mulatto* (1935), which played an astonishing 375 performances in the theatre's worst season since who knew when, albeit in the smallish Vanderbilt Theatre. Like *In Abraham's Bosom, Mulatto* told of the difficulties of those of mixed genealogy, caught between the separate behavioral codes of southern life; and, as in the Green, Rose McClendon distinguished herself. The Federal Theatre, for all its ecumenism, could not field star power. The better actors had to fight for a place in commercial precincts.

The Green Pastures' twenty-one-month run (with another star turn, from Richard B. Harrison, as De Lawd) dwarfed all other black plays. But the diffidently redoubtable DuBose Heyward capped the thirties black cycle in collaboration with his wife, Dorothy, in *Mamba's Daughters* (1939). As in the Heywards' *Porgy,* the source was a novel by Du Bose and the setting was the Charleston ghetto, where blacks avoid white law enforcement to dispense their own rough justice. Maintaining the tradition that outstanding black plays offer at least one notable performance—Gilpin, McClendon, Harrison, though *Porgy* was apparently more of an ensemble statement—*Mamba's Daughters* offered Ethel Waters in her first non-musical role. In fact the a cast was filled with names that buffs dote on, including *Porgy and Bess* alumni Anne Brown, Georgette Harvey, J. Rosamond Johnson, and Helen Dowdy, along with Canada Lee, Alberta Hunter, Fredi Washington, and our own José Ferrer. Katharine Cornell's husband, Guthrie McClintic, was the producer-director, and for a special treat Heyward wrote with Jerome Kern a bel canto blues for Waters, the lament of a jailed woman called "Lonesome Walls." It's not unlike a female "Ol' Man River."

Even without the big number, Waters' role of Hagar is quite heroic, treating a woman with intense family loyalty and a homicidal resentment of those who would cheat her. The play has few if any supporters, though it ran 162 performances at the mighty Empire, but Waters' very size in the part made the assumption all the more invigorating. What other talents might have been passed over thus far? For the revelation of Sweet Mama Stringbean—agent of song, dance, and assorted "foolnish"—as an actress of stature implied that the public's appreciation of black talent had been too narrow.

Again, the Federal Theatre widened it, just by showing how much black talent there was. From song-and-dance shows *here* and the occasional black tragedy *there*, black performers were getting around with greater ease. And surely part of the job description of a democracy's national theatre would be the furtherance of democratic values. The elite stage that Eva Le Gallienne dreamed of creating would have to be called an incorrect model.

So would the Theatre Guild, despite one virtue it claims over all the other theatre organizations mentioned in this chapter: it lasted for two generations. That aforementioned opening number of *The Garrick Gaieties* spoofed the Guild's process of play selection with "We know just what to do because we always take a chance!" Yes: on European works. Some national theatre that is. Even when the Guild adopted Americana, what exactly did the Guild stand for? Excluding the likes of *The Bat* or *White Cargo,* the Guild did everything.

This was the complaint of its most stagestruck junior staffers Harold Clurman, Cheryl Crawford, and Lee Strasberg. They thought the Guild lacked focus. This trio envisioned an alternative motivated by more than the inchoate wish to "take a chance." An alternative whose actors and technicians would forge an integrated system for the honest presentation of honest writing, completely devoid of the hokum queen and matinée idol that still thronged the stage. In 1937, W. Somerset Maugham could approvingly explain acting in his novel *Theatre* in a manager's advice: "Don't *be* natural . . . *seem* natural." The Clurman-Crawford-Strasberg actor would *be* natural.

The year was 1931, not a propitious year for the founding of a company interested in what we might call Drama of Social Inquiry. Indeed, the trio did not at first *break* with the Guild. Their launching venture, Paul Green's *The House of Connelly,* was presented "under the auspices of the Theatre Guild," for the Guild had to underwrite the ten-thousand-dollar capitalization cost. Green's play had in fact been under Guild option—what play with a sad ending and folkloric patina hadn't been under Guild option, often for years on end? Set in the south, *The House of Connelly* told of the struggle between sluggish tradition and revitalizing youth; tradition wins, in the murder of the heroine by archons of the old ways, ironically enough two black women.

As we shall see, this is exactly the material that Clurman, Crawford, and Strasberg sought to build their theatre on, though they did persuade Green to revise for a sunny ending, as the young heroine prevails. The play's preparation was unprecedented: three months of summer commune training in which Strasberg coached and drilled the company (many of them Guild bit players) into an artistry of Being Natural. There was exercise in dance and improvisation. There were all-night discussions.*

Then came the customary Runthrough For the Guild, and the Gang of Six threw its usual tantrum, demanding the replacement of several actors and the reinstatement of the original tragic finish. (One can almost imagine Lawrence Langner asking, "Whoever heard of a play with a happy ending?") Clurman, Crawford, and Strasberg held firm, however. How were they to perfect the concept of thespian ensemble if actors could be plopped in and out?; and as for the ending, the alternative was not to describe the world but to improve it.

So the Guild halved its financial support and did not put *The House of Connelly* into subscription rotation. Our three breakaways now really had to break away, raising five thousand Depression dollars, scrambling for a booking, and hiring staff. Yes, they would eventually have left the Guild, but they were forced to leave *now,* as the Group Theatre, and already we have one of

---

* In the most pointless coincidence in theatre history, that first summer was spent in a Connecticut town called Brookfield: the name of the boys' school in James Hilton's *Goodbye, Mr. Chips.*

the Group's defining elements of character: integrity. In a world so compromised by needy psyches and freaks of fortune that the bitterest enemies might be writer and director, or co-stars, or married, the Group never suppressed its value system opportunistically. The five thousand dollars that the Group's chieftain trio had to raise could prove unavailable; the loss of the Guild's subscription support could mean the difference between a one-off and the future. But when the Guild menaced Green's optimistic, progressive ending and la-di-dahed Strasberg's painstakingly coordinated thespian symphony, the Group didn't have to think it over. The answer was no: or you might as well be doing *White Cargo*.

One can love the American theatre without loving Eugene O'Neill, Eva Le Gallienne, or George Abbott; the development of overhead lighting or the revolving stage; or even free programs. But one cannot love our stage without loving the Group. So why are so many critical of the organization that tried harder than any other to idealize its art? The complaints are clichés even today:

It lasted for only nine years, presenting twenty-three different plays of which but a handful joined the national stock. At least the Theatre Guild made a campaign out of Eugene O'Neill. The Group had, mainly, Clifford Odets (with six titles, his entire early output), and (with two titles each) Paul Green, Irwin Shaw, and Robert Ardrey. The emphasis on Lee Strasberg as the Group's director (Clurman and, less often, Crawford and others also directed) overstressed Strasberg's limited interpretation of the Stanislafsky System as Strasberg's own "Method." And, of course, those Group actors were ever deserting to Hollywood. Thus, Franchot Tone, the original Will Connelly in the Group's first show, soon enough became a second-rank leading man at MGM as the Gentleman in Tails vying with Real Man Clark Gable for Joan Crawford's Shopgirl Princess. And we already know the saga of Clifford Odets.

What irritates about these criticisms is that while they're mostly true they are also entirely misleading. First of all, what is "only" about lasting nine years of Depression when virtually everything you put on is non-commercial? Keep in mind that even producers dealing exclusively in commercial attractions failed all the time; and the Group never had the Lunts to fall back on.

As for the paucity of golden names among Group playwrights, didn't the Group by its very vocation have to open its own tabernacle of writers?

How many saints are to be assembled in nine years? And regarding Strasberg's direction: yes, he so centered his teaching on the actor's personaliza-
tion of character that he created a schism within the Group (though the
division was not official till the 1950s). Indeed, Strasberg's belief that Stanislafsky's program was a concluded science warred with the Russian master's
own view of his approach as an ever evolving experiment.

However, Strasberg did bond an ensemble; even critics scoffing at Group
playwrights admired the clarity of Group actors. Theatre people found the
performances fascinating, and while Groupthink rejected glamor, especially
in its Winchellian form, certain Group actors came to win the era's highest
form of prizegiving, mention in The Column. Then, too, one cannot deny
the impressive collection of talents subsumed in Strasberg's regime. There
were an unusual number of character actors, a lack of Rollo Peters. But we
note future Lear Morris Carnovsky, Lee J. Cobb, Sylvia Sydney, Jane Wyatt,
brash young man John Garfield, Van Heflin, Charles Bickford; future directors Elia Kazan and Robert Lewis; future acting teachers Sanford Meisner
and Stella Adler, who was also the Group's Leading Lady till Hollywood star
Frances Farmer came east for *Golden Boy* and Robert Ardrey's *Thunder
Rock* (1939).

As for these and others deserting the Group for the movies (or for
higher-paying jobs elsewhere on Broadway), I've already stated how comfortable it is to call "whoring" what penniless actors think of as a shot at financial stability and professional recognition. Why do we never hear sneers
at the Hollywood pilgrimages of Theatre Guild regulars Helen Westley and
Dudley Digges, not to mention people like Bette Davis, who went Hollywood at the first invitation and seldom returned, or people like Clark
Gable, who never returned at all? A persistent Broadway legend forms a
kind of mantra for Group "disloyalty": John Garfield was so outraged when
Harold Clurman preferred Luther Adler to Garfield as Golden Boy Joe
Bonaparte that Garfield stormed off to California. True, Odets had promised the role to Garfield, who was also closer in age to Joe ("21½," Odets
says, precisely, when the play begins) than the thirty-something Adler. True
as well, Clurman was romantically involved with Stella Adler, Luther's sister. But Clurman thought Garfield lacked the range for the part. Adler had
versatility and a great reserve of inner strength; absorbing fight-game atmosphere in city gyms, he even started working out and put on a build.

This, we are told, is when Garfield walked. On the contrary, though Garfield had every right to believe that his Big Break had been denied him through office politics, he joined the *Golden Boy* cast in a small (if showy) role. And he stayed with the production for five months before leaving to seek his destiny with Warner Bros.

Now for this Strasbergian Method, which one adherent has defined as "how not to act." *Be* natural, remember? That is: no showboating or attitudinizing, and none of the automatic communication that actors call "indicating." Try, from a later time, Martin Landau's definition: "Find it. Express it. Suppress it." The character content must "leak out."

That seems sensible rather than innovative, but only because we take it for granted today. Before the Group promulgated the new style, American acting was typified in—just for example—Miriam Hopkins, a now and again stage actress who specialized in movie stardom. Her work is thus amply preserved for us, and we find in it less a series of characters than one go-everywhere character. To Martin Landau's equation, she might have replied, "Be Miriam Hopkins. Expound Miriam Hopkins. Exalt Miriam Hopkins."

Yet the woman Had Something; all the stars of her day did. Strasberg's training enabled those who Didn't to excel—Morris Carnovsky, for another example. He was never a star in the Miriam Hopkins sense, yet his reviews suggest an American Olivier.

Of course, some of our greatest actors have dismissed Strasberg's teaching as affectation, a Chinese box of processes, actorism. Jason Robards occasionally did. But isn't it likely that Robards' character prep accorded at least somewhat with Strasberg's program, only without the site-specific terminology and endless discussion?

What is more abstract than the map of portrayal? To the unbeliever, Strasberg's sin was to specify the abstract, not least in that affective memory, plowing back through the actor's life to match his responses to his character's. Such fastidious autobiography, however, created the Group's unity of style. And this unity influenced not only other actors but dramatists as well: better acting necessitated better writing, for an honest actor cannot play a false line.

We see this development leading Group playwrights in particular to minimize or eject entirely those expository tip-off statements assigned to characters who would never have cause to say them in real life. One thinks of Tom Stoppard's spoof of this old-fashioned heads-up approach in the opening line of the murder thriller in *The Real Inspector Hound,* as the housekeeper answers the telephone:

> MRS. DRUDGE: Hello, the drawing-room of Lady Muldoon's country residence one morning in early spring?

Clifford Odets all but eradicates this usage, even in *Waiting For Lefty,* though it has to tell six different tales, each with its own data to fill in— "Joe and Edna," "Labor Spy Episode," "The Young Actor." Somehow, Odets picks up each of the six actions just at the moment when all the necessary information would spill out naturalistically. And *Awake and Sing!* may be the first fourth-wall, box-set American drama without a single line of conventional exposition. The curtain rises on the Bergers at the dinner table in the lines quoted (with some deletions for space) on page 201. Note how young Ralph just starts in, giving voice to something on his mind without a single word of explanation. He doesn't say "down at my place of business" to make sure the audience will understand him. He phrases it as he would phrase it in that location to those characters: "down the place." *They* know what he means. It is up to the eavesdropping public to catch up to Odets' realism, and to learn what the family relationships are from how they treat each other.

Odets' other plays are not quite so innocent of expository announcements. *Golden Boy* starts in the middle of itself, as a guy tells a woman, "Pack up your clothes and go! Go! Who the hell's stopping you?" but then backs up for some explanations. Still, it's exciting to see a Group writer leading his colleagues on to the discovery of perfect realism.

Elsewhere on The Street, some writers merrily went on megaphoning details of the backstory through the first fifteen minutes of playing time. It will be instructive, now, to jaunt over to the Plymouth Theatre, where Clare Boothe's *Margin For Error* (1939) is playing, because Boothe is not only typically mainstream in her craft but the opposite of a Group writer in every particular.

A comic melodrama-cum-whodunit, *Margin For Error* treats comings and goings in the German consulate of an unnamed American city, where, at the end of Act One, the Consul is shot before our eyes. Because Hitler is just then ranting and screaming over the radio on an international hookup, the others on stage don't hear the shot and see nothing. *We* do—but the murder is all the same a mystery, because the Nazi was poisoned *before* he was shot: so who done it?

As Erich von Stroheim had played villainous Germans during World War I, so Otto Preminger did the honors here; the rest of the cast was also strictly typed. Sam Levene offered the scrappy, sarcastic Jewish cop who solves the murder, and the Clark Gable role of the Irreverent Reporter (whose "affected carelessness of attire," says Boothe, "merely underscores his self-assured masculine appeal") went to Leif Erickson, a sometime Group player and the husband of Frances Farmer.

Margin For Error not only hires its people off the rack but allows them to present information to characters who already have the information: to tell the audience. Thus, Preminger's of course long-suffering wife tells Preminger's secretary how his boss accepts bribes to help Jewish people in Germany and then doesn't:

> SOPHIE: What about all those other poor people who come here? . . .
> He takes their money, and never even writes a word to Berlin about
> their relatives.

She's acting like a character in a play—something we find seldom or never in the scripts the Group took on.

True, *Margin For Error* is event theatre, a mustering of troops. There were a number of such anti-Nazi plays at this time, including one from the Group, Irwin Shaw's *The Gentle People* (1939), which saw a gala Return From Hollywood, by Franchot Tone. He played the neighborhood gangster whose shakedowns rouse two dreamy immigrant Americans—the title roles—to murder him. That is: democrats must not appease but kill fascism. No words. Make war.

That brings us to another of the common criticisms of the Group: that it was simply the most prominent of the decade's many left-wing theatre companies. But once again the Group stands out, for its rejection of easy-solution propaganda pieces, whether of the Theatre Union or the *Margin For Error* kind. Clurman, Crawford, and Strasberg were liberals, but unlike many of their colleagues they did not indulge fascists of the left on that doctrine of "at least they're *our* fascists." Hallie Flanagan knew that the Communist Party was taking over middle-management positions in the Federal

Theatre to crowd out political independents, yet she did nothing to stop it. But when the Party made repeated attempts to control the Group through certain of its writers and actors—as Odets and Kazan later testified—the three Group chiefs blithely but firmly shut the Party up. This was to have a far-reaching effect, too, for it was ultimately the Group that affirmed for Broadway that the valid style in sociopolitically progressive theatre must center on human character, not on revolutionary programs.

Let us consider three samples from the Group's catalogue, to learn what thinker Clurman, practical businessperson Crawford, and teacher-psychiatrist Strasberg actually put on stage, starting with their second production, Claire and Paul Sifton's *1931—*. Produced in the eponymous year with a company of twenty-five, *1931—* had Morris Carnovsky, Stella Adler, Robert Lewis, Art Smith, and the rest of the band doubling and tripling like crazy; as John Mason Brown noted, J. Edward Bromberg appeared as "a mean foreman," a "news seller," a "meek Italian laborer," and a "mean restaurant owner." "Thus," Brown joked, "I found his impartiality just a little confusing." But Brown was impressed by this tale of a young man who quits his job in a dispute with Bromberg's mean foreman, cannot find another, and sinks into a downward spiral in which he loses everything. "Heartrending," Brown called it. For while there was "crudity in its writing" it was "beautifully acted."

On the other hand, "Seldom has a bad play stunned an audience quite so completely" was Brooks Atkinson's report. Robert Garland denounced it as a "hot-and-bothered propaganda play." The Siftons originally called it *Son of God,* referring to the first son, Adam. This is the name of Franchot Tone's protagonist, who illustrates an innovative Fall. In place of original sin we get original hardship: unemployment. From this, all disaster follows on, and Adam ends his journey by joining The Revolution. The last thing we hear, offstage, is the roar of cops' machine guns.

This would seem to contradict what I said about the Group avoiding propaganda. I bring up *1931—* because, first, it was the Group's unique venture into this territory;* and, second, because the unit set decorated by mimed intervals between each plot sequence must have appealed as sheer

---

* Yes, the *other* unique venture was *Waiting For Lefty*. But *Lefty* is a superb piece of character writing and an ensemble showpiece, irresistible to an ensemble company like the Group and itself unique in the propaganda genre.

theatre; and, third, because *1931—* recalls an elucidative anecdote. We look in on a *1931—* rehearsal, sometime between first reading and the premiere; the Siftons, sitting in the orchestra, become impatient when director Strasberg takes forever going over some piece of business with a minor player. Of course, to the others on stage, all business is equal, for any detail illuminates the epic; the Siftons see a waste of time. So Paul rises from his seat and suggests that Strasberg stop jacking off and rehearse the goddamn play.

Strasberg's reply has come to us in versions both heated and grand. I like a terse one, in which he turns, looks calmly at Sifton, and says, "We are not here to rehearse your play."

What Strasberg meant was, "We are not here *only* to rehearse your play, but *also* to train ourselves to accommodate all our future plays as well, because what *one* of us learns about acting we *all* learn about acting."

A more strictly typical Group entry is Sidney Kingsley's *Men in White* (1933), the Group's biggest hit at 351 performances. Alexander Kirkland played the protagonist, a self-sacrificing young doctor whose personal life threatens his vocation. So we have the life of an individual under scrutiny in its social context—the format that, as I say, the Group bequeathed to American drama. Of greatest interest to the Group was a sequence set in an operating room, where—with a realism to astonish Belasco himself—doctors and nurses silently went through the ritual of sterilization in "the beat and rhythm [Kingsley demands] of some mechanical dance composition." The nurses seemed like attendants at some ceremonial, the doctors like practiced custodians of totem, yet all that the mesmerized audience actually saw was the steady washing of hands, the cleaning and careful use of towels (to avoid touching flesh with infected cloth), the great lamp and its mirrors, the glove table, the "gown drum." At first entirely mimed, the scene eventually opened up into dialogue till the presiding doctor called out, "Scalpel!" As the presiding nurse grasped the instrument, carefully described an arc while passing it over, and slapped it into the doctor's hand, the stage lights went dark, leaving only the operating lamp to reveal the action. As the doctors leaned forward and the nurses at the rear stood on tiptoe to watch, the second-act curtain fell. On the first night, the house broke into one of the ovations of the decade.

Like *1931—, Johnny Johnson* (1936) typifies the Group by being atypical: because within its parameters the Group did not fear adventure. A pacifist parable that starts realistically then slips into surrealist comedy,

Johnny Johnson is also a musical. It was hoped that Paul Green (writing lyrics as well as book) and Kurt Weill would give the Group a sort of play-eretta, without choreography or Big Sing numbers. However, Strasberg could not travel that far out of his milieu, and Green's intimate picaresque was lumbered with a ton of scenery in the giant Forty-fourth Street Theatre. *1931*—was a bomb and *Men in White* a smash. *Johnny Johnson* was a valiant failure that in revival invariably notches down to bomb. It needs a champion.*

I have emphasized *1931*—, *Men in White,* and *Johnny Johnson,* but the Group was so consistent in its beliefs that any of its entries is definitive. For instance, the bluntly titled *Case of Clyde Griffiths* (1936), from *An American Tragedy,* would appeal to the Group both for its social commentary and its experimentalist challenge. Dreiser's story had already been staged (1926) and filmed (in 1931), but the Group's version adopted the style of the ancient Greeks. Alexander Kirkland again played the lead, here as the boy who feels he must murder for success, and the technical challenge must have invigorated the troupe, as Morris Carnovsky took the role of Greek chorus and the Group stock company (including Kazan, Garfield, and Luther Adler) wound up avidly submerged in panorama. The adaptation was by Erwin Piscator (and his translator, Lena Goldschmidt), a towering figure in the experimental stage of Weimar Berlin, as of course was *Johnny Johnson's* Kurt Weill.

Yet few think of the Group as sustaining links with experimental theatre, with the art of spectacle. Politics and the congested battles of affective memories sound the Group's echo today. Robert Lewis complained of the Group's failure to taste of "music, color, rhythm, movement—all those *other* things in the theatre besides psychology." When the Group finally

---

* One wonders to what extent Cheryl Crawford personally urged *Johnny Johnson* on the Group, for in her later years as a producer she favored the odd item. She could also choose sagely—three of Tennessee Williams' hits, *The Rose Tattoo* (1951), *Sweet Bird of Youth* (1959), and his one comedy, *Period of Adjustment* (1960). Crawford even tossed onto Broadway a commercial Frisbee of a play, *Oh, Men! Oh, Women!* (1953), with Franchot Tone as a Psychiatrist To the Stars in a comedy hit even further from Groupthink than Clare Boothe's *Margin For Error.* But it was in the musical that Crawford made her reputation for judgment so poor it can only be called thrilling. She veered from sure ideas like *One Touch of Venus* and *Brigadoon* to shows so weird and doomed that, in heaven, when asked if she bore any earthly regrets, Crawford answered, "Why didn't they offer me *Carrie?*"

gave Lewis a chance to direct, however, it was one of the most *other* things imaginable, William Saroyan's indescribable *My Heart's in the Highlands* (1939). "The neatest surrealist crossword puzzle of the season," Robert Coleman called it. Unfortunately, the Group turned down Saroyan's one semi-classic, *The Time Of Your Life* (1939), which Lewis also directed—at first—but for the Theatre Guild.

The Time Of Your Life is not as other as *My Heart's in the Highlands,* and can even be described: in a saloon where eccentrics cut capers, a wild frontiersman—he is actually called Kit Carson—murders the cop who threatens everyone's freedom. However, unlike our anti-fascist plays of 1939, *The Time Of Your Life* has a disconnected, otherworldly quality that soothes its own propaganda, bemusing some while offending others.

Indeed, the show's New Haven premiere was a disaster. Lewis had tried to give *The Time Of Your Life* a Group presentation, not least in the stylized setting of Boris Aronson, a Group regular since *Awake and Sing!*. One of the rare designers who function as dramatists, Aronson gave *Awake and Sing!* sheer naturalism, from the wan tchottchkes to a central window that gave on a brick wall: a place full of life and short on fun.

But *The Time Of Your Life,* like all Saroyan, is a kind of dream, and Aronson gave its saloon a hallucinatory quality, as much a crazy living room as a bar. Saroyan hated it. He hated the Group, too—"a school of theatre," he said, that could be described as "Hysterical Left-Wing." Saroyan himself took over the direction of *The Time Of Your Life* (with lead actor and co-producer Eddie Dowling) in a new and firmly realistic set by Broadway regular (if onetime Group designer) Watson Barrat. Two minor players were replaced as well, by Gene Kelly and Celeste Holm, and *The Time Of Your Life* was a hit.

Does this rebuke the Group style? *The Time Of Your Life* was right up the Guild's alley because, once again, the Guild would put on anything "arty." The Group, so much more focused in its job description, nevertheless selected its plays more widely than is generally thought. It was Clurman alone who was selecting, however, because by 1937 both Crawford and Strasberg had resigned. The divorce was hostile, less to Clurman than to the actors, who had time and again challenged the triumvirate—on politics, on the choice of plays, on the hierarchy of talent among the actors that was bound to emerge even in a cooperative, and mainly because theatre is made by clowns throwing tantrums.

So in 1940 the Group ceased production; it was all over but the influence. "I don't intend to be ashamed of my life!," a line from *Golden Boy,* seems almost to warn the next generation of thespians away from . . . what? Too much *My Sister Eileen* or *Waterloo Bridge,* but also away from the ism theatre of professional scolds? If the Group's artistic adventurism is forgot, so, often, is its humanistic view of theatre based on character rather than on agenda. *Johnny Johnson,* though pacifist in social "tilt," is not about pacifism. It's about this guy.

It took the 1930s to create a Group Theatre. The organization would have been impossible earlier not only for its emphasis on working-class reality but—however ironic this may seem—for the power of its actors. Imagine if the climactic scene of *Merton of the Movies,* when the hero falls to pieces in shame at the feet of his light of love, had been played, in 1922, with the chthonic world-scream that Strasberg would have pulled out of a Group performer. (Affective memory: go back to when you were four and helpless, and someone shot your pet fawn, Scamper.) The result would not have enlightened but shattered *Merton's* audience: most theatregoers like innovation only after they're used to it.

There were actors with this power in the 1920s, but just among the stars. So Broadway could appreciate John Barrymore in *The Jest* or *Hamlet,* but not a stageful of powerful actors that Broadway hadn't heard of. The 1930s and the Group taught Broadway how the Group needed to perform— but also what the Group needed from *writers.* This explains why, when the theatre-struck David Merrick first met Arthur Miller in the company of Mrs. Miller, Marilyn Monroe, Merrick kept staring helplessly. Not at Monroe: at Miller. Because Arthur Miller was a playwright in the Group tradition, and Miller didn't intend to be ashamed of his life.

Harold Clurman went on to become a freelance director and all-around theatrical guru. Cheryl Crawford, we know, set forth on her exhibition of the good, the bad, and the closed in Boston. As well, she joined with Kazan and Lewis in founding the Actors Studio—an offshoot of the Group, you notice, just as the Group, in a different way, was an offshoot of the Theatre Guild. Lee Strasberg came along soon enough, and thus his Method became institutionalized, useful to actors even when not preparing a role for production. We are not here to rehearse your play. It's another of the Group's achievements, really: the expansion of the profession of actor from entertainer to student.

Despite some very intense resentments in the Group's final years, most of the communicants came to realize that they had in fact shared the time of their lives, and this promoted great loyalties in a way that the Theatre Guild never did. When producer Herman Levin was looking for a director for *My Fair Lady,* his authors, Alan Jay Lerner and Frederick Loewe, recommended Robert Lewis because their mutual experience on *Brigadoon* had been so happy. Lewis turned Levin down, because he had already agreed to direct Crawford's production of *Mister Johnson,* going up exactly when *My Fair Lady* was to go up.

He turned down *My Fair Lady!* Lewis was a gent, and his word was contract. But isn't there also a feeling in this tale that Lewis and Crawford were pursuing Group ideals in *Mister Johnson?* Norman Rosten's adaptation of Joyce Cary's novel, it tells of a young African (Earle Hyman) who is destroyed by the white colonial culture that he admires. It was exactly the kind of thing the Group might have done; how could Lewis have refused? He was so involved with the project that he was listed as co-producer. His very being lay in this show, because the Group was our national theatre. So Moss Hart directed *My Fair Lady* and Robert Lewis directed *Mister Johnson,* which ran for 44 performances.

Nine

Woman and Man:

SUSAN AND GOD

AND

THE ICEMAN COMETH

Among Broadway's women dramatists of the Golden Age, Lillian Hellman enjoyed the most successful career and is the only one to remain prominent after death. In fact, Hellman's fame depends less on playwrighting than on escapades—her love affair, her defiance, her lawsuit. Of other women writers, we have met Zoë Akins, Zona Gale, Anita Loos, Michael Strange, Sophie Treadwell, and a few others less well known. The most important of all now joins us: Rachel Crothers, a genuine trailblazer. Hellman excelled in forms others were already working in; Crothers created a form. Hers was the *pièce à thèse* disguised as boulevard comedy, and she may have been the first famous American to be called a "radical feminist," decades before the term became current.

Like so many "radicals," Crothers was simply an original. A midwesterner, born in 1878, she made it to Broadway at twenty-one when teaching at the Stanhope-Wheatcroft Drama School, in a special performance of Crother one-acts by her students at the Madison Square Theatre. Her official Broadway debut occurred in 1906, with a hit called *The Three Of Us,* and already Crothers had laid out the pattern she was to follow with little variation for over thirty years: a contemporary setting (one act takes us to a Nevada mining camp), a vivacious heroine more able than men (in this case her two brothers) to conquer adversaries, a popular rather than arty star in that role (favoring for instance Maxine Elliott, Estelle Winwood, and, as we'll see, Gertrude Lawrence), and a critical eye on how American culture views the two genders.

Carlotta Nilsson was the star of *The Three Of Us* in New York; in London a year later, Ethel Barrymore claimed the part and Crothers herself staged the show. Of course, dramatists frequently served as their own directors—but not the women. Crothers was original also in her acting ability, although she played in emergencies only. During the tryout of *He and She,* in 1920, its star, Viola Allen, expressed unhappiness with her part and left, so Crothers took over the role and led the company to Broadway.

Note that title. Originating as *The Herfords* in 1920, when it closed on the road, *He and She,* the unsuccessful revision, points up the salient Crothers theme, that the sexes are not equal and are never going to be. This, she says, is partly because of the male's fear of competition, but mainly because the female is biologically destined to keep society whole through the sacrifice of her egotism. That is, it is not a male-centered culture that limits women but women themselves, because of a bloodstream cocktail of compassion, pacifism, and nesting instincts.

Thus, the Herfords of *He and She* are sculptors whose marriage is threatened when she wins a competition that both have entered and he goes bad sport on her. In the end, Mrs. Herford must turn meek and self-effacing to avoid a dangerous tipping point in her life. As *Theatre* magazine commented, "a woman of genius [should be able] to follow that genius; but . . . the genius of most women lies at home."

So Crothers may let today's feminists down; and theatre historians regret a sentimental streak in her writing. But Crothers truly was tackling difficult issues. When *He and She* was revived at the Brooklyn Academy of Music, in 1980, the mixed reviews included *Variety*'s observation that some of the play was "as strong as anything in Ibsen." Perhaps Crothers' greatest quality was her complete lack of interest in the places and things of her day, those list songs of shops, products, and people that date so many old scripts. Crothers listed ideas. In the *New York Post,* Marilyn Stasio called 1980's *He and She* a "brand-new feminist play that happens to be seventy years old." And consider this: "Entire lines from this play," Stasio went on, "are probably being spoken at this very moment at Weight Watchers meetings, in the dressing rooms in Bloomie's, in the checkout lines at Zabar's."

Besides her central gender issue, Crothers also looked at the generation divide, especially among women. *Mary the Third* (1923) got by with the uncelebrated Louise Huff in what should have been a star's parade as Mary, her daughter, and *her* daughter, one after the other. (Later, when Crothers cuts to the present day, Huff maintained the title role while different actresses portrayed her elders. It wrecks the stunt.) Ever daring in her unimposing way, Crothers questioned the very concept of marriage, as Mary the Third decides to try the flapper's virtual reality by living in sin with her fiancé. Her seniors are scandalized—and what did Crothers' public think?

Yet Crothers commanded such respect that when five of the top playwrights were asked to speak at the University of Pennsylvania, Crothers was one of them, and another was Eugene O'Neill. This is prestigious billing and Broadway in a nutshell, for as Hollywood took over the theatre's trade in the various gadget genres such as the crook and prizefighter play, what remained was O'Neill and Crothers. Highbrow and midcult.

Thus, these two writers are nearly precise opposites. A rapt visionary nourishing his own doom, O'Neill was the Great Man but not the great man of the theatre. At Provincetown, making a gesture toward communitas, he acted a tiny bit and helped on the tech, but by the time he got to Broadway he was a dramatist only. Crothers, we know, directed and (when necessary) acted: a trouper. O'Neill devoted his output almost entirely to idealistic managements, moving from the Provincetowners to the Theatre Guild with a handful of commercial producers along the way. Crothers wrote for the Shuberts, Sam H. Harris, and such. O'Neill's form was tragedy, with side excursions. Crothers wrote comedy. O'Neill preferred the relatively recent past for his settings. Crothers liked nowadays. O'Neill wrote autobiographically.

Crothers guarded her privacy. Most important, O'Neill wrapped himself in myth and eternal verities, while Crothers invaded faddish situations to analyze the culture of the everyday. She taught us how to live. He taught us how to die.

We see all this at work in two titles written in the late 1930s, her *Susan and God* and his *The Iceman Cometh*. Characteristically, Crothers wrote hers for immediate production, while O'Neill wanted his held back till the war was over. Of course: she was creating out of what was in the air at the moment, while he busied himself with the long view.*

Indeed, *Susan and God* is made of a Big Idea in chitchat form—the Oxford Movement, as it was called, in which God becomes a kind of pal and faith consists of confessing everything to one's friends. Susan is an American who has fallen under the spell of a Lady Wiggam—one of the cult leaders, one might say—who runs a sort of Sinners Anonymous at her country house in Kent. "It's *thrilling* and *alive* and *fun*," Susan declares. Taking up the cause, she wants to convert her set while neglecting her alcoholic husband and attention-starved daughter. In short, Susan is one of those people who can diagnose every personality problem except her own, all the while stirring up her own combination of maddening and enchanting. "The most intelligent *fool* I've ever known" is how one of her friends puts it. That certainly sounds like Gertrude Lawrence to me; and Crothers cast Osgood Perkins as her husband and sixteen-year-old Nancy Kelly as their daughter. During *Susan and God*'s tryout, Perkins died of a heart attack, and his understudy, Paul McGrath, went on while a replacement was sought, for while Lawrence was the production's sole headliner, Broadway etiquette demanded that her immediate male support be of some stature. In the end, McGrath excelled himself, and opened the show in New York.

Conservative in her formatting, Crothers would naturally give Lawrence a star entrance. But Susan herself needs one, as the cynosure of her coterie and

---

* O'Neill recklessly prepared only two copies of the play, retaining one and trusting the other to the safe of his publisher, Random House. The Theatre Guild's board was so eager to read the piece that O'Neill finally let Random House chief Bennett Cerf lend the Guild the house copy. Now the board was chomping at the bit to stage the first new O'Neill since *Days Without End,* in 1934. The playwright was adamant, however, postponing production till the distractions of wartime were over and one full Broadway season had passed as well.

the sort of person—we all know a few—who tinkles in and out of gatherings uttering . . . well, lines. "You darlings!" Lawrence calls out, offstage. "You darlings! You darlings!" And there she is, arms flung wide to friends and public alike in, as Crothers specifies, "a new Paris creation."*

It is when Susan begins to share her newfound spiritual mania that we realize how much Crothers is our contemporary. As Susan tells her friends of an encounter with one of Lady Wiggam's servants, who had decided to shoot his wife, Susan relates how the gun failed to go off. Sounding like one of our modern zealots who refuse to utter a sentence without some evangelical propaganda somewhere in it, Susan says, "He knew it was the hand of God that stopped him."

Of course, Susan being Susan, she lacks the vacuous commitment that marks present-day Pentecostal America. On the contrary, Susan combines the excitement of the collector of enthusiasms with the attention span of a television host—as witness Lawrence's first exit, a tiny sermonette on how Susan's latest craze will prove just the cure for "this awful emptiness." Indeed, "it is the only thing in the world that will stop war." Then, without skipping a beat, Susan tells her pal Irene as they pass through a doorway, "I've brought you the most ravishing panties."

Can Susan be cured? is Crothers' question. Can she be Saved: from taking up God as one samples canasta? Bless her heart, Crothers doesn't pretend to know. She has a feeling that the meliorators of this world are as much a problem as a solution, so the playwright deliberately neglects the Big Idea and concentrates on her heroine—fleshing out the question, so to say.

O'Neill, on the other hand, sometimes creates characters out of generalities. *The Iceman Cometh* is peopled partly with types—the self-hating anarchist who Left the Movement and never stops talking about it; the Boer War veterans who are placeless in peacetime; the black obsessed with white

---

* Joan Crawford played Susan in the film version, and while she is too earthbound for the flighty know-it-all, costumier Adrian designed airborne "creations" that count among the most created ever seen at MGM. One outfit is a white suit with matching hat that suggests a sawed-off topper. A black bowed band trims it, dropping a black mesh veil that reaches nearly to Crawford's waist. White gloves and a black cane complete the look. Even more imaginative is Crawford's entrance kit: a cloak over a dress whose bodice is adorned with a leather strap and a pouch, with sandals below and, on top, a cap supporting a gigantic vertical feather. One thinks of Chi Chi LaRue in the role of Robin Hood.

racism. But then, part of O'Neill's power lies in this very flaw: never will he "naturalize" his drama by cutting a Big Idea down to human size. He revels in grandeur. How many times, in *The Iceman Cometh,* does a character refer to "pipe dreams"—*this* play's Big Idea, meaning the illusions about oneself that help the loser to survive. Crothers never errs so; she is a master of balance. Then, too, Crothers trusted her public while O'Neill thought his simple and distracted. Yet those "pipe dream" repetitions soon become risible; and there's a fault in diction as well. It's too pat a phrase for a concept that few comprehend, much less bother to name.

However, if we set *Susan and God* and *The Iceman Cometh* next to each other, we notice that the two treat the same theme: man's desperate need to scare away "this awful emptiness" with "pipe dreams." Crothers' Susan and O'Neill's Hickey, the two protagonists, both think they know what's good for everyone else, and both are at least as troubled as those they would help.

Beyond that, the plays have nothing in common. Crothers is central Broadway; so is O'Neill. But Crothers tailored her plays—to stars, to business as usual, to a public willing to be challenged *to a certain extent.* O'Neill wrote for himself, which is why Crothers has vanished and O'Neill is more popular than ever: we're still trying to catch up to him.

Consider the first moments of contact between play and spectator. Crothers draws her curtain up on a familiar place, the terrace of a country house in summer. This one happens to be glass-enclosed, but it's essentially an upper-middle-class leisure place with a grand piano, and those in the audience who didn't have their own patios had seen plenty in plays like *Susan and God.* Populating the scene are couples returning from seasonal activity—horseback riding and tennis. It's real life among the well-to-do.

O'Neill takes us to a barroom in a slum, the tables occupied by sleeping drunks and one conscious drunk, Larry Slade (the aforementioned self-hating anarchist). The men apparently live in the bar, their existence centered on maintaining a place in the alcoholic's nirvana; and Slade is O'Neill's spokesman. Known generally as "the old Foolosopher," he is articulate and cynical, a very O'Neillian type—the Jason Robards role, though, as we'll see, Robards' *Iceman* experience led him to a very different part. The saloon is the property of Harry Hope, a God of giving, for it is Hope's booze that keeps these men alive. They dwell in a haze, literally a stupor but in effect a mess of dreams, the pipe dreams that we keep hearing of. But note that Slade sees Hope's den as being *without* hope:

SLADE: It's the No Chance Saloon. It's Bedrock Bar, The End of the Line Café, The Bottom of the Sea Rathskeller! Don't you notice the beautiful calm in the atmosphere? That's because it's the last harbor. No one here has to worry about where they're going next, because there is no farther they can go.

Alcoholism is a supremely dreary subject, but *The Iceman Cometh* isn't about drinking. The liquor that opens up the dream is a metaphor for success without achievement; or the phony denial of failure; or the sleep that is a rehearsal for death. It's The End of the Line Café, all right. However, like another remarkable work of American theatre, the Stephen Sondheim musical *Follies, The Iceman Cometh* is not to be taken literally, even though—unlike *Follies*—it is absolutely naturalistic in its action. Also unlike *Follies,* it tells of people with no future where *Follies* is concerned with people with too much past.

There is as well the conjuring up of *Follies* out of the myths of show-biz America; O'Neill seems to have used *his* play as an autobiographical exorcism of some personal demons. There really was a Harry Hope's, called Jimmy the Priest's—note, again, the association of the saloonkeeper with a religious vocation, the "hope" of salvation or simply death. Like Hope's place, Jimmy the Priest's was a tenement rooming house with a bar on the ground floor, an entire world contained within a single room of comrades, prostitutes, and drink.

Amusingly, O'Neill gives his lead a star entrance, too. Like Crothers, he primes the pump with remarks *about* his hero before he appears, but in much grander tempo. Hickey's first line—"Hello, Gang!"—doesn't occur till page 76 of the printed text (of 260 pages), nearly one-third of the running time of a very long evening. Not that O'Neill believed that length was a proof of quality: but quality did mean richness of observation, development of throughlines, and skillful use of echo texture. Dudley Nichols, an O'Neill intimate, recorded that O'Neill feared that the skittery bits of media ambience—in radio spots, "capsule news and a nervous brevity in everything we do," in Nichols' words—made it all but impossible for theatregoers to accommodate the *largo* delineations of O'Neill's Big Idea plays. Nichols particularly adduced Walter Winchell's rat-a-tat plugs and exposés to this diagnosis of attention deficit. And of course Winchell's was the voice of Broadway. Was it entirely coincidental that O'Neill's first whopper, *Strange Interlude,* came along in 1928, a few years after Winchell had conclusively imprinted his style upon the "word" that O'Neill lived in?

Pursuing our comparison of O'Neill and Crothers, let us consider titles. *Susan and God* sounds, all at once, like a worry (could Susan be partly right?), a sarcasm (and Susan gets top billing), and a hit. *The Iceman Cometh* is another of those poetic O'Neill titles, though this one carries some baggage. Do you know the old joke? Clancy calls up from the street to his wife on the fourth floor, "Did the iceman come yet?" "No," says the missus, "but he's just now reached the shoutin' stage." Literally, the title refers to Hickey's wife's infidelity. Symbolically, we look to Matthew, chapter 25, the Parable of the Ten Virgins. Verse 6 includes "Behold, the bridegroom cometh," and verse 19 "The lord of those servants cometh," and we ultimately learn who will get into "life eternal" (the generous) and who into "everlasting punishment" (the selfish). True enough, Harry Hope's is a kind of antechamber of Judgment; as Slade says, "there is no farther they can go"—in this life.* Drink postpones Judgment—but Hickey interferes with this Gorkyan lotus eating by making each of Hope's crew face up to and conquer his unique delusion. His pipe dream. To what end? Like Rachel Crothers' Susan, Hickey is the problem, not the solution. Following along with Matthew, Hickey is the bridegroom (albeit one who kills his wife) and Harry Hope is the lord of those servants. As the Parable of the Ten Virgins was well known in the America of O'Neill's youth, there does seem to be some connection between play and parable. The now irascible, now jesting Hope makes an interesting God, but, moving into heathen mythology, Hickey is a kind of Prometheus: he offends God with arrogance.

So does Susan, of course, but a comparison of final scenes reminds us how much separates Crothers from O'Neill. The tidy *Susan and God* confronts Susan with *her* arrogance, allowing the audience to forgive her when she starts forgiving everyone else, starting with her husband. The two are alone in her room at that country house, moving toward reconciliation till we hear a line that unmistakably warns the stagehands to prepare for the final curtain and the calls:

---

* There is as well the couplet in Macaulay's "Lays of Ancient Rome": "To every man upon this earth/Death cometh soon or late." Dudley Nichols says O'Neill meant *The Iceman Cometh* as *Death Comes For Hickey.*

SUSAN: I want to be so much more to you than I've ever been before. Please let me try again.

She goes to him, begging for an embrace and getting one, to our approval. Now the last line, with the merest hint that Susan fears that her busybodying days are not entirely over:

SUSAN: Oh, *dear* God—don't let me fall down again.

It's a satisfying conclusion in the "well-made" play sense, but also in Crothers' giving her star a provocative yet oddly conclusive last word. Still, that last scene is not star flattery but realistic character writing for a dysfunctional but not unloving marriage. And one Big Idea that Crothers is willing to tackle is God. He is not "something out there . . . to pray to," Susan finally realizes, like some "faith-based" fashion accessory. God is a mystery, indefinable and unknowable, and like L. Frank Baum's Oz He appears differently to each one who regards Him.

He was electricity to O'Neill (at least in *Dynamo*). However, it is not God but Man whom O'Neill regards here, and with all his themes and throughlines to put in order, and his opposition of Hickey and Hope to conclude, *The Iceman Cometh* takes its entire fourth act to do what Crothers does in five minutes. The spine of this act is The Long Speech, Hickey's account of *his* truth, the evaporation of his own pipe dream after he has tried to dispel everyone else's.

The Long Speech is a play in itself, for though most theatregoers recall it as a monologue, it is constantly hectored by outbursts from others on stage.* The entire cast is on hand, including two characters used in this act alone whose entrance O'Neill deliberately does not specify. The stage directions state only when they "come quietly forward." Moran and Lieb by name, they "look ordinary in every way, without anything distinctive to indicate what they do for a living." They are police detectives, here to witness

---

* Part of this is simply sound storytelling, for Hickey has ruined everyone's survival defenses and the bar is arguing with him. Also, O'Neill wants us to hear from the individuals of the ensemble to keep his mosaic colored in. Most important, as a true son of the theatre, O'Neill knew that the actor playing Hickey would need those intermittent cue lines to steady his voyage through the immense recitation. However much O'Neill led the Other Broadway, he was all the same steeped in the practicalities of playmaking.

Hickey's confession and arrest him. Dei ex machina, these faceless men free the residents of a place called Hope—and you in the audience—to live again. In your dreams.

O'Neill of course has yet more to close down before dropping his curtain. Even after Hickey is taken away, fifteen pages of text must be heard, with supporting lead roles to top off, one plotline to conclude, and something to fix all the play's thematic content for us—a fade-out close-up on some essential view of this palace of lying bliss. The plotline's conclusion is perhaps the most macabre moment in all O'Neill: the suicide of a young man, in expiation of his sin of ratting on his mother, a stalwart of the Movement. This is Don Parritt, the work's sole part (of sixteen for men) that can be cast with a *jeune premier*. (The young Robert Redford and Jeff Bridges have each had a go at him.) What makes Parritt's end so spooky is that Larry Slade briefly departs from his emcee's activity sheet to await with angry eagerness Parritt's jump to his death from the top of the building:

> SLADE: God damn his yellow soul, if he doesn't soon, I'll go up and throw him off!—like a dog with its guts ripped out you'd put out of misery!

and *just* then we hear the very sound of Parritt's leap of doom, right down to "a muffled, crunching thud."

Everyone in the bar hears it, but only Slade knows what has happened. Having already created a transition from the horror of Hickey to the normality of life in false Hope, O'Neill is now ready for a grand finale, as everybody but Slade breaks into song—thirteen different melodies at the same time, from nineteenth-century ballad and English music hall to Irving Berlin and a French Revolutionary fight song. Singing and shouting and laughing and banging their glasses on the table, the lifelong cast of *Harry Hope's Follies* has returned to the point at which it all began. True, the action started with almost everybody in a coma and now the cast is in full cry: but what difference does it make in the land of waiting to die? The fade-out close-up is Slade, who sees and knows all yet is no more able to improve the human condition than the rest of us. It is one of the great stage pictures in the oeuvre of a man who—once again—knew how theatre *plays*. The entire stage is in riot except for Slade, who "stares in front of him, oblivious to [the] racket." And the curtain comes down.

"To audiences accustomed to the oily virtuosity of George Kaufman, George Abbott, Lillian Hellman, Odets, Saroyan," wrote Mary McCarthy, reviewing the original production in *Partisan Review* in 1946, "the return of a playwright who—to be frank—cannot write is a solemn and sentimental occasion."

Indeed, *The Iceman Cometh* did not get the kind of welcome that *Susan and God* could count on. It's easier to pull off a play about one relatively small thing in a familiar setting in audience-friendly naturalism with a star turn. To please with an epic set in fantastical naturalism is tricky, and while *The Iceman Cometh* does have a star part, the original star was inadequate.

This was James Barton, whom we last saw playing half of *Tobacco Road*'s eight-year run and now best recalled for his Ben Rumson in Lerner and Loewe's *Paint Your Wagon* (1951), complete with his trademark soft-shoeing and drunk act. One can see why the Theatre Guild and director Eddie Dowling wanted Barton, for he utterly embodied O'Neill's Hickey: "about fifty, a little under medium height, with a stout roly-poly figure . . . He exudes a friendly, generous personality that makes everyone like him on sight." Still, even after *Tobacco Road* Barton was more an old vaudevillian than an actor per se, and while he entered well, so to speak, he could not sustain the very size of the text, especially in that big "monologue." Not only was Barton unable to discover a way to live within its rhythms; he simply couldn't remember the words, and had to take prompts from the wings.*
Dowling was no doubt dying to take over the role himself, but he had all he could handle keeping the show operating at speed. Many were those who blamed Barton for the disappointing 136-performance run.

Certainly, it was the superb Hickey of Jason Robards Jr. in the 1956 Circle in the Square revival, under José Quintero, that reclaimed *The Iceman Cometh* as an American masterpiece. Tall and slim, Robards inaugurated a new line of Hickeys, less roly-poly than dapper and even glamorous. Lee Marvin is Hickey in the 1973 film; more recently, Kevin Spacey played him in London and New York. In Yvonne Shafer's book *Performing O'Neill*, James

---

* There's a story that at one performance Barton sailed through the thing without a single hesitation, and the audience, sensing a unique occasion, gave him an ovation.
† There was truly an air of ruthless purpose in Spacey's portrayal, also a questionable lack of warmth. However, Spacey's dazzling technical command made something extra-special

Earl Jones—another Circle in the Square Hickey, Class of '73—describes Robards' Hickey as "a seducer" to Spacey's "avenging angel."[†] O'Neill himself possibly didn't realize that there is more than one way to play Hickey, or he might have wanted Barton replaced.

In any case, every major Hickey after Barton has demolished the notion of O'Neill as the actor's nightmare—"a kind of triumphant catastrophe," to refer again to Mary McCarthy. No: he's "exhilarating to play," Robards told Shafer. "All you had to do was learn the lines and you can't go wrong." And, yes, other writers who seemed so much more natural in their English such as McCarthy's oily virtuosos are in the archives (like Saroyan), or reduced to one or two titles (like Hellman), or "commercial" (like Kaufman). O'Neill is the one most regularly put back on stage, because—this is Edmund Wilson now—"he nearly always, with whatever crudeness, is expressing some real experience, some impact directly from life." When José Quintero and Jason Robards would cross paths, Quintero would tell him, "We've got to get back to the Old Man." If it seems almost capricious to compare a play by Rachel Crothers with one by Eugene O'Neill, it's not because O'Neill dwarfs Crothers. O'Neill dwarfs *Broadway;* nothing compares, especially when it comes to the *Iceman.* As James Earl Jones puts it, with wonderful lightness, "There I met a great play."

---

of *his* monologue. He gave it as an ace fighter pilot flies his plane, making a different run every time. Disdaining lesser actors' aids—the sealed-in-stone blocking used as an *aide-mémoire,* the addressing of particular lines to particular characters—Spacey challenged himself to reinvent the scene anew for each performance.

Ten

Dogs Are Sticking to the Sidewalks:

THE EARLY 1940s

The major difference between the Broadway of the 1940s and Broadway before lies in its relationship with Hollywood: so powerful in the 1930s but losing grip from now on. One reason is that after ten years of talkie the movies had reestablished their talent pool, based as much on verbal personality as on ability, and no longer needed to import actors who spoke well. True, people who were to be known exclusively as movie stars continued to invigorate their career with a Broadway launching or crank-up, even such purely celluloid developments as Jayne Mansfield and

Burt Reynolds. Broadway continued to be useful to Hollywood: but less essential.

Then, too, Hollywood no longer bought up the screen rights to plays indiscriminately. Hit shows were filmed, but now few flops attracted interest as each studio sought to create low-budget series programmers built around, say, Warner Bros.' dauntless reporter Torchy Blane (Glenda Farrell); MGM's picaresque showgirl Maisie (Ann Sothern); or detectives such as Charlie Chan, Nancy Drew, the Falcon; or the aforementioned Henry Aldrich.

One constant of the 1930s held true: the movies' genuine reverence for the stars and performing styles of the musical. To an extent, Hollywood ran intermittent commercials for bygone and current Broadwayites, most obviously in bios of everyone from George M. Cohan and the Dolly Sisters to Cole Porter and Jerome Kern, but also in resuscitations of the old ways, even a way as old as the minstrel show, an MGM obsession.

What most hurt Broadway in the 1940s was Hollywood's collapsed respect for literary prestige. Nervous about the future of the talkie in 1929 and the early 1930s, the moguls hired New York wit, lingo, eloquence. But by 1940 California wanted a community of writers native to film; knowhow trumped prestige. This led to a certain rivalry between the two coasts, a mild genuflection by movie writers when a New Yorker passed, an unreasonable intolerance on Broadway when a new byline was found to have logged movie experience. Some wanted it put into general belief that the stage was a place of idealism and film one of greed. Walter Winchell had some fun with this, telling how Moss Hart ran into Clifford Odets at a Hollywood party. Hart told Odets that, emulating Odets, all the writers in Hollywood were turning Communist. "You mean my plays converted them?" Odets asks. "No," says Hart. "Your salary."

But it wasn't just the money: it *was* the prestige. Yet more lay in it, something so abstract that it might be reduced to the simple prejudice that New York felt about Los Angeles. Isn't this why Arthur Miller billed his typescript for the movie *The Misfits* (1961) as "an original play for the screen"? A *play* by a *writer*. Of course, as we know, Clifford Odets is everybody's favorite Broadway renegade, a dramatist turned Hollywood hack. Yet his play *Clash By Night* (1941) was filmed (in 1952) in a complete revision by *another* writer, Alfred Hayes. This points up another problem in Broadway's relationship with Hollywood: in the 1930s, the movie adaptation might rival the original only supplementarily. Now, however, technical advances and the evolution in naturalistic acting empowers Hollywood to outperform Broadway in certain respects. For instance, the *Clash By Night* movie is vastly better than the play.

One reason why is the setting, the Staten Island shore in summer, when the marriage of hot Mae and dull Jerry breaks down under pressure from the fascinating Earl. A projectionist in a movie theatre, he repels but also captivates Mae with his hot-rodding small talk. Show biz has been teaching us that the erotically charged person is but a notch of civilization away from throwing off his or her clothes and scorning the Commandments on meeting another person of similar inclinations. It's why Stanley tells Blanche, "We've had this date with each other from the beginning!" when he rapes her.

So it is with Mae and Earl, but Odets' talky script and the play's modest views of the steamy environment give no scope to the explosive sexual attraction that the story tells of. The movie, directed by Fritz Lang, sees the tense need that Mae and Earl live in, contrasting the public spaces of saloon and beach with the clogged little privacy of her tiny home and his projection booth. Further, Hayes and Lang build the play's second couple, Joe and Peggy, into a kind of low-rent ideal with their bickering and pawing.

Indeed, Lang can "visualize" Odets in the first sixty seconds after the credits, with establishing shots of seals and birds at liberty in a harbor, jumping to the hard life on fishing boats or in the cannery. At last Lang cuts to a long shot of Mae trudging along a mini-labyrinth of boardwalk with a suitcase, as if about to make a choice about where to go in life. A play staged on Broadway simply has no opportunity thus to conceptualize its premise in pictures. At that, Odets' Mae is already married to Jerry, her story half over. Lang and Hayes have more to work with in bringing Mae into the beginning of the end of her voyage, teasing her with choices when she believes she has none. In a line invented by Hayes that sounds like basic Odets, Mae says, "Home is where you go when you run out of places."

True, Lang and Hayes had an ideal movie cast, each an expert in type. Barbara Stanwyck's Mae is the archetypal working-class broad too smart for her kind, and Paul Douglas epitomizes the good-natured cipher. Robert Ryan's Earl is alarming: coarse and contemptuous of all life forms but himself, he nevertheless commands a Big Guy fascination that Mae can't ignore. Opposite Keith Andes' beautiful clod of a Joe is Marilyn Monroe, just being graduated from notable bits to movie star.

However, the stage cast was also excellent, and producer Billy Rose put on, in effect, a Group Theatre production, with sets by Boris Aronson and direction by Lee Strasberg at the Belasco, a Group haunt (of Odets' plays especially). And the Group's Lee J. Cobb played Jerry, opposite Tallulah Bankhead's Mae, with Joseph Schildkraut again playing *homme fatal* as Earl. (Robert Ryan, the movie's Earl, here played Joe, opposite Katherine Locke.)

Clash By Night's Broadway opening was extra-glamorous, a genuine hot ticket in the way that actual Group shows never had been. Part of this was the work of producer Rose, a master player of the PR game; part of it was Bankhead. But part of it—perhaps—was that The Street had to wait till the Group had disbanded before it could appreciate what the Group had set in motion. This proves that the Group was a success after all: nobody in America pays attention to a failure.

Bankhead got the notices. George Freedley, in the *Morning Telegraph*, declared that Tallulah was giving "the best performance of her career." What? After *The Little Foxes,* in the role with which she is permanently associated? Yet Arthur Pollock of the *Brooklyn Eagle* concurred. "Her greatest achievement," he called it.

True, as a Staten Island hausfrau Bankhead could not rival Stanwyck in casting genetics. Yet Bankhead apparently made it work, perhaps emphasizing the lowdown in the Slumming Aristo that was her trademark front. It was the play itself that won no favor. The sole review I can locate that liked it was in the *Daily Worker,* for once forgiving one of "their" side for failing to politicize his characters. Even this review dubbed Odets' story "Triangle Plot No. 4111-A." (This critic, too, thought Bankhead superb.) Interestingly, Odets ends the action with Jerry's murder of Earl, while in the film Jerry only attempts the killing, and he and Mae reconcile. It's fitting: the constraints of theatre make it logical that this crowded, even suffocated trio find release only in a murder in a projection booth, whereas Lang so expanded Odets' setting with his harbor and beach scenes that the characters find a way out, room to live in. And while Lang did have some ten years' advantage over the original play, even in the 1940s the theatregoing class was a moviegoing class as well. They were becoming used to the sheer freedom of film.

Here's another example: *The Pirate* (1942), S. N. Behrman's adaptation of a German play of 1911, *Der Seeräuber* (literally, *The Searobber*), by Ludwig Fulda. Here was one thing Hollywood could not rival, a Theatre Guild special for the Lunts. Moreover, Alfred gave *The Pirate* one of his stunt productions, like *The Taming Of the Shrew*. Lunt saw *The Pirate* as a kind of musical, acrobatic rather than sung and, in a nod to the Caribbean setting, on Santo Domingo, utilizing a *Porgy and Bess* ensemble, but less purely lyrical than vivacious and saucy.*

Lunt shared director's credit with John C. Wilson, but the surprises were typically Luntian, such as his goof on the Star Entrance. Lynn got the first one, for she was onstage at the curtain up, fanning her dozing old slob of a husband—but the audience saw only her back, creating a buzz of whispers as the quicker parties in the auditorium started the applause. Alfred's materialization was impish, for he entered without quite being seen during a crossover parade separating the first two scenes: touring players were coming to town. Lunt was their capocomico, and as a donkey cart laden with costumes and props passed by, the audience noticed Lunt's legs hanging out from under the load.

Even the sets and costumes reflected Lunt's vision of a place so dull that everyone spends his time getting elaborately dressed. Our old friend Estelle Winwood, already in her loony-old-bag phase as Fontanne's mother, was outfitted to look—quoth the stage directions—"like the tails of nine peacocks," and the view was clogged with parasols, hammocks, and a hypnotic revolving mirror. Perhaps the busy production was meant to fill out a thin plot line: Fontanne dreams of the bloodthirsty pirate Estramudo, and believes that she has found him in Lunt. She *has* found him: but not in Lunt. Estramudo, retired, is that grumpy slug of a husband.

The script is actually one of Behrman's more adroit concoctions, devoid of sociopolitical remark but rich in Sophistication. There is a touch of Noël Coward in this exchange between Lunt and the plot's deus ex machina, the local viceroy:

VICEROY: With your passion for acting, I wonder you bother with piracy.
LUNT: I am a lazy man, Excellency. Piracy is so much easier.

---

* Musical-comedy aficionados will place, among Lunt's backup, such future leading players as Juanita Hall, Inez Matthews (of *Lost in the Stars*), and Maurice Ellis (of *Seventeen*). The true fanatic will delight in the participation of Muriel Rahn, whose fifteen minutes comprised taking over the ingenue lead in *St. Louis Woman* from Ruby Hill during the tryout and then being fired in favor of the returning Hill at the insistence of virtually the entire cast.

There are many clever touches, as when Behrman ends Act One with Lunt on a tightrope, holding his shoes and keeping his balance with one of those parasols as he sleeks his way through the air to Fontanne's bedroom. For a quaint surprise, Behrman then starts Act Three in the bedroom just before Lunt, with the shoes and parasol, came bounding in through the window.

And yet. Doesn't this kind of thing have to be a musical—a *real* one? The braggy hero, the company of players, the exotic locale and visual feast, and above all the yearning heroine? Lunt calls her "the most extraordinary mixture of fantasy and realism": isn't that a role fit for song? Isn't musical comedy by definition a mixture of fantasy and realism?

And of course it was MGM that realized *The Pirate*'s generic completion, in 1948, retaining the Broadway title for a Gene Kelly–Judy Garland Technicolor special: songs by Cole Porter, and Vincente Minnelli directing with an eye keen for the look of the piece, just as Lunt had done. However, if on Broadway *The Pirate* was gaudy, on screen it went utterly rococo, perhaps Caribbean Sophisticated, with derbies on women and pantaloons on men. Porter is not at his best, yet that ho-hum married team Frances Goodrich and Albert Hackett (later the adapters of *The Diary of Anne Frank*) throw Behrman to the winds to create a rather enjoyable script.

The Pirate lost money on first release and is still no more than a cult favorite. Still, if the thin story has any validity it would be as a vehicle for the exhibitionism of Kelly and the strangely touching comic-romantic style that no one else commands as naturally as Garland. If any duo can rival the Lunts in their form, it is Kelly and Garland in theirs, for the Lunts really were too rich a brew for this cauldron. Lunt a fraud? Fontanne yearning? It's Kelly, rather, who ham-and-eggs through life, Garland who needs. She gets a line funnier than anything in the play, when, to save the town, she must submit to the (false) pirate's advances. All are aghast, not realizing that, just between us, Garland is fulfilling her dream of becoming The Bride of the Buccaneer. As she proceeds to her "doom," one village girl gallantly offers to go in her place:

GARLAND: He asked for *me*.

Clash By Night and *The Pirate* point up something that few were willing to admit at the time: for all Broadway's high-hat, "take the money and run" view of Hollywood, some works seemed inadequate until they were filmed, further encouraging audiences to concentrate on moviegoing.

For now, however, the war years were Broadway's most lucrative since the late 1920s, as the well-to-do sought distraction from war news, and servicemen impressed their dates with a classy outing. A theatre crunch caused by the new long-run syndrome led to the rediscovery of the neglected auditoriums clustered around Columbus Circle, and a new genre appeared, loosely called "the war play." The Lunts tackled Finland versus the Soviet Union in Robert E. Sherwood's *There Shall Be No Night* (1940). Lillian Hellman advocated killing Nazis in *Watch on the Rhine* (1940). James Gow and Arnaud d'Usseau urged patience in rehabilitating a slimy Nazi kid entrusted to his American uncle in *Tomorrow the World* (1943).

The chronicle play seemed timely now. Sidney Kingsley's *The Patriots* (1943) looked in on President George Washington, Thomas Jefferson, and Alexander Hamilton in the early days of the Republic, to consider America's first principles. The show ran four and a half months and won the Drama Critics Circle Award, but its halfhearted reception disappointed Kingsley, who had worked on it for four years and seemed to regard it as more Important than *Men in White* and *Dead End*.

Howard Koch and John Huston's *In Time to Come* (1941) did even less well. Centering on the Versailles Peace Conference, it presented Clemenceau, Lloyd George, and Sonnino, but centered on Wilson (Richard Gaines). "A careful recital" was the *Christian Science Monitor*'s appraisal of Gaines' impersonation. It's a tribute to Gaines' authenticity, for Wilson—cold, stubborn, and absurdly idealistic when set against European Realpolitik—was one of our most wooden politicians.

There was far livelier entertainment in Moss Hart's *Winged Victory* (1943). It even got a cast album, actually just two twelve-inch 78s bearing the show's entire vocal score: four choral numbers, including Yale's "Whiffenpoof Song" (with relevant new lyrics in the verse) and "The Army Air Corps" (the one about "the wild blue yonder"). This recording leads some to think of *Winged Victory* as the Air Force's musical, to match *This Is the Army* (1942). But the latter is a revue with an almost wholly new score (by Irving Berlin), while *Winged Victory* is a play. Note that one of our leading Sophisticates, Moss Hart, has taken on the job of ladling out patriotic corn without a single Upper West Side sarcasm.

Like *This Is the Army*, *Winged Victory* was an intramural effort, cast entirely with soldiers (and civilian women, including many of the actors' real-life wives). A company of more than three hundred followed the progress of some half dozen inductees, as one fails his dream of becoming a pilot, one is wounded, one is killed, and one, at the very end, anticipates the coming of his firstborn. It took a bold Sophisticate indeed to declare himself unmoved by this very human epic, and again like *This Is the Army*, *Winged Victory* did sellout business till its ontological status as a national act of faith rather than a strictly Broadway attraction forced it to close up and tour. One odd note: despite the gigantic cast and technical problems (including seventeen different sets), Hart got the whole production ready for the Boston tryout in only seventeen days' rehearsal! As he explained it, he had no actory temperaments to tame: soldiers take orders, *et plus vite comme ça*.

Perhaps the best of the war plays was Paul Osborn's *A Bell For Adano* (1944), from John Hersey's novel. Although it tells and approves of an officer's insubordination, it proved extremely popular as a serious comedy with an unhappy yet inspiring ending. There is almost no plot: Major Joppolo (Fredric March), of our forces in occupied Sicily, tries to cajole, encourage, or fend off various residents of Adano, each with his own needs to be satisfied. Underlying it all is one communal need, for a replacement for the town's seven-hundred-year-old bell, melted down for bullets by the fascists. The bell was everything to Adano—timetable, protection, history. "When it spoke," says one of the locals, "our fathers spoke to us."

Joppolo manages to get a new bell for Adano—from the Navy—but meanwhile an idiot general lays down a pointless order that will do great harm to life in Adano. Osborn keeps this general offstage as a screaming terror that Joppolo is heard vainly trying to reason with. Note that while Joppolo can work with even the slyest and most manipulative of the villagers, an Army general is a thing apart, a regulation rather than a human being. So Joppolo countermands the order, saving the village. For this, he is reassigned to a punishment job in Algiers. As Joppolo departs, the new bell begins to peal out. "Listen," he cries, "it shakes the whole damn building!" Again offstage, we hear the townspeople in their excitement. Joppolo leaves, and as the bell rings out the curtain falls.

The war plays were destined to become artifacts, perhaps. Certain of the star vehicles seemed even more ephemeral, though some of the titles themselves remain vivid, if only to buffs and historians. Audiences flocked to the hideous *succès de bombe* called *My Dear Children* (1940) to see the wreckage of John Barrymore. He played the actor father of three problematic young women, wearing crazy costumes (including a Hamlet getup and an Alpine ensemble), reeling drunkenly around the stage, and tossing off ad libs aimed at latecomers and his co-star and latest wife, Elaine Barrie.

The fiery Barrie-Barrymore marriage, fanned by Barrie's noisy mother, was part of *My Dear Children*'s PR appeal, even after Barrie left the cast during the all but phenomenal thirty-three-week Chicago run during the tryout. As with the Barrymore Hamlet, no two audiences saw the same performance, and pundits clucked over the sorry choice of vehicle for the actor's first stage turn in almost a generation, in fact his farewell to art but for a few minor film parts. Yet the Barrymore wit was as sharp as ever, even through the alcoholic haze. During the Chicago stand, a fire engine siren was heard outside, and John cried, "Good God, my wife!" Immediately after, a truck backfired, and John grabbed for a topper: "And she's got her mother with her!"

Mae West was by comparison almost dull in *her* sorry choice of vehicle, *Catherine Was Great* (1944), on the famous Russian monarch. West, too, was returning after a long stay in Hollywood, but unlike Barrymore's low-rent show, West's was Big Broadway. Her producer was Michael Todd, no Gilbert Miller but a guy willing to Spend the Money. The *World-Telegram*'s Burton Rascoe thought the *Catherine* production made *The Miracle* look like something spit out by the Federal Theatre, and a glittering first-night crowd (who had paid their admission in war bonds to the tune of four *million* dollars) cheered the costumes. There was nothing else to cheer, for that premiere hosted a series of disasters—the music amplifier failed, a nervous cast muffed cues, a curtain parted at the wrong moment to exhibit a stagehand donking away on some task as the audience whooped.

Then there was the script itself. A pair of unknowns wrote *My Dear Children,* but West was her own auteur, and she let her star down with too much Russian history. "Miss West talking about men is one thing," wrote *PM*'s Louis Kronenberger. "Miss West talking about 'the people' is quite another." True, the rapaciously amorous West persona was on hand. Robert Garland found the tsaritsa relentlessly "in the Royal Bed Chamber, talking about the Royal Bed Chamber, thinking about the Royal Bed Chamber, or on her way there." In truth, the experience of West awaiting yet another handsome officer (one of them a young Gene Barry), hearing a knock, and crying, "Enta!" became a running gag for the audience. West included her usual bits—a song in Act Two, a swishy gay (Florian, the Royal Dress Designer). Still, like *My Dear Children,* this was another hit in spite of itself.

Stars were better served by Emlyn Williams and Philip Barry, respectively, in Ethel Barrymore's stint in *The Corn Is Green* (1940) and Tallulah Bankhead's in *Foolish Notion* (1945). After a long period of being miscast in flops, Barrymore secured a tremendous personal success as Williams' English schoolmarm coaching a promising young Welshman. Even Barrymore's entrance—pushing a bicycle in black dress, white blouse with man's black necktie, topped by a black-banded boater—seemed so wondrous that its photograph is *the* souvenir of early-forties theatregoing.

A year's run in New York and an even longer tour gave Barrymore the biggest commercial hit of her career; *Foolish Notion* barely broke even. But then, it wasn't a Tallulah vehicle per se. Here was another of the screwy Barry concepts: Bankhead, her fiancé, her father, and her daughter learn that Bankhead's husband, missing in battle and declared legally dead, is returning. Each in turn fantasizes what the reunion will be like. Poor Barry once again got roasted for straying from the conventional. "It is so smart, so brilliant, and so clever," said Burton Rascoe, "that I haven't the slightest idea what it was about and I was bored stiff by it."

The classics continued to turn a brisk trade. Laurence Olivier and Vivien Leigh, with *Wuthering Heights* and *Gone with the Wind* behind each, offered a *Romeo and Juliet* (1940). It was very much a family affair, what with Olivier also producing, co-directing, and even collaborating on the music; and we note with interest the Balthasar of the twenty-three-year-old John (then Jack) Merivale, who much later became Leigh's support when her marriage to Olivier collapsed. Actually, this *Romeo* turned out pure—in David Merrick's pet phrase—"turkey lurkey." However, critics really went for Eva Le Gallienne's anything-for-a-laugh staging of Sheridan's *The Rivals* (1942), featuring the shockingly heterogeneous cast of musical-comedy diva Helen Ford, musical-comedy zany Bobby Clark, old hambone Walter Hampden, and Mary Boland in the role she was born to play, Mrs. Malaprop. The Theatre Guild broke its purism-where-possible rule to present a frankly altered version, with a new prologue, a spate of songs, and some fresh misnomers for Boland. Burns Mantle saw in her a vision of Mrs. John Drew—virtually the mother of American theatre—but

Clark stole the notices. He had appeared in a Players Club showing of Congreve's *Love For Love* in 1940, so in fact Clark Going Classic was no novelty. (In 1946, he would play Molière's *Le Bourgeois Gentilhomme* as *The Would-Be Gentleman*.) Clark abandoned his trademark cigar and painted-on glasses for Bob Acres' expected finery, and Boland was all wig and beauty spot; still, this was a new Sheridan. Oddly, while *Romeo and Juliet* flopped and *The Rivals* seemed quite the hit, the one managed to last five weeks at the Mark Hellinger (then called the Fifty-first Street) while the other played the Shubert for only three weeks longer.

By far, the mistress of star Shakespeare at the time was director Margaret Webster. This formidable talent, daughter of actors Ben Webster and Dame May Whitty (who played Nurse in the Olivier-Leigh *Romeo*), staged New York's first uncut *Hamlet* (with Maurice Evans, in 1938 and again in 1939), and much of her work was comparably unusual. Not the standard-make *Twelfth Night* (1940) with Helen Hayes' Viola and Evans as a cockney Malvolio. But an Evans *Macbeth* (1941) brought forth the terrifying Lady of Judith Anderson. "I heard [her] lines as if for the first time," said George Freedley, and John Mason Brown thought the play finally worked, after 350 years.

Yet more history was made when Webster cast Paul Robeson in *Othello* (1943), with José Ferrer and Uta Hagen. Critics and public alike treated the show as a welcome act of social promotion, but George Jean Nathan, reviewing the performance rather than the event, thought Robeson "a Walter Hampden in blackface, overly rhetorical, monotonous, rigid, and given to barely concealed consciousness of its vocal organ tones." Recordings of scenes defend Nathan's view, though black Canada Lee proved a very lively Caliban in a Webster staging of *The Tempest* in 1945. (Further reinstructing the casting of Elizabethan drama, Lee played Bosola, in whiteface, in *The Duchess of Malfi* a year later.) Webster's *Tempest* was generally creative in its "speaking" of Shakespeare, giving Ariel to the dancer Vera Zorina and Trinculo and Stephano to Czech comics. Interestingly, this favorite of Shakespeare's late romances was then a rarity on Broadway. Louis Kronenberger could recall no revival after 1916, though Robert Garland mentioned a forgotten repertory troupe that gave *The Tempest* and fourteen other Shakespeare titles in a single unit set at the Jolson for half the 1932–33 season.

The Webster *Tempest* was one of Cheryl Crawford's better guesses as a producer, and the staging concept was apparently dreamed up by Eva Le

Gallienne. The plan called for a permanent structure resembling an island somewhere in ancient Greece, ever revolving to keep the action fluid in the new forties Broadway timing that sought, finally, to eradicate the stage waits so common to set changes in the past. The entire play was broken into halves separated by an intermission; whatever else one could say, the evening *moved*. The critics carped, but the show was a cognoscente's highlight and ran 100 performances, still the demarcation line marking hit from flop.

Let us close out this Shakespearean sequence with Maurice Evans' so-called G.I. *Hamlet* in 1945, a shortened version that he had toured to servicemen at the front. This, too, just got to the 100-performance mark, even at that old white elephant on Columbus Circle that had opened (in 1903) as the Majestic with *The Wizard of Oz* and then gone into eclipse as the Park, Minsky's Park Music Hall, the Cosmopolitan, and the International, among other names. It was the Columbus Circle Theatre for Evans' *Hamlet,* the last good booking it hosted till it was pulled down in 1954. The original entrance was about fifteen feet southeast of the front doorway into the present-day shopping complex containing Whole Foods.

One notable aspect of forties theatregoing is the ease with which comedy hits racked up those big runs we've been remarking on. Jerome Chodorov and Joseph Fields' *Junior Miss* (1941) is typical: a capable bit of nothing on the generation war that lasted 710 performances. As in the musical *Best Foot Forward* that same year, the cast seemed to consist exclusively of teens and forty-somethings, as the kids frazzle the grown-ups, and the audiencec recalls its own scrapes and punishments. The source was a series of *New Yorker* stories, long a fruitful garden for plays, from *My Sister Eileen* and *Life With Father* to two shows we haven't mentioned, *Having Wonderful Time* (1937) and *Mr. and Mrs. North* (1941), along with the musicals *Pal Joey* (1940) and *The Education of H*Y*M*A*N K*A*P*L*A*N* (1968).

Junior Miss is another of those "comedies" that scarcely ever utters a geuinely funny line. It's an amusing show, not a witty one. The plot generators are protagonist Judy (Patricia Peardon) and sidekick Fuffy (Lenore Lonergan), who for no good reasons decide that Judy's father is cheating on her mother and Judy's uncle is a felon. The two girls were official Broadway discoveries. Richard Watts thought Peardon "just gawky enough, just blooming enough, and just pretty enough." In short: "completely darling." Louis Kronenberger called Lonergan "easier . . . to praise than to describe," probably because of her gaudily gritty vocal tone. Although the critics noted how silly the story was, they were enthusiastic about how well Chodorov and Fields caught the fads and follies of American youth. Burns Mantle thought *Junior Miss* "a successor to the Tarkington tradition," and specified his appreciation with "Penrod and the Baby Talk Lady are with us again."*

Substitute for the sidekick figure an irritating younger sister—"Once I grew four inches in a week," she boasts—and the *Junior Miss* formula yields *Janie* (1942), which totted up a nearly comparable 642-showing run. Unlike *Junior Miss, Janie* included uniforms; by 1942, servicemen were all but de rigueur in comedy. Again, there were plenty of huge runs: *Kiss and Tell* (1943) played for 957 performances, *The Voice of the Turtle* (1943) for 1,557, and *Dear Ruth* (1944) for 683.

Kiss and Tell was a domestic comedy and *The Voice of the Turtle* a one-set, three-character talk piece. But *Dear Ruth*'s author, Norman Krasna, had thought of a genuine comic premise: a teenager (Lenore Lonergan, still in a secondary role) has been writing to a lieutenant in the Air Force overseas in her sister Ruth's name, having sent him her sister's photograph. On leave, the soldier shows up on Ruth's wedding day—so of course Ruth (Virginia Gilmore) falls in love with the soldier (John Dall). Krasna even thought of a classic comic finish, and we imagine that director Moss Hart made the most of it. After the girls' judge father gives the new couple a quickie marriage, the pair run off to finish Dall's leave as their honeymoon. All is calm. Now for the storm: another enlisted man turns up at the door, this one a sailor. He asks for Ruth.

LONERGAN: (in a spasm of remembrance) Harold!
     Harold Klobbermeyer!

So Lonergan's been a busy little correspondent; and the curtain is already coming down.

* Schmengie Footnote No. Two: Do I really have to educate any of you in America's greatest forgotten novelist and his apparently not entirely immortal characters? Booth Tarkington (1869–1946) wrote mainly of bourgeois life in his native Indiana, with emphasis on the doings of young people. Penrod, who figures in a number of Tarkington's books, was the Tom Sawyer of the early twentieth century, and the Baby Talk Lady is Lola Pratt, the visiting easterner who vamps the Indianapolis boys in *Seventeen*. Lenore Lonergan, by the way, was the third in a minor theatrical dynasty of that name; those who wish to sample her crazy voice can hear her Diana Devereaux, the vamp of *Of Thee I Sing*, in the 1952 revival, currently on DRG.

Far from all these very "wartime" comedies was a New York in-joke of a piece, H. S. Kraft's *Café Crown* (1942). Elia Kazan's first directing job after his Group days, *Café Crown* was an à clef show about—I think astonishingly—the Yiddish theatre scene. It's astonishing because how many Broadway habitués would recognize in the titular setting the Café Royal, where Second Avenue nobility held court? Would they recognize in the protagonist (Morris Carnovsky) the patriarchal actor-manager Jacob Adler, father of the Group's Stella and Luther? Yet *Café Crown* ran 141 performances, mainly on the fun that Kraft had with the mores of this sub-cultural show biz in which stars routinely speak of their "latest farewell appearance" and in which *Rain* is reset in the Catskills with a Rabbi Davidson as the heavy. Richard Watts Jr. found *Café Crown* "mellow and engaging," but it sounds quirky rather than mellow, as a critic quietly writes his notice of Carnovsky's King Lear (opposite a Mrs. Lear) before he has seen it, or as a composer writes "The Last Time I Saw Poland."*

One of the era's funniest comedies was, as one might expect, a Kaufman-Hart show—their last together, in fact—*George Washington Slept Here* (1940). Following the fortunes of city folk fixing up a dilapidated country place, it lacks *You Can't Take It With You*'s ecumenism and *The Man Who Came To Dinner*'s celebrity exposé. It also suffers from the worst and even the meanest ending of any comedy from so prominent an atelier; and I'll get to that presently.

The play's central leads, the Fullers, make an odd couple, for he (Ernest Truex) is small and fumbly while she (Jean Dixon, an alumna of the first Kaufman-Hart show, *Once in a Lifetime*) is big and in charge. The colorful types filling out the rural Pennsylvania scene include the rustic (Percy Kilbride, one of the last practitioners of the Lightnin' Bill Jones shtick and Marjorie Main's future partner in the *Ma and Pa Kettle* film series), the vicious neighbor, the evil nephew, the parasitical rich uncle (Dudley Digges,

---

* Schmengie Footnote No. Three: This is for those who don't place the reference in that song title; informed buffs will return to the text without further dawdling. "The Last Time I Saw Poland" is a joke on a number by Jerome Kern and Oscar Hammerstein, "The Last Time I Saw Mahonoy City," a tribute to "the Athens of Northeastern Pennsylvania," complete with a musical evocation of the horns of the distinctive Mahonoy City sanitation wagons on the line "I dodged the same old garbage trucks . . ." For many, the number became the anthem of the war years, and finally inspired an MGM film of 1954 with Elizabeth Taylor and Van Johnson, though for some reason the setting was changed to Paris.

later O'Neill's Harry Hope), an actor couple, an uncooperative black cook, and the dating teens so much a part of Broadway at this time. Most of the really good lines are Jean Dixon's, as her dry delivery brought out that salient wisecrack quality of the powerless seeking power. She is sensible in a sense-less world—in, basically, a dream of a country place that is a nightmare of impediments and despairs. The house doesn't even have running water:

THE RUSTIC: We've drilled down four hundred and twenty feet, and what do you think? We just struck mud.
MR. FULLER: Mud?

. . .

MRS. FULLER: Oh, I think it's wonderful, Newton. Those hot nights in August, when I say to Katie—Katie, make us a big pitcher of iced mud, will you?
THE RUSTIC: And then there's the trees, Mr. Fuller. We ought to start doing something about the trees pretty soon.
MRS. FULLER: What do we have to do about the trees, Mr. Kimber? Pay them for standing here?

Eventually, the family restores the house and conquers all adversity—and just then the vicious neighbor turns it all around. The people we have grown to love are to lose all they worked for: all the labor that we, too, feel a part of. It is genuinely calamitous, and we are unnerved when they get drunk and set about utterly wrecking their house so the vicious neighbor can't enjoy it. So, when a last-minute ruse turns it all around again and the family regains their home and a storm breaks out and the rain pours in for the frantic final curtain, we become resentful. This is not the here-we-go-again! curtain of *Dear Ruth,* but something unhappy and even offensive. *Dear Ruth* is a slice of escapist cake; *George Washington Slept Here* has an emotional reality. In some strange way, this month in the country (actually a spring-summer) rejuvenates the Fullers and draws them closer together. It's a gagfest, yes, but a lovable one—until the wrecking of the house. According to the Kaufman estate—namely, Anne Kaufman [Kiss of the] Schneider [Woman]—whenever the play is performed, the audience has a ball till the wrecking scene, and the evening ends in a resistant chill.

Serious drama was not in fettle in the early 1940s. Not only did comedy outperform it commercially, but O'Neill was not heard from at all, his prominent colleagues were in temporary or permanent decline, and the new set of Williams-Miller-Inge was not yet in play in any real sense.

Most of the interesting titles were the work of unknowns—for instance, Philip Yordan's *Anna Lucasta* (1944). Yordan told an oddly comic tale of a sort of Polish-American Anna Christie. Failing to interest a producer, Yordan ended up giving the script to the American Negro Theatre, turning it into a black story simply by changing the setting and some of the names. Perhaps this was why the *World-Telegram*'s Burton Rascoe praised the show as universal rather than ethnic; he compared the performance to "the finest efforts of the Moscow Art Theatre." Everyone agreed that it was less the story than the lively secondary characters that kept *Anna Lucasta* spirited. Louis Kronenberger compared it to Elizabethan drama and *Carmen*.

All this enthusiasm for a piece playing four nights a week during a summer heat wave in a basement seating two hundred on collapsible wooden chairs! Nevertheless, money notices and Broadway buzz demanded that the show move to The Street, and its leads of Hilda Moses Simms, Earle Hyman, and Frederick O'Neal were joined by Canada Lee at the Mansfield (today the Brooks Atkinson) in a revision and an entirely new production. The critics were less enthusiastic now; a more commercial approach with a tacked-on happy ending made a black experiment just another Broadway show with a black cast. Still, a run of 957 performances made *Anna Lucasta* the most successful black title of the age.

The more serious—indeed violent—*Native Son* (1941), by Paul Green and Richard Wright, from Wright's novel, was the age's succès d'estime, giving Canada Lee the opportunity of his career as Bigger Thomas, defiantly racist in his attitude toward whites and, in Orson Welles' slash-and-burn staging, a figure of appalling grandeur. The show's 97 performances makes a fine showing for so uncompromising a piece, played in an at the time extremely rare single act. Still, ten years after *Anna Lucasta* had closed, E. Y. Harburg could slip the title into a lyric in the Lena Horne musical *Jamaica* confident that his audience would place it; *Native Son* would have meant next to nothing by then. We should note as well that this was when Hilda Simms (who had dropped her middle name), hailed as a terrific find as Anna, was reduced to playing a maid in the comedy *King of Hearts* (1954) simply because there was so little work for non-singing blacks on Broadway.

Balancing the black show, let's try a white folk play: *Dark of the Moon* (1945), "a legend with music." This one's really white, the work of two twenty-something cousins who were nephews of the aforementioned *Clansman* author Thomas Dixon. Supposedly, there are countless versions of the folk ballad "Barbara Allen," and the cousins, Howard Richardson and William Berney, took as their plot premise the version that goes:

> *A witch boy from the mountain came*
> *A-pinin' to be human.*
> *For he had seen the fairest gal,*
> *The blue-eyed Barbara Allen.*

With a setting in the Great Smoky Mountains, characters from the spirit and human worlds, a free use of folk song, incidental music, and dance, *Dark of the Moon* was rich in atmosphere, helped by the vernacular succotash of the script, as when the witch boy tells the Conjur Woman of his first meeting with Barbara:

> JOHN: I were on my eagle, and I sailed low fer to see her. She look up
> kinda skeered like, but then she smiled and waved.

As all the fantasies tell, marrying out of your species never works out. There's a catch to the union of John and Barbara: she must remain faithful to him for a year, or he goes back to witchland and she dies the death. So far, so good. But when Barbara gives birth to a witch child, the neighbors kill it and drag her—on the last day of her trial year—to a prayer meeting at which she is raped. The spell broken, John leaps back onto his eagle and Barbara dies.

In a reversal of the usual procedure, the tryout stops saw a more blatantly erotic piece than New York did, with the rape scene presented with daring clarity. As it was, the critics all agreed that the staging had tone but the work was a little empty. It had in fact been rejected by every New York producer till it had a successful little run at the Brattle Hall Theatre in Cambridge, Massachusetts with Richard Hart and Carol Stone in the leads. Hart was unknown, but his co-star was one of Fred Stone's daughters at a time when Stone and his family were royalty. The show even got a spread in

Life magazine, which guaranteed the New York staging, by the Messrs. Shubert, at the 46th Street Theatre (today the Richard Rodgers).

This was a plum booking, especially given the wartime playhouse crunch. At 320 performances, *Dark of the Moon* proved a big hit after all, and the title remained famous, though the show was seldom seen. It turned up in New York in 1970, during that odd period just after the Stonewall Riots when, for two or three seasons, a lot of little shows appeared—mostly but not entirely on off-Broadway—whose defining feature was gratuitous nudity. A folk play might seem an odd choice, but the original had included a dance sequence for the witch boy and some witch girls, so here was an opportunity, especially with the addition of a few extra witch boys. *After Dark* fave Chandler Hill and Margaret Howell played the leads, and Rue McClanahan appeared as one of the folk.

That old question of a national theatre got yet another answer—of a sort—on West Fifty-fifth Street in 1943. Mecca Temple, built in 1924 for the Masons, was seized by the city in lieu of unpaid taxes and, on order from Mayor Fiorello La Guardia, was reinvested as a municipal auditorium, the City Center. Seating nearly three thousand, the house was really too big for anything but opera. No matter: it was there and it was available, and a "popular-priced" ticket scale allowed capacity crowds to enjoy limited runs of revival theatre, alternating with opera and dance by the companies that eventually became the New York City Opera and the New York City Ballet.

The whole shebang opened with a New York Philharmonic concert, featuring Lawrence Tibbett and Bidu Sayão under Artur Rodzinski; two nights later came *Susan and God* in its original staging with its original Gertrude Lawrence. Dancer Paul Draper and harmonica wizard Larry Adler shared one evening, a program of American folk music occupied another, the Ballets Russes of Monte Carlo paid a visit, the opera company bowed in with standard rep featuring Dusolina Giannini, Jennie Tourel, and Dorothy Kirsten, and the other plays were *The Patriots, Our Town* (with Montgomery Clift joining the original's Martha Scott as George and Emily, to the Stage Manager of Marc Connelly), and *Porgy and Bess* (in the Cheryl Crawford version, using spoken dialogue), so beloved by this 1943–44 season that *Porgy* had to extend the customary City Center two weeks by another six. Succeeding seasons hosted such events as an Eva Le Gallienne *Cherry Orchard, You Can't Take It With You* (with Fred and

Dorothy Stone and Dorothy's husband, Charles Collins), the Paul Robeson *Othello, Carmen Jones, Bloomer Girl,* and *Up in Central Park*. All the plays represented, like *Susan and God,* resuscitations of the original staging or (as with the last three titles) that very staging itself, concluding the national tour.

Within a decade, the City Center limited its theatre work to four musicals every spring. *Show Boat* and *Porgy and Bess* were perennials, along with certain fifties titles such as *Guys and Dolls* and *Wonderful Town*. But the bulk of the repertory took in forties titles, because that decade proved a treasury of classics from *Pal Joey* to *South Pacific*. However, note that for all the comedy hits in the early 1940s, there are few *classic* comedies. In fact, we can complete our précis of the form with but two more shows, Thornton Wilder's *The Skin Of Our Teeth* (1942) and Mary Chase's *Harvey* (1944).

Skin is downright apocalyptic, but we find some unusual things in even the self-effacing *Harvey*. Elwood P. Dowd, the leading role, has for a best friend a six-foot rabbit, the title role, invisible to all but Dowd, including the audience. Astonishingly, this fantasy argues in favor of alcoholism: Dowd relentlessly tipples. True, he's not a violent drunk, just a trader in whimsy, one of Broadway's least favorite things. That may be why so many stars turned the play down when it was under option. Or maybe it was the drinking, or the rabbit.

Could it have been the almost absolute lack of plot? Virtually nothing happens in Act One, and little more than nothing in the rest: Elwood's sister (Josephine Hull) wants to put Elwood away, then changes her mind.* Chase's point is that . . . well, what's wrong with having an invisible friend? Chase must have been onto something, for as the first Elwood, Frank Fay— a former tippler himself, with the airy charm of a con man who won't take your money—gave way to Bert Wheeler, James Stewart (who made the

---

* One could argue that nothing happens at all in the entire play, save one cute bit at the end of the first act, when one of those "men in the white coats," one Wilson, looks Harvey up in the encyclopedia. According to Elwood, Harvey is a "pookah," and the encyclopedia not only defines the word as a "fairy spirit" in "old Celtic mythology" but asks, "How are you, Mr. Wilson?" Correcting the whimsy to something more dramatic, a TV adaptation in 1958, with Art Carney and Marion Lorne, had Wilson read the definition aloud, as on stage. Then the Wilson, Jesse White (who had originated the part on Broadway), shivered and exited. The camera waited, staring at the open book. And suddenly it was shut by something we couldn't see.

movie), the English Jack Buchanan, second ex-tippler James Dunn, and Joe E. Brown, *Harvey* stayed for 1,775 performances.

The Skin Of Our Teeth is the optimistic counterpart to *Our Town*. In Wilder's earlier play, only the dead understand life; *Skin* tells how mankind has to keep surviving because life is all there is. Oddly, *Skin* had as much trouble getting on as *Our Town;* folks just never stop being bewildered by the unconventional, do they? At least, this one has sets, though one of them wobbles and in part falls over, to suggest the precarious nature of life on earth. After all, there was the Ice Age (in progress as Act One ends), the Flood (Act Two, set on an Atlantic City boardwalk during various conventions of the Wings, the Fins, the Shells, and the Humans), and war (Act Three), with father and son on rival sides.

Father was Fredric March, Mother was his wife, Florence Eldridge (a recurring but not invariable stage partner), their children were Montgomery Clift and Frances Heflin . . . and there was a maid, Father's harlot. This was Sabina, played by Tallulah Bankhead in one of her most famous roles and one of the most famous cases of unprofessional conduct ever to wag Broadway tongues. Florence Eldridge kept asking the director, "When are you going to do something about Tallulah?" She was speaking to Elia Kazan, hardly more advanced in his directing career than when we last saw him, staging *Café Crown.** Skin's* producer was the tyro Michael Myerberg, and Wilder himself was away on war duty. So, really, the "muscle" in the production was Bankhead. And Bankhead, like Sabina, was out of control.

We should pause a moment to consider Bankhead, for she is one of names of the age to have survived intact—and that without a great deal of notable film work. Katharine Cornell is known vaguely as one of those Actresses of Yore, and Jane Cowl is as forgotten as Rollo Peters. Bankhead has something they didn't: a scrappy, boozy, bisexual type-portrait. Legend calls her unreliable; she wasn't. Legend says she overplayed in caricature; she did so only to goad a sluggish house into responding. Legend tells that she aimed her portrayals at her gay fans; it was they who assumed control, reportedly queening it up at the slightest textual reference to the erotic, forbidden, or "different."

---

* Kazan had meanwhile suffered a ghastly flop in a more than usually allegorical piece by Paul Vincent Carroll with a title that so defies marquee sense that I refuse to cite it here. I'll work it into the text of the next chapter; be on your guard.

The truth is that Bankhead was the typical diva who can't seem to get along without making a stupid noise about trifles, getting nervous for the purpose of getting nervous, cultivating feuds, playing favorites, loving and hating without cause or transition. However, Bankhead was also passionately committed to the roles she undertook, and she got reviews as good as those of any other actress of her day. The difference between Tallulah Bankhead and, say, Helen Hayes is not that Bankhead was a joke and Hayes wasn't. It is that Bankhead created a personality that was even bigger offstage than on.

She was particularly big with Kazan on *Skin*. He allowed it at first, because Kazan was exploring a theory he was to work with throughout his career: actors' personal relationships will determine the way they play with each other onstage. In other words, human nature will overwhelm professionalism. It worked well that Bankhead and Eldridge disliked each other; so do their characters. It even worked well that Bankhead's shenanigans were disrupting rehearsals: the Sabine Woman disrupts civilizations. (This makes Wilder's own choice for Sabina, Ruth Gordon, puzzling. What did Ruth Gordon ever disrupt besides Garson Kanin?)

Still, by the time the show was running, Bankhead was simply driving everybody crazy. At one point, she took to combing her hair upstage during Eldridge's most significant speech; so March, whose throat was vexing him, decided to take his medicinal gargle in the wings during one of Bankhead's big scenes, timing his *ronron* to her best lines; so Bankhead dropped the hair combing but started tonguing March during their big kiss; and so on.

At length, Kazan stood up to Bankhead in the traditional screaming match. But Bankhead could not be tamed. She was waterfall, rainbow, earthquake all at once. Who but this lavish fiend could conceivably break character, lean over the footlights, and complain to the audience about the play? This is what Wilder has her do, and surely he hoped that, at least for a few moments, the public would fear that Tallulah had really lost it:

> SABINA: I hate this play and every word in it. . . . All about the troubles the human race has gone through, there's a subject for you. Besides, the author hasn't made up his silly mind as to whether we're all living back in caves or in New Jersey.

Much later, Bankhead told an interviewer that she truly was taken aback by the odder aspects of her part. "I'd never done such a thing," she said, referring to those sudden eruptions at the spectators. "It was like being in vaudeville."

"A fantastic comedy" is how Wilder billed the piece, and while it is no vaudeville it does game with conventional expectations. Some were offended enough to walk out; and two academics caused a scandal by claiming that Wilder had stolen *The Skin Of Our Teeth* from another writer.

The two were Joseph Campbell and Henry Morton Robinson, who had been collaborating on a trot to James Joyce's *Finnegans Wake*. Though their work was not to be published till 1944, two years after *Skin* opened, they nevertheless were able to cop a page or two of the *Saturday Review* to discern in *Skin* "important plot elements, characters, devices of presentation, as well as major themes" of the *Wake*. In fact, Wilder—one of the few educated enough to get through Joyce's polylingual metamythomaze—thought it amusing to decorate his play with *Wake* hommages. They were prim little echoes at most, and Edmund Wilson answered for Wilder in *The Nation*, pointing out that Wilder made his Joycean references "plain as anything of the kind can be."

The play won the Pulitzer Prize and went on to evergreen appeal to high-school and college groups. A 1955 television special starred Mary Martin, George Abbott, and Helen Hayes, though a perfunctory Bicentennial mounting with Elizabeth Ashley, Alfred Drake, and Martha Scott under José Quintero despoiled the work's reputation. Should it have gone musical? Leonard Bernstein, with Betty Comden and Adolph Green, couldn't make it sing; and while John Kander and Fred Ebb completed their *Skin* adaptation, it has yet to be heard in New York.

Even so, amid other classics such as *Mourning Becomes Electra, The Little Foxes, The Philadelphia Story,* and *The Man Who Came to Dinner, The Skin of Our Teeth* holds unique status as the Extremely Bizarre Play. We have seen the 1920s launch the Golden Age, with new subject matter (even in old genres), with new voices (especially that of O'Neill), and the division of the theatregoing population into highbrow, midcult, and prole (uniting for, say, *Rain* but otherwise breaking into Theatre Guild subscribers, Ethel Barrymore supporters, and those who saw *Abie's Irish Rose*). The 1930s emphasizes social drama and introduces the naturalistic acting revolution. And the innovation of the 1940s is the acculturation of genuinely breakaway styles of writing, so that such different energies as Tennessee Williams on one hand and modern French dramatists on the other are made welcome in an ever Newer Broadway. "When the breath of creative imagination blows through the theatre," wrote Rosamund Gilder in *Theatre Arts,* of *The Skin Of Our Teeth,* "what refreshment to the spirit! Doors may bang and scenery fly about; audiences may be outraged, infuriated, delighted, but the theatre is once more alive!"

Eleven

Olivier Versus Brando:

THE LATE 1940S

The war play cycle, which was to run sporadically into the 1950s, was very strong in the first years of peace, each playwright finding his special way into the subject. John Patrick's *The Hasty Heart* (1945) considered the feelings of a terminally wounded soldier, Arthur Laurents' *Home of the Brave* (1945) examined anti-Semitism using a murder plot involving servicemen, Maxwell Anderson's *Joan of Lorraine* (1946), starring Ingrid Bergman, looked in on a bare-stage rehearsal of a play about one of history's greatest soldiers, and William Wister Haines' *Command Decision* (1947) concerned the heavy losses that democrats have to endure when defeating barbarians, centering on a martinet general sending pilots out on suicide bombing missions.

None of the above quartet visited enlisted men on the ground at the front, in the line of *What Price Glory?*. Few of the World War II plays did, earlier or later. Harry Brown's *A Sound of Hunting* (1945) was one exception, with a cast headed by Burt Lancaster and Sam Levene and dealing in little more than an infantry squad in Italy trying (and failing) to rescue one trapped comrade. The critics were impressed with the writing, but the public may have found it bleak, for it ran three weeks. But *Mister Roberts* (1948) dared to kill off its hero—Henry Fonda, no less—at the close of what was to be called one of the funniest plays of the decade. That is: the audience was led along a path of guiltless and almost implausible fun, then kicked right in the teeth with Fonda's death. And the show ran nearly three years.

It started as Navy veteran Thomas Heggen's episodic novel, which then turned into Heggen's episodic script, in collaboration with Max Shulman. The latter bowed out when Air Force veteran Joshua Logan came on as collaborator and director, with Jo Mielziner's adroit evocation of a Navy cargo ship a form of collaboration as well. This unit set of the ship's main deck had to be able also to show action in separate staterooms and support a practical cargo net used for comic effect when most of the crew returned from a drunken leave borne aloft and lowered into view before the audience's eyes.

The crew's admiration for Mister Roberts, and his selfless defiance of their sadistic captain on their behalf, are why the show played so well. Yes, it is full of gags, but genuine feelings run through it, because the captain yields to Roberts' protection of his men at a terrible price: Roberts must stop trying to transfer onto a ship seeing real action *and* treat the captain with respect *and* not let the crew know why. Thus, the captain pulls off the ultimate sadistic stunt, destroying the crew's trust in the only thing they truly love, Roberts' heroism.

Fonda's Doug Roberts became so famous a portrayal (preserved, of course, in Logan's film version) that it's odd to relate that David Wayne, who as Ensign Pulver had the show's main comic role, was originally to have played Roberts. Fonda had been asked, but he was tied up with commitments in Hollywood. However, Fonda was still "theatre" enough to sit in with Wayne on one of the silliest of stage traditions, the (co-)author's Reading of the Play. Fonda was inspired to postpone Hollywood, and Wayne discovered in Pulver the role that, after *Finian's Rainbow*'s Og the previous year, would put his career into warp speed, leading on to Sakini in *The Tea-house of the August Moon* (1953) and various folksy eccentrics. (Amusingly, the captain was played by an actor twice related to musical-comedy royalty: he was the son of Edward Harrigan of Harrigan and Hart and Joshua Logan's brother-in-law.)

Fonda, one of Broadway's recurring prodigal sons, made a deceptively low-key Roberts, so tightly controlled that he could underline a dramatic statement in the same tone he used in comedy. This is no minor gift in a play that acts like a laff riot until its last ten minutes, for the crew, finally realizing what Mister Roberts gave up for them, covertly arranges for his transfer, then enjoys a letter from their friend, at last on truly useful service at the front. A second letter announces that Mister Roberts fell in action. It is up to Ensign Pulver to become the new Mister Roberts. Furiously throwing overboard the captain's beloved pet palm tree, he shouts at the captain to come out and fight as the curtain falls: tragedy with a punch line.

The question of acting—the nature of it but also the special nature of the American style—is the theme of this chapter, as it was the theme of the late 1940s, for a number of reasons. One was the acculturation of the Group Theatre's philosophy, so widespread in the half decade since the Group's dissolution that the youngest players often absorbed it unknowingly simply by working with and thus learning from their elders. Even actors prominent enough to resist changing their ways could startle with unexpected naturalistic impact—Ralph Bellamy, for instance, in Sidney Kingsley's *Detective Story* (1949). After years of those blithely under-the-top performances, Bellamy suddenly bit into the part of a self-righteous cop with a furious appetite, and while Hollywood preferred the more apparently psychotic Kirk Douglas for the movie version, it's refreshing to meet Bellamy off his turf in the first place: in a big-cast, slice-of-life melodrama set within three hours or so in the detective squad room of a New York cop shop.

Or consider the twenty-four-year-old Julie Harris, breaking a five-year series of flops just a few days into the next decade in Carson McCullers' *The Member of the Wedding* (1950). The source was McCullers' novel about a young girl so enchanted by her older brother's marriage that she wishes to be not just a "member" of the ceremony but the very content of it: attended to and loved. Critics faulted the show for lack of plot. It was still a novel, they said, beautifully written but short on drive. That's half empty. Half full is: short on drive but wonderfully enacted, especially by Ethel Waters as

Berenice Sadie Brown, the maid who runs the house; Brandon de Wilde as John Henry West, the seven-year-old cousin of Harris' Frankie Addams; and the roughneck radiance herself. Embarking on one of the last star careers to challenge the great names of the preceding pages, Harris, along with Geraldine Page, Kim Stanley, and a few others, would help define the postwar woman lead as more versatile than those who came before. Harris did have something of the old school, however: charm. Who else could play Saint Joan, Sally Bowles, and Emily Dickinson in one lifetime?

Charm was the central energy of *The Member of the Wedding*, and that was plot enough:

> BERENICE: (To John Henry) Now, Candy, how come you took our playing cards and cut out the pictures?
> JOHN HENRY: Because I wanted them. They're cute.
>
>   . . .
>
> FRANKIE: We'll just have to put him out of the game. He's entirely too young.
> (John Henry whimpers.)
> BERENICE: . . . We gotta have a third to play. Besides, by the last count he owes me close to a million dollars.

Waters was then moving into the senior phase of her voyage, a kind of Bessie Smith and Canada Lee rolled into one. She was taken for granted as being utterly brilliant. Brooks Atkinson was especially impressed by de Wilde, however. "Brandon won all the hearts in the audience," Atkinson wrote. Even that helping of sauerkraut George Jean Nathan agreed, excepting de Wilde's diction, for "much of what he mouthed sounded [like] a modern version of *Prometheus Bound* by James Joyce."

Ironically, Harris—today still famous for this show among many—was not yet fully appreciated. Perhaps she was so at one with the wistful yet rambunctious Frankie that too few credited her creation. Some apparently felt the same way about Judy Holliday's Billie Dawn in Garson Kanin's *Born Yesterday* (1946). Atkinson again: "quite wonderful," which is possibly the understatement of the decade. Is Billie the original dumb blonde in the coming fifties meaning of the term, bubble wrap in the form of Marilyn Monroe and her many simulators? And what would such an invention tell us about how men like their women?

Holliday's stage career takes in only two straight plays, *Kiss Them For Me* (1945) and *Born Yesterday* (and a City Center engagement of Elmer Rice's *Dream Girl*), and two musicals, *Bells Are Ringing* (1956) and *Hot Spot* (1963). At that, the first and last of these titles are unknown; Holliday's reputation stands entirely on the films of the two middle titles. Yet she remains one of our great comediennes, mainly because her innate warmth and intelligence made something special of Kanin's Pygmalion fable: because Kanin likes his women challenging. His triangle of corrupt money boss and idealistic lefty circling around this same Billie demands that she grow from idiot to Great American Citizen under the lefty's tutelage.

Oddly, when *Born Yesterday* went out of town, Jean Arthur was playing Billie Dawn. Kanin always claimed that as director of his own plays he saw his job as casting with precision and then keeping his actors from overplaying. But is Jean Arthur anyone's idea of a dumb blonde or, for that matter, a kept dolly? Try to imagine Jean Arthur delivering these lines, during Billie's first scene with the man who is to transform her, a writer for *The New Republic*:

BILLIE: I'm stupid and I like it.

PAUL: You do?

BILLIE: Sure. I'm happy. I got everything I want. Two mink coats. Everything. If there's somethin' I want, I ask. And if he don't come across—I don't come across. If you know what I mean.

Kanin may not have been the casting whiz he believed himself to be. In a Broadway story of the day, Kanin tells a friend that, for the money boss, he is seeking "someone like Paul Douglas." And the friend replies, "Why not get Paul Douglas?"

Kanin did so, and with Gary Merrill as the New Republican and Holliday replacing a supposedly indisposed Arthur, *Born Yesterday* sailed off on a 1,642-performance run. Holliday played most of it, replaced in the fourth and final year by Jan Sterling, but who could follow Holliday's Billie? She alone enlivened the dumb-blonde trope with a cultural learning curve: Galatea defeats systemic D.C. corruption. In her scornful treatment of Douglas, one could hear her realizing that too much money makes a goon not powerful but simply a larger goon. It's a Group Theatre perception tucked into a commercial comedy hit.

There were few such acting triumphs in comedy in the late 1940s. Even Henry Fonda's Doug Roberts was less a comic performance than the Fonda folk hero thrust into a farce. Helen Hayes tried comedy in Anita Loos' *Happy Birthday* (1946) as an aging and resentful lady nerd who enters a saloon and enjoys life-changing adventures. Tryout audiences were resentful, too: Loos had written Hayes too mean. Script revisions softened her and brought in a hit, but not a memorable portrayal. Nor did the Lunts add outstandingly to their portrait gallery in this era. They were still extremely popular, but could find nothing worthy, not even in the stunt roles of *I Know My Love* (1949). Once more in the mode of adapter, S. N. Behrman reworked Marcel Achard's *Auprès de Ma Blonde* to give Lynn and Alfred the chance to make their entrance as grayhairs, trembling and cringing, thence to undergo flashback and cosmetics to Enact the Backstory. All were ravished, the box office hummed till vacation time, and the play then vanished from conversation and memory.

As for à clef comedy, American celebrity was in transition, making it difficult to write about. Didn't Arthur Miller's "talent and the interesting rich" sum up a loop of fame that was becoming a dead end with the passing of the 1930s? The late 1940s was not a Sophisticated time. Moss Hart's backstager *Light Up the Sky* (1948) attempted (with moderate success) to revive à clef fun in a piece set entirely in the living room of the leading lady's hotel suite during a Boston tryout. The play in question, *The Time Is Now,* is—to put it mildly—experimental. (It opens in the ruins of Radio City Music Hall after the Bomb has hit New York, and the star, in rags, doesn't utter a line for the entire first act.) This accords with a traditional Broadway joke, running at least from *Me and Juliet* to *The Producers,* in which people seem to be putting on extremely strange shows. And *The Time Is Now* costs three hundred thousand dollars in 1948 money, very, very rare for a musical and unheard of for a straight play.

Note the pretentious title. It is Moss Hart's hint that the of course unseen play isn't very good, and that the people involved with it are fools and tyros. In fact, Hart's à clef subjects were major people: Gertrude Lawrence; Billy Rose and his wife, Eleanor Holm; Katharine Cornell's director husband, Guthrie McClintic, seen here as a drippy swish; and even Hart's tart-tongued mother-in-law, though his wife, Kitty Carlisle, was spared.

Hart gave his characters a disastrous opening night, which provokes a donnybrook from everyone on stage till it turns out that the critics actually liked the show. This now provokes the hypocritical hugs and kisses that Hart wanted to expose, the ugly undertone of the Broadway Melody. A cast headed by Sam Levene and Audrey Christie as the Roses, Virginia Field as the star, Glenn Anders as the director, and Barry Nelson as a gentle young playwright who comes to think of the theatre as "Murder, Inc." gave *Light Up the Sky* far more energy than the piece has on paper. Still, the genre of Broadway Thru a Keyhole had lost its power even as Walter Winchell himself was about to. *The New Yorker* magazine at least was still good for a spoof. Harold Ross was, anyway: he turned up in both *Metropole* (1949) and Wolcott Gibbs' semi-confessional *Season in the Sun* (1950), played respectively by Lee Tracy and Anthony Ross, the original Gentleman Caller in *The Glass Menagerie*.

As à clef comedy faded, a new attraction flowered: the adaptation from the French. The texts were generally less translated then transformed (if slightly), to bridge a cultural divide; S. N. Behrman alone has adapted a couple for us already. Still, the late 1940s saw the French create an active contingent on Broadway, led by Jean Giraudoux. His *Siegfried* had come to town, at the Civic Rep, as far back as 1930. Now, just after his death, in 1944, came *The Madwoman of Chaillot* (1948) and *Intermezzo*, retitled *The Enchanted* (1949).

Of Giraudoux's successors, Jean Anouilh and Jean-Paul Sartre enjoyed the most réclame, the former with a Katharine Cornell-Guthrie McClintic *Antigone* (1946), esteemed if not vastly attended, and the latter with *No Exit* (1946), *The Respectful Prostitute* (1948), and *Dirty Hands,* renamed *Red Gloves* (1948). *The Respectful Prostitute* was the hit, less for Sartre's scathing look at race relations in the American South than for a new star, Meg Mundy. *Red Gloves,* treating skullduggery in some unspecified European Communist group, offered Charles Boyer in his Broadway debut, which gave the show a "movie star" advance sale, an electric opening night in the old style, and a run of 113 performances.

Perhaps because they were so well "adapted," the French plays did not call attention to Gallic writing, or the kind of acting suitable to it, as for instance in the quibbling badinage of the madwomen in *Chaillot*. All the same, *something* was happening. On one hand, three of the greatest divas of the ancien régime—Laurette Taylor, Ethel Barrymore, and Pauline Lord—made their New York stage farewells in the 1944–45 season; on the other, Julie Harris would soon unveil the "new acting" in her Frankie Adams. And meanwhile, something else happened: a six-week visit, in 1946, by London's Old Vic.

A company headed by Laurence Olivier, Ralph Richardson, Miles Malleson, Margaret Leighton, and Joyce Redman gave the two parts of *Henry IV, Uncle Vanya,* and the oxymoron of Sophocles' *Oedipus* followed by Sheridan's theatre spoof *The Critic*. Unmissable above all was the practice of ensemble, as when Leighton and Redman slipped from Chekhof's Yelyena and Sonya to two of Jocasta's attendants in Thebes, or even when Miles Malleson contributed a bit to each of the four bills but directed *The Critic*.

The outstanding tour de force was Olivier's taking on Oedipus and Sheridan's Mr. Puff in a single night—a leap, so to say, from Edvard Munch's *The Scream* to Drury Lane dandy. Of course, George Jean Nathan maintained his role as Mr. Pan, insisting that the whole business was thrilling only the usual snobs; but Nathan's rating of Olivier overall as "competent and commendable" and Richardson as "at times competent and commendable" is an alternate snobbishness. And what are we to think when Nathan claims the company didn't pronounce English very well?

A veritable English explosion the very next year, 1947, persuaded many theatregoers that the English not only pronounced but acted very well. Donald Wolfit brought his company over in Shakespeare and *Volpone*. John Gielgud staged Euripides' *Medea* in Robinson Jeffers' version with (the Australian) Judith Anderson and himself. There was as well a Gielgudian troupe giving *The Importance of Being Earnest* and Congreve's *Love For Love,* with Robert Flemyng and Pamela Brown in both, along with Margaret Rutherford's Lady Bracknell and Cyril Ritchard's Tattle. Granted, these two comedies are easy to pull off, for the actors can play on the wit, while the language of Shakespeare or Chekhof opens upon a psychological labyrinth. Really, what have Wilde's Ernest or Algernon to reveal as they puppet about, bickering over muffins and courting the mysterious Bunbury? The strings, my lord, are false.

At that, Brits Michael Redgrave and Flora Robson let down their side in a *Macbeth* (1948), directed by Norris Houghton, that sought to reestablish the primitive world the play inhabits. Redgrave spoke of "people who slept in their clothes, had no time for haircuts, and didn't shave just before a battle for their lives." As with Lionel Barrymore's *Macbeth* in 1921, the concept tantalizes (as does the casting of the Weird Sisters, one of whom was Julie Harris). But no one was in the mood. As if supporting the George

Jean Nathan Theory of English Acting, this *Macbeth* crashed in 29 performances.

The debate swirled on—what exactly constitutes acting? Instinct and intelligence, of course. Technique, voice, imagination, but also . . . what? There was the inspiring ensemble of the Group, but how would the Group compare with those Old Vic show-offs in Shakespeare? Was there such a thing as cultural entitlement, as when our own Maxwell Anderson's *Anne of the Thousand Days* (1948) called upon Brits Rex Harrison and Joyce Redman to enact Henry VIII and Anne Boleyn?

And then the nature of American acting was revealed conclusively, by a near unknown who had been on the scene in a handful of small or secondary roles. He settled this *querelle des acteurs* with what might be the outstanding portrayal in American theatre. Then he left the stage forever.

Yet no one took Marlon Brando for a historical figure when he arrived in New York, in 1943; his attitude so lacked professional piety that he seemed to dare producers not to hire him. True, before Brando John Barrymore merrily offended with his Don't Give a Damn front. But Barrymore was protected by tradition, dynasty, lore.

Brando was protected by his lack of tradition; his talent was—there is no other word for it—startling. He could walk downstairs in *I Remember Mama* (1944) munching an apple and transfix the public. It's a famous Broadway story: they didn't believe he was acting. Had someone missed a cue? Was a stagehand pushed on to cover for him? Mama Mady Christians and crabby Uncle Chris Oscar Homolka were so busy upstaging each other they could never figure out how Brando—as one of Mama's children—got an exit hand just by saying goodnight. As I've said, Katharine Cornell adored reviving *Candida* (1946) with Brando's Marchbanks: his novelty refreshed her portrayal. But Tallulah Bankhead had Brando fired during the tryout of Jean Cocteau's *The Eagle Has Two Heads* (1947) for failing to make kowtow to the diva.

This is so much trivia. In the middle of it, just before *Candida*, Brando gave a hint of what was to come in Maxwell Anderson's *Truckline Café* (1946). A kind of proletarian *Grand Hotel,* it suffered one of the worst critical shellackings of all time. The reviews read like victim-impact statements at a murder trial, and the show closed in two weeks.

Yet it left the memory of an extraordinary scene in which Brando, having drowned his unfaithful wife in the Pacific Ocean, came roaring back onstage to break hell loose. *Truckline Café*'s director was Harold Clurman, and he and Elia Kazan produced (in association with Anderson's home firm, the Playwrights' Company). With a set by Boris Aronson at the Belasco Theatre, *Truckline Café* was virtually a Group entry after the fact, and it was Kazan who so to say "Grouped" Brando up for that last entrance with runs up and down a stairway and a blast from a pail of water: so Brando's Sage McRae would truly "be" a man coming back from a shattering experience in the ocean. It was a double-album expansion of a one-number role, and the theatre community talked of it for the rest of the season. Olivier, too, was famous for physical stunts, yet there was always something of the fop, the beau, about him—even as Coriolanus, with a genuinely death-defying fall to be caught by the heels by two terrified supernumeraries just before he hit the stage, a Shakespearean Mussolini. "A more shocking, less sentimental death I have not seen in the theatre," Kenneth Tynan wrote, in awe. So the dandy could menace. Still, Olivier was stylish. He was a pageant. He was . . . well, English, while Brando was brutish, hot, American.

So we wonder why, when producer Irene Mayer Selznick was readying *A Streetcar Named Desire* (1947), with Kazan as director, he didn't immediately suggest Brando. True, Stanley Kowalski was originally supposed to be over thirty and Brando was twenty-three; but it seems a small point. Madame Selznick, the daughter and wife of Hollywood moguls, naturally wanted to tap movie stars: John Garfield as Stanley and Margaret Sullavan as Blanche DuBois. But Tennessee Williams didn't like Sullavan, and Garfield, though the right age, made too many demands, such as agreeing to play only four months of the run. Kazan reckoned that Garfield actually wanted to take the role but couldn't face moving his family from California, and thus applied prohibitive conditions. Indeed, perhaps stirred by the success that Brando's Stanley created, Garfield went to Broadway later in *Streetcar*'s season, in Jan de Hartog's *Skipper Next To God,* a 6-performance flop. In 1952, Garfield finally got to play the role that Clifford Odets had promised him in 1937, in the title role of a *Golden Boy* directed by Odets. It was Garfield's last performance before his untimely death.

Williams himself might have demanded Brando as Stanley. However, the playwright spent so much of his time wandering around the globe enjoying himself that he wasn't up on the news along the Rialto. Williams not only knew nothing of Brando; he may not even have heard about Maxwell

Anderson's very public reply to *Truckline Café*'s reviews, in which he likened the critics to rednecks—"a Jukes family of journalism."

Not that Williams was lazy; he worked tirelessly at his art. But here is something new in this saga, a portent of the breakup of the theatre community. Imagine Ned Sheldon, in the 1910s, being ignorant of the appearance of a major new talent. But then, Ned Sheldon was a playwright because, in the world he grew up in, Broadway represented the height of glamor. Tennessee Williams was a playwright because he wrote plays; his idea of glamor was being on site when Gore Vidal slipped on a banana peel.

At that, Williams was thirty-six and still virtually unknown. His only previous show had folded on the road, and *The Glass Menagerie* was perceived at the time as mainly an actress' comeback triumph. By comparison, Ned Sheldon at thirty-six was a king of Broadway. When he ventured into a mean-streets setting, it was *Salvation Nell* (1908), realistic for its day but still somewhat glamorous. With Mrs. Fiske as Nell, how mean could it be? *A Streetcar Named Desire* was sordid: its heroine is a dithering loon and the male lead rapes her. There isn't even any redemptive social inquiry, as there is in *Salvation Nell*. Instead, there's violence and poetry, sexy and gay and crazy all together.

But it had Elia Kazan, you say. Kazan was nobody, too. Yes, he directed *The Skin Of Our Teeth* and a smash Mary Martin musical, *One Touch Of Venus* (1943). However, here as well the triumphs belonged to others.

Now this would change; it was *Streetcar* that changed it. As we know, it was Jed Harris who foresaw the shift in the public's interest from the guy who pays the bills to the guy who talks to the actors. But it was Kazan who most significantly implanted the concept of the director as the most masterly of the theatre's artists. Master*ful*? No: Kazan could not control Bankhead on *Skin*. Yet see how cleverly Kazan developed the gulf between Blanche and Stanley by giving minutiae of advice to Marlon Brando but no help at all to Jessica Tandy. It was Kazan's way of throwing the play to her in the face of Brando's spectacular "debut." Kazan knew that Brando—whom he finally mentioned when Garfield didn't work out—was going to take Stanley to the bank. And he knew that Tandy was capable enough to create a superb Blanche without his coaching. What Kazan especially knew was what Williams taught him about the Blanches of this world: they're effective only as manipulators, good with dandies and plops. They're no match for a man. To let Tandy be the protagonist of her own tragedy,

Kazan had to leave her helpless, overwhelmed by Stanley/Brando: tragic. Is this how Ned Sheldon's plays were directed? Did Olivier work this way?

As we head into the last decade of the Golden Age with Williams and Kazan, we can see *A Streetcar Named Desire* as the most influential work of that age—the one that conclusively widened the scope of Broadway's subject matter, that understood the importance of the director, that absorbed the example of the Group in the "meaning" of acting. We admire the O'Neillian lilt of Williams' title, and we need to know more about this play.

Twelve

It's About This Doctor:

A STREETCAR NAMED DESIRE AND *THE CRUCIBLE*

Ian Marshall Fisher, the impresario of London's Lost Musicals series (the equivalent of New York's Encores!), has developed the theory of the "driver" and the "facilitator" to describe the relationship between two leading characters in a play. The facilitator is all-important in an ancillary way: essential in framing the superiority of the driver. In Shakespeare's *Othello,* the title role is actually the facilitator, while Iago, the longest role in all Shakespeare, is the person who runs the play. His evil is its subject.

When Tennessee Williams wrote *A Streetcar Named Desire,* he naturally thought of Blanche as the driver, to Stanley's facilitator. For one thing, Stanley is by far the shorter role; one of John Garfield's conditions for accepting the part was a line buildup. Then, too, the Stanley that Williams envisioned wasn't quite the well-nigh Shakespearean cocktail of coiled-spring power, verbal humor, peacock beauty, and appetitive brutality that we now know him to be, because to Williams' knowledge there was no such actor in stock. Whom might Williams have had as a model? Van Heflin, perhaps. Or yes, Garfield. Then Brando appeared, and the facilitator became the driver.

That is, Stanley was written to define Blanche by encircling her ooh-la-la with a blast of the truth that she cannot live with. Is she belle of the ball or town whore? Ask Stanley: he knows. "I want magic!" Blanche cries, but in Kazan's *Streetcar* Stanley grabs all the magic. The final scene, in which a doctor and nurse take Blanche off to incarceration, finishes not Stanley's but Blanche's story: so it must be her play. Still, among them Williams, Kazan, and Brando retilted the piece in Stanley's favor by inventing the Beautiful Male. Not John Barrymore beautiful, a Great Profile, but system-override beautiful, something for straight men to worry about. This new character came complete with defining uniform (close-fitting T and jeans deliberately shrunk onto Brando's form specifically to be worn without undershorts) and unique diction. Like many gay intellectuals, Williams was fascinated by hot trash with a gift for creative lingo—Neal Cassady of the fifties beat scene is another such avatar—and Williams spent profusely of Brandospeak even before he knew the man existed:

> STANLEY: (going through Blanche's trunk to pull up a fistful of costume jewelry) And what have we here? The treasure chest of a pirate!
> STELLA: Oh, Stanley!
> STANLEY: Pearls! Ropes of them! What is this sister of yours, a deep-sea diver who brings up sunken treasures? Or is she the champion safe-cracker of all time!

Blanche is an invention as well, the first of the "gay" cartoons that homophobic commentators enjoyed discerning in Williams, Inge, and Albee in the 1960s and '70s. They note Blanche's affectations and storytelling as if these were exclusively homosexual behaviors, and all but suggest that her rape is tricking by other means. Actually, Blanche's style is not gay but southern, in the line of naggy Amanda Wingfield and secretly sensual Alma

Winemiller of Williams' *Summer and Smoke* (1948). Williams is remarking that the coquettish palaver of southern womankind is *laden:* with frustration at the limitations that the culture forces upon it. In Mike Nichols' burlesque, the typical Williams heroine suffers from "drink, prostitution, and puttin' on ai-yuhs,"* but what Blanche suffers from is insanity. The best Blanche I've seen, Jessica Lange, on Broadway in 1992, brought this forward in a portrayal so subtly long-lined that critics used to Bedlam Blanches missed her point. Her Stanley was Alec Baldwin, whose quick top-to-toe scoping of his sister-in-law when they first met gave extra point to his "We've had this date from the beginning" at the rape.

One would think excellent Stanleys even rarer than excellent Blanches, given Brando's impact; yet some felt that the touring and London Stanley, Anthony Quinn, better caught the character's animal gusto. Brando was a sometimes puzzling actor, so imaginative that he could enrich virtually any character into driver status. Quinn was simply a beast, easier to read. Brando's replacement, Ralph Meeker, hewed more closely to Brando than to Quinn. Never truly famous, Meeker did help carve out the new niche in Beautiful Male casting. When the sailors returning from leave in *Mister Roberts* were unloaded from the cargo net, director Joshua Logan was keen to include a few hunks in tattered uniform, a form of innovative ribaldry irresistible to the closeted Logan; Ralph Meeker was one of those sailors. Later, Logan cast Meeker in the hunk role in William Inge's *Picnic,* again to enter shining in his skin but also to have his shirt ripped open by Eileen Heckart in a moment of—quoting Hallie Flanagan—"Marlowesque madness." Then, right at the center of what we think of as the prudish 1950s, the *Picnic* movie, with William Holden in Meeker's role, set Kim Novak pawing a now absolutely unshirted (and shaved) Holden on the film's poster, spreading the Beautiful Male news through the culture.

Stanleys greatly vary, because it has become such a titanic assumption in its original form that few actors are right for it. Many are wholly wrong. In 1956, at the City Center, Tallulah Bankhead's Blanche faced off with Gerald O'Loughlin's ordinary Stanley, though in the end Bankhead was really contending with the giggles and shrieks of her gay following. At one performance, she actually walked downstage and dropped character to plead for a fair hearing in a silent house. More recently, Natasha

---

* Schmengie Footnote No. Four: "airs."

Richardson, under the clueless direction of Edward Hall, spent her time struggling with the accent, and her Stanley, John C. Reilly, was so miscast that the Stella got the notices. On one level, *Streetcar* is a duel between honesty and pretense—but Stanley wins not because he's honest but because, in the world according to Tennessee Williams, beauty passes the laws.

The real driver in all this was Elia Kazan; Williams (and Miller) were his facilitators, the latter in *All My Sons* (1947) and *Death of a Salesman* (1949). *Salesman* of course has its own titanic assumption in Willy Loman, originated by Group veteran Lee J. Cobb—"the greatest dramatic actor I ever saw," Miller himself wrote. Yet it would seem that the best talent outdid itself under Kazan's direction. For a time, roughly the twenty years following World War II, Kazan's name became the summoning term for the kind of director he now was: finished with screwball fun, with musicals, with Helen Hayes as Harriet Beecher Stowe, and with most unknown writers. Kazan was now the man in charge of the best plays.

Some found his productions overwrought; the authors never did, because Kazan brought out what was happening *under* the words. Of Kazan and *Streetcar,* John Mason Brown wrote, "He is able to capture to the full the inner no less than the outer action of the text." And note how easily Kazan moved between the fantasist Williams and the pedagogical socialist Miller; note how different Stanley from Willy, the dream man from the patriarch but also the turbulent beauty in utter control of his pitch from the professional loser. There is, as well, Williams the entertainer opposed to Miller the enlightener. In Paris, in 1947, Miller spent an evening at a revival of *Ondine* watching the French have a love affair with Jean Giraudoux: "The language," he wrote, "was saving their souls . . . The one unity left to them and thus their one hope." Bored with the play itself, Miller "was moved by the tenderness of the people toward [Louis Jouvet, *Ondine*'s director and star], I who came from a theatre of combat with audiences."

That is, while Williams thrilled, appalled, and loved his public, Miller kept trying to urge some sense into them, at first about the heartless and even criminal nature of American business ethics and then about the postwar purge of Communists that is very loosely referred to as "McCarthyism." To do so, Miller found a parallel in the Salem witch trials of 1692, seeing in their religious hysteria the same mix of heroism (for instance from Joseph Welch, in his definitive "Have you no shame, at long last?" to McCarthy himself) and opportunism (from those too numerous to mention) that characterized the anti-Communist era. As all my readers know, this work is *The Crucible* (1953), whose title refers to a container used for calcination and, apropos of Miller and in Webster's words, "a severe test."

When Miller researched the Salem trials, he must have—as dog handlers put it—"alerted" when he discovered John Proctor, one of the accused, who petitioned five Boston ministers to transfer his and others' cases or to send other judges to Salem, for the men they were facing had "condemned us already before our trials." This sounded very much like the attitude of those judging Miller's contemporaries under accusation. But then, tyrannies so often speak the same language that a victim of Mao Tse-tung, Nien Cheng, having seen *The Crucible* in Shanghai in 1980, told Miller that she was amazed that the play was not an autobiographical work by a Chinese. "Some of the interrogations," she explained, "were precisely the same ones used on us in the Cultural Revolution."

There is no facilitator in *The Crucible*. John Proctor drives the action all but alone, as the only fighting member of a group that will not confess to witchcraft. Just before his hanging, he is offered freedom . . . at the cost of Naming Names. One of American theatre's great heroic parts, John Proctor thus mates chronicle play with social-problem play: because the work's events have already taken place, yet the very intelligence of the piece hangs on whether or not he will pass the severe test.

Indeed, the work's events were *still* taking place when *The Crucible* went into rehearsal, in late 1952. Miller took some liberties with the record, giving Proctor a melodrama's subplot in which his marriage is ruined by his infidelity, his adulteress tries to kill Mrs. Proctor by demonizing her, and Proctor is helplessly ensnared in the case when he tries to save his wife by denouncing his whore and himself. The Greeks themselves couldn't have tied it up more symmetrically.

And what a show for Elia Kazan to chew up and spit out: the ruthless judges, the very various Salem townsfolk, the little troop of bloodthirsty schoolgirls faking attacks, and of course the love triangle of good guy, cold saint, and evil trollop. The original cast is not Kazan-famous in the *Streetcar* or *Salesman* manner. Heading the company were Arthur Kennedy, Beatrice Straight, and Madeleine Sherwood in the triangle, E. G. Marshall as a witchhunter who turns against the trials, and our old friend the now seventy-something Walter Hampden as the head judge, for whom no argument is inane if it will send someone to the noose.

It's not exactly a Kazan cast because Kazan didn't get the job: he had Informed when called to D.C., and Miller's moral code forbade collaboration between the two, especially on a work that denounces informing. This can only be called courageous, because Kazan's style was too new to claim acolytes, and for some reason that none of the communicants has explained, Miller's producer, Kermit Bloomgarden, didn't call on one of the Group stalwarts such as Harold Clurman or Robert Lewis; or one of the better journeymen like Bretaigne Windust or Michael Gordon; or one of the new hotshots like José Ferrer (mainly an actor, but also a director and for a time the head of the City Center's theatre company). Because Bloomgarden actually ended up with the worst director on Broadway:

Jed Harris. This has-been had finally alienated so much of The Street that by the late 1940s he was about to fade away, broke and without the shred of a prospect. However, Harris' mania for destructive behavior had not yet entirely beclouded his vision, and he made a comeback with a big classy hit in Ruth and Augustus Goetz's *The Heiress* (1947). An adaptation of Henry James' *Washington Square* and more recently a vehicle for Cherry Jones, the play originally went out of town with the novel's title and a tacked-on happy ending. The Goetzes hadn't wanted to rewrite James but no producer would stage it as they wrote it, with the heroine implacably treading upstairs with her lamp while her fortune-hunting beau pounds at her door. Retitled, reworked, and restaged by Harris with Wendy Hiller, the play was saved, and all Broadway knew it.

But by the time Harris got to *The Crucible,* his loony anger had overtaken whatever talent he had left. One part of him could be eloquent in discovering character relationships with the actors; but most of him was a screaming idiot, singling out Cloris Leachman with such venom that she left the show during rehearsals.* It was Harris' odd notion that *The Crucible* should avoid movement, to strike poses suggestive of Dutch painting.

---

* Leachman had been playing Proctor's lover, the scheming Abigail; this was the role that Madeleine Sherwood took over. Wasn't Leachman (Phyllis of the Mary Tyler Moore sitcom troupe) wrong for this steamy Jezebel? Sherwood made a career of sirens and termagants, such as Sister Mae in *Cat On a Hot Tin Roof* or, in replacement, Morgan Le Fay in *Camelot.* She was again hard as hickory in Arthur Laurents' *Invitation To a March;* but Stephen Sondheim wrote the show's mood music, and the Sondheim magic reformed Sherwood. Now she wished to play Saint Bernadette or a *Sound of Music* nun. No way; but she did sing Sondheim ("Lloyd tells me . . . never go by plane") as the original Mrs. McIlhenny in *Do I Hear a Waltz?*.

What, with all Miller's confrontational plotting, with people on trial for crimes they didn't commit—that do not in fact exist? At some point, Harris started skipping rehearsals, leaving the unqualified Miller to try to direct in his place. Even so, the out-of-town premiere, in Wilmington, brought the house to its feet, and at the cries of "Author! Author!" that still occasionally reverberated in theatres then, he came forward: Jed Harris, warmly greeting his public while Kennedy and Marshall, on either side of him, openly gaped in, respectively, bewilderment and disgust.

Harris later pretended to Miller that the actors had dragged him onstage, though everyone had seen him pushing on unbeseeched. Besides, the notion that actors would drag Harris anywhere but to a cauldron of boiling oil was spectacularly implausible, unworthy of the Jed Harris who once held all Broadway in fee. His jig was up, and he herewith passes out of our narrative.

Interestingly, the fancy New York audience at *The Crucible*'s first night did not share Wilmington's enthusiasm. Miller noticed an atmosphere of icy resentment settle over them once they realized that the show was not really about witches, and the reviews were all but dismissive. True, the actors never got the chance to put the play over as they might have done; Kazan would have had them blazing.* And it is true that most people don't like whistle-blowers: Miller was demanding that theatregoers discern and make war upon the new style in character assassination. (Remember Miller's speaking of his "combat with audiences"?) But it is also true that Miller's convenient parallel of witch-hunting and Red-baiting is part of the Big Lie that a portion of the American left has never admitted to. The notion of a Satanic conspiracy against Christianity is a fantasy. The notion of a Communist conspiracy against democracy is not, and the loathsome methods of the anti-Communist right do not "cancel out" the loathsomeness of Stalinism.

Complicating all this is the notion of The Names that the authorities demanded of the accused, as they do of John Proctor. Like the fresh, innocent soul you must produce to get out of your own contract with the devil, The Names constituted the only pardon. Everyone had to Name them, whether he or she had been a ruthless operative of Stalinism or an enabler of some

---

* Production really is everything. When *The Crucible* came to Paris two years later, as *Les Sorcières de Salem,* in a translation by Marcel Aymé (author of "Le Passe-Muraille," source of Michel Legrand's boulevard opera *Amour*), it was a hit. Directed by Raymond Rouleau, with Yves Montand and Simone Signoret as the Proctors, the piece ate up the stage. It was filmed with the two stars, under Rouleau, in 1958.

kind; or one who flirted with Communism at a time when it was legal and chic to do so; or one who attended meetings out of curiosity; or who once went to a cocktail party that mysteriously turned into a Communist recruitment event; or even a guy who went to meetings to meet chicks.*

In fact, so much attention has been paid to the more celebrity-studded episodes of "McCarthyism" that some may not know how much more broadly the theatre felt its impact. It wasn't just subpoenas and the movie and television blacklist. Outside the northeastern megalopolis, a chill like that of *The Crucible*'s first nighters encouraged all sorts of little tyrants to revive the American tradition of anti-intellectualism. Touring shows never knew when a local bigot might condemn anything more adult than *Abie's Irish Rose* and call for a boycott. The American Legion and certain religious organizations acted like hate groups, trying to close shows they knew nothing of, because they had "heard something." At a road performance of *Death of a Salesman*—and this was before Miller was implicated in any way—there was just one person in the auditorium at curtain time. Thomas Mitchell, the Willy Loman and therefore unofficial capocomico, told the stage manager to call places and ring up the curtain, presumably in admiration of that lone spectator's fortitude.

Worse, Chicago's mayor, police commissioner, and city council unanimously banned *The Respectful Prostitute,* and made it clear they would have liked to extend the courtesy to *A Streetcar Named Desire* and *Mister Roberts.* One always thinks of Boston as the place of the Mrs. Grundys, but that was mainly because it was such a mainstay of the tryout that the occasional battle with bluenoses made news on The Street. Indeed, "Banned in Boston" was a useful marketing blurb. Chicago was more properly a tour stop, less newsworthy when it closed its gates on a show. The last time anyone in New York noticed such doings was back in the 1930s, when *Tobacco Road,* which might easily have run ten years in Chicago, was forbidden to play.

---

* This is an important point almost entirely overlooked, and another of my personal notes may help fix a perspective for us. The university I attended divided undergraduates into the College, coeducationally, or the Wharton School, for men only. The latter took all their electives in the College, to meet women, and the course richest in dating privileges was Art 140 A and B, on the history of art. It was famously tough and good for credit only if one passed both semesters, yet the Wharton boys filled it. Now, if they went through all that just to meet women, imagine how many more men would sit in on Party meetings for the same reason.

The atmosphere in the early 1950s was so poisonous that *Mister Roberts* actually was threatened in New York. This was because of a single line, when Ensign Pulver goes off to construct a firecracker, using fulminate of mercury:

ROBERTS: That stuff's murder. Do you suppose he means it?
DOC: Of course not. Where could he get fulminate of mercury?
ROBERTS: I don't know. He's pretty resourceful.

And here comes the terrible line:

ROBERTS: Where did he get the clap last year?

During the run, Henry Fonda occasionally slipped the cut line back in when a special guest was in the house. Then some woman complained to the police, and they promised to shut the show down if the word "clap" was heard again.

Meanwhile, Elia Kazan felt bound to reply to Miller's condemnation of informers. Director Kazan and writer Budd Schulberg made their rebuttal in the film *On the Waterfront* (1954), in which the protagonist informs on the leaders of a crooked labor union. Note that, either slyly or coincidentally, Kazan employed Miller's favorite actor, Lee J. Cobb, as the head mobster, and cast as his hero Tennessee Williams' favorite actor, Marlon Brando. The latter won an Oscar, but that was the least they could give him, for at this stage of his career Brando's volatile genius was fixing his roles for us archetypally. He didn't play characters; he played gods.

And now it was Miller's turn to reply, in *A View From the Bridge* (1955). Three odd little things first: one, Miller's continuing his boycott of Kazan by going this time with director Martin Ritt was a reply in itself; two, Van Heflin finally got to play a Stanley Kowalski role, as Eddie Carbone; and, three, this now full-length piece debuted as the longer part of a double bill, with the now forgot *A Memory of Two Mondays*.* In *A View From the Bridge*, the informer is not only a villain but one motivated by personal animosity: Eddie turns in two illegal aliens, brothers from Italy who have been staying

---

* Miller made *View*'s expanded revision for the 1956 London staging, with Anthony Quayle's Eddie and Peter Brook directing.

with his family. One of them (Richard Davalos) has charmed Eddie's niece (Gloria Marlowe, earlier that year an ingenue in the musical *Plain and Fancy*), for whom Eddie bears incestuous feelings. Eddie's anonymous tip to Immigration defies parish ethics, and in retaliation Eddie is murdered by the older brother (Jack Warden).

But hadn't Miller already *defended* the informer in his own adaptation (from a plain-English translation) of Ibsen's *An Enemy of the People* (1950)? Fredric March played Stockmann, a lone honest man who takes on his community in publicizing findings that a lucrative local industry is a danger to public health. Isn't Stockmann the original informer? The whistle-blower? And isn't he not only Ibsen's but Miller's hero?

Robert Lewis directed, in case you were wondering; still, this is the Age of Kazan, one in which Broadway enjoyed the freedom to delve deeply, grandly, into emotional territory once thought too dangerous. The "over-wrought" Kazan style was simply an honesty in treating matter heretofore written dishonestly: in euphemisms and evasions. "Decadence" was the attack word used by those unprepared for Williams' innovative realism. Miller, too, occasioned frowns for his "preaching."

Is that how *The Crucible*'s first-night audience put it—"preaching"?—as it icily exited the Martin Beck Theatre? Ironically, *The Crucible* is now Miller's most popular work, a timeless classic of that old standby, good versus evil. And *A Streetcar Named Desire* is Williams' masterpiece. The two plays point back to the most influential development in American stage, the Group Theatre, which instituted the drama of social inquiry as naturalism and taught the New Acting to stimulate playwrights to elicit from that form rich statements on how we live as a society. *Streetcar* is the work that proclaimed the acting (in an apolitical context), and *The Crucible* the work that "demonstrated" social drama (despite an underpowered acting team).

And of course "McCarthyism" overwhelmed the era; yet we might edge out of that American Dreyfus Case on a neutral note. Let us return to *Streetcar,* where the worst thing that can happen to those who are "different" is rough sex with Marlon Brando. I tell you a tale known to lore, given to me by the stage manager of one of the tours. The show was nearing its closing dates, and the leading actors were unwilling to throw away any more leisure on radio interviews for PR, and even the secondary characters like the poker players and Eunice, the hard-bitten yet wise upstairs neighbor, just wanted to finish the tour and get back to their lives in New York.

At the last stop or so, everyone said no, so the actors playing the doctor and nurse who come in during the play's last minutes were hustled off to the radio station to promote the booking.

Does anyone remember how these two are billed in the program? They are called A Strange Man and A Strange Woman, so that playgoers scouring the dramatis personae would not be tipped off to Williams' grisly end, as Blanche is led off: because Stanley wills it, and Stella's job description is to will what Stanley wills.

Actually, "hustled" is not the right word, for, never having had radio time before, the Doctor and Nurse were keen. The interviewer established for the listening audience the play's title, author, and producer (who was, after all, the daughter of the third letter in MGM), and asked his guests about the subject of the play.

The man of the pair leaned eagerly toward the microphone, his Moment at hand. "Well," he began, "it's about this doctor . . . "

Thirteen

End of the Empire:

THE EARLY 1950s

s it possible that Tennessee Williams' success encouraged producers to look upon unusual projects as not only viable but more commercial than conventional pieces? For an unusual number of plays in the early 1950s are as quirky, daring, and bizarre as anything that Williams had revealed.

Perhaps Mary Chase's *Mrs. McThing* (1952) was no more than quirky, but this fantasy in which a snobby plutocrat and her son are replaced by duplicate "sticks" and sent to Shantytown to labor and learn humility was the sort of thing that producers routinely rejected as too grotesque to succeed.

Surely it got on only because ANTA* president Helen Hayes accepted the piece for ANTA's experimental theatre program *and* played the mother. (Not the title role: Mrs. McThing is the witch who creates the sticks.) At that, Hayes scheduled a brief limited engagement that was extended to 350 performances when good notices revealed that grotesque can be charming. Along with Brandon de Wilde as Hayes' son, the show boasted the goofy Shantyland gang of Ernest Borgnine, Fred Gwynne, Iggie Wolfington, Irwin Corey, and mob boss Jules Munshin. (All but Borgnine made at least one major appearance in a book musical, respectively *Angel, The Music Man, Flahooley,* and *The Gay Life.*) Hayes and de Wilde enjoyed dual roles, playing their own sticks; Mrs. McThing herself called for two actresses, the first as Crone in Wicked Witch of the West kit and the second as Fairy, a beauty in pink lighting.

Williams' own *Camino Real* (1953) was certainly bizarre, a chowder of archetypes (Casanova, Camille, Lord Byron, Kilroy, Don Quixote) served up in an unspecified sector of Latin America. Elia Kazan directed a huge cast in an exciting but incoherent evening that nevertheless lasted 60 performances, astonishing after largely blistering reviews. But then, early-fifties theatregoers at times seemed theatre-mad, supporting, if for only two months, almost anything.

For instance, they were attending one-person shows as never before—Emlyn Williams' Dickens readings in Dickens makeup (1952, then in a program devoted to *Bleak House* in 1953); *An Evening With Beatrice Lillie* (1952); Danish pianist Victor Borge's *Comedy in Music* (1953); *Joyce Grenfell Requests the Pleasure* (1955), with bit players.

Let us notice one in particular, *Paris '90* (1952). It was daring, or something: Cornelia Otis Skinner would evoke la belle époque in a pride of monologues, complete with set and costume changes, a small chorus, songs and incidental music by Kay Swift, and sizable orchestrations by Robert Russell Bennett. It was, in effect, a good-sized musical with a cast of one; who would go? The monologues, written by Skinner, opened a lavish gallery that only the most protean impersonator could paint in—diseuse Yvette Guilbert in a re-creation of her Toulouse-Lautrec; a visiting Boston schoolteacher

---

* The American National Theatre and Academy, an organization founded by Congress alongside (but separate from) the Federal Theatre in 1935. It was never clear what its purpose was, though it was productive from 1950 into the 1960s.

(with the Boston "r") who suffers a terrifying contretemps with her traveling companion; a laundress; an angel statue in a niche of Notre-Dame; a Lady of Fashion in her coach, to the clopping of hooves. "She is looking so well since her suicide," she says of one acquaintance, and "Woman's virtue is man's greatest invention."

Skinner herself was a bizarre item, one who could flourish in such rarefied entertainment only in this little age; any other would call *Paris '90*, ungratefully, self-indulgent. The daughter of the illustrious Otis Skinner, Cornelia was the Junior League with greasepaint—a lady who lunches, but with Colette. Skinner had long been a monologuist of note, but when she finally tried a real play, in *Theatre* (1941), the critics rediscovered and fell in love with her. The work of that tireless adapter Guy Bolton and Somerset Maugham, from Maugham's novel, *Theatre*—which later provisioned the Annette Bening film *Being Julia*—is obsessed with the devastating charm of its heroine. No one less than an Annette Bening dare take the role. And the critics thought *Theatre* "as phony as the twenty-five-cent watches sidewalk pitchmen peddle" and even "frankly trash." It can't be easy to win valentines as the protagonist of such a piece, yet Skinner did. And *Paris '90* actually played 87 performances. This woman must have been quite something: but her career was spotty and is now obscure. Her father is still recalled for his showpiece, *Kismet*. His daughter is recalled for her father.

Quirky, daring, and bizarre was *Mrs. Patterson* (1954). Naturalism containing fantasies, and a straight play with half a dozen songs, it was produced by Leonard Sillman as a follow-up vehicle for the most emerged of his New Faces of 1952, Eartha Kitt. Charles Sebree and Greer Johnson wrote the script, about an adolescent in Kentucky in 1920 who spends her time playing blackjack for matchsticks and weaving dreams, of both local white society and the black high life in Chicago. The fantasies actualized these dreams, as young Teddy (Kitt, of course) served tea to Mrs. Patterson (Enid Markey, Jane in the first *Tarzan* movie, in 1918) and three belles; or conjured up the devil (Avon Long) to learn of Chicago ways.

It was an unplotted atmosphere piece, very much like *The Member of the Wedding* but without Carson McCullers' wonderful ear. *Mrs. Patterson* really brightened up only in the song spots. (Helen Dowdy, as Chicago blues mistress Bessie Bolt, got one; Kitt had the other five.) From the swinging "If I Was a Boy" through the lazy jazz of "Tea in Chicago" to the slithery shuffle of "My Daddy Is a Dandy," composer-lyricist James Shelton gave the evening a variety of not plot numbers but specialty spots. Indeed, he didn't even try to fit "Be Good, Be Good, Be Good" into the show proper: after the bows, Kitt changed out of her sharecropper's cotton into cabaret red and offered the song as an encore. That *Mrs. Patterson* lasted 101 performances testifies to Kitt's star power, but also to the prevailing love of novelty.

Most daring of all were the large number of plays dealing in part or whole with gay material. What is Herman Melville's *Billy Budd* about—at least overtly, above the religious subtext—but the villain's physical idolization of the hero? To make certain that everyone got the point, Louis O. Coxe and R. H. Chapman's adaptation cast a Big Blond Boy, Charles Nolte, in the title role, first in an ANTA showcase as *Uniform of Flesh* (1949), then on Broadway as *Billy Budd* (1951). The usual Clueless Heteros could protect themselves from considering exactly how the Claggart, Torin Thatcher, viewed Billy by reminding themselves that Melville is a Classic. And Classics aren't about the Beautiful Male. Classics are . . . uh, classic. But even Euripides proved troublesome, in an off-Broadway staging of Robinson Jeffers' version of *Hippolytus* called *The Cretan Woman* (1954). This time, the hero resisted Phaedra because he preferred men; another hunk, William Andrews, bedecked in shorts, sandals with leatherman calf rigging, and a backflung cape, authenticated the sensuality.

At least John Kerr, the suspected homo prep-school student of Robert Anderson's *Tea and Sympathy* (1953), was only suspected. Anderson never tells what the kid really wants, but the homophobic housemaster's compassionate wife (Deborah Kerr) thinks she knows. Alone with the boy at the curtain, she starts unbuttoning her blouse to utter one of the most shocking lines of all time, still quoted today: "Years from now, when you talk of this . . . and you will . . . be kind."

Some of the gay matter was encoded, as in John Van Druten's comedy *Bell, Book and Candle* (1950). Van Druten was gay, and aren't the witches of this work—Lilli Palmer, brother Scott McKay, and aunt Jean Adair—stand-ins for homosexuals as members of a cult? McKay's character, Nicky Holroyd, is described as "engaging, impish, and somewhat impertinent"—pure 1950 for "gay." Another character chimes in with "You'd be amazed what's going on under your nose that you'd never suspect. . . . Some of them [flaunt it], you know. Go about dressed up so that people will recognize them." Thus, when Palmer uses craft to ensnare bachelor Rex Harrison (Palmer's then real-life husband), is this the gay beguiling the straight in crossover romance?

On the other hand, New York's first sitting at a Shaw play from 1936, *The Millionairess* (1952), offered Katharine Hepburn sparring with Cyril Ritchard and Robert Helpmann, the two mintiest Australians ever known. At a time when gays were thought as evil as—even allied with—Communists, this pair was caking around the stage of the Shubert Theatre as if to arouse a federal intervention. Even more defiant of the censor's padlock was Ruth and Augustus Goetz's adaptation of Andre Gide, *The Immoralist* (1954), with three gay characters, two of them played by parish valentines Louis Jourdan and James Dean.

Gide directs us to the arena of French theatre, more comfortable (if still seldom commercially successful) in the early 1950s than ever before or after. André Roussin's *Nina* (1951) and *The Little Hut* (1953), both comedies about a married couple and her lover, and Marcelle Maurette's *Anastasia* (1954), with Viveca Lindfors as the putative last of the Romanofs, represented boulevard style. Jean Anouilh enjoyed a veritable festival, with five titles, and Jean Giraudoux enjoyed two succès d'estime, one with that favorite Broadway thing, a brand-new world-class star. Having won big in New York   not her native Europe—in Anita Loos' *Gigi* (1951), d'après Colette, Audrey Hepburn returned to The Street with her husband, Mel Ferrer, in *Ondine* (1954). The play itself was almost a generation old—we recall Arthur Miller attending a revival in postwar Paris a chapter ago—but only now was the French love of whimsical *causerie* in style Over Here. Giraudoux's archetypal fairy tale, drawn from Friedrich de la Motte Fouqué's story of the water nymph whose love destroys a mortal prince, demands the utmost in magical spectacle, and the Playwrights' Company flattered Giraudoux with Total Production. Hepburn's naiad outfit, in fishnet body stocking pocked with caution seaweed at bosom and hips, was a talk of the town, and everyone else was in Medieval Drastic such that costume designer Richard Whorf won a Tony over all the couturiers of musicals that season. But then, *Ondine* almost was a musical, sited at the 46th Street Theatre and boasting an incidental score, by Virgil Thomson. Hepburn, too, won a Tony, as did director Alfred Lunt.

After all that, it's almost anticlimactic to record the appearance of Giraudoux's *La Guerre de Troie N'aura Pas Lieu* (*The Trojan War Will Not Take Place*), in Christopher Fry's version as *Tiger at the Gates* (1955). *Ondine* lasted 157 performances but could have run longer had Hepburn and Ferrer not departed for Hollywood; the show did such good business that it broke box-office records at a playhouse used to hits. *Tiger at the Gates* ran even longer: 217 performances. The production was from London, by our own Harold Clurman, and some of his West Enders came over with him, including Michael Redgrave, Walter Fitzgerald, Barbara Jefford, and, as Helen, Diane Cilento, who Kenneth Tynan thought was "fetchingly got up in what I can best describe as a Freudian slip."

The most European of all plays on Broadway at this time was an American work, *The Diary of Anne Frank* (1955). It was not European in style, but rather in its use of domestic drama to make a quietly epic summation of a thousand years of anti-Semitic barbarism in Europe. The Franks, the Van Daans, and a dentist named Dussel create a kind of extended family in their fragile refuge where Anne writes the diary that became one of the all-time bestselling books in Western civilization. The play's worldwide success must inevitably follow, one surely thinks.

In fact, the diary itself was not a big success at first, and U.S. publishers were inclined to turn it down. But it had a champion: writer Meyer Levin, who, while trying to arrange for theatre or film adaptation, contributed a rave review of the diary in the *New York Times*. He hadn't informed his editors of his personal involvement, in questionable ethics but perhaps on a superior historical principle. The book's sales skyrocketed, and Levin now seemed first in line of Anne Frank's potential dramatists.

However, option holders Cheryl Crawford and then Kermit Bloomgarden found Levin's script untheatrical. Carson McCullers was to start afresh on the adaptation, perhaps because of her success in adapting another plotless piece, her own *The Member of the Wedding*. In the end, the adapters were the husband-and-wife team of Frances Goodrich and Albert Hackett, with some advice from Bloomgarden's house playwright Lillian Hellman. That gray eminence only exacerbated what was already the crisis of Levin's life, for he was desperate to write the *Diary* play and saw in the sulphurous Hellman a personal enemy devoted not only to the destruction of Meyer Levin but the universalizing of the Franks and their fellows from Jewish victims of Nazis to generalized victims of fascism.

In fact, Hellman's relationship with the Hacketts, aside from her usual screaming of "What's *this*?" when opening a Christmas present that wasn't perfectly on target, consisted entirely of solving dramaturgical problems. Revising rather more than they were used to, the Hacketts did a fine and faithful job, keeping the diary's universality implicit and its ethnicity fully portioned. No one could mistake these characters for Methodists. But then, Levin was one of those who surprise a conspiracy in every agenda incongruent with their own. (He was to have another Ruckus With Just About Everyone on his only other Broadway adventure, his play *Compulsion* [1957], from his novel on the Leopold and Loeb murder case.) Levin suffered a complete breakdown, turning into a combination of Ancient Mariner and Captain Ahab, sharing his woes with everyone he encountered and chasing his White Whale Hellman. For decades after—*decades!*—Levin pursued the matter in advertisements, letters to public figures, and a hysteria so dense that he developed a nervous affliction, helplessly eructating wordless laments. Levin even took Otto Frank to court. This is like suing Bambi.

At least, by that time the play had been launched. In the little era that attended Sidney Kingsley's *Darkness At Noon* (1951), from Arthur Koestler's anti-Stalinist novel; the Nazi POW camp comedy thriller *Stalag 17* (1951); and *The Caine Mutiny Court-Martial* (1954), *The Diary of Anne Frank* was the war play no one thought of as such. The other three titles presented officers and soldiers, interrogations and betrayal. Here instead were eight people and their two protectors, the very smallest possible membership in the war. Yet their saga now stands at the forefront of chronicle. This is perhaps because Anne herself is no Saint Joan, but a merry young lady who loves life and, even in her abysmal hideout, makes the most of it.

Bloomgarden's production was standard Broadway, with an important debut that ultimately went nowhere. Garson Kanin directed in Boris Aronson's set, Joseph Schildkraut headed the cast as Otto Frank, and Lee Strasberg's daughter, Susan, won great welcome as Anne. This led her to a fabulous debacle, Dumas' *The Lady of the Caméllias* as a Winter Garden spectacle directed by Franco Zeffirelli in 1963; it all but finished young Miss Strasberg off. *The Diary of Anne Frank* won the Pulitzer Prize and the top award from both the Drama Critics Circle and the Tony voters, and it ran 717 performances. Still, the piece never seemed quite "placed" till it traversed the globe, one of the rare plays to transcend national borders and speak to everyone.*

---

* A smallish box of lore material travels along with this work—the anguished silence in German theatres after each performance, the intellectuals' calling an Anne Frank play by nature manipulative and frivolous, and, more recently, the insistent attempts by the anti-Semitic lunatic fringe to denounce the diary itself as a forgery using twisted bits of the Meyer Levin contretemps. Less well known is the urban legend of Pia Zadora's Anne

The unusual preponderance of one-offs and foreign works suggests that Broadway was undergoing another of its periodic transformations, and we find major evidence in the musical especially. After the Rodgers and Hammerstein revolution of the 1940s, this formerly lightest of forms put on the weight of character development and sensible narrative direction till it could add a brand-new business transaction to American show biz: the musical adapted from a play.

New? What of all those musicals in the 1910s and '20s based on plays? A partial list: *Very Good Eddie* (1915), *Leave It to Jane* (1917), *Going Up* (1917), *Orange Blossoms* (1922), *The Student Prince* (1924), *No, No, Nanette* (1925), *The White Eagle* (1927), *Whoopee* (1928), *Spring Is Here* (1929). However, these were all genre musicals based on genre plays. What was new in the Rodgers and Hammerstein era was the kind of play that might be musicalized: any kind. Even talky pieces like *I Am a Camera* (1951) or *The Fourposter* (1951). The early 1950s is rich in such titles. Another partial list: *The Grass Harp* (1952), *The Time of the Cuckoo* (1952), *The Teahouse of the August Moon* (1953), *Picnic* (1953), *The Rainmaker* (1954), *The Matchmaker* (1955).

There was this as well: while many Golden Age musical writers were still at work, the straight-play writers who weren't dead were doing little more than stewing prunes and chasing kids off their lawn. There were new writers, of course. But the sense of continuity in the history is slipping.

The case of Maxwell Anderson is typical. His McCarthyism piece, *Barefoot in Athens* (1951), on the last days of Socrates, failed badly. *The Bad Seed* (1954) was a hit, but two more failures followed on, one lumbered with an ignominious off-Broadway booking. *Barefoot in Athens* did at least give work to Lotte Lenya as Socrates' wife. Barry Jones played the philosopher, coolly insisting on drinking his hemlock even as friends come by to free him. ("I'll converse with them over the cup," he declares.) Alas, a

---

Frank; I retell it here to settle this matter for once and all. Various versions of the tale locate it from Glasgow to middle America, where Zadora's incompetent rendering drove her audience into comatose despair. Late in the evening, hearing the Nazi sirens, they stirred into action, shouting, *"They're in the attic!"* In fact, Zadora is not on record as having played Anne anywhere—and every version of the story that I've encountered finds the public uttering its line when the Nazis surge into view asking, "Vhere are zose hiding Jews?" *Menzogna, menzogna!* The sirens are heard, but no Nazis appear in the play; if any did, they surely wouldn't ask the public where to go. Those who wish to know more can google Zadora and click away.

plethora of endless monologues reminded many that Anderson was the guy whose verse plays might run a season without your knowing anybody who had seen one.

The Bad Seed is an expert piece, but this study of an adorable, piano-playing eight-year-old girl who is secretly a vicious killer didn't need a Maxwell Anderson to write it. Among Anderson's serious plays, this work is what the French call a "UFO" (actually an "OVNI," for "objet volant non identifié," meaning the unit in an oeuvre that is unlike all the other units). The characteristic Anderson drama (that is, not counting the few comedies) is distinguished by poetry or politics. *The Bad Seed* is simply a thriller.

Its source was William March's novel, treating the theory that one derives personality traits genetically. In Anderson's adaptation, Mrs. Penmark (Nancy Kelly) realizes that daughter Rhoda (Patty McCormack) has inherited homicidal tendencies from Kelly's pernicious mother. Kelly decides to kill her daughter and herself; we witness a drugging and hear a gun go off. But that is not the end, as Anderson offers something he never cared for before this, a plot twist. (And I especially need to reveal it here because the otherwise extremely faithful movie version alters it.) After Kelly's double-killing scene, the lights come up not on the curtain calls that the audience expected but more play. Characters discuss the terrible event:

> MONICA: She'd shot herself and given Rhoda a deadly dose of sleeping pills. She had obviously planned that they should die together.

After forty seconds more dialogue, we suddenly hear something we were sure could not again be heard: the little girl's piano playing.

> MONICA: (To Rhoda's father) You have a lot to be grateful for. If we hadn't heard the shot you'd have lost Rhoda too.

And the little darling enters, to the public's gasps. A bit of lovahugga with her unknowing father, and the curtain falls.

In effect, Anderson simply dwindled away, as so many others did. And one symbolic lurch told the theatregoing community that a certain kind of Broadway was over. This was the closing of the Empire Theatre, in 1953, after sixty years as The Street's most prestigious and even beloved playhouse. Located at the southeast corner of Broadway and Fortieth Street, the Empire enjoyed an entrance right on the thoroughfare, so dignified that it was designed without a marquee, just the theatre's name over the double doors and again atop the lintel work. The situation was historically advantageous: looking back on the Old Broadway of Herald Square and the Syndicate and up toward the New Broadway of Forty-second Street and the Shuberts.

The Empire's cultural advantage was manager Charles Frohman. As we know, he made "Empire" synonymous with glamor, elegance, and good storytelling. In a sort of anticipation of the *Follies* reunion party of Ziegfeld girls, the Empire shut its doors with a program of scenes from Empire hits, staged by Eddie Dowling and emceed by our favorite monologuist, Cornelia Otis Skinner. In the unit set of the Empire's final tenant, *The Time of the Cuckoo*—"the garden of the Pensione Fioria"—Maureen Stapleton played Camille; Brandon de Wilde and Marian Seldes played Oliver Twist and Nancy to Clarence Derwent's Fagin; Howard Lindsay and Dorothy Stickney reclaimed their roles in *Life With Father*; Blanche Yurka impersonated Doris Keane in Ned Sheldon's *The Czarina*; and, astonishingly, one of the leads from the Empire's first attraction turned up in her original part at what may have been a genuinely biblical age: Edna Wallace Hopper in David Belasco and Franklin Fyles' *The Girl I Left Behind Me* (1893).

"Broadway" itself—Broadway the idea—was losing not only real estate and artists but a percentage of its importance as The Great American Place. The dashing, dirty New York of Walter Winchell and Damon Runyon, of Sophistication and the Celebrity of Eccentricity, was all but over. True, the Runyon-inspired *Guys and Dolls* flourished, and Sidney Kingsley's hit comedy *Lunatics and Lovers* (1954), set in Runyonland's very center, a hotel in the West Forties, presented such Runyonesque studies as the shady nickel-and-dime operator (Buddy Hackett), the amiably corrupt judge (Dennis King), the clueless stooge (Arthur O'Connell), and the usual doxies (Vicki Cummings, Sheila Bond).

On the other hand, the early 1950s saw the beginning of what we might call the war on Walter Winchell—a series of controversies in which no one saw it his way, leading up to Burt Lancaster's portrayal of Winchell in the film *Sweet Smell of Success* (1957) as a megalomaniac goon. True, the film was not that widely seen, but the point is that, in the 1930s or '40s, almost no one would have dared cross that line. Now it didn't matter, and while Winchell was hated, some of this revolt against his power was cultural as well as personal. Winchell and the nation were phht, because Americans had begun to look west for their ideas: from theatre to film, from tradition to a fresh start.

One sees only hints of this in the 1950s, perhaps especially in George Axelrod's comedy *Will Success Spoil Rock Hunter?* (1955), because its Faustian plot casts the devil (Martin Gabel) as a Hollywood agent and the loser (Orson Bean) who pacts with him as a man in need of Hollywood power. Not long before, Bean would have sold his soul for success as a playwright or novelist, the professions associated with New York. And note that the show's woman lead was Jayne Mansfield, a rack diva whose *Police Gazette* looks and zany charm characterized the talent that is most comfortable on a sound stage: the opposite of, say, Katharine Cornell.

Note as well that while Mansfield enjoyed playing the eccentric, she wasn't a thirties eccentric. Another thing that Mansfield was the opposite of was Sophistication: Sophistication was over. There was still a *New Yorker* magazine. There was even *Life,* as ever obsessed with the theatre. But the celebrity of eccentricity had suddenly given way to the celebrity of cool.

Cool was an at first almost indefinably ambiguous state of nonconformity, but its classic moment of self-revelation is that much quoted exchange in the Marlon Brando biker film *The Wild One* (1954). You've seen it many times: a girl is dancing with a guy on the left of the frame while Brando, at right, plays air drums on a cigarette machine:

GIRL: Hey, Johnny, what are you rebelling against?
BRANDO: Whaddaya got?

Brando's unaggressive delivery is part of the meaning of cool: affectless, incurious, without a value system to protect and without content to express. Like Brando, the major avatars of Hollywood cool—James Dean, Paul Newman, and Steve McQueen—launched their acting careers in New York but could explore the New Detachment of cool only in the art that Hollywood made, the drama of violence or the action adventure. Brando was exceptional among them for his versatility—Shakespeare, a musical (*Guys and Dolls* again; and he did his own singing), the wily yet ultimately wise Sakini in *The Teahouse of the August Moon.* Imagine James Dean in Shakespeare, Paul Newman in a musical, Steve McQueen's Sakini.

In American acting, the myth of the Great Thespian Who Betrayed the

Higher Culture For the Mass Market remains that of John Barrymore. He's Don Juan, the gay divorcé, Adonis whom the boar slew—anything but an actor. Yet it might be time to transfer that myth to Brando, very like Barrymore in his pranks and irreverence. And surely Brando's conclusive abandonment of the theatre near the very start of a thirty-year career promotes this cultural shift from New York to Los Angeles. After all, Barrymore did, in *My Dear Children*, return to Broadway for a farewell kiss. Brando never bothered.

Fourteen

My God, That Moon's Bright:

AUNTIE MAME AND THE DARK AT THE TOP OF THE STAIRS

By the 1950s, Sophistication had devolved largely into the celebrity panelists of *To Tell the Truth,* the song stylings of Mabel Mercer . . . and the novels of Patrick Dennis. The writer's career lasted into the 1970s, and his best works arrived in the early 1960s—but the Big One landed in 1955. Sitting on the *New York Times* bestseller list for two years, this book also launched a franchise in theatre and film that raised its central character into the status of national icon: Don Quixote, Peter Pan, and Auntie Mame.

However, the Mame Dennis we know isn't exactly the one in the novel. A typical Patrick Dennis story surrounds a magnetic yet erratic figure with an assortment of cartoon types, the whole filtered through the viewpoint of a first-person narrator. In *Little Me* (1961), the narrator is the protagonist, a movie star who sleeps her way to the bottom. In *Genius* (1962), the narrator is the more characteristic Dennis onlooker, an intelligent and down-to-earth male of no personal interest to the reader, in contrast to the protagonist, a show-biz honcho down on his luck in Mexico City. In *The Joyous Season* (1964), the narrator is a small child watching his parents break up and reunite. In *Tony* (1966), the narrator is the best friend of the protagonist, an adventurer.

What made Dennis' work outstanding in its time was his odd jumble of the things that fascinated him—old-money society but also the left-outs who try to crack it; the hustler personality and the way that looks and sexual prowess can create opportunities; the ingrained bigotry and anti-intellectualism of the American bourgeoisie; the way gay folk move freely in and out of the hetero universe unbeknown to most heteros. There is an undercurrent of war in much of this—between the Sophisticated and ya-hoos, especially—that organizes Dennis' jumble.

It organizes *Auntie Mame* in particular, because the heroine becomes a crusader, battling self-righteous tyrants of the upper-middle class as she raises her orphaned nephew. He is the narrator, pleasantly vapid and less an actual person in the story than a literary device, even though he is her crusade. It is, however, an episodic one, a string of unconnected happenings. *Genius* tells a suspenseful story, *Tony* has the energy of its ambitiously phony anti-hero, and *Little Me* enjoys the wicked fun of stunt illustrations, composites made of stock shots and character studies with a guileful gay reverberation.

But *Auntie Mame* is essentially a short-story cycle—and it has almost no gay in it at all. That's odd, because it is one of our classic gay texts. And that is because "our" Auntie Mame isn't precisely the character Patrick Dennis conceived. When producers Robert Fryer and Lawrence Carr decided to turn the novel into a play for Rosalind Russell, they let Russell direct the transformation in a supervisory way, as any star might do. She would certainly have director approval. Russell wanted Morton da Costa, because he had staged Ira Levin's *No Time For Sergeants* (1955), from Mac Hyman's novel, and the result was a two-and-half-year smash. Russell saw symmetry there; now da Costa could turn Dennis' novel into a smash. Russell may also have noticed that the hillbilly hero of *No Time For Sergeants*,

Will Stockdale (Andy Griffith), sees the world in a way nobody else sees it, just like Mame, and—also like Mame—inspires allies and defeats everyone else.

In Russell's telling, she and da Costa virtually wrote *Auntie Mame* themselves, though Jerome Lawrence and Robert E. Lee were the dramatists of credit. In fact, this team did not need any help, having enjoyed their own two-year smash the same year as *No Time For Sergeants* with *Inherit the Wind*. This was a re-creation (using fictional names) of the trial of John T. Scopes, in 1925, for teaching evolution in a public high school. Note how relevant this play of 1955, on a subject from the 1920s, remains today.*

For Lawrence and Lee's tintypes of Clarence Darrow and William Jennings Bryan, as Henry Drummond (Paul Muni) and Matthew Harrison Brady (Ed Begley), represent respectively not merely scientific realism versus religious zealotry but the tolerant left against the book-burning right:

BRADY: He wants to destroy everybody's belief in the Bible, and in God!
DRUMMOND: . . . I'm trying to stop you bigots and ignoramuses from
    controlling the education of the United States! And you know it!

It's my guess that Lawrence and Lee were hired for *Auntie Mame* precisely because they already knew what Mame is up against: bankers and country-club goons without a lick of culture or socialist compassion.

In any case, *someone* saw in Mame something her creator himself had not seen, because the play's Mame is a bit like Russell's Hildy Johnson (in *His Girl Friday*) set into Dennis' milieu of money and snobs and sex and opportunists. The play's Mame is not as crazy and angry as the novel's Mame can be, and—also unlike the Dennis version—she's reasonable even when she's being unreasonable. The essential difference between novel and play is that in the former the central figure is a creature of farce, without any consistent reality. In the play, the central figure is Rosalind Russell.

Auntie Mame was the biggest non-musical production in modern

---

* It must be admitted that *Inherit the Wind*'s report is highly restyled in important details. For one instance, their Scopes, one Bertram Cates, is a quietly heroic science teacher simply working from the set text. The real John T. Scopes in fact did *not* teach evolution: because he was not only a science teacher but an athletic coach, and a field event kept him from class on the day he supposedly broke the law. Before the trial, his students had to take a special session on evolution in order to testify about it in court.

Broadway history (not counting those spectacles we saw closing out their cycle at the Century, the Manhattan Opera House, or the Center Theatre). A great deal of the capitalization covered Russell's costumes and wigs, not by the evening's costumer but run up for la star by her fellow Hollywoodite, Paramount's Travis Banton. Here was probably the greatest wardrobe Broadway ever saw, not rivaled till Robert Mackintosh created a newer line for Angela Lansbury in the musical *Mame*.

As for the sets, Oliver Smith designed the main location, the living room of Mame's Beekman Place duplex, to contain changeable parts to show the audience where Mame now was in her journey the moment the lights came up. Thus, where art had hung, bookcases now groaned with reading matter when Mame entered her literary period. The living room alternated with shallower big sets (the southern mansion, for example) and small insets at stage left and right.

The 1950s loved adaptations of bestselling novels that created "rollicking" comedies—not the *Life With Father* kind, but sexy, physical, Big Laugh shows with busy scene plots, indeed like this same *No Time For Sergeants* (which included an episode in the air as Andy Griffith and Roddy McDowall parachuted to earth) or *The Teahouse of the August Moon* (which featured the demolition and rebuilding of the eponymous teahouse right on stage). Still, with Lawrence and Lee customizing *Auntie Mame* for Russell, their piece was bound to outhit the lot. It's odd that so many stars *unlike* Russell prospered in it—Greer Garson as Russell's replacement; Beatrice Lillie as Garson's replacement and then in London; Constance Bennett, Sylvia Sidney, and Eve Arden on tour; and Shirl Conway in the first summer-tent itinerary—because they were almost all wrong, too cold or too zany. Lawrence and Lee thought Conway came the closest to Russell. Yet who but Russell knew how important it is, while opening up to one's public, to keep forty percent to oneself? We have all but *had* Katharine Hepburn or James Cagney, but we never quite collect Russell, and that makes her Mame titanic. What does this person *do* between projects, whom does she bed, what is she thinking? Where do all those crazy clothes come from— such as the evening's first, a light gray pantsuit under a black Chinese robe intricately embroidered with gold dragons and the like? (Accessories: eighteen-inch bamboo cigarette holder and gold bracelets. Wig: a short black bob with spit-curl bangs from ear to ear. Finishing touch: green fingernail polish. Cost: about equal to ten full productions of *Awake and Sing!*.)

Yet more: why does Mame enter in that getup *dashing* downstairs—because it's the star entrance or because Mame is always in a rush? To do *what*? She's a wastrel till her nephew shows up, and even then he's not unlike one of her projects till he's (almost immediately) taken out of her hands to attend boarding school. She seems heartbroken, but did this flighty professional bohemian truly welcome the responsibilities of motherhood?

I say we don't know Russell, but we really don't know Mame, either, do we? To return to the play through its movie (also with Russell) is to visit a mystery. We salute Lawrence and Lee for selecting episodes from the novel that combine in a linear narrative—Ralph Devine's progressive school; Mame's accidental destruction of actress Vera Charles' play in the tiny role of Lady Iris; the Macy's job that leads to the southern foxhunt and Mame's marriage to Beau; Mame's autobiography and the turning out of Agnes Gooch; the Upsons. Lawrence and Lee made Mame's "education" of Patrick the throughline that the novel lacks, and let his prep schooling corrupt him so the play would have a problem to solve.

And at the center stands this strange character who revives Sophistication's celebrity of eccentricity without being a celebrity herself. In the novel, the narrator introduces Mame's actress pal Vera with a blurb from his chum "Mr. Woollcott": "'Vera Charles is the world's only living actress with more changes of costume than of facial expression.'" Having Alexander Woollcott review Vera Charles—that is, mating reality with fiction—is Dennis' way of rooting his fun in the Walter Winchell–*New Yorker* magazine–Lunts' opening-night New York that was nearly gone when *Auntie Mame* opened, on October 31, 1956. The book is an act of nostalgia, but the play makes no attempt to charleston (it begins, like the novel, in 1928) or to negotiate the list song of Names with which Dennis tells us that Mame knows everyone.

In fact, if the novel looks back, the play looks *forward*, to Stonewall. Of course, all Patrick Dennis does: but in a closeted way. The play's Mame is all but biologically gay. That is, the glamor of Mame includes an inborn tolerance of and even attraction to those born "different," and the private reality of Mame is made invisible by the presentation of Mame—the clothes, the parties, the dashing-downstairs entrance, the torrent of words that silences opposition. Lawrence and Lee called Mame "a symbol of [the twentieth] century," and dubbed her a "multi-person": "From all the recent miracles of communication and mobility, a new kind of human being has emerged." Thus, modern culture and its flood of information, whether from *Life* magazine or a gossip column, from Hollywood or television, have created a new Sophistication in which the elite know more than such tidbits as Noël Coward is gay and the President has polio. The elite now know a great deal about a thousand topics, and can make a project of any of them, whether child-raising or writing autobiography. The multi-person.

But is Mame a multi-person or simply a drag queen at a party of the different? There's Vera (Polly Rowles), supposedly Mame's best friend but a treacherous egomaniac; giggly Ito (Yuki Shimoda) the houseboy; clueless hetero of southern aristo stock Beauregard Jackson Pickett Burnside (Robert Smith), not eccentric but rich and idiotic; loathsome tyrant of entrenched WASP privilege that finds a symbol in the Knickerbocker Bank, Mr. Babcock (Robert Allen); Mame's eventual secretary, Agnes Gooch (Peggy Cass); Mame's literary coach Brian O'Bannion (James Monks), a sulky boy toy. ("His eyes were turquoise blue, rimmed with thick black eyelashes," says the nephew in the novel. "The second I saw them I thought of a Siamese tomcat.") It's interesting that, with all Broadway to choose from, the producers hired journeymen rather than anyone of even secondary note. Of James Monks' Cassio in the Paul Robeson *Othello*, George Jean Nathan surmised that he "evidently once rowed on the crew in *Brown of Harvard*"; and who was Robert Smith? At least Peggy Cass sprang into fame as the living roadkill Gooch, going on to *A Thurber Carnival* (1960), more of that old-time Sophistication, and television game-show gigs.

So, in all, this play *Auntie Mame* sounds like the other rollicking fifties comedies with a peculiar central figure, just like *No Time For Sergeants* and *The Teahouse of the August Moon*. Why has it outlasted the others? Is it because Lawrence and Lee at times anticipated what would turn out to be the gay sense of humor? This strain of American show-biz jesting has by today taken over as the national style, after wisecrack comedy went through a Jewish phase in the 1960s and '70s (best exemplified in the work of Neil Simon), and also allowing for an alternative form in the dry satirical style of *National Lampoon*, *Spy*, and *Saturday Night Live*.

Gay humor is harder to describe than the others, because it mixes the wisecrack with camp interests, the erotic, and above all, the uniquely gay quality of observation and categorization. As we noted in regard to Noël Coward, gays grow up imitating straights out of sheer self-protection. Thus, they learn to identify behaviors, which makes the gay "take" on things larger and smarter than that of most heteros. This is because straights grow up thinking that they're the default setting for humanity and thus never need to develop observation skills. When, on *Will & Grace, she* offers a characteristic whine and begs him, "Be my crutch," and *he* counters with "You are so Markie Post in every single Lifetime movie," the joke draws on categorization (the genre of entertainment offered on Lifetime cable) and observation (of the sort of performer common to the genre). Note, too, that the gag depends on an expert knowledge of show biz, congenital to gay men.

The antecedents of this voice and worldview include Moss Hart and Sophistication in general, "talent and the interesting rich," Cole Porter and Ethel Merman . . . and surely Patrick Dennis but especially what the play's collaborators and Rosalind Russell made of Dennis' central invention. Some might wonder how much screwball comedy added to the mix; I say it didn't add at all. It's a Hollywood form, cautiously coded up, whereas gay humor celebrates the smashing of codes and cautions.

So, of course, does Mame, though we don't hear a lot of *Will & Grace* in her script. Much of it is sheer character comedy about a character from an alternate universe, as here, awakened by her nephew from a sound sleep:

AUNTIE MAME: Now be a perfect angel and ask Ito to bring me a very
    light breakfast: black coffee and a sidecar.

Still, there is the odd feeling that Mame Dennis—single mother, then wife, then grandmother—is teaching fifties America what would later be known as the gay lifestyle, not least in her classic line:

AUNTIE MAME: Life is a banquet, and most poor sons-of-bitches are
    starving to death!

Yet Mame herself interrupts her banquet to accommodate responsibility when it is thrust upon her. So she *does* like child-rearing: because she doesn't renounce her destiny to raise Patrick. Patrick renounces his. This is what holds the play together as a story: the conflict erupts when Mame realizes that prep-school life has turned Patrick . . . well, straight. He dines at Schrafft's and Disapproves of Live, Live, Live, especially about his aunt's relationship with housemate O'Bannion:

PATRICK: (primly) It looks very cozy.
AUNTIE MAME: For a moment there you sounded exactly like somebody from the Knickerbocker Bank.

That last remark emphasizes the We Versus They of the gay perspective, and one can argue that Mame has in effect recruited for her team, just as the stoopids of the right have imagined. And now Mame must fight to keep her We from sneaking off to They. Mame isn't only gay: she's revolutionary.

So, in different ways, were Tennessee Williams and Arthur Miller. William Inge wasn't. He takes his place in this chapter, however, not because he Knickerbocker Banked his scripts—he didn't, in fact—but because his first four fifties plays enjoyed success enough to put him onto the A list with the other two. *Auntie Mame* ran 639 performances, closing because its high running costs needed sellout-or-near business. But Inge's *Come Back, Little Sheba* (1950) played 190 performances, a fine showing for a truly depressing piece, and *Picnic* (1953) ran 477 performances, *Bus Stop* (1955) 478 performances, and *The Dark at the Top of the Stairs* (1957) 468 performances. They were four works on one story, because Inge never wrote a UFO: a strong woman tames a big clumsy fool of a man.

Or so runs the line popular today, as if all Inge were an expansion of that *Merton of the Movies* scene in which the hero breaks down in the heroine's lap. Sheba, the runaway dog symbolizing the vanished happiness of alcoholic Doc (Sidney Blackmer) and slatternly Lola (Shirley Booth), lends her name to the exception to this rule, for Lola tames no one. But *Picnic*'s Hal Carter (Ralph Meeker) is a sexy beast who gives up the little he has to run off with the town belle (Janice Rule), *Bus Stop* finds show-biz hopeful Cherie (Kim Stanley) cutting raucous cowboy Bo Decker (Albert Salmi) into bite-size pieces, and *The Dark at the Top of the Stairs* presents perhaps the classic Inge mating in sensible, anxious housewife Cora (Teresa Wright) and wild Rubin Flood (Pat Hingle), married seventeen years yet by no means Settled In. Moreover, they have two problem children who need much stronger parenting from their reckless father and less spoiling by their mother.

In a way, Inge *was* forever telling the same story: not of woman taming man but of the hopelessness of marriage with men, because every member of the gender is so self-absorbed that he is beyond communication. They're all wrapped up, like *Sheba*'s Doc. Or they're cavemen with the names of underground film stars, like the other three. Cora's sister Lottie (Eileen Heckart) envies Cora; at least Rubin's a *man*. Lottie's married to Morris (Frank Overton), the other kind of Inge male, the sexless doormat—most usually the Arthur O'Connell part. Heckart was also in *Picnic,* where she fell on her knees begging O'Connell to marry her, and he agreed to because he didn't know how to say no.

On the other hand, if Inge's alpha male can be corralled, he can't be broken. Rubin Flood charges out of *Dark at the Top of the Stairs*' first act after whacking Cora across the face, unable to bear her taunting over his girl friend in Ponca City. "Mavis Pruitt is waiting," Cora tells him, helplessly goading and punishing him. However, like the cavemen's captain, Stanley Kowalski, Rubin doesn't take well to challenge. As Elia Kazan staged it, with a near delicacy of violence, the blow occurred offstage. The audience only heard it, then saw Cora reeling backward into view, her hand on her cheek. "T'hell with you!" Rubin shouts as he slams out of the house.

Yes, Kazan. Like Williams and Miller, Inge enjoyed collaborations with prominent directors—one reason why, in the 1950s, no one questioned his membership in a trio of playwrights that no longer has any meaning. (Taking the larger historical view, the post-O'Neill trio is now Williams, Miller, and Edward Albee.) And, remember, both Williams and Miller suffered failure in the 1950s; Inge was the one with four consecutive hits. Daniel Mann directed *Come Back, Little Sheba,* Joshua Logan *Picnic,* Harold Clurman *Bus Stop;* and Kazan's work on *Dark* epitomized Inge. The writer's specialty was articulating inarticulate characters, and Kazan's Group Theatre background enabled him to draw the actors into the parts of their role that couldn't be expressed in words.

In fact, if Mame Dennis is the multi-person, we might term the typical Inge character the "mini-person," starving for life's banquet in a culture with very little there to it. A key illustration is the *Bus Stop* cowboy's complete inability to hear the European glamor in the heroine's first name. "Cherie," to her, is Sophistication. To him, it's "Cherry," not because he likes things basic but because he can't hear the difference between the two any more than he can read Shakespeare. Everyone in Inge is like that, provincial in the sense of uneducated, incurious, intolerant.

Yet Inge finds them sympathetic; had he written *In Cold Blood* it would have been about the Clutters. *The Dark at the Top of the Stairs* is set in Oklahoma City in the early 1920s. Add together the troubled Flood marriage, the two problem kids—she's absurdly shy and he's a sissy with a collection of movie-star photographs—and pile on Lottie and Morris' empty mating and one has the play whole. That is, except for one dramatic episode at its center, when the daughter's date at a country-club dance commits suicide. The apparent cause is an ethnic slur, but in fact the young man is a kind of parented orphan. Unlike the Flood kids, he's a social whiz—but it's all a front, because he's utterly alone and in despair. Is *this* the story that Inge kept telling—that no one gets a banquet out of life, that the best one can hope for is a troubled union with someone who isn't trying to understand you? Inge shows us the isolation of people in . . . what, the Midwest? The world? Generally, critics called *Dark* Inge's best play, perhaps because it most fully reveals his "story"—one that, for him, ended in real life in suicide. *Dark* might also be Inge's most basic play: he first wrote it in the 1940s, as *Farther Off From Heaven*.

However, following one of this book's throughlines, I'd say Inge's best play is a movie, *Splendor in the Grass* (1961), an original with screenplay (and a brief appearance, as a preacher) by Inge and direction by Kazan. The central romantic couple, Natalie Wood and Warren Beatty, respect the Inge paradigm of the smart woman and the appealing but clumsy man, though their problems are less of their own than their parents' making. And Pat Hingle is graduated from *Dark*'s errant but charming husband to Inge's most spectacular Wayward Male as Beatty's father, harrowingly deaf to any conversation but his own.

Auntie Mame and *The Dark at the Top of the Stairs,* while opposites in every important respect, typify fifties Broadway at its best: not so much for the chic of the Rosalind Russell star turn or the questing realism of the Kazan ensemble or even for the escapist élan of the one and the unhappy honesty of the other. They show us how well the American stage could enlighten, even as *Auntie Mame*'s "mere" entertainment or *Dark*'s bargain-basement tragedy. Intellectuals love to talk down to Broadway; Mary McCarthy's review of *The Iceman Cometh* is not showboating but business as usual, on the assumption that anything with a middle-class audience must be meretricious. It's a form of voguing, as with the teenager who tacks up a poster of Che Guevara.

In fact, this pair of plays sent out a powerful message far ahead of their time: that the unconventional family cell might succeed and the conventional one fail. Mame's family consists of a nephew, a Japanese houseman, and an Irish housekeeper; when Mame finally marries, the husband is barely on the scene and quickly gone. (He dies in a comic vignette while climbing the Matterhorn, but he rather has to, as there wouldn't be a place for him in Mame's improvisatory household.) The Floods are father, mother, daughter, son; yet the whole darn biological thing is broken every which way. Did I mention that the Flood boy, ten years old, still creeps into his mother's bed at night? When she suggests that he's too old to do so any more, he says, "I was scared." Little Patrick Dennis isn't scared. Is it possible that, accidentally or otherwise, the authors of *Auntie Mame* and *The Dark at the Top of the Stairs* were pointing out that the world of Santorum Babittry isn't as foolproof as it thinks it is?

Fifteen

The Great Sebastians Make Their Last Visit:

THE LATE 1950s

One might have expected the first years of national television to create attendence slumps at amusement parks, bars, restaurants, and cinemas. One might even have anticipated the unprecedented boost it gave to the business of its advertisers. But surely no one foresaw that TV might become in effect Broadway's biggest supporter—at first—as if to halt the steady contraction resulting from the overextended 1928–29 season and the unrelated cataclysm of the Depression. First there were too many theatres, and then there was too little money.

But now there was television, with its two centers of production, in New York and Los Angeles. The latter was closely allied with the movie industry, and the former, obviously, with Broadway. Actors, writers, and techies found their work doubling or tripling, both for headliners and those well below the glamor level. The home screen had yet to invent most of its genres or to discover the talent appropriate to them, so, throughout the 1950s, a large fraction of New York TV production was "theatre": sixty- and ninety-minute dramas and musicals taped "live" in the studios (which were usually the former theatres whose disuse was created by that overexpansion in the 1920s). On Pearl Harbor Day in 1947, the original Broadway cast of John P. Marquand and George S. Kaufman's adaptation of Marquand's novel *The Late George Apley* (1944) revived the show on NBC, heralding a major new form, Televised Broadway. Whether in such odes to Rialto events as Mary Martin in *Peter Pan* or Katharine Cornell and Anthony Quayle in *The Barretts of Wimpole Street* or in entirely new work with a Broadway flavor such as Julie Andrews in Rodgers and Hammerstein's *Cinderella,* TV was not only Broadway's employment bureau but its cultural adjunct.

The system worked both ways, so that TV writers often moved to The Street, sometimes with expansions of works previously televised. *Middle of the Night* (1956) was one such, written by Paddy Chayefsky and produced and directed by Joshua Logan. The biggest name involved was Edward G. Robinson, making his first Broadway appearance since *Mr. Samuel,* in 1930. He played a fifty-something in love with a twenty-something (Gena Rowlands) in that unique Chayefsky world in which your butcher, manicurist, or, here, clothing manufacturer turns out to be as fascinating as a big-game hunter or tango dancer. It's not unlike Clifford Odets without the ecstatic philology, a William Inge of the urban melting pot. At 477 performances, *Middle of the Night* was a hit, mainly for Robinson's expert underplaying and movie-star name; the work is utterly forgot today.

William Gibson's *The Miracle Worker* (1959) is one of the best-remembered of the straight-to-Broadway TV dramas, not least because tristate-area schoolchildren of a certain age made their first Broadway visit to this title, usually on a class trip. We've had a footnote on the food fight between Anne Bancroft and ten-year-old Patty Duke; here, now, is their strange relationship in toto, as the older woman battles the younger to get her to drop her defenses and let therapy make her whole. This happens so seldom in real life that its often rather instantaneous success on stage—as in *Lady in the Dark* (1941)—can seem silly. In *The Miracle Worker,* however, it is enthralling, and of course the audience knows that the little girl grew up to be Helen Keller.

The two leads were extraordinary. In *Theatre Arts,* Jack Balch tried to analogize Duke's "energy and fury" and came up with Judith Anderson's Medea. An extremely faithful movie with Bancroft and Duke has made constant reviving unnecessary, though in 1997 Duke took time out from her busy schedule of scolding the rest of us (because as a child star she suffered being rich and famous while we were enjoying pop quizzes on *The Last of the Mohicans*) to take Bancroft's role of Annie Sullivan in a back-to-television adaptation, opposite Melissa Gilbert.

To an extent, highbrow Broadway disdained the TV writer, as happened earlier with the Hollywood writer. Neither Chayefsky nor Gibson was welcomed aboard—and Gibson had made his debut with an original for the stage, *Two For the Seesaw* (1958), with Bancroft opposite Henry Fonda, the entire cast. Of course, highbrow Broadway still held an ace in Eugene O'Neill. Though he died in 1953 with his greatest play entrusted to his widow to withhold for twenty-five years, *Long Day's Journey Into Night* was news too big for the vault. Yale University Press published the text in 1955, Stockholm gave the world premiere in February of 1956, and Broadway took its first look at the piece at the Helen Hayes Theatre (now demolished, to Eva Le Gallienne's intense relief) on November 7, 1956.

One has little to add to all that has been written about The Great American Play, but for some notes in no particular order. First: that first production in Swedish was so big an event in Western Civilization that Dag Hammarskjöld, the United Nations secretary-general, sent a congratulatory message; imagine that happening today. Second: this "other" of O'Neill's blatantly autobiographical plays takes place exactly when *The Iceman Cometh* does, in the summer of 1912. The Circle in the Square *Iceman* revival that revealed Jason Robards Jr. as the apparent O'Neill stylist and persuaded the Widow O'Neill to let José Quintero direct *Journey* occured in May of 1956—as if guiding Broadway's attention back from Stockholm to the place where an American play earns its recognition. In his heyday, O'Neill was imposing: now he would be great.

But he would have to give too much away to get there, which is why he wanted that quarter of a century to pass before his personal memories suffered the assault of his artistry. *The Iceman Cometh* is autobiographical only in the abstract; *Journey* tells us what it was really like and how it felt at the time. So, from the play that is set far off, in a barroom, the destructive if avuncular relationship between Larry Slade and Don Parritt is revised for the play that is set close up, in the home, as the fraternal relationship of James and Edmund. We remember Slade eagerly awaiting the thump of Parritt's body on the pavement at *Iceman*'s close. Thus, as if he had spent his career peeling away the "theatre" of it all to arrive at one perfect script for Broadway's first reality show, O'Neill turns from the colorful, stagy, and allegorical *Iceman* to something unheard of in playmaking: one day in the life.

Note, too, that while O'Neill is never thought of as an Irish playwright, he is very much one here because his family background—father James was Irish-born, in Kilkenny—is *Journey*'s family background. And yet the sterotypical Irishman, so endemic to the show biz of O'Neill's youth and given mythical apotheosis in *Iceman*'s Harry Hope, was all but eradicated by the 1950s. Most James Tyrones play James O'Neill with a touch of brogue— a very world away from the pickled Clancy that Charles Winninger was still purveying in Hollywood just a decade before. Indeed, the senior Tyrone is intolerant of fun-timers and binge drinkers, of any men without a steady line of work. At one point, he excoriates "Broadway loafer's lingo" as if disapproving of *Guys and Dolls,* of the new ways to live that were to be discussed in our arts from 1919 on.

The cast that Quintero assembled for that first American *Journey* varied from sound to brilliant: Fredric March, Florence Eldridge, Jason Robards Jr., and Bradford Dillman. Mary Tyrone was actually to have been Geraldine Page, barely thirty then but an expert ager. March, however, was sine qua non, and he wouldn't work without his wife, capable but not quite the shimmering ruin that Page would have played. Interestingly, Robards also did not appear in the part that *he* was meant for, for of the two sons it was the younger James that was thought the showier, more actory role. But Robards felt an affinity for the more complicated Edmund, and it has been the "Robards role" ever since, leaving Jamie to the *jeunes premiers.* The 1962 film's lineup of Ralph Richardson, Katharine Hepburn, Robards, and Dean Stockwell is unbeatable, though Vanessa Redgrave, in 2003, found something new and striking in Mary by playing her as a drug addict. Not someone weird and wispy who is living on a pharmacopoeia, but a helpless monster trapped in the outbursts and disconnects of substance withdrawal.

There were further O'Neill disinterments to come, but the true play-wright of the 1950s would have to be Tennessee Williams. We've had mention of *The Rose Tattoo* (1951) and *Camino Real* (1953), but it was *Cat on a Hot Tin Roof* (1955), at the center of the time, that showed Williams as sharp as ever in his blend of the erotic and poetic, his compassion for his people even as he strips them of illusion. O'Neill doesn't like his characters (except in his UFO, *Ah, Wilderness!*), but then he is most often writing about his difficult family. Williams got his family out of the way in *The Glass Menagerie,* then went on to the real art of telling tales. If his glory diminishes by the 1970s, it is simply because we all sat through that interminable second act that great American lives aren't supposed to have. Williams had a long one, filled with ghastly flops.

But with Kazan directing *Cat on a Hot Tin Roof* and a cast headed by Barbara Bel Geddes and Ben Gazzara as Maggie and Brick, Burl Ives and Mildred Dunnock as Brick's Big Daddy and Big Mama, and Pat Hingle and Madeleine Sherwood as Brick's scheming brother and sister-in-law, *Cat* was a smash. It is second to *Streetcar* alone in Williams' work in immediate and lasting popularity, but here the outstanding role is not the Beautiful Male but the Resourceful Female. That's why they call her Maggie the Cat. Indeed, despite writers' common remarking of *Cat*'s Williamsiana—the South, homosexuality, alcoholism—*Cat*'s characters are unique in Williams' gallery. Big Daddy is especially unencountered elsewhere, so unlike the sex demons and mollycoddles Williams favors. Brick is a combination of the two, a former athlete who is now a drunken hater of his life; and Maggie, one of Williams' favorite children, is foreign to the style of the Williams leading lady, as a sensible person thrown into a bizarre situation who sets about taking control of it: and succeeds.

Something else worth noting: as if aware that doubters would accuse Williams of repeating himself with more southern decadence, he introduced structural novelties into *Cat,* first of all in letting each act start exactly where the previous act ended. Second, he opened Act One with a monologue for Maggie (with terse retorts from Brick) that rivals Hickey's. Third, Williams held Big Daddy's entrance till Act Two, let him dominate it, then slammed him with the announcement that he has terminal cancer and cut him out of the third act but for offstage cries of anger and pain.

However, Kazan thought Big Daddy too fascinating to shelve midway in the action. Kazan had other reservations about the third act, and while

Williams accommodated Kazan in all this, he troubled to publish his original third act as an appendix to the script as performed. One odd thing about Williams is that while he appeared on talk shows as a brain-fried loon, throwing out an arm and crying, for no apparent reason, "I cover the waterfront!," when writing about his work he was perfectly rational about his procedures. Explaining his willingness to compromise with Kazan under duress, Williams wrote, "The reception of the playing script has more than justified . . . the adjustments made [under Kazan's creative] influence. A failure reaches fewer people . . . than does a play that succeeds."

Harold Clurman directed Williams' *Orpheus Descending* (1957), a revision of *Battle of Angels* (1940), the play referred to earlier that closed out of town; it was supposedly booed right off its Boston stage. The earlier title reveals the play's religious undertow, while the later title of course suggests Greek myth. Interestingly, the hero is another Brando role (albeit only in the 1959 film version, *The Fugitive Kind*), Val Xavier (Cliff Robertson). A "savior" in snakeskin jacket with a guitar, he charms the ladies, especially the local hellion (Lois Smith) and the wife (Maureen Stapleton) of the worst villain in all Williams (Crahan Denton). Unappreciated when new, the play got a healthy jolt when Vanessa Redgrave took on Stapleton's role in London and New York in the 1990s, making a facilitator into a driver in one of her most remarkable portrayals. Still, there were doubters. On English television, all-around theatre man Stephen Berkoff merrily suggested that the play was "about a snakeskin jacket," unfortunately in the presence of Williams acolyte Maria St. Just, who ripped into Berkoff like a tiger. "And such a second-rater, too!" she concluded witheringly.

Reunited with Kazan, Williams returned to somewhat trodden ground in *Sweet Bird of Youth* (1959), filled with classic Williams types: the Big Lady (Geraldine Page); the hustler, fetchingly named Chance Wayne (Paul Newman); his childhood sweetheart, the even more fetchingly named Heavenly (Diana Hyland); and her father, the small-town fascist Boss Finley (Sidney Blackmer). Louis Kronenberger called it "a fuming and rioting depravity," perhaps because it began The Morning After, with Page asleep in bed and Newman, astir in pajamas, slippping a tape recorder under the bed, presumably to collect data for blackmail. When Page finally awoke, donned glasses, and inspected Newman, she uttered what must be the second gayest line Williams ever wrote: "Well, I may have done better, but God knows I've done worse." The gayest line followed right after: "I like bodies to be hairlessly silky smooth gold." And soon after that, Page was smoking hashish, right in front of Louis Kronenberger.

If Williams' plays seemed to form a genre all their own, the genre most opposite to Williams would be plainspoken working-class realism, in, for instance, Michael V. Gazzo's *A Hatful of Rain* (1955). The tale of a junkie hiding his addiction from his family, the piece offered Ben Gazzara, Shelley Winters as his wife, Anthony Franciosa as his brother, and Frank Silvera as his father, all in a mean-streets realism right down to the grubby clothes in which Franciosa kept house. Kronenberger took this one in his stride: "more a scare piece than a serious study." It was indeed scary, in the scenes involving pushers Mother (Henry Silva), Apples (Paul Richards), and Chuch (Harry Guardino), spreading beat lingo of the kind usually heard only on off-Broadway. Frank Corsaro was the director, and the piece ran 398 performances, long enough for Steven (so billed) McQueen and Vivian Blaine to take over the leads.

If *Hatful* typifies the gritty new naturalism, *Look Homeward, Angel* (1957), by Ketti Frings after Thomas Wolfe, gives us that old standby the literary adaptation. This presumably autobiographical treatment of a southern boy breaking away from the bad parenting of a drunken idiot father and a busily ungiving mother offered a new star as well. Osgood Perkins' son Anthony made his Broadway bow replacing John Kerr in *Tea and Sympathy* (Joan Fontaine took over for Deborah Kerr), then went to Hollywood. His return as Thomas Wolfe's Eugene Gant lent PR ballyhoo to the event, but in fact director George Roy Hill had a superb cast all around in parents Jo Van Fleet and Hugh Griffith and in Arthur Hill (later the original George in *Who's Afraid of Virginia Woolf?*) as a beloved older brother who dies of tuberculosis. The background, Van Fleet's boardinghouse, kept the action peopled and lively, and Perkins was born to play all the hesitations and wistfulness and humiliated almost-said-itism of Wolfe's alter ego, so hungry for love from his mother yet so absolute in his "drop dead" farewell to her. He's not ungrateful, mind you. He thanks her "for every hour of loneliness I've had here, for every dirty cell you gave me to sleep in, for ten million hours of indifference, and for [the last few] minutes of cheap advice."

Realism, the literary classic . . . but what was Paddy Chayefsky's *The Tenth Man* (1959)? An unsigned *Theatre Arts* review of *Middle of the Night* dubbed Chayefsky "the poet laureate of the romantically underprivileged" for his habit of assigning love plots to the likes of Edward G. Robinson, not to mention Martys Rod Steiger and Ernest Borgnine. In *The Tenth Man,* Chayefsky assigned the love plot to a young woman possessed by a dybbuk, the displaced soul of one of the undead. Yet the format was comedy.

Chayefsky set the action in a moribund Jewish synagogue way out on Long Island, where widowers hold an informal social club, cursing their daughters-in-law and bragging about the cemetery plots they have picked out. One of their number hides his granddaughter—the possessed girl—on the premises, and into the middle of all this blunders a young man with ills as modern as the girl's are Old World. He is neurotic and miserable because . . . well, who isn't? Lovingly balancing legend with contemporary life, Chayefsky constructed a one-off, a mystical folk play with a serious theme but told in jest. There's one more generic layer: the girl really *is* possessed. Interrogated by a cabalist, she replies, "You yourself will be dead before the prayers for the new moon," and such is the authority of her schizoid babblings that we have no doubt of her knowledge in this matter.

How can the work climax but in an exorcism, as the cabalist directs the blowing of a ram's horn before the necessary ten men? Yet when the demon is commanded to leave its host body, the young woman stands senseless but the young *man* falls to the floor with a bloodcurdling scream:

ONE OF THE WIDOWERS: I think what has happened is that we have exorcised the wrong dybbuk.

The fine cast was very much what one might have expected, with kibitzers Lou Jacobi, Jack Gilford, George Voskovec, and Jacob Ben-Ami and young couple Donald Harron and Risa Schwartz (granddaughter of the Second Avenue headliner Maurice Schwartz). Yet the director was the English Tyrone Guthrie, known primarily for the unusual, such as Thornton Wilder's stuffed-with-eccentrics farce *The Matchmaker* (1955) and the musical *Candide* (1956). But who better to keep Chayefsky's warring rhythms of ancient and modern as married as the Lunts? *The Matchmaker* may sound conventional, as the source of *Hello, Dolly!* (1964), and it is conventional— in a form that went out of style shortly after Feydeau. (Indeed, speaking of rhythms, some of *The Matchmaker* is deliberately verbalized in the style of Molière.) And, true, *Candide* failed, but more because it was so unexpected than because of Guthrie's staging.

Certainly, *The Tenth Man* is far more interesting than the boulevardier exhibits still very popular. Samuel Taylor's *The Pleasure of His Company* (1958), written "with Cornelia Otis Skinner," is typical. It has none of the originality or wit of Chayefsky, but doesn't need to. This play is a pastime, agreeable rather than imaginative. A bauble about the ruin of a society wedding by the sudden return of the bride's long-lost father, it shows the middle-class theatregoer how the rich live, as if we were back in the 1920s.

The setting is San Francisco, and the cast was headed by Cyril Ritchard as the bad-boy father, Skinner as his ex-wife and the bride's mother, and Dolores Hart as the daughter in question. (George Peppard played the groom.) It was the kind of piece that happily started one scene with grandfather Charlie Ruggles playing (and slyly cheating at) solitaire—a specialty bit. There was a tiny idea at the center of the work, that Hart might be too wonderful to be allowed, as Congreve's Millamant puts it, "to dwindle into a wife" without having seen the world first. And Hart actually closed the action by running off with Ritchard, risking the eventual loss of the affronted Peppard.

Tennessee Williams, working-class realism, the literary adaptation, the odd item, and a boulevard comedy: the only item missing from this précis of mainstream Broadway attendance is the English show, performed with the West End artistes. Most of the cast of Broadway's view of Terence Rattigan's *Separate Tables* (1956) had played this interrelated double bill in London. It is Rattigan's most ingenious concoction: one set (the public rooms of a residential hotel in Bournemouth), one team of support (management and guests), and two stars playing completely different roles in each of the two plays. Thus, the headliners must not only create entirely different portrayals on either side of the interval, but effect spectacular visual changes on their second entrances. The pair were Eric Portman and Margaret Leighton as, first, former lovers, he a disgraced ex-politician; and, second, a molester of women in cinemas and the terrified spinster who defies her tyrant mother to defend him.

Peter Ustinov's comedy *Romanoff and Juliet* (1957), set in one of those Lichtenburgs, didn't need a full West End cohort supplying English atmosphere, and thus came over with only its star, Ustinov himself, under George S. Kaufman's direction. The show spoofed Cold War gamesmanship in a romance between a Russian boy (whose family is forever denouncing and spying) and an American girl (whose family is diplomatic fluff). Suavely moving in and out of the action to play emcee to the public, Ustinov brought to Broadway a figure our native drama utterly lacks: the brilliant charmer with the dry wit and the deceptively soft attack.

But the big news was another visit from the Old Vic, in 1956, in nothing but Shakespeare for three months at the Winter Garden: *Richard II, Romeo and Juliet, Macbeth,* and Tyrone Guthrie's *Troilus and Cressida,* reset in Edwardian England. It made a sensation, with the Greeks turned into Prussians, and plenty of entrances and exits through the orchestra aisles, very rare at the time. Paul Rogers, Coral Browne, John Neville, and Claire Bloom headed the bills; the first two were the Macbeths and the second Romeo and Juliet. There was no *querelle des acteurs,* for American acting was now a thing in itself, and local pride could afford to be generous.

Besides, even bigger news was the Angry Young Man theatre of John Osborne. *Look Back in Anger* (1957) was the position paper, though it now seems tame next to Osborne's contemporary open letter entitled "Damn you, England." Those scathing sentiments found a home in Osborne's *The Entertainer* (1958), with Laurence Olivier in an extraordinary turn as a seedy music-hall performer in gray suit, bowler, and bow tie, with a cane, apelike eyebrows, and a lurid gap in his front teeth. Author and star together reveled in the ghastly hokum of the song-and-dance comic who goes on and on without getting a single laugh. "I've played in front of them all!" he crows. "'The Queen,' 'The Duke of Edinburgh,' 'The Prince of Wales,' and the—what's the name of that other pub?" Riding right over the silence, he adds, "Blimey, that went better first house." Also, unlike *Look Back in Anger*'s sedate construction, *The Entertainer*'s was broken into two formats, scenes of the entertainer's family life separated by the music-hall turns. It was virtually an anticipation of the musical *Cabaret,* the whole designed to portray England as corrupt and crippled.

Both Osbornes were seen in their original productions with most of the original players, and the credit for that goes to the man who got a lot more fame than Osborne out of it, David Merrick. The last of the picturesque managers creating theatre wherever they go (and not just in playhouses), Merrick honed his expertise in PR into the art of the unthinkable. Boosting *Look Back in Anger,* he hired a woman to erupt out of the audience onto the stage to smack the ranting Kenneth Haigh in the face.

Merrick put on plenty of native work, but he seemed most characteristic in buying up West End hits. *The Entertainer* wasn't just brought over: it was *brought over,* by Pan American, sets and all, from closing night at London's Palace Theatre to the Shubert in Boston, to reopen exactly ten days later.* Merrick's Europe stopped at the Channel; when he got to French or German work it was usually in their West End stagings—*Irma la Douce* (1960) and the so-called *Marat/Sade* (1965), for example, both directed by Peter Brook. Merrick did mount his own production of Jean Anouilh's *Becket* (1960), this also with Olivier, first as the Canterbury cleric opposite Anthony Quinn's Henry II, then, in a return engagement after the tour, trying out Henry to Arthur Kennedy's Thomas.

Nevertheless, Broadway's Anouilh in the late 1950s was the work of other producers, from *The Lark* (1955) to *The Fighting Cock* (1959). *The Lark* was Julie Harris' aforementioned turn as Saint Joan, and Rex Harrison led *The Fighting Cock—L'Hurluburlu* in French—as a reactionary general. Off-Broadway helped out with less well-known Anouilh: *Ardèle* (1958) and *Legend of Lovers* (1959), originally entitled *Euridice. The Lark* is the greatest work in the group, and scored Anouilh his biggest Broadway success. Lillian Hellman wrote the adaptation, given a splendid staging under Joseph Anthony. Especially helpful were Jo Mielziner's projections backing a steep rake of platforms, thus to flash back from Joan's trial to the places of her life. Following Joans of various versions Winifred Lenihan, Katharine Cornell, Ingrid Bergman, and Uta Hagen (in a 1951 Theatre Guild revival of the Shaw), Harris persuaded critics who had seen them all (or all but Lenihan) that she was the best. Typically, Harris combined fragility, power, and grace; she was radiant.

Yet another splendid staging outfitted Anouilh's *Time Remembered* (1957), originally entitled *Léocadia,* after the deceased beauty who haunts the action. This one was adapted by Patricia Moyes, and offered Helen Hayes as a dotty duchess; former matinée idol Glenn Anders as her stooge, Lord Hector; current matinée idol Richard Burton as her nephew, in mourning for Léocadia; and Susan Strasberg as a milliner hired to impersonate her. *The Lark* had enjoyed an incidental score by Leonard Bernstein, and

---

* One minor cast change from the Palace season is worth remarking, concerning a showgirl in one of the entertainer's turns: "a nude in Britannia's helmet," Osborne directs, "holding a bulldog and trident." In London, she was Vivienne Drummond, who then copped a lead in the New York *Look Back in Anger.* In New York, the entertainer's showgirl was Jeri Archer, creator of Belle Poitrine in the photographs accompanying Patrick Dennis' *Little Me.*

Time Remembered called upon Vernon Duke for not only orchestral continuity but the last new Duke vocals heard on Broadway. Hayes had the role
she was born to play—dithering yet logical, snobbish

> DUCHESS: In the war, I signed on in the nursing reserve without making
> any stipulation whatsoever about the social status of my patients.

yet endearing, as when she brings up a relative she loathes, one Patrick
Troubiscoi:

> DUCHESS: (To the milliner, perfectly naturally) You may have met him?
> MILLINER: No, Madame.
> DUCHESS: You amaze me. One meets him absolutely everywhere.

Oliver Smith was the designer for this semi-fantasy, creating *avec charme*
the park in which the Duchess has kept on retainer the sights and people
that Burton associates with his three days of love. Albert Marre directed this
most French of pieces, so sprightly and daffy while centering on a death.
"The mood is mellow," purred Walter Kerr.

By contrast, Samuel Beckett's *En Attendant Godot,* in Beckett's own
translation as *Waiting For Godot* (1956), baffled one and all and closed in
seven weeks, though it boasted Bert Lahr and E. G. Marshall as the merrily
depressed tramps of modernism's prison of nowhere. On the other hand,
seven weeks is not bad for a piece so full of . . . well, emptiness; the very
delightful *Time Remembered* was Anouilh's biggest New York hit, yet it only
lasted thirty-one weeks. Further, *Godot* was out of place on The Street,
when off-Broadway so obviously beckoned; Brooks Atkinson, arguably the
voice of the Rialto, thought it a blend of Joyce ("pungent and fabulous")
and Sartre ("black, dark, disgusted"). This is not what they call a Money
Review.

Another reflection of Rialto thinking was the cover of the monthly magazine *Theatre Arts,* where the next talking point would be anticipated with a
photographic salute. Audrey Hepburn and Mel Ferrer made it, for *Ondine;*
Rosalind Russell previewed her Indian getup from the last scene of *Auntie
Mame.* And Bert Lahr was thus honored, in his *Godot* hobo glory. But first
came a *Theatre Arts* cover devoted to Julie Andrews' Eliza Doolittle: for

Waiting For Godot opened scarcely a month after *My Fair Lady* came in from glowing out-of-town reports to be the most talked-about show in history. What could Samuel Beckett hope for after that?

Oddly, *My Fair Lady*'s tryout began direly, at least backstage, when Rex Harrison locked himself in his dressing room at the New Haven premiere and refused to go on. Though perfectly cast as Henry Higgins, Harrison had had no prior contact with the form that he disparagingly called "musical com." From the moment he left the security of the rehearsal piano for the netless trapeze act of performing with a pit orchestra at the dress rehearsal, Harrison was rattled. Yes, he got through it—but the music was so far *away* from him. There was so much it, too, violins and trombones and . . . things going every which way while he tried to stay on the melody.

Then came New Haven, and no one could dislodge Harrison from his den of fear. That is, not till the Shubert's house manager offered to go before the most expectant public since ancient Athens had heard that Aeschylus was going to introduce the Second Actor and explain exactly why no one would see *My Fair Lady* that night. Harrison went on.

We're not doing musicals in this book, but *My Fair Lady*'s success was so big it was larger than musicals. Yes, it reinvented the genre, with its classy Novelty Star who couldn't sing yet had six numbers; with its generical mating of the serious musical and the fun musical; with its definitive rejection of the venerable "girls and jokes" atmosphere, such that contemporary shows with showgirl skin such as *Ankles Aweigh, Happy Hunting* (in a "swimsuit parade" number called "For Love Or Money"), *Li'l Abner,* a couple of *Ziegfeld Follies* (the more elaborate of which never came in), and the out-of-town casualty *Strip For Action* now appear as quaint even in their time.

More important, *My Fair Lady* reasserted the power of the theatre in American culture at a time when television had finally started to adopt its audience. Fredrick Loewe and Alan Jay Lerner had done not that much more than spot songs into George Bernard Shaw—songs, however, that were so well conceived and executed that Lerner and Loewe found something that *Pygmalion* never knew it had: feelings. The transformation must have happened at just the right historical time, or with just the right amount of English in it, or looking so smart and elegant, for *My Fair Lady* arrived as the party one had to attend to maintain one's identity in the culture. *Life* magazine considered this problem by running a "human interest" story on the difficulty people had in getting tickets; and The Columns were filled with odd angles on the topic. Like the emergence of David Merrick or the remergence of Eugene O'Neill, *My Fair Lady* reinvigorated that old term "Broadway."

One thing was missing: an aggregate of new star actors to succeed the women royalty of the Katharine Cornell generation. Geraldine Page and Kim Stanley appeared to be the next in this line, and the first of the great divas to be associated with The Method at a time when Strasbergshchina had become a lightning rod for skeptics. What were they skeptical of? "Mannerisms," mostly. But isn't this another of those meaningless attack words? Olivier was mannered; acting generally is mannered. True, Spencer Tracy wasn't mannered; but did anyone want to see Spencer Tracy's Coriolanus?

For all that, would an unmannered actress succeed as, for instance, the characteristic Tennessee Williams heroine? Not straightforward Maggie the Cat, surely. But Alma Winemiller, in José Quintero's 1952 off-Broadway *Neueinstudierung* of *Summer and Smoke,* presented Geraldine Page to the theatregoing community with a flourish. Indeed, Peter Glenville's 1961 *Summer and Smoke* film makes Alma something like Page's Great Role, preserving her in her prime in something like a theatre performance.

For her part, Stanley must have been unusually creative in her first success, *Picnic* (1953), as Janice Rule's little sister, for she won important notice in the merest of along-for-the-ride parts. Immediately after *Picnic,* Stanley joined Page as performers who could draw a public to at least three months of virtually anything. Viña Delmar's dreary *Mid-Summer* (1953) and N. Richard Nash's *The Rainmaker* (1954) each ran a little over 100 performances entirely or mainly because of Page.

Stanley opened in her first starring role, in *The Traveling Lady* (1954), one night before *The Rainmaker* and right across the street. It made an arresting visual, for those two marquees might have been staring at each other thus back in the good old days, when people sometimes attended stars rather than plays. Stanley then sought better writing, returning to Inge for *Bus Stop*'s Cherie, then introducing Maggie the Cat to London.*

---

* The Lord Chamberlain wouldn't grant *Cat on a Hot Tin Roof* a license, so it played a private club, the New Watergate—and, by the way, utilized Williams' original Act Three instead of the Kazan version.

By the late 1950s, Stanley and Page held unofficial first refusal on roles of a certain type: but what type? Ethel Barrymore was a type; Stanley and Page were versatile. The former chose another major writer when O'Neill's *A Touch of the Poet* (1958) was premiered, but she couldn't bear working with the problematic Eric Portman and left early, replaced by Cloris Leachman. This meant that Stanley never "finished" Sara, daughter of Portman (and Helen Hayes), for Stanley famously mined her roles long after opening night, quarrying for ever greater clarity of character. Actors worthy of the name loved playing with her; it was like performing in real time.

Stanley's next show was an odd one, Anita Loos' adaptation of Colette, *Chéri* (1959). Barely in her thirties, Stanley was much too young to play Léa, the aging—and aging badly—cocotte who keeps a teenage lover. But then Broadway itself surely wasn't ready for this naughty French postcard of a show. Horst Buchholz came over from Germany to play the love object, and here again was the Beautiful Male set loose in the culture by Williams, Kazan, and Brando. Stanley herself was at the top of her physical form, not least in a boudoir scene, with Buchholz topless in a cache-sex and see-through leggings, making a play for her pearls. Like all of Colette, the play was a dangerous little fribble, violating the peace of the Sabbath eight times a week—but though Robert Lewis directed, the production suffered from a lack of Europe. Loos' *Gigi,* earlier in the decade, solved that problem with Audrey Hepburn and an all-English cast. *Chéri* had only Buchholz and Lili Darvas (as a panderer) for atmosphere. One can't do Colette in American.

Although it takes us beyond this book's limits, we should note a *Three Sisters* put on by the Actors Studio in 1964, translated by Randall Jarrell and directed by Lee Strasberg. Stanley played Masha and Page played Olga; Irina was Shirley Knight. Barbara Baxley and Kevin McCarthy filled out the leads, and, in homage to the Group, Chebutykin was the Golden Boy, Luther Adler. Mixed reviews (but a good run of 119 performances) revealed what many already knew by 1964: that some people, especially academics and a few of the younger Broadwayites, were tired of being upstaged by history and wanted the whole Group–Method–Actors Studio thing over.

Revolt of the Beavers. It is not uncommon for the next age to assail the previous age; rock critics routinely disparage Cole Porter, Richard Rodgers, and Harold Arlen when their names come up. But then, it's hard to glory in new music when the old music keeps hanging around, reproaching the substitution of repetitious hooks for melody and a risible incompetence in rhyme. And how can young turks create new theatre when old theatre refuses to go away?

It was perhaps in that sort of atmosphere that this *Three Sisters* traveled to London with significant cast changes but too little re-rehearsal, and with the entire company bedeviled by a sharply raked stage and impulsive lighting. It was one of the West End's most famous disasters. When the curtain went up for the full-cast call, the theatre erupted in boos and stamping, but the stage manager stubbornly kept raising the curtain again and again, as the house continued to boo and stamp. Enemies of the Group tradition reveled in it, and in the desecration of reputations. On the other hand, Kim Stanley stands vivid and unique in theatregoers' memories, and—to put it in quite a different way—Geraldine Page got eight Oscar nominations. How desecrated do these two deserve to be?

At least the Lunts went out in style. They could be our Golden Age Couple, because they not only spanned but dominated it, reaching Broadway at just about 1919 and remaining through 1959 an objective correlative for what "Broadway" meant in talent, glamor, and Sophistication. Like Eugene O'Neill and the Theatre Guild, Katharine Cornell and the Barrymores, Clifford Odets and Kaufman and Hart, the Lunts made something of themselves that could have obtained only *in the theatre* and *at that time*. Weren't they multi-persons, too, in all the things they managed to be in a lifetime—Cornell as Candida but also as Anouilh's Antigone, taking on the State out of conscience; or Odets balancing a writer's public obligations with his personal needs? They were there when it happened, but not out of luck entirely, because it could not have happened without them: they were impassioned. And when Lee Strasberg very shockingly says, "The Lunts *are* the Method," isn't he pacifying all of Broadway's interior contradictions? Doesn't he mean, We *all* were part of it?

True, some might sniff at the Lunts boulevarding their way through Howard Lindsay and Russel Crouse's *The Great Sebastians* (1956), about a mind-reading act. She was the English Essie and he the Czech Rudi, and they opened the show in harness, in play-within-play style, Lynn in radiant gold-trimmed white and blindfolded on stage and Alfred, in tails, working the house from the aisles: "Madame," he calls to Lynn, "there is a gentleman at the back. He is holding up something—can you tell me what it is?"

The Lunts in fact put on a genuine show, using members of the ANTA Theatre audience and a verbal code. "Quickly, Madame, quickly" signified that Lunt was holding a key.

For the play itself, the authors came up with something rather elegant and contemporary, a political snafu embroiling our two stars in the Communist takeover of Jan Masaryk's democratic government. There was even a surprise ending, but as so often the critics carped at the humdrum quality of the writing. The public, however, was delighted, and the run of 174 performances misleads, for the theatre scaled its prices for a new straight-play top of $6.90, and the Lunts did land-office business till they closed for the summer before the fall–winter tour.

After a career like the Lunts', how to go out—more boulevard fluff, taking the kiss canoe to Candyland? One could hardly expect the Great Sebastians to go modern and black comic all of a sudden. Yet that is what the Lunts did, in a piece about a fabulously wealthy old beldam who returns to her native Swiss village to offer it a fortune for the murder of the man who seduced and betrayed her long before. She has made the temptation extra enticing by using her millions to buy up and wreck the place over the years. Their life is no life. Of course, they immediately and adamantly refuse; that's Act One. Then they start to think it over.

Friedrich Dürrenmatt's *Der Besuch der Alten Dame* (The Old Lady's Visit) was done as *The Visit* (1958), in Maurice Valency's translation, under Peter Brook. The Lunts and Peter Brook? But Brook at this time was intrigued by all sorts of theatre; so were the Lunts. Remember, they played O'Neill, Chekhof, and Shakespeare. *The Visit* could be thought of as the trio's meeting place: boulevardier modernist. And, after all, but for the old lady's murderous intentions, *The Visit* in outline is *Reunion in Vienna* with the sexes reversed.

It was decided to play London first, but British tryout audiences *hated* the show. The Lunts reached Dublin and Edinburgh but couldn't come in: the West End was barred to them because of the work's brutal character. The English stage apparently wasn't "contemporary" yet, and it underscores the adventurous nature of fifties theatregoing, as I've noted, that Broadway ate this show up. The first night was one of the last really great ones, not least because Charles Dillingham's Globe Theatre had been wholly refurbished as the Lunt-Fontanne for the occasion. Once again, ticket prices went high (as they did in Dillingham's day, which is why he built his house with that extra-large orchestra: to take advantage of six-dollar tops for Fred Stone's musicals).

The critics were extremely appreciative even while suggesting that they had never seen the Lunts do anything important before. "Our two most gifted comic actors," said Brooks Atkinson, "look like our most gifted dramatic actors." The problem was the old mistake of taking one's false assumptions about a thing for the thing itself. Because it seems sensible that lighter fare calls for "lighter" talents, actors who frequent comedy are assumed to be less gifted than actors of drama. It isn't sensible. Talent is talent; its portion is not counted by genre. Was Judi Dench less "talented" when she played Sally Bowles in the first London *Cabaret,* and then *more* "talented" when she tried Madame Ranyefsky in *The Cherry Orchard*? Are there two Judi Denches?

There may be two Londons. After *The Visit*'s New York triumph, a tour, and a City Center return for the usual two weeks so that wise New Yorkers could collect this historic farewell one last time, the Lunts took *The Visit* to the West End after all. The critics were simply amazed. Most of it was because the Lunts really were stupendous. Some of it was because Alfred played Anton Schill (changed from Dürrenmatt's obviously unsuitable Alfred Ill) in a magnificent arc even as his fortunes fell ever lower. He was the guilty man who denies and resists, then attempts a meticulous little frenzy of an escape. None of the crowd "seeing him off" physically stops him, yet Lunt played the scene as if fearful of rescue and judgment at once: maddened by the destiny he chose. At length Lunt resigned himself to what he came to see as justice, a messy old coot yet huge, Greek, symbolic.

Then, too, some of the fuss was because Lynn softened Dürrenmatt's Baal of an old lady, an implacable god of destruction. Lynn's Claire Zachanassian hailed from a combination of Norse saga and fairy tale, less old and inhuman than a beauty in love with Lunt and vengeance at once.

There were many great moments; the company took away a career's worth of insights from the experience. Perhaps the most arresting of the Luntian touches was that last minute or so of Act One, where, at a banquet before more or less the entire town, the lady makes her evil offer:

CLAIRE: I want the life of Anton Schill . . . I am willing to pay one billion marks.
(The Burgomaster stands up, very pale and dignified.)

BURGOMASTER: Madame Zachanassian, we are not in the jungle. We
   are in Europe . . . In the name of the town of Güllen, I decline your
   offer. In the name of humanity, we shall never accept.

The town breaks into wild applause, which emphasizes Dürrenmatt's
ironic recollection of Nazism ("We are in Europe") by growing into an angry clapping fascist unison. The lady rises, thanks the Burgomaster, gives
him a long look, and says only

CLAIRE: I can wait.
(She turns and walks off, and the curtain falls.)

At least, so runs the script. The Lunts and Brook decided to make far
more of the pause before Claire's last line and to cut Claire's exit. Brook had
toyed with the unnervingly long pause at Stratford-upon-Avon, in 1949, in
Measure For Measure. The director determined to goad the play's conflicting
themes of justice and mercy with what Kenneth Tynan described as "half a
dozen long pauses, working up a new miracle of tension Shakespeare knew
nothing about." The last of these pauses, after the Duke asks Isabella if she
will plead for the villain, so concentrated attention on Barbara Jefford's Isabella that, said Tynan, "every heart in the theatre [was] thudding" for, as he
counted it, thirty-five seconds.

Brook now decided to top even that, perhaps because *The Visit,* too, concerns the meting out of justice—this time without mercy. A brilliant actress
might have held the pause after thanking the Burgomaster, eventually to turn
slowly to her lover and victim, thence to the Burgomaster again, and utter the
final line. A genius actress might have found a way to do all this without
quite looking at the two men, or at anyone, perhaps treating the audience to
a gnomically unfathomable look.

But *this* actress—Lynn Fontanne—did nothing, and did it for so long a
time that the public became as nervous as the citizens of Güllen. Of course,
Fontanne's "nothing" was like Garbo's in the last shot of *Queen Christina.*
Supposedly, Fontanne varied the length of the pause according to how in-
tently she felt the audience had followed Act One; a truly captivated audience got the longest, most occupied nothing of all time, till even Lunt
himself might fear.

Only then did Fontanne channel the stage manager, perhaps by astral projection: *ready the curtain*. Without moving her head, without even changing any of her two thousand simultaneous and contradictory expressions, she delivered the last line. "I can wait." She waited, immobile, for another eleven seconds.

And then the curtain came down.

❧ Index